DATE DUE

FEB 1 2 2013		
MAR 2 1 2013		
		APR 2 3 2013
MAY 8 2013		

HIGHSMITH #45115

JACKSONIAN ANTISLAVERY
AND THE POLITICS OF FREE SOIL,
1824–1854

Jonathan H. Earle

Jacksonian Antislavery &

WHIG - ABOLITION
PLATFORM.

SA

the Politics of Free Soil,
1824–1854

THE
UNIVERSITY
OF NORTH
CAROLINA PRESS
CHAPEL HILL &
LONDON

DEMOCRATIC PLATFORM.

VER.

Designed by Eric M. Brooks
Set in New Baskerville, Bulmer, and Grotesque
by Keystone Typesetting, Inc.
Manufactured in the United States of America

The paper in this book meets the guidelines
for permanence and durability of the Committee on
Production Guidelines for Book Longevity of
the Council on Library Resources.

Library of Congress Cataloging-in-Publication Data
Earle, Jonathan Halperin.
Jacksonian antislavery and the politics of free soil,
1824–1854 / by Jonathan H. Earle.
p. cm.
Includes bibliographical references and index.
ISBN 0-8078-2888-2 (cloth: alk. paper)
ISBN 0-8078-5555-3 (pbk.: alk. paper)
1. Antislavery movements — United States — History — 19th
century. 2. Free Soil Party (U.S.) 3. Slavery — Political
aspects — United States — History — 19th century.
4. United States — Politics and government — 1815–1861.
5. Politicians — United States — Biography. 6. Political
activists — United States — Biography. 7. United States —
Race relations — Political aspects. I. Title.
E449.E17   2004
324.2732 — dc22   2004007423

Portions of Chapter 4 appeared in slightly different form
in *Massachusetts Historical Review* 4 (2002): 61–88.

cloth   08 07 06 05 04   5 4 3 2 1
paper   08 07 06 05 04   5 4 3 2 1

For

L . R . T .

CONTENTS

List of Illustrations and Maps ix
Acknowledgments xi

INTRODUCTION
Jacksonian Antislavery
and the Roots of Free Soil

1

CHAPTER ONE
Dissident Democrats in the 1830s
William Leggett, George Henry Evans, and Thomas Morris

17

CHAPTER TWO
Set Down Your Feet, Democrats
Politics and Free Soil in New York

49

CHAPTER THREE
Making Hay from Democratic Clover
*John P. Hale and the New Hampshire
Independent Democracy*

78

CHAPTER FOUR
Marcus Morton and the Dilemma of
Jacksonian Antislavery in Massachusetts
103

CHAPTER FIVE
David Wilmot, the Proviso, and the
Congressional Movement to Abolish Slavery
123

CHAPTER SIX
The Cincinnati Clique, True Democracy,
and the Ohio Origins of the Free Soil Party
144

CHAPTER SEVEN
Free Soil, Free Labor, Free Speech, and Free Men
The Election of 1848
163

CONCLUSION
Free Soilers, Republicans, and
the Third Party System, 1848–1854
181

Appendix 199
Notes 211
Bibliography 247
Index 269

ILLUSTRATIONS AND MAPS

ILLUSTRATIONS

1. David Wilmot   3
2. Abijah Beckwith   11
3. William Leggett   21
4. Barnburner politicking   64
5. "Smoking Him Out"   76
6. "Wilmot, the Wizard"   140
7. "The Modern Colossus"   166
8. "A Modern Democrat"   183

MAPS

1. Free Soil in New York, 1848   170
2. Free Soil in Ohio, 1848   173
3. Free Soil in Massachusetts, 1848   174
4. Free Soil in New Hampshire, 1848   176
5. Free Soil in Pennsylvania, 1848   178
6. Election of 1848: Free Soil Vote by Counties   179

Historians of antebellum politics know that in order to win an election, favors had to be granted, financial support cobbled together, arguments articulated and rearticulated, and debts of gratitude duly acknowledged. The same holds for completing a work of scholarship, and it is my pleasure to thank the many people and institutions that helped me write this book.

Like so many before me, my interest in the antebellum period began while I was an undergraduate at Columbia College. Eric Foner and the late James P. Shenton shared their vast knowledge of the period with me and introduced me to what it meant to be a scholar. At Princeton, James McPherson, John Murrin, Daniel Rodgers, Christine Stansell, and Stephen Aron pushed me in several different (and fruitful) directions, and Sean Wilentz directed my doctoral dissertation with insight, patience, and humanity. He also shared his excellent seats at Yankee Stadium far more often than I deserved. Thanks also to fellow travelers Sharon Block, Walter Johnson, Gary Hewitt, Steve Kantrowitz, Michael Millinder, Henry Yu, and Eric Love, who made spending seven years in suburban New Jersey far less onerous and helped make my work better in various ways.

I was extremely fortunate to land my first academic job at the University of Kansas, and my colleagues here have immeasurably improved this book. Victor Bailey, Angel Kwolek-Folland, Tom Lewin, Eric Love, Jeffrey Moran, Phil Paludan, and Bill Tuttle have all offered their time, excellent advice, and friendship. Ted Wilson is an absolute mensch—he read the entire manuscript at a time when I was short on confidence and declared it "finished." Peter Mancall was the best faculty mentor any junior hire could ever wish for. I will be forever in his debt for the mountains of good advice he gave me after my arrival in Lawrence.

The library and research staffs at the Library of Congress, the National Archives, the New-York Historical Society, the New York State Historical Society, the New York Public Library, Massachusetts Historical Society, the Historical Society of Pennsylvania, the Library Company of Pennsylvania, the New Hampshire Historical Society, Cornell University Libraries, Dartmouth University Libraries, Columbia University Libraries, the University of Kansas Libraries, the Bradford County Historical Society, the Albany County Historical Society, and the Herkimer County Historical Society each added depth to this book and made my time researching it significantly more fulfilling.

At the University of North Carolina Press, I wish to thank Lew Bateman for his early interest in this project, Michael Morrison for perhaps the most intricate and helpful reader's report in the history of academic scholarship, and Chuck Grench for supporting the project through to the end. Stephanie Wenzel improved the final product with deft copyediting.

Generous financial support came from Princeton University, the Friends of the Princeton University Library, the Hall Center for the Humanities at the University of Kansas, the General Research Fund and the Vice Chancellor's Book Subvention Fund at the University of Kansas, and the Massachusetts Historical Society. Fellowships from the American Council of Learned Societies, the National Endowment for the Humanities, and the Henry E. Huntington Memorial Library and Botanical Gardens provided a year's funding to improve and revise the manuscript. Special thanks to Roy Ritchie of the Huntington for making my year in Southern California so rewarding intellectually and gastronomically.

For their expert advice on portions of the manuscript, I wish to single out Daniel Feller, Iver Bernstein, Christopher Clark, James Huston, and John Mack Faragher for special thanks.

Finally, I want to thank members of my family for the years of love and support while I wrote this book. My late grandparents Phil and Dorothy Halperin came through with timely financial help in graduate school; my journalist brother Geoff Earle made some professional-quality research forays to the Library of Congress on short deadline; my father, Richard Earle, provided love and money; my mother, Janice Earle, did the same and, as a special bonus, advised me on dissertation writing; and my in-laws, Jerry and Carol Tuttle, delivered all sorts of practical help. My wife, colleague, best friend, and partner-in-all-things, Leslie Tuttle, has been at the center of my personal and professional life since the first day of graduate school, when she sat across the table from me at the inaugural meeting of a course called "History 500: Introduction to the Professional Study of History." By the time the syllabus reached Gramsci (or was it Ladurie?), she had captured my heart as well as my head. It is to her I dedicate this book.

JACKSONIAN ANTISLAVERY

AND THE POLITICS OF FREE SOIL,

1824–1854

Jacksonian Antislavery and the Roots of Free Soil

The dinner table conversation at Masi's rooming house on Pennsylvania Avenue rarely, if ever, centered on the food. Politics was the main course on the evening of August 8, 1846, as it was most other nights when Congress was in session. Every one of the house's residents was a member of the 29th Congress, a northerner, and a Democrat. Yet on this sultry Saturday night, the penultimate night of the session, the housemates' conversation was particularly heated. At issue, each lawmaker believed, was whether millions of acres of western land would remain free (as it had been since 1821) or fall into the hands of slaveholders.

Earlier that day, President James K. Polk had submitted a message to both houses of Congress requesting $2 million to make peace with Mexico and to purchase California and New Mexico.[1] To a growing number of the Democrats representing northern districts — for years the South's staunchest political allies — the president's request seemed the latest in a series of moves intended to increase slave territory (and the power of slaveholders) at their constituents' expense. This feeling was particularly intense for Democrats known as Barnburners, who believed slaveholders had been responsible for defeating their leader, Martin Van Buren, in 1840 and 1844; for capitulating on extending Oregon's northern boundary; and for carving out a new empire for slavery in Texas and the Southwest. The Barnburner Democrats in residence at Masi's and elsewhere on Capitol Hill seized on Polk's request as the moment to make their increasing opposition to new slave territory heard.

Uneasy with the prospect of dealing squarely with the controversial addition of new territory so late in the session, a group of northern representatives moved to kill the president's request by referring it to committee.

Failing this, they unsuccessfully attempted to table it. Finally, in confusion, the House agreed to take up the matter at the evening session on August 6.[2]

During the brief dinner recess, separate groups of disgruntled northern Democrats lamented that the southern wing of their party seemed poised to snatch yet more territory for slavery. At Masi's, a first-term congressman from remote northeastern Pennsylvania named David Wilmot announced that if the Speaker introduced Polk's request as a bill, he would move "an amendment to the effect that slavery should be excluded from any territory acquired by virtue of such an appropriation." Opinion on Wilmot's plan was far from uniform. Robert Dale Owen of Indiana objected, fearing the amendment would tear apart the Democratic Party. Two other companions, Robert P. Dunlap of Maine and Jacob S. Yost of Pennsylvania, heartily approved of Wilmot's proposal.[3]

On the short walk back to the Capitol, Wilmot encountered Democrats Martin Grover of New York, Jacob Brinkerhoff of Ohio, and Hannibal Hamlin of Maine, who were plotting a similar strategy while standing in the street. This new, larger group agreed to "advise with our northern friends" when the evening session began and to press the measure "if it met with their approbation." Apparently it did, since Wilmot recalled that during a brief canvass on the House floor, "Northern Democrats were unanimous in favor of the movement."[4]

The $2 Million Bill was called up just before 7:00 P.M., and the core group of northerners, joined by Preston King of New York and James Thompson of Pennsylvania, again gathered "to agree on the form and terms" of the amendment. Different drafts of the slavery-restricting amendments were submitted, discussed, and altered, the final draft being "the result of our united labors," according to Wilmot. The wording and strategy chosen to introduce the amendment were hardly unusual; in fact, they were lifted straight from Thomas Jefferson's Northwest Ordinance, which the group hailed as a founding document of Democratic antislavery.[5] After agreeing on language, each member of the cadre wrote out a copy and attempted to gain control of the floor during debate. As Brinkerhoff had predicted, Wilmot, heretofore "a favorite of the Southern members," was the first of the group so recognized.

Wilmot's speech was brief. He fully endorsed the ongoing war with Mexico and the annexation of Texas (accomplished three years earlier) as a slave state. If territory from the free nation of Mexico was gained by a peace treaty, however, Wilmot thundered, "God forbid that [Congress] should be

the means of planting this institution upon it." He concluded by endorsing the president's request for funds, "*Provided*, That, as an express and fundamental condition to the acquisition of any territory from the Republic of Mexico by the United States . . . neither slavery nor involuntary servitude shall ever exist in any part of said territory, except for crime, whereof the party shall first be duly convicted."

The quiet House chamber quickly sprang to life. A small group of women fanning themselves in the gallery was quickly joined by capital luminaries such as Gen. Winfield Scott, Senator James Buchanan, Postmaster General Cave Johnson, and Secretary of the Navy (and historian) George Bancroft.[6] After a loud, angry, and hurried debate, the proviso passed the House 77-58 — but the margin itself did not make the vote significant. Every member from a district south of the Mason-Dixon line or the Ohio River, excepting two Kentucky Whigs, opposed the proviso. Put another way, the Northwest and Northeast united almost unanimously behind Wilmot's proviso, as acrid party distinctions melted away. For a brief moment in the Congress of the United States, the North and West, led by a band of disenchanted Democrats, stood united against an angry and defensive South.[7]

Herrenvolk Democracy?

This first vote over the proviso placed slavery squarely at the center of American politics, where it was to remain until the ratification of the Thirteenth Amendment in 1865. Yet for the recalcitrant and little-known northern Democrats who hatched the scheme to halt the expansion of slavery in 1846, the events of that sweltering evening proved more of a culmination than a beginning. Antislavery Jacksonians like Marcus Morton of Massachusetts traced the origins of the revolt against the "Slave Power" to the congressional debates over the Missouri Crisis in 1819–21, at which time he had joined a determined group of northern Jeffersonians to marshal Constitutional arguments opposing the extension of slavery into the new state.[8] These arguments—that the federal Constitution was an antislavery document and that Congress had the power and duty to bar slavery's extension into territories of the United States—resurfaced a quarter of a century later in debates about land gained during the war with Mexico. In the interim, controversies over the censorship of abolitionist mailings in 1835, Texas annexation, the throwing aside of their political leaders, and the growing willingness of slaveholders to defend their "peculiar institution" as a positive good convinced a growing number of northern Democrats that the South had begun to trample on the rights of white freemen as well as black slaves.

Consider Morton's comments of 1837: "To say that I am utterly opposed to slavery in every form, civil, political, or domestic, is saying very little," he wrote in a published letter to fellow Jacksonian George Bancroft. "I deem slavery to be the greatest curse and the most portentous evil which a righteous God ever inflicted upon a nation; and that every effort . . . be made to mitigate, and, if possible, to extirpate it from the land."[9] Avowals of such sentiments by a prominent Democrat fly in the face of recent historical portraits of the party of Thomas Jefferson and Andrew Jackson. Indeed, numerous studies have focused on the Democracy's domination by slaveholders and the vicious racism espoused by various groups within the Jacksonian coalition.[10] Yet this interpretive stance ignores those Jacksonians who, beginning in the 1830s, took stands against slavery and, in many cases, the racial prejudice that supported it. It also obscures the vital contributions these "free-soil" Democrats made to the antislavery political battles of the 1840s and 1850s. The views espoused by Morton and his compatriots recall an older historical vision of the Democratic Party, one memorably conjured up by Arthur Schlesinger Jr. more than a half century ago. In *The Age of Jackson*, Schlesinger famously claimed that "the Jacksonian tradition . . .

supplied the most solid foundations for political antislavery" and that "the group which took the lead on the political stage in combating the slave power were the radical Democrats in the straight Jacksonian tradition."[11] Numerous historians have found fault with Schlesinger's thesis, pointing out that Democrats as far apart on the slavery issue as David Wilmot, Stephen Douglas, and Jefferson Davis each claimed to fall within the "straight Jacksonian tradition."[12] Furthermore, critics have demonstrated that the Jacksonian legacy regarding the issue of slavery was at best mixed and at worst fundamentally tainted.[13] More recently, some scholars have suggested that Schlesinger's radical Democrats were, in fact, *pro*slavery. Instead of the progressive, hard-money reformers of Schlesinger's *Age of Jackson*, Democratic leaders and their followers are depicted as committed above all else to white supremacy and to slavery's perpetuation.[14]

This study proposes a more nuanced understanding of the radical Democratic tradition. While there remains little doubt that Schlesinger overstated the Jacksonians' protoliberalism, his most recent critics, by making white supremacy and proslavery the underpinnings of Jacksonian political thought, have distorted the history of both Jacksonianism and the antislavery movement. This book examines how Democratic veterans of the antibank and antimonopoly battles of the 1830s fashioned their own arguments against slavery and its extension. These arguments, rooted in Jacksonian notions of egalitarian democracy and producer's rights, were political and economic and owed far more to the radicalism noted by Schlesinger than to the evangelical perfectionism commonly linked with the antislavery movement.[15] This Democratic strain of antislavery thought and action, born and nurtured far from the abolitionist salons of Boston and Philadelphia, greatly enlarged the antislavery movement by injecting it with that dynamic political ideology called free soil. Free-soil Democrats went beyond simple hostility to the Slave Power and its pretenses, linking their antislavery opposition to a land reform agenda that pressed for free land for poor settlers, in addition to land free of slavery. The resulting union between radical Jacksonianism and the antislavery movement, as will be shown, is far more important than historians have allowed. Blending hostility to slavery with traditional Democratic ideas like land reform and hard money, free-soil Jacksonians brought hundreds of thousands of new voters to the antislavery political coalition. Free soil, as an ideology and a movement in its own right (one that often acted in concert with its better-known cousin, free labor) forced a major realignment in local, state, and national politics between 1846 and 1854, greatly intensifying the sectional crisis.

Slavery and Expansion

As Marcus Morton asserted, several of the hallmarks of Jacksonian anti-slavery and free soil were imprinted during the contentious debates over Missouri's admission to the Union. A bloc of northern Jeffersonian congressmen, including the young Morton, contributed arguments opposing slavery in new states that differed significantly from those set forth by antislavery northern Federalists. Specifically, they rested on a view that the U.S. Constitution, despite its straightforward allowances for slavery, was essentially an *antislavery* document that left an opening for Congress to restrict slavery's expansion by barring new slave states. Strict construction, these Jeffersonians said, could help right the wrongs mistakenly allowed by the founders.[16]

The anti-Missouri Jeffersonians and their Federalist allies were, of course, defeated. House Speaker Henry Clay was able to muster majorities to admit Missouri as a slave state along with the free state of Maine despite the prohibition of new slave states north of 36°30'. Joining the compromisers was New York's newly selected senator Martin Van Buren, who after the crisis over Missouri cast about for southern allies to revive the old Jeffersonian bisectional coalition by relegating sectional issues to the political sidelines. In a famous letter to Richmond editor Thomas Ritchie, Van Buren proposed an alliance of "the planters of the South and the plain Republicans of the north" that would form "a complete antidote for sectional prejudices."[17] Of course, by the late 1820s, times had changed, and most surviving members of the old national Jeffersonian coalition were more than willing to lay aside their differences about slavery to combat the corrupt "Money Power" they saw as a more immediate threat to democracy and the Union. Van Buren's coalition succeeded in electing Andrew Jackson to the presidency in 1828.

Almost immediately, however, the Jacksonian coalition began to fray at the seams. In 1830, proslavery vice president John C. Calhoun broke with the administration. Then, in the mid-1830s, antisouthern and antislavery northerners began to fear that slaveholders held too much sway in the coalition. In Ohio and New York City, small groups of Jacksonians broke with party leaders who supported the gag rule (which tabled antislavery petitions sent to Congress), barred abolitionist material from the mails, and cheered on mobs who attacked abolitionist meetings and black neighborhoods. The Democratic Party leadership generally treated antislavery Jacksonians as heretics and often banished them from the party. Yet every dissident claimed that the proslavery leadership had abandoned true Jacksonian principles, not the dissidents themselves. The events of the 1840s—Texas annexation, the Mexican War, and the Wilmot Proviso—amplified these arguments, persuading a growing number of northern Democrats that their party was increasingly dominated by southerners. These Jacksonians (dubbed "the Undaunted Democracy" by Walt Whitman) anxiously viewed southern mastery within the party as a threat to their *own* liberties.

This anxiety was focused squarely on the western territories and the question of slavery's expansion there.[18] By recasting the slavery debate into a battle over expansion and western lands, antislavery Democrats hit upon a popular political weapon that would later be known as free soil. Originally a slogan for agrarian land reform, by 1846 free soil encompassed a hodge-podge of reinforcing ideas about patriarchal landownership and slavery restriction. By moving the political debate away from slavery's immorality and toward its future in the territories, Free Soilers were able greatly to enlarge the antislavery movement's political constituency. Eventually this expanded movement ensured that the Republican Party—acutely responsive to these Democratic sensibilities—emerged victorious in 1860. The Jacksonian element within the Republican Party was by no means a majority or even a dominant voice. But the genius of the new party was its ability to attract various free-soil Democrats, Liberty Party men, and Whigs under a single antislavery banner.

From the Money Power to the Slave Power

Free Soilers' opposition to slavery did not imply the abandonment of other established ideas or positions. Indeed, this particular antislavery impulse grew straight from the roots of the Democracy's long-standing commitment to egalitarianism or, put in opposite terms, the rank and file's ingrained hostility to centralized power and its perceived tendency to promote social and economic inequalities.[19] As Marvin Meyers noted in the 1950s, radical, hard-money Democrats developed a shorthand description for this inter-locking set of powerful individuals and institutions they called the Money Power. Vaguely defined and characterized in pictures and prose as a multi-tentacled monster, the Money Power exerted its majesty through privileged access to the nation's banking system. In fact, the radical Jacksonians' original raison d'être had been to elevate the nation's farmers and laborers at the expense of the Money Power, which supposedly exploited them.[20]

By the mid-1830s, however, Democratic dissidents, reasonably satisfied that Jackson and his administration had the Money Power on the run, discovered that another enemy—slavery—had arisen in its place. To make matters worse, this Slave Power (a phrase coined by Jacksonian dissident Thomas Morris in the 1830s and popularized by Abraham Lincoln and the Republicans in the 1850s) was allied with the New England textile barons to ensure a profitable future for cotton, market capitalism, and slavery. "The slave power of the South and the banking power of the North, are now uniting to rule this country," Morris told the Senate in a speech attacking the gag rule and defending organized abolitionism. "The cotton bale and the bank note . . . have at last met and embraced each other, both looking to the same object—to live upon the unrequited labor of others."[21] Instead of adhering to the orthodox Democratic view of slaveholders as upright producers, the dissidents saw them as grasping aristocrats who endangered the American experiment.[22] "The northern man must be false to his education, and blind to his interests, who does not, inch by inch, and hand to hand, resist the extension of the slaveholding power," wrote the Jacksonian Theodore Sedgwick III. "The institution is in every way a blight and a curse [that has] plunged the laboring class into degradation, and made labor itself dishonorable."[23] Thus, dissidents like Sedgwick pointed to the Jacksonian principles of political democracy and economic equality as the foundation of their hatred for slavery.

Of course not every radical, hard-money Democrat came to Morris's or Sedgwick's conclusions about slavery and slaveholders. In fact, many of them veered off in an opposite direction. Jacksonian labor editor Orestes Brownson, for example, embraced the thinking of the slaveholding John C. Calhoun after the Democrats' defeat in the election of 1840. The devastating loss altered Brownson's long-held views about the virtue of popular majorities. "Experience proves," he wrote in 1842, "that the more extended the suffrage, the greater will be the influence and more certain the triumph of wealth, or rather the business classes." If workingmen and their champions constituted a minority only, he reasoned, then other minorities should constitute their natural allies. This new, antimajoritarian view drove Brownson into the arms of Calhoun, who had long volunteered the "minority" South as a bulwark against the tyranny of the northern business elite.[24] By 1843 Brownson described the master-slave relationship as "of a more generous and touching nature" than that between employer and worker.[25] Fitzwilliam Byrdsall, the former secretary of the Democratic splinter Locofoco Party—a group inspired by William Leggett's editorials for the *Evening Post* and *Plaindealer*—went further still. In 1842 he launched a "free-trade association," supported by several veterans of the New York labor movement, that was little more than a front for Calhoun's presidential campaign. Five years later, while many of his former allies were forming the national Free Soil Party, Byrdsall wrote to Calhoun that "never was there any social institution more unfairly vilified than that which is termed Southern slavery."[26]

Byrdsall's and Brownson's political evolution, as much as Leggett's and Morris's, prompts a thorny question: How could committed Democrats — who shared nearly identical beliefs on centralized authority, workers' rights, egalitarianism, and the Money Power — come to such different conclusions about the threat of slavery and slaveholders? Put another way, Why did some Democrats who held these same principles and hostilities to centralized power in any form become Free Soilers while others did not? The answers to these questions lie at the heart of the study of political ideology. The simplest answer, echoing the critiques of Schlesinger's *Age of Jackson*, is that every antebellum Democrat (or Whig, or Know-Nothing) fashioned himself and his allies adherents to the "true" and "pure" principles of his political party. As Major Wilson and Michael Morrison have shown, party members who shared the same beliefs commonly wound up on different sides of an issue, especially one as contentious as slavery. Conversely, party members could arrive at similar beliefs for very different reasons — witness the variety of (often contradictory) arguments mobilized by Democrats against the Second Bank of the United States. Hard-money Virginia Democrats, for example, opposed the bank because they believed paper money robbed planters and workers of the value of their crops or labor. Soft-money Ohio Democrats, however, also opposed the bank but believed restricting the use of paper currency to commercial transactions would likely choke off western development.[27]

Responses to the Slave Power proved to be as varied as earlier reactions to the Money Power. The comparison is particularly apt because free-soil Democrats adapted (in a process Lawrence Kohl calls "transference of feeling") the rhetoric and substance of the Money Power ideology and used it to make sense of, and formulate a critical response to, the emergence of the Slave Power. At the same time, other Democrats reached the opposite conclusion about the relation between slavery, slaveholders, and national politics. They charged that Free Soilers were dangerous latitudinarians intent on enhancing centralized power (in this case, the power of Congress to ban slavery in the territories) against the rights and liberties of individuals. These anti-free-soil Democrats fashioned their opposition to central power into the formula of popular sovereignty, which allowed residents of a territory to decide whether to admit or ban slavery.

How, then, is it possible to explain the rising hostility to slavery among some northern Democrats and not others? Obviously, opposing centralized authority and the paper economy was not, in and of itself, enough to prompt a Democrat to become a Free Soiler. Historians have long privileged the political causes of the free-soil revolt, focusing on one Democratic faction's desire for "revenge" against the party's southern wing and its office-seeking northern allies.[28] No doubt for some Free Soilers, the decision to bolt their party was based on naked political maneuvering. But this study will show that by 1848, northern Democratic dissidents—even those who were politicians—sincerely believed their party had been hijacked by southern aristocrats bent on subsuming the party's goals to one issue: the expansion of slavery.

Party politics, however, was seldom the sole factor in a Free Soiler's making. Other influences, often in combination, were necessary to motivate this type of action, as well as to influence the timing with which it was taken. Searching for explanations of who bolted—and who stayed—prompts the historian to look for hitherto unexamined similarities linking those individuals who became Free Soilers. To begin, an analysis of the areas where the free-soil revolt emerged in the 1840s offers a picture of political antislavery vastly different from the one historians usually present. Free-soil voting clusters stretched from the remote, eastern border of New Hampshire, through upstate New York, and west to the recently settled towns in Wisconsin territory. Although there were no "typical" free-soil areas, they tended to be long settled, fairly isolated, and off the mainstream of western migration. They were largely untouched by the speculative mania that caused wildly fluctuating land prices, and they suffered from chronic shortages of cash. The depression of the late 1830s and 1840s was especially severe for the people who lived in these communities, leaving them extremely hostile to banks, joint-stock corporations, and paper money. Not surprisingly, these districts provided the Democratic Party, especially its radical, hard-money wing, with some of its largest electoral victory margins. After 1854 these former Jacksonian strongholds—in places such as New Hampshire, northern Pennsylvania, central New York, and the northern borders of Ohio and Illinois—were solidly, and suddenly, in the Republican column. Many of them still are.

In addition to these socioeconomic similarities, a number of other factors emerge repeatedly—although not universally—in the intellectual biographies of free-soil politicians and the constituents with whom they corresponded. The most significant of these include nonevangelical religious affiliations (sometimes verging on deism, free thought, and "irreligion"),

FIGURE 2

Abijah Beckwith (1784–1874).
Beckwith, a lifelong farmer in central
New York state, voted for the Democratic
ticket in every election between 1805 and
1846 "without erasing a single name." In
1846 he left the party and became a Free
Soil "hotspur" when proslavery Hunkers
took control of the state nominating
convention. (Herkimer County [N.Y.]
Historical Society)

radical ideas about landownership, and an outsider relationship to the emerging market economy. Again, not all Free Soilers exhibited these characteristics, and not all those who did became Free Soilers. Nevertheless, each of these factors emerges as a leitmotif in free-soil editorials, manifestos, speeches, and correspondence.

No historian could realistically hope to find a single person that exemplifies each of these various components. Yet imagine this author's surprise when Abijah Beckwith's handwritten "Autobiographical Record," composed for his grandson in 1847, came to light. This upstate New York Free Soiler's background and story fall well beyond the purview of traditional antislavery narratives featuring eastern urban elites, evangelical Protestants, and Whigs. Beckwith, a freethinker who spent his entire adult life farming marginal land in remote Herkimer County, was none of these things. Politically, he was a dyed-in-the-wool Jacksonian. Between 1805 and 1846 he voted the Democratic ticket in every election "without erasing a single name." Yet in 1847 Beckwith abandoned the party of Jefferson and Jackson for good, becoming a Free Soiler and, after 1854, a Republican. The reason for his defection, he wrote, was his belief that slavery had become "our nation's worst evil," far eclipsing the dangers posed by monopolists and bankers. To him, slavery was perpetuated by "aristocratic men" out of a "detestable lordly pride" — a pride that he believed would lead to a bloody, yet just, slave uprising in the South.[29]

Notably absent from Beckwith's antislavery critique is the evangelical and perfectionist rhetoric used by middle-class reformers associated with Rev. Charles Grandison Finney. Beckwith's memoirs contain no talk of sin, moral suasion, or redemption. In fact, his antislavery views barely resemble those of his neighbors in western New York's "Burned-Over District," whom the freethinker described as "restless, renegade and priest-ridden Yankees." Beckwith's autobiography is full of respectful praise for greater New England's clever teachers, enterprising peddlers, and hard-working farmers, who are "always stirring and doing something to better their condition; or that which they think will better the condition of others." But he felt only scorn for the advancing tide of evangelical reformers, whose "zeal for the Bible and their religion . . . inculcate[s] their notions [on] people who have not what they consider, the true religion."[30] Whether they knew it or not, these people aided the forces of what Beckwith called the "aristocracy," a class in which he included landlords, speculators, bankers, priests, and slaveholders. Not every Free Soiler was irreligious — many of them, in fact, were quite pious.[31] Yet as a group they stood apart from the evangelical, Finneyite tide of benevolent reform sweeping the North, associating it with Whiggery, aristocracy, and inequality.

It should also be noted that Beckwith's free-soil appeal extended well beyond slavery restriction and (white) territorial ambition. As his autobiography makes clear, he opposed the perpetuation of slavery in any form, in any part of the country. He even went so far as to ruminate about slavery's violent end in North America, in what he foresaw as a "general rising of the slaves and a strike for freedom" by integrated troops. Suppose the slave states ever attempted to separate from the Union, he pondered in early 1848. "The north should march an army to where they have the largest slave population," he wrote, "and proclaim freedom for the slaves who would join them and fight their former masters and oppressors. What chance would the Southern slaveholders have of success under this state of things?"[32] Such sentiments placed Beckwith squarely in the company of the more radical opponents of slavery in the late 1840s, but as an antimonopoly farmer who cast three presidential ballots for Andrew Jackson, Beckwith hardly fits the profile of a typical antislavery partisan. This study will argue that the free-soil antislavery appeal articulated by Beckwith and thousands of other Democrats proved to be of crucial importance to the rise of antislavery as a northern mass political movement.

Abijah Beckwith, of course, is unusual. Few grassroots or low-level party men left written records of their political, ideological, and moral transformations. The new social historians of the 1960s and 1970s have given us many statistical and mathematical accounts of the way the Beckwiths of the mid-nineteenth century voted, lived, paid their taxes, and died. But even the most impressive regression analyses cannot bridge the still-yawning gap between high- and low-political history or tell us why people change their minds about significant issues. Pursuing the inclusion of elements of both traditional social and political history between the covers of this book, I have benefited from the work of social historians, combining their findings with the methods of more traditional political history. I have adopted a hybrid approach: each chapter focuses on the career of one (in some instances more than one) state-level political leader. Some of these politicians and writers achieved national reputations (like U.S. senator and presidential candidate John P. Hale and proviso author David Wilmot); some have been all but forgotten (Massachusetts governor Marcus Morton and New York scribe Theodore Sedgwick). Still, these antislavery Jacksonians left records of their political careers and offer historians the possibility of following the trajectories of their ideological transformations.

As I intend to show, free soil possessed decidedly social and economic components. In other words, where you came from had more than a little to do with whether you became a Free Soiler. Abijah Beckwith's Herkimer County, shaped like a stovepipe stretching from the Mohawk River Valley into the northern reaches of the craggy Adirondacks, was a prototypical free-soil bastion (see map 1). Counties with large free-soil voting bases varied, but they tended to be poorer, farther from the main lines of immigration and transportation, and more hostile to financial institutions such as banks and joint-stock companies.[33] They also tended to have fewer ties to the revivals of the Second Great Awakening and voted more solidly Democratic than their counterparts.[34] The social origins of free soil, then, are markedly different from those of immediate abolitionism and evangelical reform.

Jacksonian Free Soil

Because "free soil" is one of antebellum America's most elusive terms, one of this study's ambitions is to clarify its origins and meanings. Coined by labor radical George Henry Evans as a slogan for land reform, it later became shorthand for Jacksonian antislavery. In the late 1840s the term variously described an ideology, a party, and a movement—often all three at once. Given these ambiguities, it is not surprising that both contemporaries and historians have misunderstood free soil. In his pathbreaking study of the antebellum Republican Party, Eric Foner used "free soil" as a virtual synonym for his more developed concept of free labor, an ideology he closely linked with the rise of capitalism in the North.[35] But many Free Soilers, including Abijah Beckwith and William Leggett, came from remote rural areas or radical labor backgrounds and felt nothing but contempt for Whiggish free-labor views. Foner also surveyed the Republican coalition (and the ex-Democrats who made up a large minority within it) from the vantage point of the 1850s. Though valuable, his analysis overlooks the long and complex roads Jacksonians traveled before entering the Republican Party. This study approaches the story of free soil by focusing on the 1830s and 1840s, seeking to account for some of the continuities between what historians call the Jacksonian and Civil War periods. It will also attempt to integrate the social and economic transformations in American society into the story of free soil.

While free soil always retained shades of its original meaning as a way to relieve urban social problems by dispensing "free" homesteads to needy settlers (a prominently featured plank in the Free Soil Party's 1848 platform), its meaning continued to evolve throughout the 1840s. From its beginnings in the labor politics and radical land reform movement in the 1830s, free soil matured as a concept that conveyed both agrarian (free farms) and antislavery (land free of slavery) meanings. Free-soil ideas first exhibited notable political potential during the movement to abolish perpetual leases and widespread tenant farming in New York state in the mid-1840s known as the anti-rent wars. Later, when it became clear that the war with Mexico would likely add millions of square miles to the United States, free soil took on far greater significance as a political movement devoted to barring slavery from the new territories. Embodied in the Wilmot Proviso, free soil became the basis of a political party that challenged Democratic and Whig candidates on national and state levels in 1848 and 1852.

Eric Foner has also noted that the Free Soil Party was the first antislavery political organization to remove the issue of equal rights for blacks from its national platform. Other historians have recently argued that the Free Soil Party weakened the antislavery movement by diluting it with northern racism, yielding a Negrophobic and land-hungry ideology that actually legitimized slavery by striving only to limit its expansion. While it is beyond dispute that many Free Soilers were racists (a trait they shared with most white Americans in the nineteenth century), it is inaccurate to view the party and ideology as unprincipled and cynical retreats from the far preferable goal of racial equality. Even Free Soilers such as David Wilmot, a favorite target in recent years because of his frequently voiced antiblack views, made it clear he opposed slavery in any form, and in the South as well as the West. Restricting slavery was, for many northern Democrats, the first step toward its eradication — a move that would, as Wilmot stated, "at no distant day . . . insure the redemption of the Negro from his bondage in chains."[36]

Among Free Soilers, racial views fell along a wide spectrum, ranging from outright Negrophobia to a minority's belief in racial equality. While far from enlightened regarding racial matters from a twenty-first-century perspective, a great majority of Free Soilers opposed the perpetuation of slavery wherever it existed, rejected racist arguments justifying bondage, and insisted on the basic humanity of African Americans. Providing the center of gravity under this wide banner was opposition to slavery — the belief that no person, black or white, should be forced to live as a slave, uncompensated for his or her labor and subjugated to the whims of another. Democratic antislavery ideas had a fundamental impact on American ideas about slavery, equality, and the Union, a legacy most clearly seen in the ideology's twin triumphs: the Emancipation Proclamation and the Homestead Act, both enacted during the Civil War after southern states seceded. It is worth pondering how different the history of the postbellum United States might have been had free-soil programs like free homesteads been extended to ex-slaves and Indians, as some radical Democrats envisioned. Instead, as Foner has demonstrated, self-ownership — "nothing but freedom" — was the point at which free laborites (and many abolitionists, including William Lloyd Garrison) declared victory over slaveholders.[37]

Previous historians have shown that by the 1850s, the Democratic Party had become the primary national political instrument of what its opponents called the Slave Power. Southerners, especially wealthy planters who had originally gravitated to the Whig Party in the 1830s, defected in large numbers to the Democrats, giving birth to the "solid South," while sycophantic northern would-be officeholders (often called "doughfaces") curried southern favor. "All democracy left the democratic party," recalled Massachusetts Jacksonian Frederick Robinson in 1862, "and every democrat that was too intelligent to be cheated by a name, deserted its ranks."[38] Indeed, by the time the Kansas-Nebraska controversy unleashed new levels of violence and mass political desertions that would practically guarantee larger sectional conflict, Jacksonian Democracy was dead as the dodo.

Four years after the introduction of the Kansas-Nebraska Act, Abraham Lincoln observed of the expanding Republican alliance that "much of the plain-old democracy is with us, while nearly all of the old exclusive silk-stocking whiggery is against us."[39] This was, of course, a slight exaggeration, since a large majority of former Whigs, even of the silk-stocking variety, became solid Republicans. But the Republican Party, and its ultimate success, owed a substantial debt to radical Democrats like Abijah Beckwith (who at age seventy-six was chosen as one of Lincoln's New York electors). These former Jacksonians, in conjunction with the Douglasses, Garrisons, Grimkés, and Welds, brought an end to slavery in North America.

CHAPTER ONE

Dissident Democrats in the 1830s

William Leggett, George Henry Evans, and Thomas Morris

As Andrew Jackson delivered his farewell address in 1837, the Democratic Party was at its apex. Even though the president, less than two weeks shy of his seventieth birthday, railed passionately against the Second Bank of the United States and privileged men who meet in "special conclaves" to buy and sell elections, most Jacksonians agreed that the dreaded Money Power was in retreat. The bank's charter, after all, had expired in 1836, making Nicholas Biddle's "monster" just another private bank headquartered in Philadelphia. The $5 million federal surplus had been returned to the states, and Jackson's Specie Circular, Democrats believed, weakened the dangerous power exercised by speculators on the frontier. There were other reasons for optimism as well. Jackson's handpicked successor, Martin Van Buren, had won a majority of the popular vote and 58 percent of the votes in the electoral college, capturing states in every region of the country. More important, the opposition was hopelessly divided: three Whig candidates had combined to win just ten states in 1836, while the Democracy appeared to most observers to be united and strong.

Yet rumblings of discontent could be heard throughout the victorious party. Some western Democrats questioned the wisdom of Jackson's hard-money policy on land sales, and others feared that the "pet" banks that succeeded the Bank of the United States would be unable to coordinate monetary policy for Jackson's successor. And, perhaps surprisingly, a few Democrats objected loudly to the party's popular positions on slavery. Such objections were both isolated and rare, and the party's policies of banning abolitionist material from the mail and tabling every antislavery petition sent to Congress remained in effect, robbing abolitionists of their Constitutional freedom to speak publicly. Democratic chieftains at the highest levels helped enforce "the correct state of public opinion" by cheering on mobs that attacked abolitionist meetings and newspapers.[1] But discontent within the party over the gag rule, mail violations, and the treatment of abolitionists by angry mobs — though muted — solidified into arguments to counteract slavery's expansion that would become important in later decades. This chapter will focus on three antislavery Democrats who broke with the party in the 1830s, well before the debate over slavery extension prompted the Free Soil schism in the 1840s and 1850s. Significantly, each of these early dissidents arrived at his antislavery position as a result of battles over abolitionism in the North, and not over the issue of slavery in the territories — the issue that swelled the movement in the decades before the Civil War. More important for the argument advanced in this study, early dissidents provided specific lines of argument that would later help galvanize and significantly expand the Free Soil movement.

Ohio senator Thomas Morris, for example — the first senator from either party to defend abolitionists on the floor of the U.S. Capitol — formulated and popularized the concept of a Slave Power. The term quickly came to encompass the entire range of anxieties and hostilities northerners harbored toward slavery and the South, and for many antislavery Jacksonians it replaced the Money Power as a master symbol for the aristocracy's ascendance. New York editor William Leggett, who eventually came out as a full-fledged abolitionist, fashioned compelling antislavery arguments from his pro-producer and antimonopoly views, making him a hero to many Free Soilers. George Henry Evans — a freethinker, mechanic, editor, and land reformer — set in motion a reform movement over the future settlement of the public lands that brought two fundamental tenets of Jacksonian ideology (universal landownership and protection of slavery within a disciplined, national coalition) into irreconcilable conflict.

During the 1840s and 1850s, the arguments set forth earlier by Jacksonians such as Leggett, Morris, and Evans were to be amplified by external events such as Texas annexation, the Mexican War, and the Wilmot Proviso. These arguments, compounded by the increasingly aggressive actions of their onetime proslavery brethren, persuaded a growing number of northern Democrats that the South could no longer be trusted as a political ally. When they came to believe their party was in the hands of a proslavery conspiracy, they quit — and laid down arguments that would cause much larger defections in the years to come. These Democrats formed the backbone of the Free Soil coalition that helped bring an end to the second party system.

William Leggett

No other Jacksonian, however prolific or zealous, could match William Leggett's eloquence in articulating arguments against centralized authority, whether embodied by monopolies, "fanatical" reformers, or the Money Power. Leggett's writings for the *New York Evening Post* and his own *Plaindealer* arc among the most polemical and memorable of the antebellum era, each editorial laying the intellectual groundwork for the system of antimonopoly, hard-money, and free-trade beliefs that came to be known as Locofoco egalitarianism. Leggett's arguments against concentrated power in any form, grounded firmly in concepts of natural law and liberty, led him first to champion the classes of producers over capitalist enterprise, making him a hero to the Democratic Party's labor wing. When he applied this same reasoning to slavery in the mid-1830s, the former antiabolitionist underwent a conversion so absolute and unexpected that it took him beyond the stance of most Garrisonians to a passionate advocacy of racial equality. Leggett thus pushed both Democratic egalitarianism and antislavery to their outer limits, confirming Arthur Schlesinger Jr.'s description of him as "the Democrat in whom social radicalism and antislavery united most impressively."[2]

Leggett's formidable hostility to centralized authority began in his youth. In 1825, at age twenty-four, he was court-martialed out of the navy for insulting his commanding officer with, among other things, "abusive verses" from Lord Byron.[3] Yet his naval career, disastrous as it was, provided the young writer with material for *Leisure Hours at Sea,* a volume teeming with wrenching scenes of captains' wanton authority visited upon innocent sailors. At least one reviewer of the work made a connection between life on a ship and on a plantation: "After reading this book and reflecting on its subject, we came to the conclusion that to be master of one of our [naval] vessels is very much like being a negro driver, and to be a ship owner very much like being a slave holder."[4] In "The Squatter: A Tale of Illinois," Leggett moved onto dry land and confronted directly the issue of race. Unlike his other stories, which feature black characters only in supporting roles and contain abundant racist stereotypes, "The Squatter" places Mungo, an elderly black servant, in the role of protagonist. One of Leggett's techniques in the story is to contrast Mungo's shrewdness and humanity with the white characters' ignorance, expedience, and bigotry (one white character calls Mungo "that cursed piece of Indian ink"). Intentionally or not, by making Mungo's intelligence and decency invisible to his white "superiors," Leggett effectively undermines their racism and gives his story an unlikely hero. Like his earlier attempts at poetry, Leggett's stories were critical and popular failures. But his sympathy for the downtrodden, be they despised slaves, luckless squatters, or terrorized sailors, was emerging as a recurring theme in his writings.[5]

Literary failures or not, Leggett's fiction attracted the attention of William Cullen Bryant, the owner of the Democratic *New York Evening Post.* Bryant invited the young author to write literature and theater reviews for the paper in June 1829; Leggett accepted on the express condition that he would not be asked to write about politics. This arrangement was apparently temporary, for Leggett's first political editorials — sparkling with a wit and eloquence absent in his earlier attempts at fiction and criticism — appeared two months later.[6]

Leggett's political writing has been dissected in print many times. Conservative diarist Philip Hone commented that Leggett "disgraced the once respectable columns" of the *Evening Post* "by the most profligate and disorganizing sentiments. This unblushing miscreant makes himself popular . . . by administering to the vitiated appetites of his fellow men nauseous doses of personal slander." A century later, Richard Hofstadter had reduced the "unblushing miscreant" to a "bourgeois radical." Although he never delved into Leggett's antislavery writing, Marvin Meyers was closer to the mark in pointing out that each of Leggett's editorials centers on concern for both rights and power.[7] These two concepts were at the root of his developing worldview: Leggett saw the potential of corrupt central authority everywhere, from the seemingly innocuous functioning of state charities to the delivery of the mail in rural areas (which, he argued, fattened political machines with patronage and encouraged rapid settlement in remote places, thus benefiting speculators).[8] What truly distinguished the young scribe, however, were his relentless attacks on the Money Power, the interlocking collection of financial institutions and capitalists that, he asserted repeatedly, preyed on the labor of farmers and laborers. His editorials, picked up by Democratic papers throughout the country during the 1830s, solidified the *Post*'s position as the party's leading organ in the nation's leading city.

The "banking system," Leggett wrote in 1834, "is essentially an aristocratic institution [that] bands the wealthy together, holds out to them a common motive, animates them with a common sentiment, and inflates their vanity with notions of superior power and greatness." Idle bankers made their money, he explained in his merciless editorials, out of the hard earnings of poor people and funneled political as well as monetary power to the rich. This concentration of "exclusive money privileges" was, according to Leggett, in "direct opposition to the spirit of our constitution and the

FIGURE 3

William Leggett (1801–1839). The intellectual Leggett, a leading Democratic editor in the 1830s, pushed Jacksonian egalitarianism and then Jacksonian antislavery to their outer limits. His ideas were adopted by antislavery Democrats and Free Soilers throughout the antebellum period. (Library of Congress)

genius of the people. Unless the whole system be changed, [the rich] will rise in triumph on the ruins of democracy."[9]

Despite their reddish tinge of class warfare, Leggett's editorials on free trade, banking, and monopolies generally supported the Jackson administration's policies, and Bryant felt confident enough in his young partner (Leggett used a loan to buy a half share in the paper in 1831) to leave him in charge when he left for a tour of Europe in 1834.[10] Bryant had been gone barely two weeks when antiabolitionist mobs attacked antislavery meetings and black homes and churches in the "July Days" riots, beginning Leggett's yearlong, zigzagging conversion to abolitionism. For three days, rioters ruled the streets of Manhattan, destroying more than sixty dwellings, wrecking at least six churches, and causing untold personal injuries.[11] Although at the time he called abolitionism a "scheme" designed to promote the "promiscuous intermarriage of the two races," Leggett could not see how their meeting "furnish[ed] . . . justification for invading the undoubted rights of the blacks, or violating the public peace."[12]

As one looks back on Leggett's "preconversion" editorials attacking abolitionists as "fanatics" (a virtual synonym for abolitionists in both the Democratic and Whig presses), it is clear that he was most anxious about the danger mobs posed to the rights of free discussion guaranteed by the Constitution. Later, the increasingly repressive tactics employed by southern politicians to silence their abolitionist critics (such as the gag rule and the banning of abolitionist material from the mails) pushed Leggett even further toward the antislavery position. Eventually, he decided the slave system itself was the wellspring of a growing wave of southern-led assaults on the nation's founding document. "Not only are we told that slavery is no evil," he wrote in 1835, but that it was a "violation of the spirit of the federal compact, to indulge even a hope that the chains of the captive" may one day be broken. Next, he joked, the "arrogant south" would call upon northerners to "pass edicts forbidding men to think on the subject of slavery," on the ground that even meditation on the topic violated the spirit of the Constitution.[13]

When the southern states' rights faction of the Democratic Party, led by Governor George McDuffie, attacked northern supporters of Martin Van Buren as "pro-abolitionist," Leggett was stunned. As he familiarized himself with antislavery literature during the mid-1830s, he gradually stopped insulting abolitionists as "amalgamators" and instead described them as "men of wealth, education, respectability and intelligence, misguided on a single subject, but actuated by a sincere desire to promote the welfare of their kind."[14]

A particularly violent antiabolitionist mob in Haverhill, Massachusetts, finally brought about Leggett's heretical conversion. In a scene that bore a chilling resemblance to the previous summer's riots in New York, a large mob dragging a loaded cannon and carrying other explosives marched on an abolitionist meetinghouse. Leggett again claimed that such attacks would only fortify the abolitionists; this time, however, he warned that blood shed in the battle against slavery threatened to "engender a brood of serpents which shall entwine themselves around the monster slavery, and crush it in their sinewy folds." With this editorial, the "monster slavery" replaced in Leggett's mind monopolies and the "scrip nobility" as the most serious aristocratic threat facing the nation's democratic institutions. The next evening, Leggett shocked Jacksonian New York by announcing he had read and almost wholly endorsed the program of the immediatist American Antislavery Society.[15]

According to abolitionist lore popularized by John Greenleaf Whittier, Leggett's conversion hit him like a bolt of lightning after he read the Antislavery Society's *Address* on September 3, 1835. "He gave it his candid perusal, weighed its arguments, compared its doctrines with those of the foundation of his political faith," Whittier wrote, "and rose up from its examination an abolitionist."[16] Actually, some time elapsed before Leggett would call himself an abolitionist, with all the overtones of middle-class reform and perfectionist zeal that the term implied. In the months after his conversion to antislavery, in fact, the editor insisted he was nothing more than a particularly dedicated Jacksonian Democrat. Leggett bristled at accusations from other Democratic presses that his antislavery pronouncements meant that he had deserted his party; editorials on topics other than slavery bore him out on this point. For example, Leggett enthusiastically endorsed Martin Van Buren, Jackson's handpicked successor, in 1835 and marked the passing of the Old Hero's time in office with a tribute to a "period that will shine in American history with more inherent and undying luster, than any other which the chronicler has yet recorded."[17]

After 1835 Leggett became even more doctrinaire in his calls for hard currency and free trade, establishing himself as the godfather of the radical wing of the Democratic Party.[18] So Leggett's politics were in flux on a wide variety of issues in 1833–37. He continued to claim that his radical hard-money and antislavery stances grew organically from his Jacksonian views.

Leggett's attacks on the city's proslavery Democratic and Whig presses rhetorically echoed his earlier editorial tirades against monopolies and the bank. In fact, his strong adherence to the Jeffersonian concept of strict construction led to one of Leggett's most important contributions to political antislavery: an argument framed within the bounds of the U.S. Constitution.[19] As a strict constructionist, Leggett agreed with many southern politicians that the Constitution forbade direct federal interference with slavery where it already existed.[20] But he argued that the framers had never intended to make slavery a permanent feature of the American landscape. Why else, he asked, would they purposely avoid the words "slave" or "slavery" in the Constitution?[21] All that was decided in the compromising spirit of 1787, Leggett came to believe, was covert recognition of an unfortunate institution. Certainly the framers had left to Congress the explicit authority to abolish slavery in the District of Columbia, and to the American people the option to discuss openly any matter pertaining to slavery, whether or not it threatened the institution.[22]

Leggett insisted that Constitutional property rights be separated from the specific right to property in slaves. He claimed that the Constitution did not recognize slaves as absolute property; instead, it merely recognized the institution (albeit tacitly) and gave slave owners certain legal rights, such as the recovery of runaway slaves. "Nowhere," he wrote, does the Constitution "give any countenance to the idea that slaves are considered *property* in the meaning of the term as used" in the Fifth Amendment, which states that private property will not be taken for public use without just compensation.

"They are not *taken*," he continued, "but enfranchised; and not *for the public use*, but for their own; or rather, not *for use* at all, but in compliance with an exalted sense of the inalienable rights of humanity."[23]

Leggett's "divorce" of constitutional property rights from the right to hold slaves as property, as well as his observation of the limits in the Constitution's recognition of slavery, would be taken up in the following years as a central tenet of the political antislavery movement. Political abolitionists such as the Democratic-leaning Gamaliel Bailey and Salmon P. Chase would insert the call for the divorce of the federal government from slavery in every Liberty Party platform up to 1848. Abolitionist Alvan Stewart took the argument even further when he insisted that the Constitution was, in fact, an *antislavery* document.[24]

Once Leggett reasoned that slavery was inherently hostile to Constitutional rule, it was but a small step to denouncing it as a social and economic evil. Using a familiar technique borrowed from Alexis de Tocqueville and other travelers, Leggett contrasted "garden"-like Ohio and its "lethargic" neighbor Kentucky as proof that slavery "withers what it touches." By removing slaveholders from the category of producers, a concept upon which the Democratic alliance was built in the 1820s, Leggett helped to portray them as another face of the antidemocratic monster threatening the equal rights of the white male citizenry.[25]

Leggett did not stop with slavery's assaults on white Americans. His later editorials — written for his independent *Plaindealer* in early 1837 — extended Jacksonian equal rights doctrine to blacks, a mammoth departure from the Democratic mainstream and the almost universally held assumptions of white supremacy. In the prospectus for the new paper, he reiterated his loyalty to the party of Jackson and Van Buren and its "cardinal principle" of equal rights. By then, however, he included within that term the rejection of slavery as evil and the absolute defense of abolitionists' attempts at free expression a necessary part of democracy. Democrats, Leggett insisted, were far more likely to be "true" abolitionists because slavery was a repudiation of "the fundamental article of the creed of democracy, which acknowledges the political equality, and unalienable right of freedom, of all mankind."[26] Echoing the arguments of free black newspapers in New York and Philadelphia, Leggett pointed out that "the oppression which our fathers suffered from Great Britain was nothing in comparison with that which the negroes experience at the hands of the slave holders."[27] By defining slavery in such political terms for both blacks and whites, Leggett pioneered a strain of abolitionism that bore little resemblance to the perfectionist "fanaticism" he had once scorned. Even his most radical demand—the call for black suffrage in addition to emancipation—was based on Democratic equal rights doctrine. He ridiculed the property qualification imposed on free blacks under New York's 1821 constitution: "May not the black man, who has only one hundred dollars, possess as much capacity, honesty, and love of country, as he who has twice or thrice that sum?"[28] Only when the freed slave's "enfranchised spirit" was allowed "to roam on the illimitable plain of equal liberty," Leggett argued, would the United States live up to the promises uttered by the founders.[29]

Editorials favoring black enfranchisement and racial equality were intolerable to the men who ran the Democratic Party. First Leggett was attacked in the *Washington Globe*, the national party's semiofficial organ. Then he was publicly read out of the party by the New York County Democratic organization. Finally, Democratic sachems forced Bryant to cut Leggett loose from his financial share of the *Post* by withdrawing all government patronage from the paper, a move that threatened it with bankruptcy. Leggett, already in declining health, wrote that he had been unjustly purged for attacking slavery in the very same way he had railed against monopolies and the Second Bank of the United States, "on account of the prejudicial influence slavery exercises on the morals of the people, for the manifold vice which it fosters, and for the paralyzing effects which it has on enterprise and industry in every walk of life."[30]

Despite his excommunication from the regular Democratic organization, Leggett remained a hero to the equal rights wing of the party. After famed Shakespearean actor Edwin Forrest, Leggett's close friend and patron, declined the regular nomination for Congress in 1838 (preferring to remain on the more lucrative theatrical stage), a significant number of radicals and ex-Locofocos moved Leggett's name for the nomination. This Leggett boomlet was only possible because conservative, probank Democrats such as Gideon Lee and Richard Riker had bolted the regular ticket to support Whig William Seward's campaign for governor. In their absence, such radicals as Alexander Ming Jr., Charles Ferris, and Levi Slamm were free to strike a deal with moderates like C. C. Cambreleng and Stephen Allen. In a move that would have seemed impossible three years earlier, the Tammany General Committee adopted the entire Locofoco *Declaration of Rights* (inspired by Leggett in 1835) and declared that monopolies inherently "violated . . . the equal rights of the people." Within this "new" Tammany Hall, a sizable number of Democrats were ready to accept Leggett's economic and political leadership *despite* his abolitionism.[31]

Members of the nominating committee, however, remained unconvinced. In an ironic echoing of the tactics of the abolitionist Liberty Party, the committee sent Leggett a questionnaire to determine, once and for all, the extent of the once feisty editor's antislavery. Leggett's supporters, including Bryant and Richard Adams Locke of the *New Era*, tried in vain to suggest that his opinions on slavery in the District of Columbia "precisely coincide[d] with that of the President of the United States." But Leggett's official statement, which was read aloud to the committee, clearly stated his belief that "Congress has full constitutional power, by express provision, to legislate [with regard to the District] . . . and that slavery is as much a subject of this power as anything else." Although toned down from his radical writings in the *Plaindealer*, Leggett refused to compromise his slavery views. His brief candidacy was over.[32]

Leggett was deeply embarrassed by his supporters' disavowal of his abolitionism in their attempt to make him a more palatable congressional candidate. One booster even went so far as to declare in print that "Mr. Leggett is *not* an abolitionist." This forced Leggett's most explicit declaration on the matter: "I am an abolitionist. . . . I would not have this fact disguised or mystified. Rather, I again meet the denunciations of Tammany Hall and be stigmatized with all the foul epithets with which the anti-abolition vocabulary abounds, than recant, or deny one tittle of my creed. Abolition is, in my sense, a necessary and a glorious part of democracy."[33] In the same letter, Leggett also predicted the rise of an imminent movement for the overthrow the slave system "in the next three years — or, if not three, say three times three." He would not live to see his prediction borne out.

By early 1839 Leggett was again battling illness, as he had for the last half of 1835 and most of 1836, and his money had run out. Forrest, who had already sunk $15,000 into Leggett's publishing ventures, found his friend contemplating suicide. He covered Leggett's most immediate debts and installed Leggett and his family in a house in New Rochelle. In the winter of 1839, Van Buren (indebted to Leggett's doctrines for his signature economic contribution, the Independent Treasury) arranged a position for Leggett as consul to Guatemala, where it was hoped the tropical air would help him regain his health. Leggett never made the trip, as he died from an attack of "bilious colic" on May 29, 1839.[34]

Yet William Leggett became more of a hero in death than he had been in life. He was eulogized in verse by Whittier and Bryant, toasted in the White House, and praised in countless Jacksonian journals. In a strange turnabout, Tammany Hall expunged Leggett's 1835 excommunication from its official minutes and two years later erected a bust of him in the room where the denunciation took place. The irony was not lost on Whittier:

> . . . Well is it now that o'er his grave ye raise
> The stony tribute of your tardy praise,
> For not alone that pile shall tell to Fame
> Of the brave heart beneath, but of the builders' shame.[35]

In the following decade, praise like this helped Leggett become the patron saint of antislavery Democrats such as Whitman and countless others throughout the North.

George Henry Evans

George Henry Evans, a freethinker, mechanic, newspaper publisher, and land reformer, personified the radical tradition in antebellum America, artfully bridging the intellectual and temporal gaps between Tom Paine and Henry George. From the inauguration of his *Working Man's Advocate*, the leading organ of America's first labor movement, to his plan, still unrealized at the time of his death, to parcel out western lands to homesteaders, Evans spoke for eastern producers who feared the changes transforming the nation before the Civil War. After emerging as a leader of New York City's Workingmen's Party, Evans focused his attention on winning more influence for workers in the Democratic Party. Like William Leggett, Evans was a leader in the battle against monopolies and banks and for hard money, land reform, and the separation of church and state. As his political ideas matured, Evans became increasingly convinced that the concentration of land in the hands of a few wealthy Americans—what he called the "land monopoly"—constituted a more dangerous concentration of power than any bank, religious denomination, or political party. Evans's proposal to distribute public land for free to settlers as homesteads contributed an essential component to the ideology of Free Soil that, by the 1850s, became inextricably linked with antislavery. Yet more than a decade before Evans proclaimed his movement for free homesteads, he had already concluded that the principles of the Democracy were incompatible with slavery and that southern slaveholders posed a serious threat to the well-being of the republic.

George Henry Evans was born in Herefordshire, England, in 1805, the eldest child of George and Sarah White Evans. His father was a British officer in the Napoleonic Wars; after serving in Egypt, he operated a modest brickworks in the town of Bromeyard. Sarah's family had done well enough raising sheep to acquire a large house with several servants. In 1820, after Sarah's death, the elder George Evans moved with his two sons to America, joining his brothers in Chenango Point (now Binghamton), New York. After he remarried a year later, the father again moved the family, this time to a small farm on the Oswego Turnpike, near Ithaca. Sixteen-year-old George Henry, endowed with a solid English "scholastic" education, was apprenticed to a local printer.[36]

While working in Ithaca, which had a reputation as a haven of free thought, Evans first read the writings of Tom Paine, who became his hero. In 1824, nearing the end of his apprenticeship, Evans jointly published the biweekly *Museum and Independent Corrector*, later described as a "chatty" free-thought paper.[37] Evans moved to New York City, probably in late 1827, to work for the free-thought *Correspondent*. In March 1828 the paper carried the notice that it was printed by the George H. Evans Printing Co., at several successive addresses, the last of which was the Institute of Practical Education, directed by Robert Jennings. Jennings introduced the young journeyman printer to Frances Wright, the brilliant and eccentric Scottish "priestess of Beelzebub" who would lead Evans into the Workingmen's cause.[38]

Wright had recently abandoned her communal settlement at Nashoba, Tennessee, where she had purchased several slaves and planned to have them earn their freedom with the farm's profits. When the profits did not materialize and local hostility toward her experiment endangered the entire enterprise, Wright moved to New Harmony, Indiana, the community founded by English industrialist Robert Owen. (She later accompanied her former slaves to Haiti, where they were given land by President Jean Pierre Boyer.) Wright and Owen's son, Robert Dale Owen, took over the settlement's newspaper, the *New Harmony Gazette*, and as its fame grew (mostly due to Wright's scandalous notoriety as a female lecturer), moved it to New York. With Jennings as his contact to Wright, Evans became the printer of the newspaper, which was renamed the *Free Enquirer*.[39]

Owen and Wright had reprinted articles during 1828 from a small Philadelphia weekly called the *Mechanics Free Press*, the nation's first labor newspaper. New York was experiencing similar labor conditions, with journeymen and laborers agitating for a ten-hour day, a mechanics' lien law, the abolition of imprisonment for debt, and improved educational opportunities for the city's working people. As a freethinker and a mechanic, these issues were all exceedingly important to Evans. On October 31, 1829, Evans published the first issue of the *Working Man's Advocate*, "edited by a Mechanic," in which he proposed to fight against "any further encroachments on our equal rights . . . and seek the means by which all may be placed on an equal footing."[40] One week later, twenty-four-year-old Evans became an American citizen.

After a remarkable showing in the 1829 elections, the Workingmen's movement split into three factions, the largest of which was connected with Evans and Owen. The other two were associated with the regular Tammany Democrats and Thomas Skidmore, a fiery mechanic who advocated a re-distribution of property. The Evans-Owen faction began publishing a new newspaper, the *New York Daily Sentinel*, with the *Advocate* continuing as the *Sentinel*'s "country edition." By the early 1830s there were more than fifty newspapers in the East, South, and Midwest that imitated, endorsed, and reprinted portions of Evans's papers, making it far more important than its small circulation (around 2,000) would suggest.[41]

The radical insurgency of the early labor movement virtually ceased to exist after December 1829, but the Workingmen's Party, born out of a mar-riage of convenience between the Owen-Evans wing and a group of entre-preneurial craftsmen, continued well into the 1830s. By early 1832, however, much of the old "Workie" constituency had returned to the establishment politics of Tammany, which had shrewdly passed limited legislation appeal-ing to New York's journeymen. While some of the entrepreneurial craftsmen who helped take over the Workingmen's Party broke off to support the politics of Henry Clay, Evans led the remnants of the old insurgency slowly and carefully into the radical wing of the Democratic Party.[42]

This did not mean Evans was casting his lot with the politicians of Tam-many and Martin Van Buren's Albany Regency; on the contrary, Evans al-ways maintained a high level of contempt and suspicion for the local party. He even remained cool to Jackson before the 1832 election, dubbing him a "violent party man" and a "caucus candidate."[43] "The times demand an-other Jefferson who will take the side of the people," Evans wrote in June 1830 in an editorial urging the nomination of Richard M. Johnson of Ken-tucky, an anti-Sabbatarian congressman who fought against imprisonment for debt. But it was not long before Evans was comparing Jackson to the sage of Monticello, and tributes to Johnson faded from the pages of the paper.[44]

Evans began warming to Jackson in the spring of 1832. "Although many of the working men might not approve of all the conduct and measures of Andrew Jackson, there are few who do not *prefer* him [over Henry Clay and the Whig opposition] for his support of some of the most important mea-sures which the working men advocate."[45] These "measures" were the overthrow of monopolies in general and banks and paper money in particular, cited increasingly by the Workingmen as causes of their anxiety and declining status. The equal access to education so touted by Evans and Owen in 1829 was quickly giving way to calls for an end to the Second Bank of the United States and other "chartered monopolies."

While Evans and his faction were moving gradually toward the Democracy, the party was preparing to welcome them. By 1832, Democrats had adopted the political language of the Workingmen, arraying "producers" and "mechanics" against the new aristocracy of privilege and moneyed corruption. To be sure, the goals of the Democrats were less radical than those of the Workingmen of 1829, but by the time of Andrew Jackson's famous bank veto message in 1832 — the rhetorical high-water mark in the battle between the "republican small producers" and the Money Power — most of the former Workies were squarely in the Democratic camp.[46]

For George Henry Evans, however, the antibank, antiaristocratic message emanating from Washington — while positive — did not square with the administration's embrace of the South's system of slavery. Evans always maintained that he was more concerned with the welfare of white, urban workers than of black slaves in the South (a stance that has earned him attacks from recent historians), but on several notable occasions he was unmatched in the boldness with which he attacked the peculiar institution. During the decade of the 1830s Evans twice staked out a position as an antislavery radical. The first was in the aftermath of Nat Turner's rebellion in Virginia, when Evans stood alone — even compared to William Lloyd Garrison — in justifying the violent actions of Turner and his followers. The second was during the July Days of 1834, when for more than a week antiabolitionist mobs ruled the streets of New York. Only Evans and William Leggett — both radical Jacksonians — condemned the rioting and rioters at a time when the leaders of both parties blamed the abolitionists and fanned the flames of mob violence.

Word of Nat Turner's slave rebellion in Southampton County, Virginia, reached New York on Monday, August 29, 1831. Evans's response to the bloody rampage was remarkable in its sympathy for the murderous slaves. While condemning violence, Evans focused on the rebels' goals: freedom from servitude. If their acts were ignorant, he said, it was because the education of slaves was forbidden by law. Evans's was the only journal in New York to defend Turner's band, and his stance brought withering criticism from the mainstream press, which blamed abolitionist agitation for the Southampton disaster. Turner's famous *Confessions*, recorded in Southampton's jail by a white lawyer, are silent about the ultimate plan of the rebels. There was gossip in Southampton of an attempt to seize the town of Jerusalem or to sail to Africa or the free states or even simply to "rise and murder all the whites."[47] Hundreds of miles north in New York, George Henry Evans claimed absolute certainty about Turner's aims: "What can be more natural than human beings destined to perpetual slavery, should commit excesses in attempts to better their condition?" Evans asked on August 29. "And how can the whites be better secured against such excesses than by affording the degraded slaves the prospect of gradual but effectual emancipation, and by capacitating them for the enjoyment of freedom?"[48]

Responses of other papers to the killings illustrate Evans's radical stance on this point. Local reactions to the uprising were mostly intended to dispel rumors and pacify anxious whites. One Virginia paper pondered how a group of "deluded wretches" with no cause for revenge could rise against such "kind and indulgent masters."[49] Virginia governor John Floyd blamed the affair on black preachers and the "Yankee pedlars [sic] and traders" who traveled the Virginia countryside. "They . . . tell the blacks the black man was as good as the white; that all men were born free and equal; that the white people rebelled against England to obtain freedom; so have the blacks a right to do." To curb the problem, Floyd proposed confining slaves to their owners' estates, prohibiting black preaching, and deporting all free blacks from the state.[50]

Gallons of the strongest anti-Turner vitriol, however, were spilled in the pages of the northern press. The *New York Journal of Commerce* painted the rebels as highly sexualized savages gleefully hacking at children and "weltering in their gore." In a far cry from Evans's justifications of black-on-white violence, one editor called for the execution of every slave even suspected to have participated in the "diabolical transaction": "When the lives of a whole community are in jeopardy," he asserted, "severe measures are not only justifiable, but necessary."[51] The *Albany Argus*, the Regency paper edited by Edwin Croswell, used the occasion to assuage southern fears of (mostly imagined) northern hostility to slavery. Croswell even offered northern help in putting down a future rebellion: "The men of the North will come to the aid of their fellow citizens of the South [because] the cause is a common one; and the claim upon us . . . is the claim of humanity and patriotism."[52]

Not surprisingly, the most vicious and rabid attacks on the rebels came from the pen of James Watson Webb, famous for his antiabolitionist and antiblack — as well as anti-Jacksonian — views. Much of Webb's wrath was directed at abolitionists. "What do they mean, and where do they intend to stop? . . . Do they mean to array the black against the white? Do they mean, by preaching up the equality of the two races, to blend them with each other in a mongrel breed of crisp-haired mullatoes?" Webb's suggestion for preventing future slave uprisings was to occupy the South with proslavery troops and "distribute them that the slaves shall feel that to attempt an insurrection will be attended with certain punishment. The property in slaves is guaranteed to their masters by the Constitution of the United States . . . and this can only be [enforced] by the presence of regular troops."[53]

Even William Lloyd Garrison, whose *Liberator* had debuted just eight months before, stopped short of justifying the actions of the Southampton "brutes." "In all that we have written, is there ought to justify the excesses of the slaves? No. Nevertheless, they deserve no more censure than the Greeks in destroying the Turks, or the Poles in exterminating the Russians, or our fathers in slaughtering the British."[54] That same week, Garrison reiterated to a friend that "I do not justify the slaves in their rebellion; yet I do not condemn *them*, and applaud similar conduct in *white men*. I deny the right of any people to fight for liberty, and so far am a Quaker in principle."[55] To Garrison, slavery was a terrible sin and the Constitution a proslavery document. The only way to accomplish the "great work of national redemption" — the abolition of slavery — was for righteous "Christians, philanthropists and patriots" to persuade the rest of the nation of the evils of slavery.[56]

Evans saw the events in Southampton differently. Three weeks after the insurrection, he wrote a scathing editorial condemning the "Daring Outrage of the Virginia Slavites." Far from damning the nation's founding documents as the tools of slaveholders, Evans penned an eloquent defense of the rebellion based on natural rights. Invoking his idols Tom Paine and Thomas Jefferson, Evans declared that, since freedom is the "birthright of man," the violent response of the rebels to lives of perpetual servitude was justifiable. "However absurd or cruel were their proceedings, if their *object* was to obtain their freedom, those who kept them in slavery and ignorance alone are answerable for their conduct. They were deluded, but their cause was *just*."[57] Indeed, it was upon the shoulders of the slaveholders, who had kept their human chattel in a state of ignorance and misery, that the guilt lay. "Have they done what they could and should do for eradicating the evil of slavery? Have they diminished the number of slaves? Have they prepared the present generation, or made provision for preparing the next, to enjoy freedom? The answer to each of these questions involves them in guilt."[58]

Adding to the "outrages" of the Virginia slaveholders, Evans printed the diary of a New York lawyer who was forcibly driven out of Virginia for statements he made during the rebellion. After maintaining in a conversation that "blacks, as men, were entitled to their freedom," the lawyer was, in full view of the mayor and other town officials, dragged from his room, taken out of town, stripped naked, and nearly murdered by an angry mob. "I asked [my captors] whether this was the country in which 'all men were born free and equal' — in which 'the freedom of speech' was guaranteed to everyone; and, also, whether this was their reward for my flying to arms, last Friday [during the insurrection] in defense of their wives and their children?" After narrowly escaping a lynching at the hands of his captors, the narrator eventually fled to Richmond and boarded a steamer bound for New York. Evans, who was acquainted with the lawyer, even printed the names of several of those "slave-holding desperadoes of Petersburg" most responsible for the episode.[59] Evans and Garrison stood out among the editors of the North in their condemnation of the slaveholders for causing Nat Turner's uprising, but Evans alone found justification in Turner's actions. Evans's natural rights critique of slavery and his comparison of the rebels with the soldiers of the American Revolution were the opening shots of a new, Democratic assault on the peculiar institution.

In the weeks after the Turner uprising, Evans continued to print editorials attacking southern slaveholders and to call attention to rumors of copycat slave rebellions.[60] Evans also published a circular by "A Free Colored Floridian" titled "Prejudice Against Color," which urged equal protection under the law for free blacks and argued all prejudice stemmed from ignorance. "Constitutional protection to person and property are granted to all free people in all civilized countries, with one exception . . . the United States," the author wrote. The Free Colored Floridian specifically chastised states such as Ohio, which passed legislation hostile to the free black population in the late 1820s. But instead of calling for equal justice in the United States, the author urged free blacks to move to Mexico, where he claimed there was ample land for purchase, settled "by people who are mostly colored *and entirely free from all prejudice against complexion.*"[61]

When faced with the proslavery writings of Whig editor James Watson Webb, Evans responded with some of the strongest abolitionist rhetoric of the 1830s. To Webb's fear-mongering about the dangers of miscegenation, Evans replied that "if a mixture of the races *would* be the consequence of that equality which the immortal Jefferson declared to be the birthright of all mankind, we should still contend for equality." Evans then tried to rebut Webb's claim (which was also Garrison's) that slave property is specifically protected by the Constitution. Here Evans was on shakier ground, but his attempt was quite spirited. First, he pointed out, the word "slave" was not to be found anywhere in the document. After reprinting Article I, Section 2, which set out that political representation be determined by adding to "the whole number of free persons, including these bound to service for a term of years[,] . . . three-fifths of all other persons," Evans argued that while it admitted to slavery's existence, the section in no way acknowledged a "right" to property in slaves, as Watson had asserted. In an analysis of Article IV, Section 2, the famous "fugitive slave" clause of the Constitution, Evans wrote that "the idea is too absurd for belief, that the framers intended even to *recognize* the right of the minority of the people of any state to hold the majority as *property,* and it is monstrously absurd to suppose that it was intended to *guarantee* the right to *such* property." Evans believed it to be a bitter irony that there were "slaves in a land of freedom," and in this editorial he was desperately searching the nation's founding document for passages hostile to legalized chattel slavery. This was a unique course of attack, since at the time it was almost universally argued that slavery was subject to "state jurisdiction," as were all powers not explicitly mentioned in the Constitution. Later in the decade, radical Jacksonian William Leggett would expand upon the course first taken by Evans and argue even more persuasively that the Constitution was an antislavery document.[62]

Evans followed his Constitutional arguments by explaining why the *Advocate* supported the Southampton rebels and by voicing limited support for the much-maligned abolitionists. "The 'fanatics' of whom the Courier speaks must answer its questions for themselves. We answer that we believe it our duty to take the part of the oppressed, against the oppressor, whatever may be the kindred or country of the oppressor and the oppressed. In relation to the question of slavery our kindred are mankind — our color is the color of freedom." Evans also derided the goals of the American Colonization Society, which attempted to end slavery and rid the nation of free blacks by colonizing them in West Africa, as "the most absurd of all absurd projects."[63] Since there was little evidence slaveholding states would consent to give up "their assumed right of property in human flesh," Evans concluded forcefully that slavery must be "abolished . . . by means of the general government, or by the general government withholding the means of perpetuating it." This was an important leap for Evans, who as a small-government Jacksonian abhorred excesses of federal power. He understood that slavery would not be given up lightly, even in places like Virginia that at the time were mired in economic decline. One place slavery could be abolished fairly simply, he suggested, was the District of Columbia.[64]

More significant than his defense of racial equality and the Turner rebels, however, was Evans's program to distribute public lands to landless homesteaders, a program he called, among other things, Free Soil. During the 1840s and 1850s, homesteads became unalterably fused with the issue of slavery expansion in the minds of northerners and southerners alike. This link underscored Free Soil's rhetorical elusiveness and ambiguity. The potent term was appropriated by a host of other groups, movements, and political parties, including the Free Soil Party and, later, the Republicans. No matter who appropriated it, however, Free Soil always potentially implied the double meaning Evans intended: land free of charge and at the same time free of slavery. Free Soil managed to speak directly to the anxieties of poor or vulnerable northern whites, creating a new source of support for limiting slavery's expansion.

As recent scholars have pointed out, Evans and his followers were far more concerned with the plight of free white labor, which Evans termed "white slavery," than with enslaved blacks.[65] Too often, however, this point has been made in an attempt to indict antebellum white workers on charges of racism, one to which many—even most—would have surely pleaded guilty. Still, Evans's careful plan to parcel out the public lands into inalienable homesteads for settlers—be they urban workers, Indians, free blacks, or ex-slaves—fused democratic ideas of universal landownership with attempts to contain the expansion of slavery. "I am as much an *abolitionist* as any man in the land," Evans wrote in the first number of his land-reform journal the *Radical*. "I think Slavery is a disgrace to the republic, black slavery as well as *white*." He went on to promise that he would not "truckle" to southern slaveholders "by asserting *that the negro is not a man*," but he made it clear that his priorities were the equal rights of white labor. "If we would abolish southern slavery, let us set the slaveholders an example," he wrote, "by emancipating the white laborer, *by restoring his natural right to the soil*."[66]

Much of this story will be taken up below, as territorial expansion into Texas, the upper Midwest, Oregon, and finally, land won from Mexico became interlocked with the movement for free homesteads. To be sure, not every southerner (or every slaveholder) opposed the notion of free homesteads. But as the issue of slavery's expansion heated up and homestead planks buttressed the platforms of parties as varied as the Liberty League and the Free Soil, Free Democratic, and Republican parties—each desirous of confining slavery—land reform's staunchest opponents proved to be slaveholders. George Fitzhugh wrote that free land, like free love, "tended to dissipate civilization," while the fire-eating *Charleston Mercury* railed that an early version of the Homestead Act was the "most dangerous abolition bill which has ever indirectly been pressed in Congress."[67]

Just what posited free farms opposite slave labor? There were several factors. First, the people whom homestead legislation targeted were free, white workers who had little desire to compete with black labor. This is not to say that they had an affinity for black people. Most clearly did not. In these respects they were similar to the immigrants from Virginia and Kentucky who populated the free states of the Old Northwest. Second, land reformers continually made theoretical connections between homesteads and Free Soil, playing on the term's duality. New York abolitionist and landholder Gerrit Smith, who became one of Evans's most stalwart converts, explained in a broadside the connection he saw between land reform and abolitionism: "I hardly need say that I am an abolitionist," Smith wrote in 1848. "But, abolitionist though I am . . . to abolish chattel-slavery is not to abolish land-monopoly, to abolish land-monopoly is to abolish chattel-slavery." He went on to argue that the division of the West into farms totaling 50 to 100 acres, worked by families of free white or black farmers, would leave no room for plantations, auctions, or slavery. "Abolitionist though I am, I regard Land-Monopoly, take the world together, as a far more abundant source of suffering and debasement, than is Slavery," Smith continued.[68]

Slavery's potential advance into new territory kept the two movements linked in the 1840s, as factions as varied as the Industrial Congress and the Free Soil Party adopted Evans's land reform ideas. Workers saw homesteads on the public lands as a potential safety valve for labor surpluses and compressed wages, while farmers in both East and West viewed that same territory as a way for their offspring to replicate a yeoman farming life for at least another generation. Key members of each of these groups began, in the mid-1840s, to fear that expansionist slaveholders were threatening the futures of their families and even the republic. One farmer in upstate New York feared that unless slavery was contained, his grandson might never own productive land of his own. The homestead principle alone, Abijah Beckwith wrote to his young namesake, ensured the "equal distribution of our lands into convenient farms, and the generally equal distribution of wealth," which he believed would "prove favorable to liberty [in our] lately acquired possessions on the Pacific."[69]

That farmers such as Abijah Beckwith were conversant with the land reform principles of a New York radical was significant, and mostly due to Evans's brilliant propagandizing. "Are you an American citizen?" Evans asked in his most famous land-reform circular. "Then you are a joint owner of the public lands. Why not take enough of your property to provide yourself a home? Why not vote yourself a farm?" Copies of the circular were plastered over the walls of New York City in the fall of 1845 and made their way upstate in the periodicals dedicated to abolishing tenantry in the state.[70]

Evans's contributions to the Free Soil and free labor ideologies of the 1840s and 1850s have been almost overlooked by modern scholars. Yet his nonevangelical, working class, and Jacksonian critique of slavery and its expansion had important consequences for the city of New York, the state of New York, and the nation in the decades before the Civil War.

Thomas Morris

Thomas Morris's eulogists were convinced that the senator's memory would be honored by unborn generations of Americans. Salmon P. Chase, who later held Morris's seat in the U.S. Senate, credited Morris with awakening him and countless others to the character of the Slave Power and insisted that "his memory should be kept freshly living among the lovers of liberty and progress." Another eulogist prophesied that "so surely as justice is an attribute of the Supreme Being, the generation will yet be born that will bless the memory of THOMAS MORRIS."[71] Such predictions of immortality, however, have not been borne out. Thomas Morris, the first political martyr of the antislavery movement, has received scant attention from historians. This is undoubtedly due to his relatively brief appearance on the national scene and to the absence of any sizable body of personal papers. But it is also true that such men as Thomas Morris have generally left historians baffled. On one hand, Morris was a typical administration Democrat: he stood solidly with President Andrew Jackson in the nullification crisis and shared Jackson's hostility to banks, tariffs, and chartered monopolies. Yet he became a zealous opponent of slavery and an advocate of black suffrage — positions anathema to his party and to a large majority of the American public in the 1830s.

Morris opposed slavery on moral as well as political grounds, but in a manner very different from that of the middle-class reformers and Finneyites who made up the immediatist abolition movement. Though a deeply religious man (and the son of a Baptist preacher), Morris resented as meddlesome the abolitionists' attempts at reforming slaveholders. Instead he focused on slavery's immorality to slaves and its potential threat to the liberties of northern and southern whites. "That *all* may be safe," Morris told the Senate, "I conclude that *the negro will yet be set free.*"[72]

Morris's influence on the development and fulfillment of antislavery sentiment was political. First and foremost, he introduced the phrase and concept of the Slave Power into American political culture. Just as the Monster Bank served as the master symbol of the Age of Jackson, the Slave Power became the personification of political evil during the ensuing era of American sectionalism. Like the Money Power represented by the bank, Morris's symbol encompassed the rising tide of fear and hostility northerners felt toward slavery and the South. The connection drawn by Morris between one master symbol and the next was instrumental in turning northern Democrats against slavery and its expansion. When Morris was denied re-election to the Senate because of his abolitionist views, his political "martyr-dom" provided further evidence for anxious northerners of the growing influence wielded by the slaveholders.[73]

Thomas Morris's early life mirrors the efforts of many early Americans to preserve a life based on freehold ownership of small farms, even if it meant constant mobility and instability. Morris was born in rural Berks County, Pennsylvania, on January 3, 1776, exactly one week before Tom Paine published *Common Sense* in nearby Philadelphia. Morris's father, Isaac, was a Baptist preacher whose family traced its American origins back to seventeenth-century Massachusetts. His mother, Ruth, was the daughter of a small-scale Virginia planter. According to Morris's son and biographer, Ruth Morris instilled hatred of slavery in the boy; she apparently learned about the horrors of the Middle Passage and forced labor by talking with some African-born slaves on her father's plantation. Whether or not the story is true, Morris's feelings about slavery did not affect his behavior, political or otherwise, until his years in the U.S. Senate.[74]

Soon after Thomas's birth the family moved to a small farm in the mountains of western Virginia. The boy's formal education was minimal, consisting of three months at a common school. At age seventeen he joined Captain Levi Morgan's company of Wood Rangers and unsuccessfully trailed bands of Indians through the wilds of eastern Ohio. In 1795 Morris crossed the Ohio River and settled in the frontier town of Columbia, where he clerked in a store owned by the Reverend John Smith. When Smith emigrated from Pennsylvania in 1790, he was only the second regular pastor in the Ohio Territory. Most of Columbia's earliest settlers were committed

Baptists (many of whom were preachers like Morris's father), and one of the town's first official acts was to organize a church and engage Smith. After just a few months, the congregation passed a resolution allowing Smith to split his time between the Columbia church and another one erected five miles away in Cincinnati, Columbia's main rival for supremacy in the Miami country. Smith quickly became known for more than his mastery of the Gospel, however. He was locally famous for his superior skills in pursuits as varied as ox driving, logrolling, horse racing, and especially, politicking.[75]

The pastor became Morris's political and spiritual mentor. The young adventurer appears to have experienced a religious conversion while in Smith's employ and found an outlet for his feelings in pietistic verse. Smith encouraged Morris in all his religious, intellectual, and political pursuits until the former's 1802 removal to Washington as one of Ohio's first U.S. senators.[76] Two years after Morris's arrival in Ohio, he married Rachel Davis, the daughter of one of Columbia's pioneer Baptist families. In 1800 the young couple moved to the frontier town of Bethel, located between Columbia and Cincinnati, after Morris was arrested and served a short prison term for debt. In an effort to improve his finances, Morris read law in a rough-hewn office in Bethel in 1802 and was admitted to the bar two years later. The proprietor of the hamlet was a devout Virginia Baptist who deeded two lots for a Baptist church, for use by believers "who do not hold slaves, nor commune at the Lord's Table with those who do practice such tyranny over their fellow creatures."[77]

Morris quickly developed a successful practice as a frontier lawyer, relying on his strong personality and ability to make legal arguments clear to a frontier jury. In this respect his early career parallels those of Andrew Jackson and Henry Clay, who, as did many of the rising stars of the young republic, honed their political skills in western courtrooms. Before a jury Morris was said to be "clear, able, powerful . . . and not uncouth." He also developed a reputation among the lawyers in southern Ohio for his ability to sway juries with skillful (and accurate) quotations from scripture.[78]

Politically, the young lawyer (like the vast majority of those living in the new towns of southern Ohio) was a steadfast Jeffersonian. He was elected to the state assembly in 1806 on the basis of his growing reputation and would occupy a seat in the legislature for all but two of the next twenty-four years. Ohio's Jeffersonian chieftains began to view Morris as an ideal state legislator. He relished his positions at the head of various committees, took pride in crafting legislation, and projected little outward ambition for higher office. Issues that interested the young legislator were the abolition of imprisonment for debt (the offense for which Morris had served time in the Williamsburg jail), the establishment of common schools, direct election of judges, opposition to increasing state debt for canal construction, and an end to the establishment of all chartered monopolies and legislation that "gave one class civil privileges above another."[79]

As his support for these issues indicates, Morris was the very embodiment of a Jeffersonian Democrat. His record in the state legislature is, however, nearly silent on the issue of slavery. Slavery had been prohibited in the states carved from the Northwest Territory by Jefferson's 1787 ordinance, but with slavery thriving just across the Ohio River in Kentucky, the question was often debated in the halls of the state capitol. There had been several attempts to introduce slavery into the Ohio Territory before 1800, but antislavery forces succeeded in writing the Northwest Ordinance into the state's Bill of Rights in 1803. On one occasion during Morris's tenure a bill was introduced to prohibit the immigration of "free Negros and mulattoes" into the state, but Morris strongly opposed the bill, calling it "unjust, unconstitutional and odious." The bill was later rejected by the legislature.[80]

Late in his career as a state legislator, Morris had another occasion to examine his views about slavery when he sat as chair of a select committee appointed to report on attempts to colonize the free blacks of Ohio in Liberia. Morris's "Report on Colonization," delivered just after Nat Turner's rebellion swept across Southampton County, Virginia, urged that Congress "adopt such measures as may be within their constitutional powers for removal of the colored population from the several states, and their resettlement in Liberia." Morris also recommended that the citizens of Ohio form colonization societies to aid in the relocation of the state's free black population.

By the 1820s, Ohio was well settled and commanded substantial national political clout due to its sixteen electoral votes. John Quincy Adams, Henry Clay, and Jackson each had strong followings in Ohio, but after some equivocation, Morris decided to support the Tennessean. At the time Morris was publishing the weekly *Benefactor and Georgetown Advocate* in Brown County, which was the most populous county in the 5th District and one of the fastest growing in the state. In January 1824 Morris transferred ownership of the *Benefactor* to his adopted son Thomas Hamer, who quickly swung the paper into the Jackson camp. The journal was known as one of Ohio's staunchest Jacksonian papers, and Morris, for a time, was "the presiding genius of the Democratic Party in Ohio." Four years later Morris helped

Jacksonian editor Samuel Medary of Bethel establish the *Ohio Sun*, which became one of the most prominent Democratic journals in the West.[81]

After an unsuccessful run for a congressional seat in 1832, Morris returned to his law practice. The election was a boon for Ohio's other Democrats, however, who won control of the legislature on the coattails of Jackson's reelection. With Morris temporarily out of public life, some of the state's political leaders decided to back him for the state's vacant U.S. Senate seat. Not only had Morris been a loyal Jacksonian since 1824, but Ohio's political chieftains saw from his long legislative record that Morris would stand behind the administration in two important areas: the bank war and the nullification crisis. He was sent to Washington to support the administration.[82]

Morris's animosity toward the Second Bank of the United States—and banks and paper money in general—was well known. At the Democratic state convention in January 1832, Morris had authored a strident antibank resolution and led the subsequent floor fight for its adoption. Morris received national attention for the resolution, including one letter from a national officeholder that credited him for "placing Ohio in the front rank of the Democracy of the country, redeeming her character from the imputation of being governed by the influence of a Monied Monopoly."[83] Even after Jackson's bank veto, Morris continued to attack banks and corporations in general. In a speech before the Ohio legislature in December, which was reprinted in the nationally prominent *Washington Globe*, Morris claimed that "all corporations are aristocracies, and in their very nature and essence opposed to the principles of free Governments. . . . Their very design is to make an artificial distinction in society, and to give a few individuals rights and privileges not enjoyed by the citizens at large."[84] Morris had also taken a strong stand against the South Carolina nullifiers. At a time when many Ohioans (and northerners in general) were anxious about backing the president against South Carolina's "states' rights" men, Morris expertly shepherded a set of antinullification resolutions through the legislature. The state's legislators elected him to the Senate in 1832 by a vote of 54-49.[85]

Morris quickly satisfied the Ohio Democratic Party by voting consistently with the administration. His first impressions of the capital city were disappointing. He was unimpressed by the stature of the "great men" he had heard so much about, and he found the Senate chamber "small and . . . not very convenient." He did, however, rejoice in Jackson's removal of national deposits from the national bank. "Never has any curse fallen on this Republic equal to the Bank," he wrote to his eldest son. "If it triumph now it will rule for ages. I trust the majority of the House will stand firm [on the removal of deposits]."[86]

During the first three years of Morris's term, the Senate was preoccupied with the bank war, the aftermath of nullification, and debates on how to dispose of the public lands and build internal improvements. Outside the Senate, however, the issue of slavery was increasingly gaining importance. In Virginia the legislature was debating the future of slavery in that state after the Nat Turner rebellion; in New York City the American Antislavery Society was printing thousands of petitions and abolitionist tracts and mailing them South; and antiabolitionist mobs were sacking presses and disrupting abolitionist meetings in New York City, Utica, and Cincinnati. On a quiet day early in the term, Senator John C. Calhoun stood at the desk he occupied next to Morris's and called for a special committee to answer President Jackson's request for new federal laws to halt the spread of abolitionist material in the mails. With no other senators voicing objections, the committee was formed.[87]

There was no other mention of slavery in the chamber until Thomas Morris presented a routine petition from his constituents for the abolition of slavery in the District of Columbia. There was nothing unusual about the presentation of abolitionist petitions; it was a duty performed by most members of Congress in their capacity as representatives of the people. Morris's petition, however, was the first such measure introduced into the 24th Congress.[88]

By 1836 a massive petition-writing campaign initiated by the American Antislavery Society was flooding Congress with up to 100,000 petitions a year.[89] The petition movement enraged southerners and made it more difficult for northern politicians to remain expediently silent on the slavery question. Since a large majority of the petitions focused on abolition in the District of Columbia, which fell under congressional jurisdiction, the usual argument that slavery was a matter for the states to decide did not apply. As soon as Morris presented his petition on January 7, 1836, Calhoun was on his feet, attacking the petitioners as "fanatics" and demanding the Senate ban all such memorials. He accused Morris of fomenting rebellion in the South, since presenting abolitionist petitions would "compel the Southern press to discuss slavery in the very presence of Slaves, who would be induced to believe that there was a powerful party in the North ready to assist them." He added that receiving petitions was "sundering the ties" that bound the Union together. Morris, who had shown no sign that he supported the abolitionists' cause, quickly responded that whether Calhoun agreed or not, the Constitution authorized congressional authority to abolish slavery in the District of Columbia. He objected to Calhoun's call to silence the people's right of petition. "If you are to tell the people that they are only to petition on this or that subject, or in this or that manner," Morris said, "the right of petition is but a mockery."[90]

Morris's response to Calhoun took many of the other senators by surprise. To many of them he had violated the unspoken gentleman's agreement to refrain from debate on the slavery issue. Morris's Democratic allies were especially puzzled that he had seized the antisouthern mantle in 1836, for up to that time Morris had shown no antipathy toward either the South or its peculiar institution while in Congress. But there are hints from various sources that Morris felt that Calhoun and his "Southern majority" carried too much influence in national affairs and that this threatened the Union. He also complained repeatedly to his son about the stuffiness of the Upper Chamber, calling it the "aristocratic branch of Government" and expressing disappointment in the "appearance and management of the great men." Clearly Calhoun's call to ban his constituents' antislavery petitions struck him as both arrogant and "aristocratic."[91]

Morris remained quiet for the next three months as the Senate debated Calhoun's bill to bar "incendiary material" from the mails. He did, however, speak out twice in defense of antislavery groups. In March 1836 he chastised Senator Felix Grundy of Tennessee for intimating that the only things abolitionists understood were the "whip and the rope." In April, Morris defended the petitioners' motives and joked that the best way to stop agitation on abolition in the national capital was to move it either north or south.[92]

In a speech on April 14, 1836, Morris formally voiced his opposition to Calhoun's bill. Morris reiterated his Constitutional arguments for opposing a ban on antislavery mail. But the most striking part of Morris's speech was its political rhetoric. The speech marks one of the first uses of a Slave Power conspiracy to condemn the South and slavery. The dismissal of abolitionist petitions to Congress and the prohibition of abolitionist materials in the U.S. mail was, Morris claimed, yet another example of an increasingly powerful southern delegation attempting to protect slavery by weakening others' rights. What would Calhoun have said, Morris asked, "if an act of Congress had been passed to prevent the proceedings of [nullification societies] from being sent by the mail to any citizen of South Carolina?" Morris also raised the specter of slavery's expansion, even suggesting that Calhoun's

Constitutional arguments could someday be used to introduce slavery into the free states themselves. "They [the South] are attempting to overwhelm us by the power of this Government," Morris said.[93]

Morris's presentation of an aggressive, conspiring band of slaveholders willing to overwhelm northerners' freedom for the sake of slavery struck a powerful chord. Until the speech, the idea of a Slave Power had only been advanced by abolitionists like James G. Birney, and even then only in small-circulation journals like the *Philanthropist*. This new formulation made slavery into a *political* problem, and therefore one that demanded a political solution. The speech also marked a watershed in Morris's career. For the rest of his term (and his life), Morris was committed to the cause of antislavery.[94]

When debate on Calhoun's bill ended in June, the Senate refused to grant the "special protection" he sought for the southern mails by only three votes. But the southerners in Congress were just getting warmed up. The House passed the first of its gag rules on abolitionist petitions on May 18, 1836. After that date, petitions were tabled without debate until December 1844. The Senate rejected Calhoun's proposal to follow the House's example, partially due to Morris's speech, but preserved sectional harmony by independently tabling each petition as it arrived in the chamber. When the Senate adjourned in July, Morris returned to Ohio a changed man. Although he was not yet a political abolitionist, he had shed his role as a dutiful supporter of the administration.[95]

Morris returned to southwestern Ohio in the summer of 1836 to some of the most violent antiabolitionist activity the nation had ever seen. Most of the controversy swirled around James G. Birney, a slaveholder turned abolitionist, and his newspaper, the *Philanthropist*. On July 12, about the same time Thomas Morris arrived at his home in nearby Clermont County, a mob gathered in front of Birney's Cincinnati office, and a few men dismantled his press. In the weeks that followed, Birney's paper was attacked a second time, black neighborhoods were burned, and abolitionist meetings were disrupted.[96]

Morris saw the escalating lawlessness in Cincinnati as further proof that a southern conspiracy was afoot, and he slowly began to drift into the orbit of organized antislavery. On November 23 he attended the inaugural meeting of the Clermont County Antislavery Society, and although he chose not to become a member, the delegates passed a resolution thanking Morris "for his valuable suggestions to this society in the remarks he has just made." He also publicly endorsed the resolutions adopted at the meeting, one of which vowed that members would work until the stain of slavery was removed from America. Another promised they would "alert fellow Americans to the ominous threat of the Slave Power."[97]

Not surprisingly, Morris became the darling of Ohio's antislavery movement. His attendance was coveted at antislavery meetings and conventions, and he was thanked by meeting after meeting for his efforts in fighting for the right of petition. But the patience of the local Democratic political machine was wearing thin with the antislavery senator. When Andrew Jackson visited Cincinnati in March 1837, local officials left Morris's name off the guest list for a reception honoring the president. Formerly genial party men stopped greeting him at gatherings, and local Democratic papers (except for Hamer's *Benefactor*) began to ignore his speeches.[98]

Morris began to expound publicly the idea of a Slave Power conspiracy, provoking angry editorials in regional Democratic and Whig journals. He ominously predicted that, once entrenched in power, the slaveholding minority would secure laws making slavery legal in Texas, future territories, and even the North itself. "I have seen [the Slave Power] attempt to subvert the constitutional liberty of the citizens," Morris wrote to a friend, "and to extend its influence into every state of the Union. . . . It has established a system of Espionage, by which the very sanctuary of the domestic fireside may be polluted by its unhallowed tread." Morris promised his antislavery friends he would step up his fight against the Slave Power when he returned to Washington in December 1837.[99]

During the opening days of the 25th Congress, Calhoun proposed a series of resolutions recognizing slavery as an "integral part" of the nation and prohibiting any constitutional or legal restrictions on its extension into the territories, and then he strongly urged his colleagues for unanimous support to mollify southern anxieties. Morris grabbed the floor and introduced his own resolutions guaranteeing slavery's immunity within state lines but reiterating Congress's power to abolish it in the District of Columbia and the territories, as well as to put an end to the interstate slave trade. According to William Morris, Calhoun replied to Morris's resolutions by saying "Yes! here was displayed the *absolute creed* of the Abolitionists, fully developed." The South Carolinian was successful in portraying Morris as an abolitionist, and five of his six proslavery resolutions were passed by the full

Senate. The resolution prohibiting restrictions on slavery's expansion, however, was tabled. The lines for the fight over slavery's expansion into Texas and other new territories were already being drawn.[100]

Morris's resolutions enraged the leaders of the Ohio Democracy. In an attempt to calm the fears of Democratic voters, the state party sent Morris a letter demanding that he go on the record with his views about slavery and other important issues. His replies to the questions about the Independent Treasury and the bank revealed him to be a loyal hard-money Democrat. But even though Morris toned down his antislavery rhetoric, denouncing specific abolitionist groups as well as political and social equality for blacks, his answer to the question "Are you for or against Modern Abolitionism?" sealed his fate with the party. "*I am opposed to slavery in all its forms,*" Morris replied, "and against its further extension in our country. . . . I believe it to be the *duty of the States as well as their interest, to abolish slavery where it exists.*" There is no evidence as to who gave the official order, but on December 21, 1838, Ohio's Democratic legislators voted to replace Morris in the U.S. Senate with Benjamin Tappan, a Jacksonian who had little in common politically or religiously with his famous abolitionist brothers, Lewis and Arthur.[101] Morris accepted his ouster graciously, saying he had no wish to hold any position in which "all the powers of my mind, may not be fully exercised in this high, and permit me to say, holy duty . . . to oppose slavery, [and befriend] the poor, trodden down, and broken hearted slave."[102]

Morris's excommunication from the Democracy released him, at last, to speak freely about the subject of slavery. Upon his return to Washington for the lame duck session of the 25th Congress, he wrote to one Democratic associate that, having fought the "power of concentrated wealth," he was ready to devote the rest of his career to battling slavery, "an interest which . . . is more powerful and dangerous to the peace and prosperity of the country, than Banks or any other interest, that has ever existed among us."[103]

Morris received his first opportunity to speak out in February 1839. In an attempt to shore up support for his upcoming presidential bid, Henry Clay had delivered a speech denouncing antislavery agitation, while presenting petitions from Washington slaveholders begging Congress to silence slavery's critics.[104] Two days later, standing alone in the Senate, Morris replied to Clay. Without the shackles of party limiting his antislavery rhetoric, Morris made what was unquestionably his greatest speech. Claiming Jefferson's mantle, Morris brushed off the hisses and epithets of his southern detractors. "Sir," Morris exclaimed, "if I am an abolitionist, Jefferson made me so. I only regret that the disciple should be so far behind the master in both doctrine and practice." He asked how, in the previous session, Calhoun's proslavery resolutions were received, printed, and voted on, while his antislavery resolutions were laid on the table without debate. The answer, he said, was that a conspiracy of slaveholders had seized control of the federal government: "The power of SLAVERY . . . is aiming to govern the country, its Constitutions and laws. . . . The slave interest has at this moment the whole power of the country in its hands. It has the President . . . the cabinet . . . five out of nine judges of the Supreme Court . . . the President of the Senate, the Speaker of the House . . . the army and the navy." Morris then drew a direct connection between the two master symbols of antebellum America, the Money Power represented by the bank and the slaveholding power that, he said, posed an even greater threat. Both banking and slavery, he said, were based on the "unrequited labor of others." He continued: "Let it be borne in mind that the Bank power, some years since, had influence sufficient in this body, and upon this floor, to prevent the reception of petitions against the action of the Senate. . . . The same power though double in means and in strength, is now doing the same thing. . . . The slave power of the South, and the banking power of the North, are now uniting to rule this country." At several points, Morris's rhetoric presaged that used by Abraham Lincoln two decades later: "I am not now contending for the rights of the negro, rights which his Creator gave him and which his fellow man has taken away No, sir! I am contending for the rights of the white person in the free States, and am endeavoring to prevent them from being trodden down by that power which claims the black person as property." In his conclusion Morris insisted that if democracy and human progress were to continue, enslaved people must be set free.[105]

Copies of Morris's speech were printed in newspapers throughout the North, helping to place the phrase "Slave Power" permanently into the national political lexicon. Morris left Washington a hero of the nation's abolitionists. He would have a second career in the 1840s as a Liberty Party politician and would run for vice president on the ticket in 1844.

Morris's contribution to political antislavery was twofold. First, he helped coin and popularize the idea of the Slave Power conspiracy. Most Jacksonians were quite comfortable with planters as political allies, but Morris's slogan and rhetoric starkly illustrated the potential dangers of an expansive slave system. Though Morris agreed with abolitionists that slavery was immoral, the Slave Power thesis transformed slavery into a *political* threat as well, one with potentially disastrous outcomes for the North's farmers and workers. Second, the story of Morris's political excommunication illustrated the reach and potency of the Slave Power. Because of a heretical stance on one of many issues, Morris was read out of the party he helped to found.

With the antislavery defections of Jacksonians such as Leggett, Evans, and Morris in the 1830s, the intellectual arguments were set that would underscore a series of political realignments in the next decade.

↑

CHAPTER TWO

Set Down Your Feet, Democrats

Politics and Free Soil in New York

For Martin Van Buren, a canny veteran of New York politics and in 1827 a U.S. senator, slavery was not the problem. According to the tavern keeper's son, the gravest threat facing the republic was—and always had been—aristocracy. During the Revolution and again in the 1790s, Van Buren believed, the forces of aristocracy had come within a hair's breadth of thwarting the nation's democratic experiment. First, the Revolutionary patriots beat back the British army and their Tory allies. Then, two decades later, the Federalists built an intrusive central government, favored the British in international affairs, and encouraged policies that catered to the nation's elite. Jefferson's triumph over Federalism in 1800, Van Buren reasoned, saved the new republic from impending aristocratic calamity.

The history lesson absorbed by Van Buren and his allies was that the only way to counter the constant encroachments of aristocracy was with more democracy. Never, he reasoned, had the forces of democracy been more successful than during Jefferson's battles against Federalism in the 1790s. As the "Little Magician" saw it, Jefferson's Democratic-Republicans had defeated Hamilton and the Federalists because of their organization into a disciplined party and their trust of "the people" in electoral affairs. Yet the nation did not enter a glorious democratic age after Federalism's collapse in 1815. Instead, noted more than one Jeffersonian, Congress enacted a series of Federalist programs, including a second Bank of the United States. During the next decade, the country experienced a perilous financial panic, flirted with disunion during the Missouri Crisis, and witnessed a "winning" presidential candidate lose the office in a swirl of capitol intrigue. For Van Buren, the "era of good feelings" was a misnomer.

To right the ship of state, Van Buren argued for a return to old-style partisanship and for party discipline that would transcend sectional tensions. Fighting a two-front battle against disunion and the forces of aristocracy required bisectional coalitions, he told Thomas Ritchie, editor of the *Richmond Enquirer*, "and the most natural and beneficial to the country is that between the planters of the South and the plain Republicans of the north." Looking back nostalgically, he reasoned that "the country has once flourished under a party thus constituted & may yet again." Van Buren suggested capitalizing on the personal popularity of slaveholder Andrew Jackson — who had won the popular vote in 1824 but lost the presidency to John Quincy Adams in the House of Representatives in what Jacksonians called the "corrupt bargain" — with the surviving remnants of Jeffersonian partisanship. Such a combination would have two important consequences: the "wrongs" of 1824 would be instantly undone, and the sectional tensions loosed by the Missouri controversy would be buried under a Jackson landslide. "If [old party loyalties] are suppressed," he wrote, "geographical divisions founded on local interests or . . . prejudices between free and slave holding states will inevitably take their place." Once and for all, Van Buren argued, such a coalition could potentially banish privileged insiders and unreconstructed Federalists from the nation's halls of government. If discipline was ruggedly maintained, a truly bisectional party could indefinitely keep "clamour [against] Southern Influence and African Slavery" ineffectual in the North. In other words, a political union between slaveholders and northern workers and farmers would keep the aristocracy at bay and keep politics from dissolving into sectional warfare over the issue of abolition.[1]

The years that followed were full of stunning successes for Van Buren's new party based on "old distinctions." After Adams's single term, the Democracy won the next three presidential elections. It succeeded in destroying the Second Bank of the United States and forced the Money Power into retreat. Jacksonians also returned budget surpluses to the states, faced down nullifiers in South Carolina, lowered the price of public lands, and helped abolish imprisonment for debt. Yet as this chapter will show, Van Buren's considerable energy and political acumen failed to silence "clamouring" over slavery within the Democracy itself, especially in his home state. As previously demonstrated, some Jacksonians broke with their party's stands on the South and slavery even as the party was enjoying its most important victories, setting in motion the formation of a new ideology that would bring down the second party system in the 1850s.

For hundreds of thousands of New York Democrats — and eventually for Van Buren himself — slavery came to eclipse all other political issues, representing an insidious brand of aristocracy that threatened the union should it be allowed to expand. Any story centering on antebellum New York politics is Byzantine and mercilessly complex, "a vast deep," according to one historical observer. The state's intricate partisan maneuverings have been described as "a labyrinth of wheels within wheels . . . understood only by the managers." The present narrative seeks to make the complicated compelling, and to make new sense of old stories. What is clear, despite the complexity, is that the battles over canals, banks, and land tenure had by the mid-1840s given way to debates about slavery and its expansion. This shift in Empire State politics had significant consequences for the nation.[2]

New York was, without a doubt, the beating heart of the national Free Soil movement. The state's politics became the setting for a unique combination of urban dissent and populist rural radicalism that precipitated, first, an intraparty schism, then the formation of a new party, and finally a multistate movement based on the Free Soil concept. As demonstrated in the preceding chapter, Free Soil's ideological origins were largely the work of urban New York dissidents such as William Leggett and George Henry Evans. The state's remote hinterland also proved fertile ground for Leggett's and Evans's ideas. Tenant farmers in the mountainous central part of New York, for example, were quick to adopt Evans's notion of a land monopoly and his prescription for abolishing it: free homesteads for settlers on the public lands. Communities in remote Herkimer and St. Lawrence counties applied Leggett's hard-money ideas to local and state fiscal policies. Smaller towns like Buffalo, Herkimer, and Utica each hosted significant Free Soil conventions populated by antislavery Democrats from across the state. When voters cast presidential ballots for Martin Van Buren and the Free Soil Party in 1848, a lion's share came from communities throughout upstate New York. Free Soil, then, was not simply an intellectual movement orchestrated by Manhattan-based dissidents; it had a significant rural component as well.[3] Against a backdrop of the urban and rural components of Free Soil, this chapter revisits the antebellum political history of New York state, recasting oft-told narratives of Bucktails, Hunkers, and Barnburners to tease out the various strands of Jacksonian antislavery. Other northern states experienced a similar redrawing of party boundaries. But the story begins in New York, where a convergence of ideas and electoral possibilities made resistance to slavery's expansion the paramount issue of the 1840s and 1850s.

Free Soil in New York had both rural and urban branches. Both were nourished by the writings and ideas of Jacksonian antislavery dissident William Leggett and were peopled by steadfast partisans of Martin Van Buren.

In New York City, Leggett's former partner and benefactor William Cullen Bryant led a coterie of young urban Democrats that included lawyers David Dudley Field and Samuel J. Tilden, Theodore Sedgwick III, and the young Brooklyn newspaperman, Walt Whitman.[4] These young Democrats, many of whom also participated in the Young America literary movement, were among the first to bolt their party to become Free Soilers. Yet while their literary hero Leggett was mainly concerned in the 1830s with the numerous attacks on abolitionists' rights of petition, assembly, and speech, his successors in the 1840s focused on opposing Texas's annexation and the addition of any new slave territory. Significantly, they also stopped short of Leggett's embrace of organized abolitionism.

Upstate, Leggett's Democratic followers were more influenced by his hard-money economic ideas than by his antislavery writings. Building on these and other established critiques of monopolists, bankers, and corporate privilege seekers, these rural radicals fashioned an egalitarian critique of slaveholding and of southern power within the Democratic Party and the Union. Preston King, an editor and postmaster from the North Country town of Ogdensburg (more than 400 miles from New York City) became a leader of the radical upstate Democrats at home and, later, in the U.S. Congress. Both rural radicals such as King and urban writers such as Sedgwick found new political homes in the Barnburner revolt and Free Soil movement of the 1840s.

The Urban Crucible of Free Soil

William Leggett's antislavery legacy is most clearly visible in the ideas and writings set forth by New York City's young and radical Democratic writers and intellectuals. Many of these men clustered around poet and editor Bryant, whose *Evening Post* carried on his former partner's attacks on laws favoring the rich and powerful and his defense of abolitionists' right to assembly and speech. "We are resolved," Bryant wrote, "that the subject of slavery shall be as it ever has been, as free a subject for discussion and argument and declaration, as the difference between whiggism and democracy, or as the difference between the Arminians and the Calvinists."[5]

But it was Theodore Sedgwick III, a New England transplant like Bryant, who most clearly advanced and preserved Leggett's political contributions. Just twenty-eight years old when Leggett died, Sedgwick painstakingly collected his former boss's far-flung editorials for publication in a two-volume set that, to this day, remains the best source for Leggett's writing. Sedgwick's background seems at first glance an unlikely springboard for a career in the chaotic world of urban Jacksonian politics. His family was among the first to settle in Massachusetts Bay Colony, and his grandfather and namesake was an ardent Federalist who served as a justice on the state supreme court and as Speaker of the House in the 6th U.S. Congress.[6] Yet the elder Theodore Sedgwick's descendants were notably unorthodox in matters of both politics and culture. While his son Theodore II followed his father into the law, he became an able amateur economist, a champion of wage laborers, and an outspoken supporter of the plantation parvenu Andrew Jackson. Even more surprising, Theodore II's sister, Catherine Maria Sedgwick, was one of the country's most popular authors, whose novels and short stories frequently questioned traditional gender roles.[7]

Theodore II's son (and Leggett's precocious protégé) Theodore III attended George Bancroft's school at Round Hill but was expelled for bad behavior. This early educational misfire, however, did not prevent him from graduating from Columbia or traveling to France as an American attaché in 1833–34. While there, he dined with Lafayette and assisted Tocqueville (whom he had met in his hometown of Stockbridge two years earlier) with the preparation of parts of *Democracy in America*. After a year abroad Sedgwick presumptuously wrote his father's acquaintance Vice President Martin Van Buren of his desire to return to the United States to live "under those institutions which make us all if not Agrarians or Owenites — at least — Workies." Fortunately for Sedgwick, he returned to New York in 1834 to find William Leggett shorthanded at the *Evening Post*, and so commenced his career in egalitarian politics and pamphleteering. According to almost every account, Sedgwick was smart, attractive, and an excellent wordsmith. He impressed Fanny Kemble and appeared even to Whig Charles Sumner to be "the cleverest and most gentlemanly person I have seen in New York." High praise indeed for a budding Jacksonian radical.[8]

Sedgwick's pieces for the *Evening Post* appeared under the name "Veto." Several in 1834 on the topics of hard money, banking, and monopolies were published as an oft-quoted pamphlet titled "What *is* a Monopoly?" He also took over Leggett's editorial duties during the increasingly frequent spells when Leggett was too ill to put out the newspaper.[9] Like many Jacksonians, Sedgwick admitted a "strong attachment to the South," citing his mother's family's heritage and the fact that many of "our ablest men" had sprung from that part of the country. But in defiance of Jacksonian orthodoxy, he also blamed the South and its peculiar institution for sowing fears of dis-union throughout the history of the republic. "Is not the most melancholy tendency of slavery to create . . . discordance and incompatibility of interest [between North and South]?" he asked his parents, from France. "I am convinced that unless the sore be cauterized or cut out speedily by bold and able hands, its consequences will defeat the whole system. The prejudices which control the South . . . degrade the blacks with us."[10]

Sedgwick's views on slavery were never far beneath the surface of his writings, even as he addressed issues like the rights of labor, the national bank, or religious freedom. But when the issue of Texas annexation returned to the fore during the early 1840s, Sedgwick published a blistering series of essays in the *Evening Post* explaining how, in the minds of a growing group of New York City Jacksonians, annexation threatened — not enhanced — the future of democracy. Such arguments, of course, flew in the face of those expounded by the large majority of expansionist, pro-annexation Demo-crats, who claimed that a democracy of states' rights and limited federal powers could be extended indefinitely. They also latched onto the rumors (devised in part by Texas president Sam Houston) that Great Britain desired an independent Texas as a buffer against further southwestern American expansion.[11]

Sedgwick refused to concede that the Texas question was about anything besides the naked expansion of slavery. "Give us the real issue," Sedgwick wrote in 1840, "*is Slavery a good or an evil to the free citizens of these States?*"[12] Most of Sedgwick's contributions to the *Evening Post* were devoted to proving the latter. Annexation would "incalculably increase the slaveholding inter-est," which, Sedgwick took pains to say, was different from what he saw as the "southern interest." Slaveholders, he argued, not southerners in general, were responsible for "plung[ing] the laboring class into degradation, de-priv[ing] the operative of every stimulus to exertion, mak[ing] the master idle and reckless." Again decrying the sectionalism of pro-annexationists and slaveholders, Sedgwick appealed to *northern* sectionalism in an attempt to derail Texas statehood and future slave states. "The northern man must be false to his education, and blind to his interests, who does not, inch by inch, and hand to hand, resist the extension of the slaveholding power."[13] By applying Leggett's views on slavery and slaveholders to the issue of an-nexation and slavery's expansion into new territory (in this case, Texas), Sedgwick had helped construct an important piece of the larger ideology of Free Soil.

In upstate New York, ideas about monopolies, banks, chartered corporations, and hard money—subjects vigorously championed by William Leggett in the 1830s—had a similarly important effect on the development of the Free Soil and the antislavery movements.[14] Upstate Democrats based their opposition to slavery and southern expansion on what they called aristocratic abuses, centralized power, and other affronts to egalitarianism. Moreover, the remote, agricultural New York communities that became bulwarks of Free Soil ideas—and, later, votes—barely resembled the middle-class, evangelical, and Whig locales of the famed Burned-Over District covering the western parts of the state. Many of them, in fact, were isolated and economically stagnant—more passed-over than burned-over.

The most active Free Soil counties in New York included St. Lawrence (on the Canadian frontier), Herkimer (which stretched for more than a hundred miles into the wild Adirondacks), Delaware (populated largely by Catskill tenant farmers), and Chemung (on the Pennsylvania border). Each of these upstate counties was rugged, densely wooded, and among the last to be settled in the state. Shallow, acidic soil made traditional staple agriculture difficult in many of these areas, especially those of higher elevation. As the crow flies, some of these communities were quite close to the bustling Erie Canal, but the famed "artificial river" might as well have been a thousand miles away. In fact, its completion in 1825 actually made matters worse for farmers removed from the canal district, as western competition, soil depletion, and crop diseases dealt consecutive blows to small-scale New York farmers.[15]

Just how different were these out-of-the-way places from their sister communities nearer the bustling canal? New York state's thorough antebellum censuses offer some clues. Nineteenth-century state enumerators asked New Yorkers about their "market gardens," that is, acreage devoted to the production of vegetables and fruits for urban markets. Census figures on market gardens are one way to see how much energy farmers in a specific community devoted to production for immediate cash sale (as opposed to family or community use). In Oneida County, for example, which was neatly bisected by the canal that contained the booming new city of Utica, residents devoted 247 acres to market gardens that produced $49,258 worth of goods in 1855. Erie County, which contained the emerging city of Buffalo, had 482 acres that produced $39,130 for its owners. By contrast, the Democratic, hard-money county of Herkimer had only 9 acres devoted to market gardens, yielding just $1,133; St. Lawrence County had 31 acres with $4,730; and Delaware county in the Catskills had 5 acres with a scant $69. These figures suggest how unlikely farmers in Herkimer, Delaware, and St. Lawrence were to find buyers for their produce. The material value of the dwellings and farms in the hard-money districts was also far less than in the bustling counties of Oneida and Erie. The average dwelling (stone, brick, frame, and log) in radical Democratic St. Lawrence and Herkimer counties was worth $392 and $536, respectively; the averages for the bustling counties of Oneida and Erie were $705 and $1,154. More telling, perhaps, is data regarding construction materials. In 1855, 28 percent of St. Lawrence's and a majority (53 percent) of Herkimer's dwellings were built of logs, compared with 10 percent of Erie's and just 3 percent of Oneida's.[16]

The populations of most hard-money counties had leveled off as well. Between 1825 (the year the Erie Canal opened) and 1845, Oneida County's population grew 42 percent; Erie's exploded by 82 percent. By contrast, Delaware County's population grew by 20 percent and Herkimer's by an anemic 14 percent.[17] Among these new residents, very few in the radical Democratic counties called themselves bankers. According to the census, there were two bankers in Delaware, six in Herkimer, and none in St. Lawrence in 1855; Oneida, meanwhile, had twenty, and Erie contained thirty-six.[18] In fact the 4th Legislative District in St. Lawrence County, which elected Preston King to Albany as a state legislator in 1834, had the least bank capital — $700,000 — of any in the entire state.[19]

Mired in comparatively stagnant communities, residents of Delaware, Herkimer, and St. Lawrence grew wary of paper money, joint-stock corporations, and state-sponsored credit, from which they benefited less than their downstate neighbors. Politically, these communities remained bastions of Democratic electoral strength: in election after election, residents voted overwhelmingly for the party of Jackson. Many of the politicians who served this constituency first entered politics in the 1820s as part of a faction of Democratic-Republicans known as Bucktails after their trademark deerskin caps. The Bucktails, led by Martin Van Buren (from Columbia County in the Hudson Valley) and Silas Wright (from St. Lawrence County) often hailed from families that had been excluded from politics in previous generations. They also tended to thrive in parts of the state farther from established markets. Their political raison d'être was opposition to the fiscal policies of Governor DeWitt Clinton, who used public funds for internal improvements like the Erie Canal and facilitated the incorporation of banks, insurance companies, and other so-called privileged corporations.[20] Van Buren and his allies had nothing against canals or other examples of human enterprise and ingenuity per se; it was government intervention in the form of chartered corporations, they believed, that transformed "instruments of progress" into agents of oppression. Artificial chartered monopolies, the Bucktails insisted, amassed the resources of the many for the enjoyment of the few—in this case canal district merchants, stockholders, and the corrupt legislators who authorized their privilege.[21]

In 1821 the Bucktails secured the election of Van Buren to the U.S. Senate. Back in New York, Wright took over what became known as the Albany Regency. Many historians have commented that the Bucktails played a major role in making partisan politics an acceptable, even glorious practice. They were pioneers in initiating and perfecting the political devices that defined a generation of American public life, including the legislative caucus, the official party newspaper, and the unconcealed (and unapologetic) use of patronage to ensure loyalty. "When our enemies accuse us of feeding our friends instead of them," instructed Wright, "never let them lie in telling the story."[22]

One of the great strengths of the Albany Regency was its top-down organizational structure, which coordinated a loose constellation of county-level clubs into a political party able to contain and balance antagonistic elements, at least for a time. Some of the strongest of these county clubs emerged in areas left out of the economic revolution that followed the completion of the Erie Canal and the resulting credit boom. A solid block of New York counties, including Delaware, Herkimer, and St. Lawrence, became a stronghold of the Regency's radical wing and, later, the antislavery Barnburner movement. Neither commercial nor urban, these communities were the same types of postfrontier, settled agricultural communities that spawned radical movements such as Shays's Rebellion and the anti-rent wars of the 1830s and 1840s. In these communities hard money and, later, Free Soil ideas took root, amid political battles over land titles, internal improvements, and banks.

Upstate hard-money ideologues represented the radical fringe of the state Democratic Party, at least on economic issues. Regency radicals in St. Lawrence County, for example, vociferously blamed the Bank of the United States and paper currency for ruining farmers there in 1834, as the central bank called in its loans and caused a sharp panic in the countryside. Notes issued by local banks quickly became known as "shinplaster"—worth less than the paper they were printed on.[23] In the wake of this panic, Wright's

North Country protégé Preston King authored a series of radical resolutions in 1834, reminiscent of policies touted in Leggett's editorials, calling for the immediate abolition of all bank notes less than $20. Such a law was necessary, King reasoned, in order to give "the yeomanry of the land a reacquaintance with a constitutional hard money currency" and put an end to the "immense moneyed power [able] to oppress the common man, embarrass commerce, derange trade, prostrate public and private credit, and put an end to public confidence."[24] Unlike lists of resolutions drawn up by Democratic conventions in New York City or along the canal route that relied on ambiguity and compromise to promote party unity, King's Canton Resolutions demanded the eventual abandonment of all paper money.

Just to the south, in Herkimer County, hard-money Democrats drew up another set of radical resolutions, proposing that every proposition to increase the state's debt must be submitted directly to the voters and approved by them before the money could be borrowed. These so-called People's Resolutions, written and shepherded through the legislature by Herkimer Democrats Arphaxed Loomis and Michael Hoffman, flew directly in the face of Whig development plans (which, in fact, they intended to hamstring). The resulting Stop and Tax Law of 1842 effectively halted work on canals in New York, dramatically reducing state expenditures and debt. Hard-money Jacksonians applauded, because they increasingly viewed state-sponsored development as beneficial only to well-connected people in select, privileged areas. They did not oppose development, for that matter, but resented seeing stockholders and land speculators reap the benefits of state expenditures.[25] In the state legislature, upstate and urban radicals united to resist every corporate charter as a form of economic privilege, to open up banking to people and groups without legislative charters, and to propose a plan, later adopted by the Van Buren administration, to "divorce" bank and state under an independent treasury.[26] William Leggett's rural and urban legacies had collided in Albany.

The Agrarian Component: The Anti-Rent Wars

The ideas of Leggett's fellow Jacksonian dissident George Henry Evans also had a profound effect on New York's urban and rural politics in the following decade. Evans's agrarian and antislavery ideas inspired another group of New Yorkers — tenant farmers in the central part of the state — to attack a homegrown system of "unfree" labor and land distribution. Introduced upstate via the political agitation of the National Reform Association (NRA), the organization founded by Evans to push for the free distribution of land to settlers, these ideas provided the foundation for a powerful new basis for opposition to slavery's expansion.

Evans's antislavery evolved significantly after he retired from Democratic labor politics during the depression following the Panic of 1837. While farming melons on his New Jersey farm, he hit upon a scheme to solve problems as varied as unemployment, tenantry, slavery, and what he called the land monopoly: the free distribution of the public lands to poor settlers, in the form of inalienable homesteads. By offering each head of household a free homestead, Evans hoped simultaneously to enhance democracy (by enlarging the number of yeomen), raise wages (by moving surplus urban labor onto the land), and contain slavery (by doling out the West into farms worked by free men). Evans's vision included the distribution of land to ex-slaves and Indians as well as whites. One of the many names Evans gave his scheme for land reform was Free Soil, and before the term was attached to the Free Soil Party, it became shorthand for his concepts of land reform. Central to these concepts, tirelessly promoted by Evans, was the belief that a man had a natural right to enough land to support a family.[27]

Evans had to look no further than the Hudson River Valley to find an example of a very real land monopoly—and a chilling vision of what he feared the expanding West might look like if speculators, land magnates, and slaveholders were allowed to dictate the terms of settlement. Unlike most of the antebellum North, where farmers usually owned their land, nearly one in twelve New Yorkers worked property leased to them (and often to their fathers and grandfathers) by a handful of great proprietors. In 1839 upstate tenants inaugurated a movement to break up these immense estates and redistribute the land to the people who worked it. This anti-rent movement began with attempts by hard-pressed tenants to purchase their land; when the great families refused to sell, some anti-renters took to the courts to challenge the proprietors' titles, while others turned to rent strikes and, eventually, paramilitary tactics. In a series of violent confrontations with sheriff's posses, anti-rent tenants disguised as Indians (representing the original proprietors of the land metaphorically, if not accurately) pre-vented evictions, distress sales, and arrests. Eventually three counties in central New York were declared to be in a state of rebellion, and the militia was called out to put down the insurrection.

Through nearly constant agitation by NRA lecturers and their converted anti-rent allies, thousands of manor tenants signed on as supporters of land reform, flooding the offices of newspapers like the *Anti-Renter* and Evans's

Young America and even the U.S. Congress with letters, petitions, and resolutions claiming each citizen had "natural right to the soil."[28] The result of this agitation was a movement that simultaneously appealed to the New Yorkers' hunger for land and committed them to favoring the use of the constitutional powers of the state to undermine both unfair and unfree systems of land distribution and labor. This combination was a potent one: an agrarian-based antislavery centered on the anxieties and desires of free state producers.

Anti-renters founded newspapers and their own political party and rapidly became a significant force in New York politics. In 1846 one-eighth of the representatives in the state assembly were identified with the anti-renters, which briefly handed the tenants and their leaders the balance of power in the Empire State.[29] The anti-renters' contributions to the *national* ideology of Free Soil, however, far outweigh their eventual success in abolishing an atavistic landlord-tenant system in New York. Under the influence of Evans's NRA, some tenants' goals evolved from the mere desire to purchase land they farmed into a belief that each head of household should own enough land to support a family. This idea became the foundation of the decades-long push for a homestead act that would eventually distribute pieces of the public lands to settlers, one of the central tenets of the Free Soil and Republican parties. Evans clearly intended his land reform program as an antidote to both wage (by which he meant white) and chattel (by which he meant black) slavery and as a force for the abolition of all forms of unfree labor. "The black as well as the white must, in my opinion, have his right to the land restored to him before he can be free," Evans wrote to abolitionist and philanthropist Gerrit Smith in 1844.[30] A West (or an upstate land patent) broken up into small family farms would be a strong impediment to the migration of slaveholders, according to both Evans and, subsequently, Smith.[31]

Who were the agrarian anti-renters most apt to adopt Evans's ideas about land reform and antislavery? A recent study of the movement suggests that, compared with those tenants whose only goal was to own their own land, NRA anti-renters differed only slightly in age, occupation, or wealth. Leaders of both factions tended to own some property and head a household.[32] One difference stands out, however. A large majority of those who threw their lot with the agrarians were Democrats from the party's hard-money wing — that is, they supported policies on public debt, banks, internal improvements, and centralized authority similar to those of their radical upstate neighbors. For example, of those Albany County anti-renters whose previous party activities were known, NRA supporters were nine times more likely to have been Jacksonians than Whigs. Non-NRA supporters were only 60 percent more likely to be Democrats, a figure much more in line with the political makeup of the county.[33]

By 1846 a split had developed within the anti-rent movement between the agrarians, who continued to push for wider reforms like homesteads, and more conservative tenants who wanted to work with the existing political parties. Both liberal Whigs and Hunker Democrats offered themselves as allies to the more conservative anti-renters. When the regular anti-rent party nominated a Whig for governor, NRA anti-renters cast about for new allies. They found them among the state's growing population of political abolitionists, including Gerrit Smith and William Chaplin. Smith, following a long correspondence with Evans, had come to believe that the eradication of land monopoly was a necessary first step to abolishing chattel slavery. Chaplin, the editor of the *Albany Patriot*, wished to move abolitionism beyond the Liberty Party's "one idea" (abolition) and work for other reforms. "We trust the day may not be so distant," he wrote, "when [land reformers], Liberty Men and all earnest, sincere reformers . . . will see that the mighty power of reform lies in the faithful and full application of the simple principles of radical democracy in all the relations of the social state."[34]

The anti-renters, land reformers, and abolitionists cemented their new alliance at the Albany City Hall in the fall of 1846, proclaiming themselves the Free Soil Party—the first to use the name. At this inaugural gathering, the rag-tag Free Soilers fumbled toward articulating a political formula that, less than two years later, would disrupt the second party system and pave the way for the sectional crisis. The delegates labeled both land monopoly and slavery "combinations of wealth against the liberties of the masses" and called for an abrogation of all leasehold contracts, an equalization of rewards to labor, and a homestead law. Evans's *Young America* and Chaplin's *Patriot* both trumpeted the Free Soil slate, which included nominations of land reformer Lewis Masquerier for governor, ex-Chartist anti-rent radical Thomas Devyr for Congress, anti-rent leaders John J. Gallup and Thomas Shafer for the assembly, and Chaplin himself for lieutenant governor. "I regard the question of Free Soil reform as vital to the progress of an enlightened, stable, Christian Democracy," Chaplin wrote just before the election.[35]

With election day just two weeks away, the Free Soilers came together far too late to affect the 1846 races. But the platform and resolutions presaged a larger political movement that would fare better in the near future. Linking the Free Soil parties of 1846 and the one christened in 1848 were commitments to two distinct yet complementary ideas: free homesteads on the public lands for needy settlers and hostility to the spread of slavery. What made 1848 so different from 1846 were two factors: the addition of thousands of square miles of territory to the United States as a result of the war with Mexico and a full-bore schism within the once mighty New York Democracy.

Hunkers, Barnburners, and New York Democrats on the National Stage

At the same time anti-renters were claiming the right to own their farms, New York's Democratic Party famously came apart over old issues (bank charters, canals, and other hallmarks of development) and new ones (the extension of slavery). Prodevelopment Democrats in New York state became known by the nickname Hunkers (after those who hanker or "hunker" after the spoils), while they scorned their opponents within the party as Barnburners (after an apocryphal and overzealous Dutch farmer who burned his barn to rid it of rats). Both names stuck.[36] The initial reasons for the split were squarely economic: whether and how to fund internal improvements, support the national bank, or charter more state corporations. These fissures over hard money and canals began to center more and more on sectional issues or, more accurately, how each faction viewed the strength of slaveholders' power within the national Democratic Party. Hunkers, who shared the slaveholders' economic conservatism and looked southward for political patronage, were quite comfortable playing the role of junior partner to Democrats such as John C. Calhoun of South Carolina and Robert Walker of Mississippi. As the 1840s wore on, Barnburners—many of whom had earlier counted themselves among the South's strongest allies within the party, often at the expense of their own constituents' views—were less willing to follow the South's lead. This latter group, led by the recently defeated ex-president Martin Van Buren, was the faction that would later supply the Free Soil Party with a lion's share of its votes at the national level.

During the first half of the 1840s, Barnburners became increasingly angry and alienated within the state and, later, national party. Much of this bitterness stemmed from the presidential election of 1840, when many Van Burenites blamed their candidate's defeat at the hands of William Henry Harrison on lackluster support by Hunkers in New York and southerners in general. Four years later, Barnburner partisans again saw foul play at the root of their candidate's defeat for the Democratic presidential nomination. This time they felt southerners had engineered their candidate's defeat on a technicality: even though Van Buren's supporters arrived at the party's national convention with more than a majority of delegates, southerners were able to block the nomination through eight ballots by employing a rule requiring a two-thirds vote.[37] Significantly, Van Buren's opposition to immediately annexing Texas — a position strongly advocated by antislavery Jacksonians like Sedgwick, Bryant, and Jabez D. Hammond but bitterly opposed by nearly every southern Democrat — was the key reason for the evaporation of his support south of the Mason-Dixon line. With Van Buren's candidacy fatally wounded, Tennessee slaveholder James K. Polk emerged at the convention as the first "dark horse" candidate, winning the nomination on the ninth ballot. Polk, a hard-money Jacksonian who had heretofore been a strong Van Buren supporter, was palatable to nearly every southerner as well as to northern Democrats like George Bancroft.

Still, Van Buren's New York supporters felt the harsh sting of betrayal. A dejected Silas Wright turned down the vice-presidential nomination, while James Wadsworth of Geneseo denounced the "dictation and selfishness of the south." Still, the Van Burenites prided themselves on one thing: neither John C. Calhoun (who had earlier that spring justified Texas annexation by proclaiming slavery "essential to the peace, safety, and prosperity" of the South) nor their northern nemesis, Michigan's Lewis Cass (the first choice of many of the southern delegates) had captured the nomination in their man's place. "Some of us," wrote John L. O'Sullivan to Van Buren, "are weeping with one eye while we smile with the other at the overthrow of the intrigues of traitors."[38]

With the excitement of the contentious 1844 convention behind them, most Van Burenites coolly resolved to support the ticket. Polk was, after all, their battle-tested ally on issues like hard money and banks — "a man of . . . right views in regard to the questions on which the two parties of the nation are divided," according to Bryant. Yet Van Buren Democrats continued to reiterate how "deplorably" wrong Polk remained on the vital question of Texas, and how the row at the convention seemed to have underscored their worst fears about rifts within the party. Before the Baltimore meeting, Wright, King, and even Bryant thoroughly believed that northern and southern Democrats were equal partners within the party, and that each side depended on the other to combat the people's real enemies: the bankers, stock jobbers, and speculators represented by the Whig Party. For these

New Yorkers, this old view seemed no longer to match reality. Congressman
Lemuel Stetson fretted that the party would consistently lose votes — and
elections — in New York if it did not quickly shed its "prosouthern" image.[39]
In Manhattan, Bryant and six other Van Buren Democrats composed and
sent a confidential letter to like-minded party members backing Polk but
blasting the party plank on Texas annexation. "The Convention went beyond the authority delegated to its members," Bryant wrote in the letter,

"and adopted a resolution on the subject of Texas which seeks to interpolate into the party code a new doctrine hitherto unknown among us — at war with some of our established principles, and abhorrent to the opinions and feelings of a great majority of northern freemen." When the "Secret Circular" inevitably found its way into print (in the Hunker daily *Plebeian*, which editorialized that the signers should be expelled from the party unless they declared themselves in favor of annexation), its signal effect was to widen the rift between New York's Hunkers and Barnburners.[40]

Polk won the election, thanks in large part to Barnburner Silas Wright's reluctant decision to leave the Senate and run for governor of New York. Wright's name on the ballot provided the Democratic ticket with the political coattails Polk needed to capture the state's pivotal electoral votes and the White House. With solid support from radical upstate Democrats, Wright beat his Whig opponent by more than 10,000 votes statewide, while in the presidential race Polk outpolled Clay by just 5,000.[41] Though pleased with Wright's triumph, Barnburners worried that the controversy over Texas had alienated enough antislavery Democrats to allow the abolitionist Liberty Party an opportunity to capture those votes in the future. In either case, the election results sufficed to convince still more Barnburners that it was time to distance themselves from the slaveholders in their party. Association with southern slaveholders had become so politically distasteful to these Democrats, wrote Barnburner Congressman Lemuel Stetson, that if the Van Burenites did not take a stand, "before one year is over, the Northern Democracy will have so strong a smell of niggers that ¼ of our friends will be drawn to the abolition ranks, and the next contest for the presidency would be a great sectional war between north and south."[42]

Antislavery Democrats seized two opportunities to break with the prosouthern administration in the weeks after Polk's election. First, in a stunning reversal, northern Democrats refused to open the congressional session by providing their usual votes to perpetuate the gag rule on abolitionist petitions to Congress.[43] When annexation (with Polk's election, a fait accompli) came up, leading Van Burenites and future Wilmot Proviso supporters George Rathbun, Lemuel Stetson, and Preston King spoke out forcefully against Texas. King, for one, was startled at the intensity of his own feelings on the matter: "I was . . . surprised at my own repugnance to Texas on the single point of slavery. The southerners do not want Texas without slavery — I would take Texas tonight without slavery and upon this point alone am I embarrassed about Texas."[44] King and twenty-six other Van Buren Democrats (all fourteen from New York) risked being branded as hypocrites and defectors and voted against Texas annexation. They were, of course, in the minority; Congress passed the resolution just before Polk took office, and Texas became the fifteenth state in December 1845.[45]

The Dark Horse in Power

Increasingly touchy Barnburners perceived every action of the Polk administration, whether in the realm of patronage, diplomacy, or expansionist belligerence, as the Slave Power puppet master manipulating the president's strings. Much of the Van Burenites' fury over patronage matters could be attributed to that faction's excessive — almost obsessive — belief that they were the only "true" Democrats and had delivered the nation for Polk in 1844. When the president doled out offices to Hunkers in a gesture of fairness, the Barnburners felt only betrayal.

Barnburners (and northern Democrats in general) also felt short-changed in matters of territorial expansion. Even though Polk ran on a platform to win for the United States all of Oregon and Texas, he compromised only on presumptively free Oregon.[46] Polk was, however, willing to risk war over the slaveholding republic of Texas. When Polk precipitated a border crisis with Mexico by placing American troops on land most observers believed belonged to Mexico, northern Democrats felt pressed. Almost all of them had wholeheartedly supported expansion, and yet with each additional acre of territory the question of slavery expansion arose anew. Barnburner John A. Dix saw the events before the outbreak of war as the "work of speculators and bankrupts": "a magnificent scheme has been devised to invade and conquer Mexico," he told Azariah C. Flagg. Van Buren also saw how the coming war would place his faction in a tight spot, politically. In a war against Mexico for the purposes of territorial expansion, he told Navy secretary George Bancroft, "the opposition shall be able to charge with plausibility, if not truth, that it is waged for the extension of slavery." This kind of war would force northern Democrats "to the sad alternative of turning their backs upon their [southern] friends, or of encountering political suicide with their eyes open."[47] The status quo was clearly no longer working. "The time has come, I think," wrote Connecticut Democrat Gideon Welles, "when the Northern Democracy should make a stand. Every thing has taken a Southern shape and been controlled by Southern caprice for years. The Northern states are treated as provinces to the South. We have given in, too much."[48]

Such was the political climate that surrounded the introduction of the

Wilmot Proviso on August 6, an event discussed at length earlier. The preponderance of New York Barnburners present at the proviso's creation, however, is worth noting here. Six of the eleven instigators of the proviso restricting new slave territory were either New Yorkers or members of Barnburner leader Preston King's mess in Washington. Each was a Van Buren Democrat. New York's newspapers, furthermore, were the earliest and loudest trumpeters of the proviso's creed. Walt Whitman of the *Brooklyn Eagle*, for example, bragged that he was the first to call it the Democrats' "duty . . . to take an unalterable stand against the allowance of slavery in any new territory, under any circumstances, or in any way."[49] Before his editorials brought him into conflict with the *Eagle*'s owner (costing him "one of the pleasantest sits" of his life), Whitman offered himself as another of Bryant's and Sedgwick's urban army of Free Soil editorialists.[50]

As did his upstate compatriot Preston King, Whitman hoped a movement to stop slavery in its tracks would begin in Congress and then spread to the Democratic electorate at large. "Let the Democratic members of Congress (and Whigs too, if they like,) plant themselves quietly, without bluster, but fixedly and without compromise, on the requirement that *Slavery be prohibited in them forever*," he wrote jauntily in December 1846. But Whitman's next line was more wistful and tinged with trepidation: "We wish we could have a universal straightforward setting down of feet on this thing, in the Democratic Party. *We must.*"[51]

Two weeks after Whitman's editorial appeared in the *Eagle*, Preston King kept his promise to reintroduce the proviso on the first day of the new congressional session. King's speech, reprinted and distributed throughout the North, prompted President Polk (who had long claimed to see no connection between territorial expansion and the slavery issue) to confide in his diary that "the slavery question is assuming a fearful and most important aspect. The movement of Mr. King today, if persevered in, will be attended with terrible consequences to the country and cannot fail to destroy the Democratic party, if it does not ultimately threaten the union itself."[52] In King's incarnation of the proviso, Wilmot's lofty and Jeffersonian language was pared down; he aimed, instead, directly at the anxieties of potential northern emigrants. "Shall the territory now free which shall come to our jurisdiction be free territory, open to settlement by the laboring man of the free states, or shall it be slave territory given up to slave labor?" King asked on the floor of Congress. "If slavery is not excluded by law, the presence of the slave will exclude the laboring white man. The young men who went with their axes into the forests, and hewed out of the wilderness such states as Ohio and Indiana and Michigan and Illinois and Iowa and Wisconsin, would never have consented, in the workshops or the field, to be coupled with negro slaves."[53] King's mention of western pioneers was no accident. In what would become a mainstay of Free Soil rhetoric (borrowed from anti-rent and land-reform journals), antislavery Democrats like King referred again and again to slaveholders choking off potential immigration to new and old territories. Arguments such as these were especially powerful in rural New York. Many of the farmers in King's district (and those surrounding it as well) had sons and daughters moving westward at a truly furious pace, especially to Michigan and Wisconsin Territory. Dozens of King's and Wright's own relatives in the North Country had already moved or were planning to leave soon.[54]

The Barnburner Schism

The demise of the old Jacksonian coalition in New York occurred in 1847. The year began with King's speech reintroducing the proviso and ended with the Barnburners' commitment to make containment of slavery the "cornerstone" of a new Free Soil Party. In the eighteen months between King's speech in January 1847 and the 1848 Democratic convention in Baltimore (where Barnburner delegates walked out), there were no less than five Democratic mass meetings in New York state. In these mass gatherings the Free Soil ideology coalesced within the Barnburner revolt and led to the formation of a new, more powerful antislavery party.

The Barnburners' leader at the beginning of 1847 was Silas Wright. Despite losing the governorship in 1846, Wright was seen by many observers as the Democrats' leading presidential candidate for 1848. Van Buren ally Thomas Hart Benton of Missouri, bowing out of the 1848 race to make way for the New Yorker, loudly attacked John C. Calhoun's antiproviso resolutions and urged the Democracy to nominate a candidate from a free state. Bryant's *Evening Post* proudly reprinted Benton's letter and called attention to other papers' early endorsements of the ex-governor. Wright's sudden death in August 1847 left the faction without a leader of national renown and plunged it into disorganization and apathy. Barnburner John Dix shared his dismay: "To his friends, the [loss of Wright] is serious indeed; but to the country in its present unhappy condition, it is far greater. I see no hope of rallying the Northern democracy [for 1848], unless it be on Mr. Van Buren."[55]

The Hunkers used their opponents' bad luck and momentary disarray to

seize control of the state Democratic convention, which convened in Syracuse on September 29. After gaining control of the state central committee
and expelling several Barnburner delegates, the Hunkers succeeded in tabling a resolution declaring the Democracy's "uncompromising hostility to
the extension of slavery."[56] By the time the convention disbanded, many
antislavery New York Democrats had had enough. One Barnburner recalled
how the Syracuse convention, which at one point threatened to dissolve into
a brawl, provided him with a political conversion. "If it was barnburnerism
to stand up for the rights of free labor to the soil," said future congressman
James R. Doolittle, "I am a barnburner. . . . If it was barnburnerism to stand
by those who had stood between the people and the rapacity of those who
would thrust their hands into the public treasury, I am a barnburner."[57]
Doolittle's experience was not atypical. Other antislavery Democrats across
New York noticed how, for them, the issue of slavery in the territories was
trumping old feelings of party loyalty. "All ordinarily 'weighty issues' are
insignificant before this," wrote Walt Whitman in the *Brooklyn Eagle*. "It
swallows them up as Aaron's rod swallowed the other rods [and] involves the
question whether the mighty power of this Republic . . . shall be used to root
deeper and spread wider an institution which [our forefathers] anxiously
sought the extinction of."[58]

For their part, the Hunkers left the Syracuse convention with an important political victory: the territory issue was, for the time being, buried; the
machinery of the Democratic Party was firmly in their hands; and the state
Democratic ticket was packed with Hunker candidates. Yet the Barnburners
sensed they held a political trump card in the Wilmot Proviso, one that
could, if played deftly, bring them victory in New York and, perhaps, within
the party as a whole. Veterans like C. C. Cambreleng and Azariah Flagg were
slower to realize this new political reality, but younger Barnburners were
not. Led by King and Van Buren's son John, they pushed hard to convene a
separate meeting to nominate a rival antislavery Democratic ticket and denounce the Syracuse convention as a fraud. The next day the Barnburner
paper, the *Albany Atlas*, publicly endorsed the meeting, signaling an open
party breech.[59]

From the start, the Barnburners' hastily called meeting was open to
charges of illegitimacy. The state Democratic Party had already met and
named a ticket. As well, the display of overt disloyalty within the Democracy
went against everything Van Buren's old Albany Regency had stood for — if
there was backstabbing to be done, the Regency had done it in back rooms,
behind closed doors.[60] The editors of the *Atlas* proposed adding a more

official air to the new meeting — scheduled for October 26 in the free-soil stronghold of Herkimer — by having the call issued by the dissatisfied delegates from the earlier convention.

Grassroots support for a political organization for antislavery Democrats grew during the fall of 1847. Three separate assembly district meetings in King's home county of St. Lawrence in mid-October had repudiated the state ticket and endorsed the Wilmot Proviso, just as both Herkimer districts and one in Cayuga had done in previous weeks. Still, the old guard was worried. Veteran Azariah Flagg preferred to let the spontaneous meetings speak for themselves and urged against the nomination of any new slate of candidates. "These movements in the assembly districts will have a much stronger moral effect than an organized opposition got up by leaders at headquarters," Flagg insisted. He remained steadfastly opposed to the "action of . . . these hotspurs, from whose indiscretion we have suffered as much as from any source."[61]

One of the hotspurs Flagg mentioned by name was Abijah C. Beckwith, the sixty-three-year-old farmer from Herkimer County. Beckwith's life and career perfectly illustrate the changes in both society and politics that were propelling rock-ribbed Jacksonians into the antislavery movement. Born in Columbia County in 1784 to a Methodist mother and an "Armenian" father, Beckwith married young and moved to a "considerably new" fifty-acre farm in Herkimer County in 1809.[62]

During his long career as a farmer and "student of politics" Beckwith was a Democrat of unquestionable loyalty. "Whether it was out of habit or due to the bumps on my head," Beckwith recalled, he had voted for Democrats in every election between 1806 and 1846. The events of the Syracuse convention prompted the antislavery Beckwith to leave his party, and he quickly joined the more radical Barnburners in calling for independent, pro-proviso nominations.[63]

Beckwith's Jacksonianism and opposition to slavery were closely linked; both flowed from his belief that "democracy" relied upon an "equal distribution of lands into convenient farms." In other words, both the tenantry of the anti-rent districts and the chattel slavery of the South were "aristocratic evils" and should therefore be abolished by a people's government. For years, he reasoned, New York's great families ("aristocrats who contrived to own all the land") and the South's slaveholders ("wealthy men . . . who [possess] a lordly pride of having human beings as their property and under their control") had posed a two-pronged threat to northerners' prosperity and democracy. As a state legislator in 1816 Beckwith had voted in favor of gradual emancipation (in a vote he remembered as his proudest legislative moment); three decades later he referred to the victory of pro-slavery Hunkers at Syracuse as an "eavle [*sic*] consequence following from the moral curse of slavery." Of course, Beckwith said, antislavery Democrats should nominate new candidates.[64]

This idea that slaveholders were, by definition, aristocrats flew in the face of the older idea, advanced by Van Buren himself in the 1820s, that only an alliance of "plain republicans" and "planters" could challenge resurgent inequality. Across the state Democrats like Walt Whitman were echoing Beckwith's sentiments. "Will the exclusion of slavery from the new terri-tory deter [nonslaveholding southerners] from going with their axes and ploughs into its forests, and making their houses on its unfurrowed sur-face?" he asked his Brooklyn readers in 1847. "The only persons who will be excluded will be the *aristocracy* of the South — the men who work only with other men's hands."[65]

Pressure from rank-and-file antislavery Democrats like Whitman and Beckwith encouraged younger, more radical Barnburners to plunge head-first into a new Free Soil movement. Martin Van Buren, Azariah Flagg, and older Barnburners, fighting the last political war, continued to underesti-mate the value of slavery containment as a political issue. Despite a plea from David Wilmot for the ex-president publicly to endorse his proviso, Van Buren instead wrote an open letter disavowing rumors of his presidential ambitions and endorsing Polk's war measures without a single reference to the slavery issue.[66] But the more Van Buren and the old guard tried to derail the Herkimer movement, the stronger it became. Van Buren and his friends were no longer leading New York's Democrats; they were being led by them.

The schismatics' mass convention convened on October 26, 1847, in the Herkimer railroad station, the largest building in town. The meeting has merited only passing attention by historians but was significant for the fu-tures of both Democratic and antislavery politics. First, it was the first mass meeting composed solely of antislavery Jacksonians.[67] Each of the 4,000 delegates who crowded into the sleepy Mohawk Valley town was committed to Free Soil in principle as well as name. Second, its proceedings provide a picture of the evolution of the Free Soil ideology from a program for land reform to a bulwark against slavery extension. Antislavery advocates and politicians across the country watched the proceedings with interest. Ohio antislavery politician Salmon P. Chase, for example, wrote to Massachu-setts's Charles Sumner that he knew of "no event in the History of Parties in this Country, at all approaching, in sublimity and moment, the Herkimer

Convention, or rather the great movement of which the Convention was the most signal, visible expression." Lastly, the Herkimer meeting was important for the maturation of the Jacksonian antislavery impulse. David Wilmot traveled from his home in northern Pennsylvania to the meeting, joking that he wanted to "see if my namesake would survive the buffetings it had received at Syracuse." What he saw and heard at Herkimer, he said, inspired him "with new hope and new courage" for the antislavery movement.[68]

The Herkimer platform of resolutions amounted to a potluck containing every radical Democratic reform measure of the previous fifteen years. Presented to the assembled crowd by New York lawyer David Dudley Field (author of the cornerstone resolution tabled at Syracuse), they included attacks on the "factious majority" of the Syracuse convention, urged the "divorce" of the federal government from banks, and endorsed free trade, limited public internal improvements, cheap postage, the war effort, and the superiority and dignity of free white labor. The Herkimer delegates then unanimously passed Field's cornerstone resolution and adjourned with a new motto. In addition to presenting an inclusive summary of the principles of Jacksonian antislavery, it was also a mouthful: "Free Trade, Free Labor, Free Soil, Free Speech and Free Men."[69]

The immediate effect of the Barnburner revolt was a humiliating Democratic defeat in the 1847 election. Majorities for Whig gubernatorial candidate Millard Fillmore numbered more than 38,000, making 1847 the highwater mark of Whig power in the state. No one was fooled about the real reason for the ignominious failure of the regular Democratic ticket: the complete desertion of the party's antislavery wing. Surprisingly, though, Democrats did not cross lines and vote the Whig ticket. Azariah Flagg, the state's most astute political observer, noted that the total Democratic tally was 104,000 votes less than in 1844, while the Whig vote was down by only 56,000. In St. Lawrence County, for example, the local Democratic assembly candidate (who was not nominated by the Syracuse convention) received 3,914 votes, while the Syracuse ticket polled only 844 votes in the entire district, famous as a Jacksonian stronghold.[70] This suggests that more than 3,000 St. Lawrence Democrats came to the polls, voted for their local candidate, yet refused to vote for the regular statewide ticket. Flagg wrote to fellow Barnburner Dix that in six St. Lawrence towns combined, the Syracuse ticket polled 13 votes, while the local Democratic candidate, who had not been nominated in Syracuse, won 367. "The Democrats of the county know that the ticket was got up under the dictation and management of those who defeated Silas Wright," he wrote, "and they trampled it in the dust."[71]

The Barnburners were generally delighted with the blow they had dealt their Hunker foes. In Brooklyn, Walt Whitman was optimistic about the faction's electoral future. "The day is not far distant," he told readers of the *Eagle,* "when politicians will be as eager to prove that they were in this matter on the side of freedom, as ever were men to escape companionship with the cholera or yellow fever!"[72] The only way for the Democracy to regain its former glory, Whitman asserted, was for it openly to adopt the antislavery doctrines of the late William Leggett. "[Leggett's] ideas — once derided, but now widely worshipped — form the best elements of the Democratic creed, and of the Democratic Party," Whitman wrote. Making Leggett's "progressive spirit" central to party doctrine would herald a day, he concluded, "when monopolies shall be things that *were,* but are not — when the barbarism of restrictions on trade shall have passed away — when the plague spot of slavery, with all its taint to freedmen's principles and prosperity, shall be allowed to spread no *further,* and when the good old Democratic Party . . . shall flourish over the grave of this fleeting Whigism."[73] Whitman's editorial no doubt irked many of Brooklyn's Hunkers, none more than Whitman's own boss, the owner of the *Eagle.* By January 1848, Whitman had involuntarily joined the ranks of the unemployed and boarded a steamboat for New Orleans.

Southern Democrats similarly rejected Whitman's prescription for a resurgent party based on Leggett's antislavery principles. They ridiculed the Barnburners as a faction of "disorganizers."[74] Still, as 1848 dawned, both Hunkers and Barnburners knew that the time had arrived for a showdown. First, the schismatic antislavery Jacksonians met again, this time in Utica, to elect their own slate of delegates for the Democratic convention. Then they began to discuss forging political alliances across the old party lines. The Barnburners were, after all, seasoned party men — they knew they could not win elections on their own. But who would they join? And around what candidate could they rally?

Liberty Party members, still smarting from their anemic electoral tallies of 1844, hoped to win the Barnburner support for their candidate John P. Hale, the ex-Democratic senator from New Hampshire.[75] None but the most radical young Barnburners, however, were even remotely interested in uniting with the Liberty Party in early 1848. With the death of Silas Wright, Democratic conversations over who would make the best candidate kept circling back to Van Buren, who had recently come out of retirement to hammer out Barnburner strategy from a suite at Julien's Hotel on Washington Square in Greenwich Village. Connecticut congressman Gideon Welles, a close ally of the Barnburners, wrote Flagg that he supported a third Van Buren candidacy, "to right, in 1848, the wrong of 1844." This was less for reasons of revenge, as many historians have characterized the schism, than the inability of any other available candidate to rally antislavery Democrats.[76] As the national Democratic convention approached, more antislavery Democrats set their hearts on Van Buren. This is one reason why, when events at the Baltimore convention unfolded as they did, Barnburner delegates found it easy to walk out of the party many of them had helped to found.

The Little Magician Reappears

As was becoming a quadrennial tradition, New York's delegation was at the center of political intrigue in the months before the national Democratic convention. The leading candidate appeared to be Michigan's senior senator, the frowning, droopy-eyed Lewis Cass. For Barnburners, Cass was the ultimate symbol of scorn: a doughfaced westerner who had traded all principle for southern support. Many blamed him personally for engineering Van Buren's humiliation at the 1844 convention.[77] At the Free Soil meeting in Utica in February 1848, Barnburner George Rathbun replayed for the cheering assembly step-by-step how Cass had abandoned the Wilmot Proviso and "turned traitor to the North, to freedom, and became a soldier under the black banner of Aggressive Slavery."[78]

Meanwhile, in the war room at Julien's Hotel, the Little Magician saw an opportunity to demonstrate the Barnburners' hold on the Democratic electorate in New York and a way to lend legitimacy to their slate of irregularly chosen delegates. Van Buren drafted an address that Free Soil newspapers later christened the "Barnburner Manifesto" or the "First shot for Free Soil." He summoned the young Barnburner lawyer Samuel J. Tilden to his chambers and handed him the manuscript, saying, "If you wish to be immortal, take this home with you, complete it, revise it, put it into proper shape, and give it to the public." Except for a brief introduction by Prince John and a small insert by Tilden, it was left virtually unchanged.[79]

After six years of equivocation, Van Buren was finally ready to come out for slavery restriction.[80] His address systematically presented the history of the slavery issue and argued that only a party committed to opposing its extension could speak for the Democratic voters of New York. The document opened with a legal defense of the Wilmot Proviso, which had come under attack by southerners, Hunkers, and even the ailing John Quincy

Adams. In response, Van Buren wrote that only a law barring slavery from the territories would halt slavery's spread. The proviso was even more necessary due to "new and startling doctrines" passed by meetings in Alabama, Florida, and Virginia that demanded northern Democrats adopt the view that a person has a guaranteed right to hold slaves in the territories. "We ask [the southern Democrats]," he wrote, "to believe that the principle of extending slavery to territories now free from it can never be made acceptable to the freemen of the North."[81] Anticipating some of the key arguments of the next decade, Van Buren asked if new territories shall be free or slave. "They cannot be both," he wrote. "Free and slave labor . . . cannot flourish under the same laws. The wealthy capitalists who own slaves disdain manual labor, and the whites who are compelled to submit to it . . . cannot act on term of equality with the masters."[82] Concluding the address with a political masterstroke, the ex-president demanded that the upcoming Democratic national convention seat *only* the Barnburners' irregularly selected delegates. Van Buren thus offered the party a choice: either admit the Barnburner delegation exclusively or hand New York and its electoral votes over to the Whigs.[83]

After Tilden and John Van Buren finished editing the address, the elder Van Buren instructed them to read it to the Democrats in the state legislature, where it received overwhelming approbation on April 12. John was so pleased with its reception that he asked his father if he would allow the more radical Barnburner delegates to offer his name to the Baltimore convention and bolt if it was rejected. The Little Magician's reply was an unequivocal no, and he scolded his son for suggesting such a "rash and unadvised step."[84]

Far more important than the nominee, Martin stressed to John, was the full admission of the Barnburner delegation at the convention. The convening gavel had barely fallen in Baltimore when delegates raised the question of which New York delegation to admit. Hunkers and Barnburners swept all gentility aside, each loudly claiming exclusive rights to represent the Democrats of New York. Convention leaders proposed a compromise: each delegation would present its side, and the full convention would vote on which faction to seat.[85] Preston King used his address to argue that if the party unseated those Democrats who opposed slavery's extension, Free Soil delegates from other states would have to be excluded as well, bringing antislavery voters' wrath upon the party in the coming election. "If all the other States were prepared to make the democratic party the carrier of slavery over this continent," he said, "the democracy of New York would take no part in such an alliance. . . . Alone or in company [we will] fight this battle of

FIGURE 5

*"Smoking Him Out" (1848). This dramatic cartoon depicts Martin and
John Van Buren, like mythical Dutch farmers, burning down a barn to rid it of rats.
Trapped on the roof is popular sovereignty Democrat Lewis Cass. John exclaims,
"We'll rat 'em out yet. Long life to Davy Wilmot." (Library of Congress)*

freedom from beginning to end."[86] In a compromise that satisfied no one,
both New York delegations were seated, and each delegate was given half a
vote. The compromise, along with the decision to allow South Carolina's
sole delegate to cast his state's nine votes, poisoned the convention for the
Barnburners. Bad feelings intensified when the convention nominated the
Van Burenites' archfoe Lewis Cass on the fourth ballot. The Barnburner
delegates dramatically rose in unison and marched out of the convention
and the Democratic Party.[87]

After the Barnburners stormed out, the remaining delegates adopted a
platform that completely dodged the territorial issue by repeating verbatim
the 1840 and 1844 planks insisting Congress could not interfere with slavery in the states. Chastened by the exodus of delegates from a state particularly rich in electoral votes, delegations from Alabama and Virginia, who

had previously insisted on a positive guarantee for territorial slavery, accepted the platform. In the eyes of the Barnburners, however, the platform explicitly repudiated the letter and spirit of the Wilmot Proviso.[88]

The results of the Baltimore convention torpedoed any hopes for a quick reunion among New York's Democratic factions. Tilden drafted an address explaining the "injustices" committed at Baltimore and condemned Cass as unfit for New York. At a boisterous rally in New York's City Hall Park, 12,000 Democrats cheered the call for another state convention (also planned for Utica) where a strategy and more acceptable candidates might be chosen.[89] Older Barnburners like Dix and Flagg continued to oppose an independent Free Soil ticket, but the younger radicals had won a powerful new convert: Martin Van Buren himself. A third party effort suddenly appeared to be the best way to enhance the faction's political influence while, at long last, accurately reflecting their constituents on the question of slavery extension.[90]

In Utica for the second time that year, New York's Barnburners received telegrams promising the support of like-minded Democrats in Indiana, Illinois, and Pennsylvania. The meeting's delegates formally nominated Martin Van Buren for president, despite his earlier refusals, and a new platform urged all Free Soil New Yorkers to participate as delegates in any free state convention called to unite the antiextension forces. Delegates also resolved to form local "Jeffersonian Leagues" for "Free Soil and free principles."[91]

Over the next two weeks, in a move that would have been unthinkable to most Barnburners just a year before, plans were laid for a political union of all Free Soil forces to be launched in August, in the city of Buffalo. In New York, what were once muted local protests against slavery and tenancy had taken the state by storm. And once Free Soil ideas and rhetoric reached prominence in state politics, they were quickly adopted by the Barnburners looking for ways to regain control of the state Democratic Party. Barnburners opposed to the spread of slavery such as King, Whitman, and Beckwith led the faction headlong into the growing antislavery movement. A tumultuous political season had severely wounded Martin Van Buren's second party system and set the stage for a national antislavery alliance built on the political ideas of Thomas Morris, William Leggett, and the radical Democrats of New York state.

CHAPTER THREE

Making Hay from Democratic Clover

John P. Hale and the New Hampshire
Independent Democracy

While Free Soil ideas in New York stemmed from long-standing land disputes and political rivalries, the origins of New Hampshire's version of Free Soil were tied to one divisive issue: Texas annexation. Public opposition to annexation spread across New Hampshire like wildfire in early 1845, leading to a statewide political insurgency directed against the regular, pro-annexation Democratic Party. Before 1846 was over, a new, "Independent Democratic" coalition, comprised of antislavery advocates from all parties and led by dissident Jacksonians, banded together to halt annexation and slavery. Unlike the Liberty Party, which took its organizational structure from local abolition societies, the Independent Democracy was launched as a centralized political party. New Hampshire's Free Soil insurgency thus gave the antislavery movement a new model of political coalition with which to expand its constituency. At least one member of this coalition remarked on the differences between the tactics of abolitionists — whom he chided as "malignant scolds" — and those of the masculine, Jacksonian antislavery of men "giving blow for blow" in the public sphere to elect candidates pledged to halt southern expansion. Finally, New Hampshire's political revolution provided the movement with the first antislavery Democratic leader of national stature: John P. Hale.[1]

As Good a Democrat as There Was in the World

After an extended visit with a Unitarian minister on January 4, 1845, New Hampshire congressman John Parker Hale decided to ignore the explicit instructions of the state Democratic Party and vote against annexing the republic of Texas to the United States. Despite dubious assurances from leaders of both parties that annexation would "add more free than slave states to the Union," Hale had become convinced that the admission of Texas meant only one thing: the extension of slavery. To Hale, the spread of slavery was both a political and a moral catastrophe.[2]

Hale's decision to oppose annexation provided the antislavery movement—and his political career—with one of its defining moments.[3] Hale's vote against Texas's admission on antislavery grounds ignited a political revolution in New Hampshire that brought dissident Democrats, Liberty Party members, and Whigs into a formidable statewide coalition. Thus, New Hampshire became a political battlefield on which the Jacksonian coalition broke apart into pro- and antislavery factions. Throughout the North, these shifts led to new, free-soil alliances. Nowhere did this type of realignment occur more perfectly than in the Granite State, long regarded as the greatest northern bulwark in defense of southern principles. Far from the genteel abolitionist salons of Boston, dissident Democrats in the New Hampshire hills converted the "South Carolina of the North" into an unlikely hotbed of antislavery agitation.

John P. Hale was the central figure in New Hampshire's antislavery revolution. Hale had risen through the ranks of the New Hampshire Democratic Party as a staunch opponent of railroads, corporate privileges, and abolition. He did not arrive at his decision to oppose Texas annexation lightly, knowing a "nay" vote would likely end his political career at home.

It was a career that had manifested considerable promise. Hale was born in Rochester, New Hampshire, in 1806, the eldest child in a downwardly mobile family.[4] Hale's father, an impecunious lawyer, died in 1819, leaving his wife and thirteen children to rely on relatives. Lydia Hale eventually sold the family home and operated a boardinghouse, saving enough money to send her son to the Phillips Exeter Academy. The young scholar did well enough there to go to Harvard, but instead he chose to attend the less expensive Bowdoin College in Brunswick, Maine. Among his college classmates were Franklin Pierce (already president of a pro-Jackson debating society), Nathaniel Hawthorne, and Henry Wadsworth Longfellow.[5]

Hale decided early to study law and enter politics. When he did, he bucked the family Federalist tradition and became a Jacksonian Democrat. Hale moved to Dover, the bustling Strafford County seat, and joined the Jacksonian political machine managed by the hunchbacked editor Isaac Hill. After a brief stint as a state legislator, advancement came in the form of political patronage: President Jackson, at the advice of Hill, appointed Hale U.S. attorney.[6]

Hale was nominated and elected to Congress in 1843.[7] Upon his arrival in Washington, Hale was, in his own words, "as good a Democrat . . . as there was in the world." He voted for the Independent Treasury bill, repeatedly opposed federal appropriations for internal improvements, spoke against imprisonment for debt, and joined in sponsoring a resolution that called the very idea of a national bank "hostile to the spirit of our [democratic] institutions."[8]

The only time Hale voted differently from the rest of the New Hampshire delegation was on the infamous gag rule, which automatically tabled all anti-slavery petitions sent to the House. The gag was already on its last legs in 1843 due to the tireless efforts of Whig congressmen John Quincy Adams, Joshua Giddings, and Seth Gates. In early December 1843, Hale had sounded out his plan to vote against the gag to his northern Democratic messmates and had been pleasantly surprised by the results.[9] Hale couched his opposition to the gag in states' rights language, arguing that the federal government had no power to interfere with slavery, either by assisting in its perpetuation or by silencing debate. By Hale's reasoning, the gag rule, by avoiding direct votes on the receipt of abolitionist petitions, gave unnecessary federal assistance to slaveholders. Even with Hale's vote, the gag rule was sustained a final time, with ninety-one voting for repeal and ninety-five opposed.[10]

Despite Hale's fears of political retribution for his vote against the gag, the reaction to his votes in New Hampshire was mild. Edmund Burke's *Argus and Spectator* and Isaac Hill's new *Hill's Patriot* predictably denounced him, but Hale's hometown *Dover Gazette* and the *Exeter News-Letter* praised his course. When the official party organ, the *New Hampshire Patriot*, finally registered its disapproval, Hale's name was left out of the article. Hale also received an influx of warm support from Democrats (and some Whigs and Liberty men), mostly from the eastern parts of the state, where party conventions in Strafford, Rockingham, Carroll, and Merrimack counties backed Hale's "manly and independent stand."[11]

Congress permanently abandoned the gag rule, again with Hale's vote, in December 1844. But the victory against the gag was ephemeral. Already the issue of the admission of Texas loomed before Hale and his colleagues. This time, when the young congressman took an independent stand, the results in New Hampshire were not mild at all.[12]

After nearly a month of agonizing over Texas, Hale informed his wife, Lucy, of his as yet "secret" decision to defy the leaders of his own party and oppose annexation. "I am convinced beyond the shadow of a doubt that I am right & I cannot barter the conviction of my conscience for any peace," he wrote. He resolved to vote against annexation and to "prepare a letter to the people of the state giving the reasons for my conduct, and requesting them, if they do not concur . . . to select some other person to carry out their views."[13] Expecting to incur the wrath of the state party and be forced out of New Hampshire politics forever, Hale quietly began making plans to open a law practice with New Yorker and fellow Democratic dissident Theodore Sedgwick III.[14]

Hale's retirement plans were premature. His *Letter to the Democratic Republican Electors of New Hampshire* appealed directly to the state's voters, over the heads of party leaders. Published widely across the state, the letter struck a chord with Democrats dissatisfied with the state party's aggressive appeasement of the South and slavery. Franklin Pierce, chairman of the State Central Committee, made plans to replace Hale with a more "suitable" nominee for Congress. Over the next three months, Hale's letter sparked a realignment in state politics that incorporated all antislavery voters under one umbrella, led by dissident Jacksonians.[15]

The South Carolina of the North

During the 1830s, New Hampshire's Democratic Party was without peer in the North as a defender of its southern allies and their peculiar institution. In constant pursuit of southern goodwill and the national patronage it inevitably bestowed, New Hampshire's Democrats melded a states' rights philosophy and antiabolitionism into a successful political combination that complemented a deep-seated hostility to banks, corporations, and railroad construction.

Democratic governors and congressmen won their elections by wide margins, making New Hampshire an anomaly among the New England states. Jackson soundly defeated Henry Clay in 1832 with 56.8 percent of the total ballots cast.[16] Moreover, the state's leading Democrats — editor Isaac Hill and the evasive Senator Levi Woodbury — were two of the Jackson administration's most trusted northern associates.[17]

While the state was solidly Democratic, however, major rifts over economic issues threatened to split the party. Conservative Democrats, clustered in the southwestern corner of the state and led by Hill (a director of the new Concord railroad), agreed with Whigs that the state should aid economic development. More radical Democrats such as Pierce, however, insisted there was nothing "public" about train lines and corporations and passed legislation designed to slow the railroad boom and hobble the entire Market Revolution in the state. Hale aligned himself with Pierce's wing of the party, making a name for himself as a staunch opponent of subsidized railroad development. In 1840 Hale attacked the nearly ubiquitous northern practice of eminent domain, urging his friends to "resist the arbitrary and tyrannical proceedings of the rail road . . . in their illegal and high handed usurpations of the rights of land holders in taking their freehold from them by the hands of violence." This type of New Hampshire Jacksonianism resonated well with the poorer farmers in the mountain and northern frontier areas, who tended to oppose legislation favoring corporations as well as moral reformers telling them what to do. Judging by the election returns, the Democratic Party in New Hampshire spoke for a large majority of the population. Throughout the 1830s and early 1840s, Democrats tightened their electoral hold on the state.[18]

Slavery had never found much of a purchase in the Granite State, and a judicial interpretation of the state constitution outlawed the institution in 1783. Due to the tiny number of slaves and free blacks in the state, emancipation proceeded with few of the conflicts common in other northern states.[19] While New Hampshire was one of only four states to allow adult black men to vote on an equal basis with whites, assumptions of white supremacy were nevertheless widespread. At least as prominent as New Hampshirites' distaste for chattel slavery was a strong belief in states' rights, which held that it was unwise and even unconstitutional to meddle in the affairs of the slave states. Leaders of the Democratic Party went further still, waging a multileveled assault on organized abolitionism. In Congress, New Hampshire representatives were instrumental in hatching and sustaining the federal gag on abolitionist petitions in the late 1830s and early 1840s.[20] Isaac Hill, for years the undisputed Democratic Party leader in the state, went even further, remarking on the "moral superiority" of slaves to free blacks and explaining how "mutual relations between slave and master . . . endear one to the other."[21] State legislators voted repeatedly to support the gag rule and routinely passed resolutions attacking the abolitionists' "fanatical" and "inflammatory" actions. At the grassroots level, antislavery organizations were systematically harassed and, worse, assaulted by vigilante mobs.

Hale's early career, as well as those of several future Democratic Free Soilers, was marked by public opposition to abolitionism, as one violent incident in 1835 demonstrates. In August, the Reverend George Storrs, an agent for the tiny New Hampshire Antislavery Society, traveled to Dover to deliver a series of abolitionist lectures. The first two meetings took place without disruption, but before the third, handbills appeared around town claiming to reveal the "secret" goals of the meeting as a wicked combination of "abolition" and "*disunion.*" Protesters packed the church to heckle the visitor. After Storrs finished his speech, Hale rose to demand the floor and then to rebut "the fallacies of the doctrines of the abolitionists" and the "evils" emancipation would bring upon the citizens of the South. Hale concluded his "short but animated address" by dismissing slaves as "beasts in human shape . . . not fit to live free," the last word, according to Storrs, uttered in a barely audible whisper. The demonstration that followed forced Storrs to cancel the final lecture in the series and flee Dover, to the delight of the local Democratic press.[22]

An Antislavery Conversion

How did Hale, then, a typical antiabolitionist in the 1830s, become the nation's leading advocate of political antislavery during the following decade? As with most of the other Jacksonian antislavery dissidents, it was a gradual and anguished process, the effect of a combination of intense soul-searching, religious belief, and the unceasing force of outside events.

More than for his future Free Soil allies David Wilmot and Marcus Morton, religion and rigorous introspection were central facets of Hale's life. He was born and raised a Unitarian and eventually became a deacon of the Dover Unitarian Society. A devoted churchgoer from childhood, Hale was constantly in search of an uplifting and fulfilling sermon. Yearnings for spiritual satisfaction led Hale to attend other churches, including Catholic, Congregational, and, especially, Freewill Baptist. This latter sect, alone among New Hampshire denominations, was an early and vocal opponent of slavery. Hale doubtless heard many fiery antislavery sermons at the Dover church as early as the mid-1830s.[23]

Hale carried on an intense correspondence with his wife, the former Lucy Lambert, to whom he confided his increasingly agonizing attempts to synchronize his religious beliefs and his politics. During December 1844, when Hale realized he would have to vote on the annexation of Texas as a slave state, he began to attend church even more regularly. He worried about the "temptations" of political ambition and the difficulty of making spiritual progress in his worldly vocation. "The more I have reflected upon the subject," he wrote, "the more I am convinced that a correct appreciation of that great central truth of Christianity will induce such a government of the heart and life as cannot fail to continually advance us in the path of holiness and happiness."[24] A vote to admit Texas and extend the reach of slavery, Hale feared, would topple this "government of the heart."

Hale also found a religious and moral sounding board in the person of the Reverend John Parkman, who came to Dover from Boston in 1840 as the minister of the First Unitarian Church. Before he moved to New Hampshire, Parkman had been vice president of the Massachusetts Antislavery Society, and he unabashedly carried his hatred of slavery into his new home, a bastion of Democratic doughfaces. Hale had initially detested the new pastor's abolitionism, but in 1842, when Parkman's job was in jeopardy because of protests over his antislavery sermons, Hale drafted resolutions backing the minister's right to address the "moral questions of the day," including slavery.[25] Even if the ideas were unpopular, Hale wrote, Parkman should not be silenced. The pastor was retained, and the incident inaugurated a close friendship between the two men. Parkman quickly became the person in whom Hale confided about moral questions. In turn, it seems, Parkman gradually convinced Hale of the necessity for action against slavery and the Slave Power.

Parkman's letters to Hale during his first term in Congress illustrate his method of prodding the young representative to stand up to party leaders on the question of slavery. In one letter, he related how local antislavery voters were debating whether Hale would "go right" or vote with two well-known New Hampshire doughfaces to extend the gag. "My reply generally was 'We shall see.' "[26] Parkman, like Lucy Hale, provided commentary on the moral, rather than political, ramifications of Hale's actions and eventually convinced him that there might be room in New Hampshire politics for a moderate Democratic antislavery leader. One Dover Democrat, Parkman related, was already "more than half an abolitionist," as a result of Hale's stand against the gag, while "your Democratic friends — so far as I can hear — are now all for the right of petition. I think some of them, if you had voted differently, would have been quite as zealous the other way."[27] Hale's mind was changing, as were the minds of some of his constituents.

Religion aside, Hale began to view harassment of abolitionists and restriction of their speech as violations of their civil liberties. Gag rules and mob violence helped cure Hale, like Leggett a decade earlier, of his antiabolitionism. In New Hampshire, Hale upbraided the legislature for voting overwhelmingly and repeatedly against granting incorporation to a Freewill Baptist printing establishment in Dover on account of the sect's abolitionism.[28] Restrictions on free expression, such as those that were attempted against John Parkman in 1842, had always incensed Hale. Incrementally, by the mid-1840s he had come to agree with the views expressed by one anonymous constituent who wrote to him in November 1843, that the votes to uphold the gag rule were a "ruthless assault on the inalienable rights of man: when Democrats, professing 'equal rights to all,' instead volunteer in the service of oppression, then, sir, the English language is barren of emphasis in expressing the infamy which they deserve and will ultimately receive. Among them your name, sir, is not yet written."[29] By Christmas 1844, Hale understood he would likely be forced to choose between his changing convictions and his political career. On December 27 the New Hampshire legislature voted to instruct the state's congressional delegation to work toward annexing Texas. In this season of goodwill toward men, Hale decided he could not in good conscience cast a vote he believed would expand the reach of slavery.

Hale's change of heart paralleled the growing legitimacy of the New Hampshire Liberty Party and political abolitionism in general. Although membership in antislavery societies lagged far behind other New England states, ten antislavery societies in New Hampshire reported a total membership of approximately 3,000 by 1837. The state's abolitionist paper, the *Herald of Freedom*, had a circulation of 1,400.[30] By the time Hale entered Congress in 1843, forty towns boasted antislavery auxiliaries, and the Liberty Party vote had increased its 1840 showing by twenty-seven-fold, commanding 3,400 votes. Both New Hampshire and Hale had begun a shift on the issue of slavery.[31]

The Independent Democracy

The New Hampshire legislature's resolutions instructing the state's congressional delegation to work to annex the republic of Texas placed Hale in the most politically awkward position of his career. After he decided to ignore the legislature and his state party, the former district attorney pleaded his case directly to the electorate in the form of the *Letter to the Democratic Republican Electors of New Hampshire*, dated January 7, 1845. In a stinging rebuke to the legislature's "fond delusion" that annexation would benefit northerners by adding "more free than Slave states to the Union," Hale suggested that the opposite was true: "[Annexation] is advocated here," he wrote, "as the sure and effectual means of sustaining slavery." His lawyerly analysis of the Texas constitution (which required that "all persons of color held in bondage, shall remain in a like state of servitude") concluded that the only way a free state could ever be formed out of the immense territory of

Texas was to make abolition a *legal condition* of annexation. In other words, annexation offered precious little for the people of New Hampshire. Could the founders of the Granite State, he asked his constituents, have foreseen the day when their "degenerate sons should be found seeking to extend their boundaries and their government, not for the purpose of promoting freedom, but sustaining slavery?"[32] Fully expecting the Democratic Party leadership in Concord to cast him out for his apostasy, Hale franked his letter and began tidying up his affairs in Washington. Despite a desire to continue his career in politics, he admitted to one friend that he had "no more idea of being returned to Congress again from New Hampshire than . . . of succeeding to the vacant throne of China."[33]

Hale was right about one thing: the swift and furious response of the state's Democratic Party leaders. Franklin Pierce scheduled a special convention for February 12 to "review" the party's congressional nominations, the first step in a well-coordinated campaign to "throw Hale overboard."[34] Fearing for the state's political patronage from the incoming, strongly pro-annexation Polk administration, he reprimanded Hale for his "rude, sweeping denunciation" and party irregularity. In a scathing article published January 16 in the *New Hampshire Patriot,* he publicly condemned Hale's "factious, selfish, and disorganizing" course and accused him of acting in collusion with Massachusetts abolitionists and Whigs.[35]

Scores of Democratic voters, however, did not agree. Although its author remained 500 miles away, Hale's letter precipitated a reshuffling of parties that has shaped New Hampshire politics to this day. Despite Pierce's best efforts, the initial response to Hale's stand was overwhelmingly positive. The circular "is better received than I had thought," Hale confided to his wife in the days after its publication. "I expected to be denounced for it in no measured terms. But today I received commendations . . . worth vastly more than all the wealth and honors government can confer."[36]

Over the next three months, parallel campaigns — one designed to sustain Hale, the other to bury him — electrified the state, with each faction intent on prevailing in the spring elections. Much of Hale's initial support came from eastern and northern parts of the state, the same areas that had supported him in 1843 after his vote against the gag rule.[37] S. B. Parsons in Coös County, in the remote, northernmost corner of the state, told Hale his stand had inaugurated "a new era in the history of New Hampshire — when the politicians will not dare use the word 'democrat' as a cloak for actions of iniquity and oppression."[38] Exeter lawyer Amos Tuck informed Hale that New Hampshire had been "cursed with the dictation of small men for years" and that he was "willing for a division, if that becomes inevitable in consequence of you doing your duty."[39] A farmer from Hampton Falls assured Hale that "every democrat in this town of a majority democratic district" was for him, while a young Whig editor promised significant Whig and Liberty support in the coming election.[40] A Concord dry goods merchant who had opposed Hale in 1843 weighed in strongly against the admission of Texas: "The main objective of annexation is to increase and perpetuate slavery—here in Concord it is the only thing talked of . . . [and] many more approve of your course than condemn it."[41]

Rushing to beat the next round of inclement weather (and Pierce's scheduled convention), Hale's supporters in far-off Coös County, a region physically isolated from the southern part of the state by the White Mountains, convened in Colebrook on February 4. Hilly, heavily forested, and cut off from regional agricultural market centers, communities in Coös remained dependent on subsistence farming well into the 1850s. Fiercely Democratic (the county had given 79 percent of its votes to Andrew Jackson in 1832, with one town even changing its name from "Adams" to "Jackson" to honor its hero), the farmers of Coös County had no intention of splitting their party in 1845. Yet Hale's flagrant "decapitation" at the hands of party leaders demanded urgent action.[42]

At least forty-eight Democrats representing towns across the county attended the February 4 meeting, which praised Hale's "correct and manly course" and "freely, impartially, and fully" condemned annexation, "a measure fertile in evils to our beloved country, and of an inevitable tendency to consolidate, increase and perpetuate the crime and curse of slavery." The proceedings of the convention, published in pamphlet form and titled *Democracy and Patriotism*, placed antiannexation in a long line of positions taken by the radical Democrats of Coös, including opposition to policies including rechartering the national bank, imposing a high tariff, limiting the right of suffrage, distributing surplus revenue, and "favoring the rich at the expense of the poor." The address made clear the wishes of the party's rank and file: "We are collectively cultivators of the soil—we are laborers and tillers of the ground—we are men who work for our daily bread. . . . As freemen, we are now to decide whether a future population shall receive that boon which is dearer than life, or whether by extending the limits of slavery we shall doom them to a harrowing and hopeless bondage." Only by supporting Hale, then, would the New Hampshire Democracy regain the confidence forfeited by the "driving, blustering clique of party-leaders" and their "subserviency to the interests of the Southern slaveholders."

The address ended with a call for a movement of "lovers of Freedom," with Hale as leader, made up of "independent men who don't bow to the party press."[43]

Coös's enthusiasm, however, brought Hale's official Democratic candidacy no reprieve. The state Democratic Party "decapitated" Hale on February 12, replacing him on the ballot with pro-annexation party loyalist John Woodbury.[44] Nevertheless, enthusiastic pro-Hale meetings continued across the state throughout the winter. In Ossipee, near the eastern border with Maine, dissident Democrats assembled to support Hale, just as they had the previous winter when Hale voted to end the gag on antislavery petitioners. "The [party] press will not rule the ballot box in March," the meeting's chairman assured Hale. "It cannot, at least, *in righteous Ossippee.*"[45] Another letter informed Hale that seven-eighths of the Democrats, a quarter of the Whigs, and all the abolitionists in Conway (also in eastern Carroll County) were devout antiannexationists.[46]

Nine days later, Democrats in the town of Rochester met in convention to declare slavery a local institution and resolved that Texas annexation was a trick by southern Democrats to force their northern brethren to approve of their "evils": "All attempts to make [slavery] a national affair, and to make the free states partake of its criminality, should be met with the just and severe rebuke of every Democrat and friend of equal rights." This reasoning was peculiarly Jacksonian; the Rochester meeting, in effect, accepted John C. Calhoun's states' rights contention that all slavery was local. Turning Calhoun's reasoning on its ear, however, the Rochester Democrats declared that annexation was an attempt by slaveholders to win national support for their peculiar institution. They refused to acquiesce in the scheme.

After agreeing unanimously to support Hale in the upcoming elections, the Rochester Democrats turned to the question of territorial expansion, usually poplar among both northern and southern Jacksonians. "We also oppose the addition of territory to the republic," the meeting resolved, since there were already "billions of unsettled acres," and Rochester's Democrats feared a drop in the value of the public lands if Texas were added to the Union.[47] This idea that additional territory—especially slave territory—was actually *bad* for the republic was also echoed in other Democratic meetings in the winter of 1845.[48]

One lesson Hale's supporters learned after Pierce's defenestration of their candidate was the need for a permanent, statewide organization. Since Hale insisted on waiting in Washington for the "people's verdict," New Hampshire's dissident Democrats were forced to act on their own. Aside from the remote northern and eastern Hale outposts in Coös and Carroll counties, the populous southeastern towns of Exeter and Portsmouth were hotbeds of dissident Democrats. Each town had its leading Hale partisan — John L. Hayes in Portsmouth and Amos Tuck in Exeter — who was willing to give up lifelong membership in the Jackson party for the antislavery cause. Hayes, the clerk of the federal court in Portsmouth, said he was tired of being told to "eat" his antislavery sentiments by leading Democrats, while Tuck had vowed as a state legislator in 1842 "never again to let [antislavery] convictions be overruled by party leaders." Ironically, Pierce had first informed Tuck that Hayes held similar views on slavery and Texas. The two subsequently met in the jury room of Exeter's Old Court House to plan New Hampshire's antislavery revolution.[49]

First, the duo issued a broadside, later signed by 263 Rockingham County Democrats, calling for Hale's supporters to meet in an Exeter church on February 22 "to make a full declaration of their sentiments, and take into consideration the present position of our party."[50] Several hundred dissident Democrats (mostly farmers, mechanics, and merchants) crowded into the church vestry to hear speeches by Hayes, Cram, and Joseph G. Hoyt, a professor of Greek and mathematics at Phillips Exeter Academy, as well as to pass a series of unusual resolutions. Some speakers praised Hale and decried his ouster. But others directly addressed the type of Democracy advocated by William Leggett in the 1830s — a combination of antislavery and radical egalitarianism. A broadside published after the meeting asserted that "we stand upon the broad platform of the Democratic party" and vowed to maintain the principles of Jefferson and Jackson. "A direct or indirect advocacy of slavery, or support for measures which will foster and encourage it, is wholly inconsistent with the Democratic doctrines of human equality and universal justice," the leaflet proclaimed.[51]

The assembled Jacksonians agreed to become "Independent Democrats" and dedicated themselves to maintaining all the principles of the Jackson party *except* its unwavering loyalty to the South and slavery. The new organization quickly received national attention. In the *New York Tribune*, Horace Greeley reported that meetings of "Loco Focos who are not prepared to be transformed into the mere instruments of slavery fanaticism" had been held across New Hampshire.[52] William Lloyd Garrison printed Hale's letter to his constituents in full, and in February a pro-Hale headquarters was opened in Boston. From John Greenleaf Whittier, antislavery's poet laureate, came a flattering ode comparing the Independent Democracy to New Hampshire's Revolutionary heroes:

God bless New Hampshire! From her granite peaks
Once more the voice of Stark and Langdon speaks.
The long-bound vassal of the exulting South
For very shame her self-forged chain has broken,
Torn the black seal of slavery from her mouth. . . .[53]

Abolitionists across New England watched with glee as the Independent Democrats threatened the future of Democratic hegemony in New Hampshire.

A New Hampshire Hale Storm

The congressional election of March 11, 1845, proved embarrassing for Pierce and the regular Democrats. Three of the four Democratic candidates won by large margins, but Hale, running as an independent, received enough votes to deny John Woodbury's majority (and election) by 827 votes.[54] As a result, ownership of the seat would be decided in a September runoff election between Woodbury, Hale, and Ichabod Goodwin, the top Whig candidate. Even though Hale finished third, the Independent Democrats had defied the odds, and for the first time since 1829, Democrats had no statewide sweep at the polls. A Carroll County stage driver proudly told Tuck the day after the election, "There had been a *terrible Hale* Storm" in New Hampshire.[55]

From whence did Hale's support come? By comparing how various Democrat, Whig, and Liberty candidates fared in the election, it is possible to trace approximately 90 percent of Hale's votes and piece together a snapshot of the embryonic New Hampshire Free Soil coalition. The Democrats who cast ballots for Hale are the easiest to trace, since the Independent Democratic and regular Democratic ballots were identical, except Hale's name was substituted for Woodbury's. Since Woodbury ran almost 2,200 votes behind the ticket's top vote getter (Mace Moulton), it is likely that approximately this number of Hale's votes (32 percent of his total) came from disgruntled Democrats. In other words, about 1 in 12 Democrats that day bolted the regular ticket to vote for Hale. Hale's Whig and Liberty supporters are slightly more difficult to trace. Since ballots were usually cast by straight ticket, for Whigs or Liberty Party members to vote for Hale, they had to cross another candidate's name off their ballots or use a special ballot already printed with Hale's name in place of another candidate's. Using this logic, it appears Hale received somewhere between 729 (10 percent) and 1,758 (25 percent) of his votes from Whigs.[56] The Liberty tallies tell a similar story. Congressional candidates Cilley and Perkins ran almost 1,000 votes behind gubernatorial candidate Daniel Hoit; most of these votes almost certainly ended up in Hale's column (14 percent of his total). The rest (approximately 22 percent) of Hale's total came from the large number of voters (1,536) who scattered their votes.[57]

The congressional race was clearly the big draw in the election: Hale's vote combined with the tally for each party's *weakest* candidate shows that about 2,000 more votes were cast than in the gubernatorial contest. While Hale received most of his votes in the spring elections from Democrats, his total was the result of a new type of political coalition — one that relied heavily on anti-Texas (and antislavery) voters from all parties.

Hale learned of the election results while in New York making arrangements for his political retirement. According to one associate, the news instantly "released him from his bonds" of inactivity. Hale now took over an active role as leader of the Independent Democracy from the dissidents who had launched it in his name.

With Hale determined to stump the entire state "in the Western fashion," Amos Tuck decided the time had come to publish an Independent political journal. The first issue of the *Independent Democrat* (based initially in Manchester) appeared May 1, 1845. Though edited by Robert C. Wetmore, whose brother had provided most of the money for the paper, most of the early editorials were written by Tuck and Professor Hoyt.[58]

The new paper's prospectus declared it would be "both Democratic and Independent, opposed to all dictation, monopoly and oppression." Its stance toward slavery fit squarely within the strict constructionist mode set forth by William Leggett, which set it apart from the Garrisonian antislavery journals. Wetmore promised to "look upon slavery as a moral, social and political evil, but yet such an one as our forefathers, in a spirit of compromise, consented to recognize in the formation of our Constitution." Slavery in the South, then, was (at least initially) to be left alone. The prospectus concluded by urging support and patronage for Hale, whom Wetmore described as a "Democrat of the Jeffersonian school" and the representative of "a great set of Radical and Republican principles."[59]

Hale did not wait to read the first issue of the *Independent Democrat* before hitting the campaign trail. In his first address since returning home (at the

Exeter Congregational Church on April 21), Hale went well beyond the issue of Texas annexation and came out wholeheartedly as a Jacksonian abolitionist.[60] Hale took Tuck's advice and avoided the political arguments against annexation in favor of "the moral aspects of the question" and delivered what one antislavery reporter described as a "thorough-going abolition speech, in spirit, doctrine and denunciation."[61] Yet Hale's antislavery was clearly different from that which filled the columns of the *Liberator* or the local *Herald of Freedom*. First, in contrast to Garrison's characterization of the Constitution as a "pact with the devil," Hale held up the document as sacred and claimed to accept as a given its compromises with slavery. Thus, while he called slavery a "political, social and moral evil of the highest turpitude, and a curse to our country," Hale reminded his listeners that "our fathers tolerated it for other great advantages to be derived from union."

Second, in contrast to abolitionists' rhetoric, Hale defined the controversy over slavery and its continuation as an issue between aristocratic slave owners and "sturdy republicans" rather than between innocent slaves and sinful masters. For example, Hale stated he was for giving "no more to the slave power of the South than the Constitution gives." To the delight of the predominantly "sturdy" audience, however, Hale ridiculed one of the central compromises of 1787, the Constitution's clause awarding slaves three-fifths representation in Congress: "The poor man, when he went to the polls in New Hampshire, could say to the rich man, my vote is worth as much as yours; but the poor man who did not own slaves could not say so to the rich man of the South. The rich planter would tell him, I have got five slaves, and your vote, saucy white man, counts but one-forth as much as mine!" But while Hale seemed at first to defend the compromises the founders made with slavery, he still argued passionately for its ultimate eradication. The fastest way to accomplish the end of the "*black spawn*" of slavery, he argued, was to refuse "that the eagle of America, when she stretches her wings over other lands, should carry in her talons, chains and whips and scorpions to scourge and oppress the down-trodden." After Hale concluded his speech, John L. Hayes took to the podium and called for a formal union of "good men and conscientious men, of all parties" to join the movement for a "purer Democratic party." In this new, "purer" party, it was still possible to oppose bank charters and aristocratic privilege, but heckling and baiting abolitionists while supporting the South would no longer be tolerated.[62]

Hale campaigned throughout the state during the spring of 1845, spreading the Jacksonian antislavery message to tiny outposts like Colebrook, Ossippee, and Bristol. Although Hale officially addressed only Independent Democrats during his campaign swing, the regular Democratic press was already spotting various "signs of coalition" between the Hale forces, Liberty men, and antislavery Whigs. John T. Gibbs, the editor of the formerly pro-Hale *Dover Gazette*, reported that many Whigs privately admitted that they hoped Hale would be a member of the next Congress. "Think of it Whigs! Think of it Liberty men! . . . Such remarks as these cannot but foreshadow an intention on the part of the Federal Whigs to make Mr. Hale the candidate for their party in the spring elections, and to invite the Liberty men into a coalition!"[63] Hale planned to crown his campaign swing with a large address and rally in the state capital. Not wishing to let Hale's charges go unanswered, Franklin Pierce agreed to debate his former friend in Concord's Old North Church. The result was one of the most celebrated debates in the state's history, as well as one with national implications. In the words of one Hale partisan, the debate made Hale senator and Pierce president.[64]

During the debate Pierce claimed Hale had entered an "unholy" alliance with abolitionists designed to make him a U.S. senator and destroy the party of Jackson. He also bristled at Hale's accusation that the New Hampshire party was subservient to the South, calling the annexation of Texas a "national necessity." Pierce's remarks were printed and distributed throughout the South, greatly enlarging his popularity there and clearing the way for his presidential candidacy in 1852.

Hale defended himself as a good Democrat, pointing to his congressional votes on issues such as the tariff and the distribution of the public lands to settlers. His only divergence from the rest of the state's delegation, he said, was his vote against Texas annexation — "for this and only this, I have been denounced as an Abolitionist, a Federalist, renegade and traitor to the ranks of the Democracy." For his conclusion, however, Hale the lawyer and legislator stepped aside in favor of Hale the churchgoer anxious about his salvation. Denigrating earthly ambition and anticipating the judgment of God and posterity, Hale said he hoped his children would read on his tombstone that "he who lies beneath surrendered *office, place and power*, rather than bow down and worship slavery."[65]

By almost every account Hale won the day. "The meeting has carried terror into the hearts of the clique, which no bragging or whistling can conceal," wrote George G. Fogg from the Gilmanton Iron Works. "I know of a number of men who went to that meeting strongly prejudiced against your course who are now open and zealous friends."[66] But more important than who won the debate in Concord was the event's immense national significance: two former allies, both staunch Jacksonians, had demonstrated beyond a doubt the existence of unbridgeable rifts within the northern Democracy. One, a future president, argued that party harmony necessitated the suppression of the slavery issue. The other, a future senator and presidential candidate, insisted that no party was worth saving if it demanded the debasement of free men's rights and consciences in defense of a moral iniquity. The battle lines of the sectional conflict, carved in New Hampshire granite, were on display in sharp relief.

After months of relentless campaigning to increasingly large audiences, Hale and the Independent Democrats again prevented Woodbury from attaining a majority in the September runoff.[67] Two months later, in yet another runoff, Hale still ran third; but this time Woodbury was even further short of a majority than he had been in March. By the reasoning of the *Independent Democrat*, this meant that the "slavery candidate" was defeated by a "glorious majority of more than *Two Thousand*."[68]

The most significant shift in the voting between the first two elections and the November runoff was Hale's steep decline in strong Whig towns and his simultaneous gain in traditionally Democratic towns like Gilmanton, Ossippee, Hopkinton, Epsom, Northumberland, Deerfield, Candia, and Pittsfield. These towns in the southeast uplands were a perennial linchpin in the state's Democratic electoral majority. It was this increase among Jacksonian votes for Hale that the *Independent Democrat* valued most: "Next to the defeat of the Slavery Clique, this is what gives us the most pleasure — and carries the voice of doom beyond any contingency into the camp of the enemies of Liberty and True Democracy."[69] These voting shifts over the course of 1845 illustrated the increasing "Democratization" of the New Hampshire antislavery coalition. Whigs, sensing potential weakness in Pierce's party, generally stuck with their own candidates and hoped for a future coalition that would give them partial control of the state government. Dissident Democrats, however, lined up behind Hale in larger and larger numbers.

At base, then, the Independent Democratic Party was an unmistakably democratic political organization. It owed little to Whiggish appeals and even less to abolitionist camp meetings. Instead, the party operated at the grassroots level, with supporters signing petitions, passing resolutions, writing letters, debating editorials, and holding endless meetings in taverns, courthouses, churches, and homes. As a candidate, Hale crisscrossed the state, taking the message directly to the people; Pierce and Woodbury, by contrast, spoke mostly through the party press. New Hampshire voters have always been — and continue to be — fond of "retail" politics, and the Independent Democrats took popular democracy back to the winning ways of the early 1830s. This energized a core of support and helped immeasurably on election day.[70]

The Voters of "Righteous Ossippee"

What did these Democratic "Hale storm" towns have in common? Except for Northumberland (in northern Coös County), they were clustered in the eastern part of the state, north of the southern tier of counties, in areas known as the southeast uplands and the lake district.[71] Each town had given Andrew Jackson more than two-thirds of its votes in 1832, and several had supported Hale in 1843 when he voted to end the gag rule.[72] The towns were predominantly agricultural; the exceptions were Gilmanton (which had an ironworks) and Pittsfield (which had some cotton mills).

Among these communities, Hale ran strongest in Ossippee in Carroll County, about eight miles east of Lake Winnipesaukee near the Maine border. Ossippee provides a glimpse into the socioeconomic and religious base of the Independent Democracy. The town reached its peak population during the 1840s; in common with many northern New England towns, it would lose citizens in droves after the Civil War.[73] An 1830 inventory noted an economy based on "small subsistence farming and grazing" and an almost total absence of industrial production. The 1850 U.S. Census backs this up. It reported that 360 family heads owned farms and only 30 percent of the town's acreage had been cleared. The industries mentioned included tanning, lumber production, furniture making, and small-scale spinning. Ossippee in the 1840s, then, was a remote farming community barely touched by the Market Revolution.[74]

It was in the realm of religious belief that the farmers of Ossippee differed most remarkably from their counterparts in the Connecticut River Valley, which from the days of the Great Awakening had been the epicenter of evangelical Protestant revivals. The community was a bastion of Freewill Baptism, a resolutely Arminian sect that originated in New Hampshire and took hold mostly among remote rural farmers.[75] The sect was founded in 1780 by the Reverend Benjamin Randall, a New Castle sailmaker's apprentice who joined the Congregational church after hearing George Whitefield preach in nearby Portsmouth. After making a reputation as an open-air preacher, Randall left his church to join a Calvinistic Baptist congregation in Berwick, Maine, where he provoked conflict for refusing to preach the doctrine of predestination. Having decided his theology did not match any existing denomination, he moved with seven followers to New Durham, New Hampshire, to found the first Freewill Baptist religious community.[76]

The sect grew quickly. Randall organized numerous Freewill Baptist revivals along the Maine–New Hampshire border, including several in Ossippee, where his father lived. One revival in Ossippee in 1806 was remembered as the largest ever assembled in that part of the state.[77] By 1810 there were 98 Freewill Baptist congregations in New Hampshire and Maine and 2 more in Vermont; by 1830 the number had grown to 466 churches with 21,499 members spread across New England, New York, Ohio, and western Pennsylvania.[78]

Freewill Baptism is significant in the history of New Hampshire and of Jacksonian antislavery for two reasons: its radical and organized abolitionism and its members' overwhelming propensity to vote for Democrats.[79] As Donald B. Cole has shown, Whigs tended to do well in New Hampshire communities that were prosperous and accessible to markets and in which orthodox Congregationalism predominated. Conversely, Jacksonians routinely carried areas that were more rural and less prosperous and had fewer Congregational churches.[80] Cole's model ideally fits eastern New Hampshire in general and Ossippee in particular. The town was overwhelmingly rural and isolated from markets, and only two of the town's fourteen churches were Congregational. Nine of them, however, were Freewill Baptist.[81]

From its earliest days the sect's followers identified with the party of Jefferson and Jackson; in fact, one contemporary writer asserted that "there has been no sect whose churchity has been more consistent with the Democratic party."[82] Another reasoned that "they have generally arranged themselves politically with those who have seemed most to favor equal rights . . . [because] the communicants of this church have been confined mostly to the poorer classes, and were subject to various privations and wrongs imposed on them by older and more wealthy denominations." Freewill Baptists were also the first New Hampshire sect to embrace abolitionism, as well as the most ardent in doing so. The first churchwide resolution in favor of immediate emancipation was passed in 1834; at the next yearly meeting more than 3,000 members unanimously passed another stating that abolition was "consistent with the word of God."[83]

Not surprisingly, the sect's adoption of a radical brand of abolitionism quickly soured relations with the Jacksonian leaders Freewill Baptists had long supported. Congregations and their clergy "incurred the hate and displeasure of men who . . . took it upon themselves to harness Democracy and Slavery in the same team forever." When the sect requested an act of incorporation for its newspaper, the *Morning Star*, in 1835, the Democratic legislature rejected it by a vote of 184-34, fearing the press would "flood" the state with "incendiary" material.[84]

While abolitionists like Garrison and Theodore Weld were quick to praise the church for its brave opposition to slavery, Freewill Baptist abolitionism was a far cry from the evangelical type found in the pages of the *Liberator*.[85] Freewill antislavery was centered more on political equality and anxious about the effects slavery and slave labor might have on Christian producers. In fact, Freewill Baptists viewed the entire Market Revolution as an anti-egalitarian abomination — from the cotton boom that intensified southern slavery to the "sepulchral" factories that exploited (and entombed) New England workers. One series of articles in the *Morning Star* urged members to boycott all products of slave labor, including tobacco, sugar, and especially cotton. This radical, Jacksonian abolitionism called the entire emerging capitalist system into question. In 1841 one contributor surveyed the balance sheet of gains and losses for New Englanders in the transformation from household to factory production and found it wanting. Instead of "cultivating our own soil, rearing herds of flocks, [and] operating household looms . . . *rich* capitalists have become richer. . . . *We* may safely calculate these losses to be large."[86] The human cost of cotton production and use, calculated by adding the suffering of plantation slaves to that endured by northern mill workers, was simply too much to bear.

John P. Hale was deeply affected by the egalitarian abolitionism of the Freewill Baptists. He often attended sermons at the church in Dover; it appears that he occasionally found them more spiritually sustaining than the fare at his Unitarian church. With the aid of the Freewill Baptists of Ossippee, Hale's November 1845 total there increased to 213 of 303 votes cast (70 percent), up nearly 50 percent from the previous election. These were the people who gravitated to New Hampshire's Independent Democracy in 1845.[87]

Shifting Coalitions

After the November runoff, every politician in the state understood that a union of anti-Woodbury forces from several parties would be enough to defeat the Democrats in 1846. This antislavery coalition began to take shape during the winter of 1845–46 with the primary goal of winning control of the legislature, and with it the right to select New Hampshire's next senator and, perhaps, governor.[88] To this end, Independent Democrats and Whigs secretly placed one member of the other party on their tickets in Concord, and they repeated the practice in other towns as well.[89] Independent Democrats and Liberty Party supporters worked even more closely, holding simultaneous conventions in January. Both conventions nominated popular abolitionist Nathaniel S. Berry for governor.[90]

The March 1846 election gave the new coalition a tremendous victory. For the first time since 1828, the Democrats failed to elect a governor or control either house of the legislature, which would elevate candidates to the vacant seats. Woodbury again failed to secure a majority (leaving Hale's old seat vacant), and the Democratic gubernatorial candidate was 1,564 votes short of election.[91] Most striking, however, were the results of the legislative races. A total of six of twelve state senate seats went unfilled, and the seats won by Independent Democrats, Liberty men, and Whigs in the lower house gave them a slim majority of fourteen. John P. Hale was elected to the New Hampshire house of representatives from Dover.[92]

John Greenleaf Whittier called the election results "glorious" and penned yet another poem in New Hampshire's honor. This one took the form of an apocryphal letter from Pierce to Democratic congressman Moses Norris Jr.:

> 'Tis over, Moses! All is lost!
>   I hear the bells-a-ringing;
> Of Pharaoh and his Red Sea host
>   I hear the Free-Wills singing.
> We're routed, Moses, horse and foot,
>   If there be truth in figures,
> With Federal Whigs in hot pursuit,
>   And Hale, and all the "niggers."
>
> . . . I dreamed that Charley [Atherton] took his bed
>   With Hale for his physician;
> His daily dose an old "unread
>   And unreferred" petition.
> There Hayes and Tuck as muses sat,
>   As near as near could be, man;
> They leeched him with the "Democrat;"
>   They blistered with the "Freeman."

The ides of June! Woe worth the day
   When, turning all things over,
The traitor Hale shall make his hay
   From Democratic clover!
Let Hale exult, and Wilson scoff,
   To see us southward scamper;
The slaves, we know, are "better off
   Than laborers in New Hampshire!"[93]

The Independent Democrats, Liberty Party adherents, and Whigs soon divided the spoils of office. They sent Whig Anthony Colby to the governor's mansion and elected Hale Speaker of the New Hampshire house. But Hale's demotion to politics at the state level was temporary. One week later, the same coalition united to send him to the U.S. Senate for a six-year term. The Independent Democracy had its first leader on the national stage.[94]

Hale used his brief stint as Speaker to reverse the previous house's course and make the New Hampshire legislature a laboratory for antislavery political action. First, Hale proposed a joint resolution to denounce the war with Mexico and Texas annexation. The resolution also pledged the state's cooperation in "every just and well-directed effort for the suppression and extermination of that terrible scourge of our race, human slavery."[95] House Democrats bitterly opposed the new resolution, and Hale stepped down from the Speaker's chair to deliver a two-hour harangue against the war, calling it "*unparalleled in infamy in modern history.*" It was a convincing speech; both houses passed Hale's resolution in July.

To the dismay of the regular Democrats, the legislature passed another joint resolution asking the state's congressmen to work for the exclusion of slavery from territories, an end to the domestic slave trade, and abolition in the District of Columbia. The allies also passed a personal liberty law making it illegal for private citizens to aid in the capture of fugitive slaves. Whig governor Colby pleased the allies by reversing his former antiabolitionist stance and signed each of the legislature's measures into law. The South Carolina of the North had abruptly changed its tune on slavery.[96]

The 1846 summer session of the New Hampshire legislature marked the high point for the new Independent Democrat–Whig–Liberty coalition. Two areas of weakness plagued the allies. First, major differences on economic policy between the Whigs and former Democrats constantly threatened to disrupt the alliance. (Independent Democrats and Liberty men, on the other hand, had been working together since the previous year, and since most post-1844 Liberty converts were former Democrats, there were fewer points of departure on economic issues.) While Whigs were content to cooperate in the legislature and during elections, they were not yet ready to dissolve their organization to form a permanent alliance.[97]

The second major weakness was the threat from without: the Democrats, temporarily stunned by their failure, began regrouping after the summer of 1846. First, the state party went on record in support of David Wilmot's popular proviso, introduced in August 1846.[98] This pragmatic move stole much of the allies' thunder, but the Independent Democrats and the Liberty Party were already planning a more permanent antislavery union.

Beginning in June 1846, the Liberty *Granite Freeman* abandoned its formerly tepid support for Hale and extolled the senator-elect as the "embodiment . . . of the principles of Liberty." Hale in turn spoke at Liberty meetings throughout the summer. In September, to crown this new spirit of cooperation, Independent Democrats and Liberty men met in joint convention in New Market and formed a single political organization. With Whittier and Henry B. Stanton on hand as observers, Amos Tuck (the allies' new nominee for Congress) called for an expanded national movement on the Independent Democrat–Liberty model.[99] In spite of the loss of electoral momentum since 1846, however, the antislavery opposition could claim two members of Congress and U.S. Senator John P. Hale.

Senator Hale

Senator Hale arrived in Washington on December 4, 1847, giving the upper house an antislavery spokesman for the first time since Thomas Morris's ouster in 1839. The two senators had much in common: belief in strict construction of the U.S. Constitution, fear of an unchecked Slave Power, deep religious convictions, and a strong adherence to the tenets of Jacksonian Democracy. But there was one major difference: Morris converted to antislavery after his election to the Senate. For this, he was read out of the Democratic Party.[100] Hale, on the other hand, was elected *because* of his antislavery views, by a coalition of dissident Democrats, Liberty men, and Whigs. This election-by-coalition had another consequence as well. Unlike most of his Senate colleagues, who had to mollify voters on a multitude of thorny issues such as internal improvements, the tariff, and the Independent Treasury, Hale represented a constituency with one common denominator: opposition to slavery. Thus, Hale was a man without a party. He could devote all of his time to fighting the Slave Power and speak his mind freely without fear of reprisal from party leaders or angry whips.[101]

Concurrent with Hale's arrival in Washington was the campaign (masterminded by Salmon P. Chase) to combine the North's disparate antislavery groups into one political organization. Hale, already the reluctant presidential nominee of the national Liberty Party for 1848, would figure grandly in Chase's scheme. So would many of the other contributors in New Hampshire's antislavery revolution of 1845–46, including Tuck, Hayes, and Fogg, all of whom had known Chase from their Dartmouth College days in the 1820s. These Independent Democrats, the first to organize a statewide antislavery coalition, were instrumental in giving birth to the national Free Soil coalition.[102]

Forty years later, pioneer Independent Democrat Amos Tuck (then a retired businessman) was invited to address a reunion of the "Free Soilers of '48" in Boston. Given the gathering's locale, Tuck found himself the only former Jacksonian amid a hall full of self-congratulatory former Conscience Whigs. With this in mind, Tuck used his address to suggest to the old Whigs (each of whom, including Tuck, was a stalwart Republican) that the wholesale political realignment that produced both the Republican Party and the Civil War began in New Hampshire, not in Massachusetts. To "prove" this contention, Tuck produced a yellowed copy of the call he and Hayes printed for the inaugural meeting of the Independent Democracy in February 1845 and read off the resolutions—principled statements that bore an uncanny resemblance to the 1856 and 1860 Republican platforms. "While we cannot claim much in our little state," Tuck said, "we are very jealous of what we can claim," he told the crowd. Continuing this argument, he insisted that the origins of their common Republican Party were more Jacksonian than Whig: "We insisted on organizing as Democrats," he said, "[and] refused to leave the Democratic party on account of our declaration of sentiments. And we refused to leave to this day, until we have got a majority of the Democrats of New Hampshire to the Republican side."[103]

Still later in Tuck's long life, he recalled his good fortune "to be at the fountain of a movement which soon agitated the whole country, controlled parties, created the Republican party and finally saved the government" from slavery and aristocracy. But even half a century after the Hale storm, Tuck continued to resent abolitionists for taking the credit for emancipation. "Garrison and his followers had preached antislavery for years," he wrote, but failed to inspire "men professing love for church or state [to] rise spontaneously and unanimously to purify both from the sin of slavery." The institution's demise, he argued, was instead accomplished by "taking hold as active men, fighting at the polls, giving blow for blow, and at length electing antislavery men to office." In other words, Tuck believed a politically oriented, masculine antislavery — with clear Jacksonian antecedents — fulfilled the mission that the evangelical abolitionist movement, with its feminine tactics of moral suasion, could not. "It never seemed to me," he added, that abolitionists like Garrison and Phillips "were anything but a hindrance, most of them impracticable, malignant scolds, incapable of concerted action and a stumbling block to others."[104]

Whether or not Tuck's old-age reminiscences are fair to the heroes of abolitionism, he gets one thing right: the roots of Free Soil in New Hampshire, like other states in the Northeast, were deeply Jacksonian and antievangelical. They were also strongest in communities that missed out on the rising tides of the Market Revolution. These origins yielded an ideology that placed greater value on political activity (waged mostly by men) than religious agitation and protest (waged mostly by women). As John Hale's odyssey proves, however, it was not an irreligious one.

CHAPTER FOUR

Marcus Morton and the
Dilemma of Jacksonian Antislavery
in Massachusetts

Massachusetts justly earned a reputation as the historical center of the movement to end slavery in the United States. Bay State abolitionists such as William Lloyd Garrison, David Walker, and Theodore Parker demanded immediate emancipation for slaves and, oftentimes, equal rights for blacks. They kept the issue of slavery squarely before a skeptical American voting public in the decades before the Civil War and never wavered in their attack on the South's (and, it could be argued, the nation's) central institution. Nonetheless, at the movement's height abolitionists accounted for only the tiniest minority of voters, even among the middle-class evangelicals who provided the lion's share of their financial and numerical support. The overwhelming majority of antislavery partisans — those Americans who eventually stood up to slavery and its extension — never belonged to any antislavery organization.

In other words, it took far more than professed agitators to overthrow slavery in the United States. Hundreds of thousands of Americans of many stripes — black and white, rich and poor, Whig and Democrat — came to oppose slavery and its expansion in the second quarter of the nineteenth century. They reached this position for a variety of reasons. Exemplifying this complexity was the career of one Massachusetts antislavery politician, jurist and two-time Democratic governor Marcus Morton. The story of how Morton defended his antislavery position — as well as the often tortuous path he followed into the Free Soil and Republican parties — encapsulates the social and political transformation of northern politics and public opinion on the greatest issue of the day. Far removed from the righteous abolitionists of Cambridge's Brattle Street, Morton's career in rough-and-tumble Democratic politics brings to life a vital moment in antebellum U.S. history—a moment when layers of loyalties, patronage ties, and political coalitions dissolved in the face of slavery's continued expansion.

In a decades-long political career during which he occupied both federal and state offices, Morton navigated a rocky course among the demands of the national Democratic Party, his constituents in Massachusetts, and his own conscience. Each fall between 1828 and 1843, Morton moonlighted as the Jacksonian candidate for governor, making his yearly appearance on the ballot—and his frequent defeat at the polls—as predictable "as the fall of the sear and yellow leaf." Except for two nonsequential terms in 1840 and 1843, Morton lost each race, first to a succession of National Republicans and then to Whigs, members of the dominant parties in Massachusetts politics. He was the William Jennings Bryan of the Bay State.[1]

During these years, including the two in which he held the governorship, Morton downplayed but did not deny his strong opposition to slavery in order to prioritize Democratic Party issues such as expanded suffrage and the secret ballot, relief for debtors, repeal of an unpopular temperance law, and an end to state credit to private corporations. Like most antebellum Democrats, including many discussed in this study, Morton believed that organized abolitionism distracted public attention from more important problems facing the United States; in particular, he shared with other radical Jacksonians the conviction that the influence of a "monied Aristocracy" posed a far more serious threat to the republic.[2]

Nonetheless, Morton's aversion to slavery—a feeling common among New Englanders—underpinned his political career, functioning sometimes as a boon and surfacing at other times as a liability.[3] Morton's political successes in Massachusetts depended to a significant degree on his antislavery reputation. He won the governorship twice in part by siphoning off the votes of antislavery Workingmen, Antimasons, Whigs, and even Liberty Party supporters in the 1830s and 1840s. In 1845, as Morton awaited confirmation in the U.S. Senate to the federally appointed post of collector of the port of Boston, that reputation became an Achilles' heel. Southern members of his own party, determined to excise any hint of dissent on the topic of slavery, attempted to derail his political viability with public accusations.[4] If Morton's enemies had charged him with corruption or theft, Morton could easily have proven his innocence. But the charge leveled against Morton was abolitionism.[5] Morton responded by retreating from his outspoken criticisms of slavery and distancing himself from organized abolitionism, thus demonstrating how little room existed in the Massachusetts (or, for that matter, the northern) Democracy for an outspoken antislavery politician.

Morton possessed the unusual ability to maintain a public career spanning several decades on the differences—subtle as they may appear—between antislavery and organized abolitionism. In fact, the story of Morton's Jacksonian antislavery and his leading role in Massachusetts's Free Soil schism in 1848 is instructive about trends within the Democracy, the antislavery movement, and northern politics at critical junctures in the antebellum era. First, it shows how political antislavery in Massachusetts initially (and curiously) bore a Democratic stamp, as Morton won votes from slavery-averse Bay Staters of various stripes. Second, it illustrates the struggles among Democrats trying to remain viable as a party in "Whig" New England as the national politics of slavery expansion forced candidates and appointees to extemporize, adapt, and, finally, evolve into distinctively northern Democratic (and, later, Free Soil and Republican) wings. Finally, Morton's tortured self-defense in the face of the charge of abolitionism, echoed by his supporters and numerous other Free Soil Democrats, provides an object lesson in the realities—as well as the dilemmas—of Jacksonian antislavery.

The Making of a Jurist

Marcus Morton was born in Freetown in Bristol County in 1784. His mother, Mary Cary, descended from the pious early settlers of Bridgewater; his father's ancestors arrived in Plymouth Colony in the 1620s. Morton's father, Nathaniel, a self-taught "farmer of narrow means," provided for his family with only economy and "unremitting toil."[6] Like other yeomen in the Taunton River Valley, the Mortons watched their agricultural yields and status decline precipitously during the last years of the eighteenth century in sharp contrast to the bustling markets and maritime might of Boston, Salem, and New Bedford. According to one historian of the area, poor soil quality and weak domestic and overseas markets made life difficult for farmers in Plymouth and Bristol counties, where sentiment ran strongly toward Daniel Shays's rebels in the 1780s. The region's settlers mostly tilled the "thinly populated waste of pine forest and cedar swamp," raising timber, wool, and corn.[7]

Despite his homespun rural background, Nathaniel served in both the General Court and the commonwealth's Executive Council, while Mary, who had a "good education for those days," was a mainstay at the town's Congregational church. Marcus, the couple's only son, recalled being reared in the "orthodox Congregational faith" and educated at the local common school while his sister became a missionary. When Marcus turned fourteen, his parents sent him to Rochester, New York, to split his time between the lesson room and the Reverend Calvin Chaddock's farm. In 1801, with Chaddock's recommendation, Morton gained admission to Brown College.[8]

While at Brown, Morton became an ardent follower of Thomas Jefferson. Morton publicly displayed his Jeffersonian beliefs during a commencement oration in 1804, embarrassing his teachers and classmates by condemning their "collective extravagance" and arguing that wasteful expenditure of public moneys inevitably created privilege and inequality within the body politic.[9] Morton's decision to attend Brown was in itself a political act — Massachusetts students who passed over Harvard and its conservative Unitarianism for Brown's heterodoxy and tolerance tended later to become opponents of traditional Massachusetts Federalism, National Republicanism, and Whiggery.[10]

After college, Morton attended Tapping Reeve's famous law school in Litchfield, Connecticut. There he became acquainted with the school's most outspoken student, John C. Calhoun. Morton was in awe of his southern classmate's "brilliancy of intellect," and the two built a close personal and political friendship based on their shared political antipathy to central authority. They corresponded regularly after law school, and the independent-minded South Carolinian served as a political mentor to Morton and many other Massachusetts Democrats.[11]

After graduation Morton returned to his hometown of Taunton to practice law. Although it was the fourth-oldest settlement in Plymouth Colony, Taunton was far less affluent than its Bay State neighbors. In Taunton, Morton further honed his antiestablishment politics, especially in his frequent clashes with Bristol County's Federalist town fathers (he was an outspoken supporter of Jefferson's embargo). Nonetheless, he maintained good relations with all his peers. What one historian called his "fineness of temper" provoked goodwill even among his political opponents.[12]

The county's Democratic-Republicans nominated Morton for the U.S. Congress in 1814, but he lost his bid for office; pro-war supporters of President James Madison won few popularity contests (or elections) in Federalist New England. Two years later, however, he did win, surprising political experts who thought he could not carry a rural and longtime Federalist district. He arrived in Washington in 1817 to begin two terms in Congress, a time he later described to a friend as "the lamest part of my life." He offered his support to Andrew Jackson, then under attack for conduct during the Seminole War. In his first direct engagement with antislavery politics, he took an active role in opposition to the admission of Missouri as a slave state during the Missouri Crisis of 1819–20. Morton voted to prohibit slavery outright in Missouri and then to free all slaves there at age twenty-five. He later voted to keep the 36°30′ provision, which stipulated the line north of which slavery was prohibited in the compromise, in the measure after various southerners had proposed to strike it. He maintained his position during the second session, voting against Missouri's admission with the 36°30′ stipulation and slavery. Years later, Morton expressed regret that but for the "extraordinary influence and extraordinary efforts" of Henry Clay, "who was supposed by some to have resorted to extraordinary means to accomplish his purpose," the antislavery side might have prevailed in the Missouri Crisis.[13]

Morton also recalled another experience that at this time shaped his attitudes about slavery: he saw "two droves of human beings manacled and chained together, driven like cattle by a drover, under the walls of the Capitol, in which were assembled the representatives of the people proud and boastful of their liberty." This spectacle, he later admitted, convinced him Congress had the right—even the obligation—to abolish slavery in the territories and the capital city: "I can entertain no doubt . . . that the congress has the control of the whole subject within the District of Columbia."[14] He saw a clear distinction, however, between Congress's jurisdiction over slavery in the District of Columbia and its lack of jurisdiction in southern states. Despite his strong and public antislavery feeling, Morton insisted that only slaveholders themselves could put an end to slavery. Although this ability to parse so delicate an issue may strike modern readers as a contradiction, it was one maintained by scores of antebellum politicians. In 1822, after returning to his law practice in Taunton, Morton put this belief into action. When Massachusetts officials imprisoned a Virginia slave owner named Camillus Griffith on criminal charges for attempting to reclaim a runaway slave, Morton successfully defended the planter in court. More than two decades later, as Morton attempted to deflect charges of abolitionism, he invoked the Griffith case: "When no member of the bar would appear for him, I came forward and, at the risk of reputation and business, bailed him out of jail, defended him before the court, and successfully vindicated the law against prejudice and violence."[15]

Morton entered state politics in 1824 when he received the nomination for lieutenant governor under William Eustis, with whom he had served in Congress and who had been a member of Jefferson's cabinet. He became governor when Eustis died later that year, but with the supposedly nonpartisan National Republican Party drifting toward a political alliance with

John Quincy Adams and many other Old Federalists (men Morton called "aristocrats"), Morton refused to stand again in 1825. His successor, Levi Lincoln Jr. — the last governor able to unite Old Republicans and Old Federalists — appointed Morton to the state supreme court later that year. Although he was the lone Jeffersonian on the bench, Morton wrote several significant opinions, including *Charles River Bridge v. Warren Bridge* (in which the court invalidated the Charles River Bridge Company's monopoly charter); a few involving disestablishment of the Congregational Church; and *Commonwealth v. Kneeland*, a successful blasphemy suit. For the latter, Morton wrote a dissent that won praise in legal circles.[16]

Safely ensconced on the state bench, Morton turned his attention to forging a political coalition to oppose what he called the Aristocratic Faction, the powerful combination of ex-Federalists, conservative National Republicans, financiers, and manufacturers that ran the state from Boston. The supremacy of this financial and political elite, which firmly controlled the state house, the bench, and from 1825 to 1829, the White House, further radicalized the diehard Jeffersonian. Morton subscribed wholeheartedly to what James L. Huston has termed the "political economy of aristocracy": the belief that inequalities of wealth resulted from exploitative "aristocrats" using government to transfer the fruits of others' labor to themselves.[17] Morton saw the Second Bank of the United States and the exclusive clique of interrelated Lees, Otises, Higginsons, Cabots, and Perkinses that controlled business and politics, especially in Boston, as the embodiment of the new aristocracy. "We always have had a powerful monied Aristocracy," Morton wrote to his friend John C. Calhoun, "which by the influence of wealth has attached to itself a great force of talents and no inconsiderable share of moral worth. Wealth is here more regarded and draws to its possessor more consideration and respect than in any other free Country. This is the weakness or fault of N[ew] England character."[18] Like many other "hard money" Jeffersonian and Jacksonian Democrats in the 1820s and 1830s, Morton viewed the growing Money Power as the most serious threat facing the republic — far more serious than slavery or slaveholders.

Morton, perhaps naively, believed that enough votes and energy existed across Massachusetts to drive the National Republican (soon to be Whig) majority from power. He saw potential in the existing — though fragmented — opposition, which drew most of its support from groups that had long opposed Federalism. They included farmers from southern counties like Morton's Bristol and neighboring Plymouth, Barnstable, and Norfolk;

fishermen from Nantucket, Martha's Vineyard, and Cape Cod; descendants of the Shays rebels in the western parts of the state; and mechanics, ship caulkers, and day laborers in the growing seaport cities. Other disgruntled Massachusetts men, including banker David Henshaw, who began his career as a modest druggist and felt continually snubbed by Boston's Unitarian financiers and manufacturers, joined these groups in opposition to the governing elite.[19] Morton applauded when Henshaw established the anti-Adams (and antiaristocratic) newspaper *Statesman* in 1821 and quickly became the acknowledged leader of the state's nascent Democratic Party. In 1827 both Henshaw and Morton sought an alliance with the managers of Andrew Jackson's ongoing presidential campaign against Adams.[20] Immediately after a pro-Jackson rally on January 8, 1828, the leaders of the state's opposition movement initiated a gubernatorial campaign for Morton and published a list of "Republican Jackson" candidates for the state senate.[21] Morton won majorities in only eighteen towns, most of which were in the southern and western parts of the state, but the Democratic Party in Massachusetts had begun to coalesce.[22]

South Carolina slaveholder John C. Calhoun, seeking reelection as vice president in 1828, helped draw together the various opposition groups in Massachusetts. Morton, who remained close to Calhoun after their days together at law school, became his chief source of Bay State political information.[23] Between 1828 and 1831 he also lent his support to Calhoun's presidential ambitions. Morton believed that Calhoun, an outspoken champion of "Southern rights," had the best chance at uniting New England's rural Jeffersonians, urban artisans, anti-Adams commercial interests, and the handful of ex-Federalists who had supported Andrew Jackson in 1828. He also viewed the South Carolinian as a potential moderating influence on the Tennessee parvenu occupying the White House, whom most New England Democrats considered "rash and violent."[24]

Morton was especially drawn to Calhoun's ideas about states' rights and the protection of minorities.[25] "My opinion is the danger most to be feared is encroachment by the powerful upon the weak, and by the rich upon the poor — and not the reverse," he wrote to Calhoun in February 1834. "The greatest vigilance is needed to protect the common people of the community, the industrious, quiet, producing classes of Society against the overbearing influence of the rich and the powerful. . . . As one means of accomplishing this object, care should also be taken to protect individual States from the combined power of the whole."[26] By the "industrious, quiet, producing classes," Morton meant the type of people that voted for him each year—farmers, ship caulkers, and New Bedford factory workers—a group that clearly did not include enslaved African Americans. In fact, before 1831 Morton dismissed Calhoun's well-known proslavery pronouncements as essentially inconsequential. For example, when he advised Calhoun that his views on slavery damaged his support in New England, Morton added that such opposition could be overcome. "There are two subjects permanent and unavoidable operating against you," Morton confided. "These are the Slavery subject and the Tariff subject. Altho' the efforts [of] the Federalists have been untiring to excite a prejudice against Slave holders; yet that prejudice is principally confined to that party. . . . The spirit of democracy with the aid of party discipline and the patronage of the National Administration will ride over both of these."[27] Calhoun, of course, did not become the Democratic presidential candidate in 1832. Andrew Jackson ran for a second term and won in a landslide, while breaking once and for all with his mercurial vice president over nullification and other issues.[28] The public break with Jackson marked the end of Calhoun's career in the executive branch.[29]

Although Morton privately claimed he supported Calhoun in the dispute with President Jackson, he dramatically broke off political relations with him in March 1831.[30] What caused the rift? Surely a portion can be explained by political expedience on Morton's part: the Massachusetts Democracy depended on federal patronage more than on Calhoun's political skills. More importantly, to Morton, Calhoun's recent actions supporting the South Carolina nullifiers and praising slavery revealed that he had "depart[ed] . . . from original [Democratic] principles": "If I am not always found on the side of the weak against the strong, whether in reference to Governments, corporations, or people, it will be cause I err in finding which side that is. I cannot but fear that you and I might differ in the application of the above principles more than the principles themselves."[31]

On nearly every issue before the public, from internal improvements, to banks, to the need for constitutional protection for minorities "from the combined power of the whole," little disagreement existed between Morton and Calhoun. Morton had expressed support for Calhoun's opposition to high tariffs and even his devotion to South Carolina's economic interests; he also seconded Calhoun's views on states' rights and internal improvements.[32] He stood apart from Calhoun, however, on one vital, deal-breaking difference in "principle": the tenet that a state, acting on its own, could declare null and void any federal law it declared unconstitutional.[33] Morton concluded that the protection of *slavery*, not states' rights, lay at the heart of

Calhoun's doctrines. He also determined that slavery supported a political and economic class that bore more than striking resemblance to the monied aristocracy he battled in Boston.

As far back as 1828 Morton had chided Calhoun for an earlier dalliance with New England's monied class; by 1831 he saw Calhoun's political moves as nothing less than the justification of an aristocracy of slaveholders. He coolly predicted that either Calhoun or Clay would represent the "aristocratic" party in the next presidential election.[34] Morton's break with Calhoun split the Massachusetts Democratic Party. One faction, loyal to Collector Henshaw, continued to support the South Carolinian; Morton's group backed Jackson's new lieutenant, Martin Van Buren.

Slavery and Massachusetts Politics

By the mid-1830s the second party system had solidified in Massachusetts. Both Democrats and Whigs boasted complete rosters of professional politicians, newspapers, and patronage pecking orders. Although they disagreed on many issues, they came together — squarely — on one: that slavery should be kept outside state and national politics. For large majorities in both parties, the issue sapped strength that was needed for other battles, such as the tariff question or abolition of imprisonment for debt.

The sliver of antislavery voting that existed in the parties gravitated toward Marcus Morton, whose position on the matter was strikingly different from those of his Whig opponents — especially that of Representative Edward Everett. In March 1826 the former minister and Harvard professor had taken to the floor of Congress to defend the slave system. "Domestic slavery is not, in my judgment, to be set down as an immoral and irreligious institution," he told the House in his second speech as a U.S. congressman. "I would cede the whole continent to any one who would take it — to England, to France, to Spain — I would see it sunk in the bottom of the ocean, before I would see any part of this fair America converted into a continental Hayti."[35]

While the three-hour oration won Everett friends among the state's conservative textile barons, many voters hostile to slavery supported Morton, despite the national Democratic Party's dismal record on slavery and race relations. Other parts of Everett's 1826 speech were soon forgotten, but this portion was cited well beyond the Whig orator's dying day. One Everett supporter correctly predicted that his position on slavery "will make him infinitely odious to many people who wished him well," while Ralph Waldo

Emerson noted of his former idol that "in case of a servile war, he would buckle on his knapsack to defend the planter."[36]

Moderate antislavery voters fortified Morton's growing electoral coalition in the mid-1830s.[37] In 1835, for example, Morton answered a formal query from abolitionist minister Gardiner B. Perry on the topic of slavery, a request that Everett refused. Although Morton's answers fell far short of the abolitionist position, his reply clearly demonstrated his opposition to the institution: "I have a deep and strong conviction of the unrighteousness of holding our fellow men in servitude," he wrote, "and of the magnitude of the curse of slavery to our country." But he feared the question of how to rid the nation of slavery raised "appalling if not insurpassable difficulties": "Can we interfere with the conduct of the slave holder towards their slaves? The power of holding slaves is guaranteed to a portion of the union by the sacred instrument which we are all bound to support. And we have great reason to fear that any interference with what the slave holders deem to be their domestic rights and their legal property will in any degree, tend to ameliorate the condition of the slaves to facilitate their eventual emancipation." In addition, Morton worried that further agitation by abolitionists would excite slaveholders' prejudices and "retard the growth of, if not entirely extinguish" their "humane" principles.[38]

Morton scripted his reply to Perry against the backdrop of slavery's explosion onto the Massachusetts political scene in the mid-1830s. First, abolitionists had flooded the mails and Congress with massive postal and petition campaigns. Closer to home, antiabolitionist Bostonians filled Faneuil Hall to overflowing in August 1835 to convene a meeting called by both the Whig *Atlas* and the Jacksonian *Morning Post.* In the keynote address, Whig Brahmin Harrison Gray Otis railed against abolitionists for forming a "dangerous association" that incited blacks to rebellion and women to "turn their sewing parties into abolition clubs." Worse, according to Otis, this "revolutionary society" was becoming a "political association" that "interrogated" candidates (just as minister Perry had Morton) about slavery. Within weeks of Otis's speech and Morton's reply to Perry, the city's antiabolition fervor climaxed when a mob dragged William Lloyd Garrison through the streets of Boston at the end of a rope.[39]

Many (if not most) local abolitionists held the governing Whig Party responsible for the riots. "The mobs of 1834–5, and especially the great outbreak of October 1835, when 5,000 'gentlemen of property and standing' broke up the female antislavery society prayer meeting, were *Whig* mobs," wrote Joshua Leavitt in the *Emancipator.* "The ferocious proslavery meeting in August of that year, in Faneuil Hall . . . was got up, officered, and addressed by Whigs. In the following January, Gov. Everett, the Whig governor . . . recommended that the abolitionists be indicted at common law. . . . During all these years of Whig proscription, the country Democratic press, and the *Daily Advocate*, of Boston . . . took sides with the abolitionists and in favor of free speech."[40]

As the Whig Party made itself especially repugnant to antislavery Bay Staters, some turned to the Democrats, who afforded them some alliance with Morton's reputation. Morton increased his vote totals by 14 percent in the 1835 gubernatorial election, picking up several formerly Whig towns — his largest one-year increase in nine tries for the office. The next year, Morton added another 7 percent, bringing his total to a competitive 46 percent of those voting. Constant agitation by the state's abolitionists added to Morton's totals by keeping the slavery issue before the public, even though many Garrisonians refused to vote. From 1830 to 1839, the year Morton won the governor's chair by a single vote, Morton's vote increased from an anemic 32 percent to 50 percent (see Appendix, Table 1). Many of those votes were provided by nominal Whigs and Democrats angry about their parties' expediency in regard to slavery.[41]

Whatever popular outcry existed against slavery, both Whig and Democratic leaders ignored it. Like most Democrats, Morton believed no action could be taken against slavery where it already existed except by slaveholders themselves. He repeatedly stated he would take no active part in agitating against it. Unlike his fellow party leaders in Massachusetts, however, Morton publicly attacked slaveholding on numerous occasions and argued that Congress had the right to abolish the institution in the District of Columbia and in the territories. "To say that I am utterly opposed to slavery in every form, civil, political, or domestic, is saying very little," Morton wrote. "I deem slavery to be the greatest curse and the most portentous evil which a righteous God ever inflicted upon a nation; and that every effort consistent with a moral duty and the constitution . . . ought to be made to mitigate, and, if possible, to extirpate it from the land."[42]

During the eight days before the 1837 gubernatorial election, Morton received requests from several abolitionists — including poet John Greenleaf Whittier and "the colored citizens of New Bedford" — to state his opinion on issues connected with slavery.[43] The queries reflected a more concentrated strategy by politically minded abolitionists to poll issue-evading candidates for their positions in regard to slavery. Morton declined to answer the various inquiries during the last week of the 1837 campaign, fearing "it would do myself and the democratic cause more injury than benefit." Despite this reticence, his attitudes about slavery reached a public forum on November 8, 1837, when the *Boston Advocate* printed a personal letter he had written to Morton Eddy on September 28. Although the letter accurately represented his views, Morton would live to regret it.

In the missive to Eddy, which Morton later described as a "very hasty and rather slovenly reply . . . designed expressly for private use," the jurist reiterated his previously published advocacy for the freedom of petition and speech and his opposition to slavery in the District of Columbia and its extension into new territory. The letter also provides something different: a clear glimpse into Morton's hard-to-discern personal views on the topics of slavery, race, and religion. "For one human being to hold others, whom the Almighty has created his fellows, in bondage, is entirely repugnant to that principle of equality which is founded in religion as well as in natural right," he wrote. "That principle of equality knows no distinction of race or condition, [and] includes in its benevolent embrace the whole human family."[44] Unlike most other Democratic opponents of slavery, who consistently emphasized the institution's deleterious effect on *white* people, Morton suggested his opposition was based on a principle of equality he saw as guaranteed by both natural rights doctrine and Christianity.[45] This, of course, does not mean Morton thought of African Americans as socially equal to white people; there is no evidence that he did, and if indeed he believed in absolute racial equality, it would have been unusual even among abolitionists. Still, it is clear that Morton held this principle of equality as the centerpiece of both his religious and political traditions and saw it threatened by aristocratic combinations in the North and the South.

Two years after this incident, Marcus Morton won his first race for governor, defeating the incumbent Everett by a single vote.[46] To Morton's slowly growing coalition were added those Bay Staters (including many new immigrants) incensed by an ill-conceived Whig law to limit the sale of liquor to quantities of fifteen gallons or more, effectively outlawing the sale of alcohol over bars in saloons. In his inaugural address, Morton avoided all mention of slavery, instead focusing on tried-and-true Jacksonian themes: economic retrenchment, an end to the practice of lending state credit to private corporations, suffrage extension and the introduction of a secret ballot, the abolition of capitol punishment except in cases of murder, and relief for insolvent debtors. Ever the politician, Morton also called for a swift repeal of the "fifteen gallon law."[47] Although "joyfully received as text books of the Democracy in all [of Massachusetts's] sister states," Morton's program had little chance of passage with both houses of the legislature under firm Whig control.[48] He did, however, win the admiration of many peers and constituents. Historian and fellow Bay State Democrat George Bancroft glowingly recommended Morton for national office, writing that "he has gained in the hearts of his political friends so strong a hold, that they will remain restless till justice shall be done to his genius, his consistency, his patriotism, and his virtues."[49]

During the next gubernatorial campaign, Morton found himself battling for reelection on the opposite front. A new political party devoted to slavery's demise made its debut in Massachusetts: the Liberty Party. Consequently, Bay State antislavery voters had candidates of their own — candidates who were far less evasive than Morton on abolitionists' questions regarding slavery. The Liberty Party polled 6,382 votes in the 1842 governor's race, enough to force the election into the legislature.[50] Normally, the house of representatives would pick two candidates for the upper house to vote on for governor, but the Liberty candidates had scored well enough to leave sixteen of the forty senate seats unfilled. Thus, the job of filling the empty seats fell to a combination of the legislators who had won clear majorities, and the six new Liberty representatives suddenly controlled the balance of power. "They [Whigs and Democrats] must look for the young giant hereafter," Liberty editor Elizur Wright wrote to New York abolitionist Gerrit Smith.[51]

Liberty men knew that if they managed to keep Whigs and Democrats evenly divided, they had a realistic chance of elevating their own candidate — Samuel Sewall — to the governorship and choosing one of their own as Speaker of the house. The plan fell one vote short of success. A solitary Whig member crossed party lines and voted with the Democrats, filling each of the senate vacancies with Jacksonians.[52] The Whig *Daily Advertiser* editorialized that Whig members preferred another year with Morton as governor to an abolitionist candidate who won barely 7 percent of the vote; perhaps this was the motivation for the lone Whig turncoat.[53]

After the election of 1842 but before the legislature's vote to return him to the governor's chair, Morton sought the political advice of a famous abolitionist. "[I have] long wished to confer with some candid, intelligent Abolitionist, on the best mode of ameliorating the condition of the slaves, and of eventually accomplishing emancipation," he wrote to poet John Greenleaf Whittier. Morton declared that he was "no political abolitionist" and accused abolitionist leaders of "selfish and sinister designs"; but, he said, he was "as ready to take any measures which are right in themselves, and give any rational promise of relief to the slaves, as the highest toned Abolitionist in the country." Whittier's reply is lost, but Morton's statement survives as testimony of his intention to pursue a more deliberate and active antislavery course.[54]

These sentiments are not surprising. Morton and other statewide candidates undoubtedly viewed the Liberty Party as a serious rival for votes after the 1842 election. Morton must have known that he had far more to lose than his Whig opponents, having long been the beneficiary of antislavery votes. The growth of the Liberty Party's support in the 1840s suggests that an increasing number of its votes came from disgruntled Democrats who, presumably, had previously supported Morton.[55]

Morton's loss in the 1843 campaign was to be his last. Within a few years, the demands of national politics and the struggle for control of the Democratic Party would pull him away from state elections. Henshaw's faction of the state party, now firmly allied with President John Tyler and John C. Calhoun, continued to wrestle with the Morton–George Bancroft faction. The contest became more heated after the new Polk administration favored the Morton-Bancroft group with patronage appointments in early 1845. Polk made Bancroft secretary of the navy and appointed Morton, for his sixteen years as a Jacksonian standard-bearer, collector of the port of Boston.

The Charge of Abolitionism

Recognizing the shift in the balance of power, Henshaw's followers went on the offensive. Their strategy precipitated the crucial political battle of Morton's career. Using the *Statesman* and the *Post* as their amplifiers, Morton's enemies charged that he was anti-Catholic, that he had removed people arbitrarily from positions at the Customs House, and that he was an abolitionist. In the political climate of 1845, with southern Democrats increasingly defensive about slavery and strengthening their hold on federal power, the charge of abolitionism had the potential to wreck a political career, even one as distinguished as Morton's.

Morton refuted the first two charges with ease. He wrote to New Hampshire senator C. G. Atherton that "from the days of the [1798] Alien law, when I was a school boy, I have advocated the principle of the naturalization laws, and the rights of the naturalized citizens and especially *Catholics*."[56] Morton had routinely captured large majorities of the Irish vote in the state and was popular among Catholics. The charge did not stick. His accusers had a similarly difficult task proving that Morton had been arbitrary in his removals at the Customs House while collector. Morton argued that he had looked to the entire Democratic Party when dispensing patronage: "In my nominations were included Van Buren men, Calhoun men. . . . Now, I believe, there are more than twice as many Calhoun and Tyler men than Van Buren men." Very few people believed Morton had behaved improperly as collector.[57]

The charge of abolitionism proved much more dangerous. The attack forced Morton to defend his record in public or risk going down to defeat in his senate confirmation vote and losing the position of collector. So Morton took up a campaign of his own to demonstrate, beyond a reasonable doubt, that he was no abolitionist. Although Morton had never been a member of the Liberty Party or any abolitionist society, he was known to be hostile to slavery and, increasingly, to the southern wing of the Democratic Party. In January 1845, when he first heard of the accusation, Morton was not surprised: "It is not very strange that Southern men should think the language of [the letter to Morton Eddy published in 1837] somewhat inflammatory. As it was printed, it certainly appears pretty sharp." But, Morton insisted, it "clearly showed no connection with the abolition movement." He added that he regretted the haste with which he wrote the letter and the lack of "cautious" language.[58]

In the opening salvo of this battle, Morton's opponents charged him with secretly favoring abolitionists in his appointments as a quid pro quo for Liberty Party support during the deadlocked election of 1842. In his defense, Morton appealed to various high-ranking Democrats, promising them that "not a single abolitionist, in any form directly or indirectly, cast a vote in my favor [in the Legislature]." He asked them to "be assured, that though I am strongly opposed to slavery on principle, yet no one here has given less countenance to the democratic party or been more cautious not to recommend abolitionists for office."[59] Morton received several queries from Washington and Boston about the antislavery views held by some of his appointees, and to each he responded in a similar manner. "I have made inquiries into the moral character of Mr. Worth, the candidate for postmaster of Nantucket," he wrote in one letter, "and I am informed, by men of great respect and worth, that there is not the slightest foundation for the [abolitionist] charges made against him."[60] Morton's earlier correspondence confirms that he had carried out inquiries into the views of his appointees but not that he favored or passed over supposed abolitionists. In the case of Mr. Worth, the Nantucket postmaster, Morton seems to have been aware that he was one of seven members of the "abolitionist faction" on the county Democratic committee. In a letter that might be viewed as presaging the McCarthyism of the 1950s, one angry Nantucketer fingered Worth as an influential abolitionist, writing Morton that "none were more active [than Worth] in attracting votes for the amalgamation or negro ticket," and that Worth had received his office only because local Democrats were "not aware of the new character which he had in the meanwhile adopted." Nonetheless, Worth retained his postmastership at the recommendation of Marcus Morton.[61]

By the end of 1845, Henshaw and his ally B. F. Hallett had ratcheted up their charges against Morton, hoping to poison his position with southern senators. In December they outstripped the argument that he had favored abolitionists for office and accepted their votes, instead accusing him of out-and-out abolitionism. In a remarkable issue of the *Boston Post*, Democrats leveled salvo after salvo at one of their own for, while serving as governor, refusing to surrender a Virginia fugitive, acquiescing in antislavery and anti-Texas resolves passed by the state legislature, and approving an act to repeal the state's law prohibiting marriages between blacks and whites and another to punish any state official who aided in apprehending a slave. "Standing in relation of secret cooperation with prominent Abolitionists," the *Post* piece concluded, "Mr. Morton has often obtained a larger vote than the strength of the Democratic Party proper." This statement must be among the first complaints by a party organ that its own candidate had attracted *too many* votes.[62]

Morton could hardly deny the specifics of Henshaw and Hallett's charges, since he did accomplish each of these measures while in the governor's chair. Instead, he recycled the once effective strategy of stressing how he opposed both abolition *and* slavery: "Any charge of *Abolition* against me, is entirely without foundation; and I have no fear that abstract opinion against slavery is any objection to a northern man. If a non-slaveholder is to be opposed for an opinion *against* slavery, a slaveholder may just as reasonably be opposed for his opinion in favor of slavery."[63]

During the 1830s, this defense would have sufficed to save Morton's appointment. Yet by 1845, much had changed in Massachusetts and the nation. Texas had won admission to the Union as a slave state. The rift between northern and southern Democrats had widened when northerners watched their southern brethren spurn Martin Van Buren at the 1844 Baltimore convention. More to the point, abolitionists had gained significant force in northern (and national) politics, and southerners had become

Antislavery in Massachusetts

increasingly insistent that the federal government use its power to silence them, to extend slavery into new territory, and to return fugitives to slavery. In response, a growing number of northerners believed that these actions represented the machinations of a conspiratorial Slave Power intent on dominating every corner of American political life.[64] Because the concerns of southerners still increasingly steered the party at large, Morton had to defend his views and actions in public and demonstrate his hostility to organized abolitionism in any form. Otherwise, he would have no future in the Democratic Party.

In this fresh bout, Morton began by marshaling his forces. When the Suffolk County Committee, under Henshaw's control, submitted a petition to the U.S. Senate declaring Morton "unacceptable" to the Democrats of Massachusetts, Morton solicited aid from northern Democratic senators Benjamin Tappan of Ohio, John M. Niles of Connecticut, and John Fairfield of Maine, each of whom had his own misgivings about the Slave Power. Morton also requested support from proslavery northern Democratic stalwarts C. G. Atherton and Franklin Pierce of New Hampshire.[65]

At the same time, Morton allowed his defenders to publish a thirty-two-page pamphlet titled *A Refutation of the Charge of Abolitionism . . . Against the Hon. Marcus Morton* in an attempt to salvage his appointment and political career. A "defense pamphlet" straight out of the honor culture of a waning era, the document addresses, line by line, the various charges made against Morton.[66] "Against no man in the Commonwealth, can the charge of Abolitionism be made with less truth, than against Marcus Morton," stated the anonymous author. "Governor Morton has always expressed the greatest alarm at the rash thoughtless course pursued by this band of modern fanatics."[67] The Marcus Morton portrayed in the pamphlet resembles a conservative northern doughface like Franklin Pierce or James Buchanan more than the principled, if only modestly successful, governor-jurist of the 1830s.

Occasionally, the pamphlet overstates Morton's distance from abolitionist positions and willfully misreads their presses in an attempt to shield him from association. "The Abolition party in this state, knowing [Morton's] opinions hostile to their views, have ever opposed him in their prints, and by their votes," the pamphleteer stated. Quite to the contrary, Joshua Leavitt had come to Morton's defense in the *Emancipator* in 1845, using the imbroglio as a challenge to antislavery Democrats to disavow "the proslaveryism of [Henshaw and Hallett's] Boston clique . . . the unscrupulous vassals of the overseers": "What shall we say of the masses—the men who are

Democrats because they are men, and not because they expect preferment and office? . . . Can you, as honest men, any longer submit to the lead of men who openly avow such a policy as this—a policy which virtually excludes from the party a majority of the party itself?" Even if the *Emancipator* exaggerated the percentage of men with "abolitionist tendencies" in the Massachusetts Democratic Party, it made a spirited defense of that "old and faithful servant, Ex-Governor Morton."[68]

On the issue of prohibiting the use of state jails for the imprisonment of fugitive slaves, the writer suggests that "the existing laws of our State point to the acts which enclose a citizen within the walls of our prisons;—and the constitution declares, that being a slave is not one of them." Thus, the extremely volatile issue of fugitive slaves appears in the guise of civil liberties alone.[69] All told, Morton's views on questions central to the slavery debate become neatly severed from that debate and especially from abolitionism. His campaign to save his commission and clear his name is notable for its energy, its effectiveness, and its extreme backpedaling on the greatest issue of the day.

Bancroft informed Morton in May 1846 that he had been confirmed by the Senate, despite the furious campaign against him, after he was able to "make representation" of much of Morton's "inflammatory" antislavery rhetoric as "untrue." Morton's defense had succeeded. The timing, however, proved ironic: the Mexican War and David Wilmot's famous proviso just three months later—planned and introduced by antislavery northern Democrats in the U.S. Congress—placed the issue of slavery and its extension in the center of American politics for the next fifteen years. The old strategy of relegating slavery to the political sidelines was no longer effective or even remotely possible. Morton, clearly uncomfortable with the centrality of the slavery issue, feared for the future of the Democracy: "the dreadful question about Slavery appears to have assumed a worse aspect than on any former occasion," he wrote to Bancroft. "We should all do well to have our robes folded for a graceful fall."[70]

A divided state Democratic Party met in Worcester to pick candidates in the spring of 1847, and an attempt by Morton's ally Amasa Walker to place the convention behind the Wilmot Proviso never made it off the table. "As a matter of preservation," Walker said over the shouts of his opponents, "the Democracy cannot *thrive* in the Bay State if it must be forever bound to the shameless, *undemocratic* institution of chattel slavery." Despite having "more than four fifths of the Democracy" behind the resolution, it was tabled by the Henshaw partisans who controlled the party's machinery.[71]

After the convention, Morton turned his back on state politics and began a rich correspondence with Martin Van Buren's New York Barnburner faction. This group, Morton concluded, had the best chance to overpower the southern wing of the party and set the Democracy on what he deemed to be the correct path. "The Northern Democrats have conceded and submitted till they have lost the respect of their Southern brethren," Morton wrote to Van Buren lieutenant John Dix. "It is quite time they asserted their rights and let the South know that a man who disapproves of slavery is to stand on equality with a man who approves of it."[72]

In 1848, when the Free Soil schism splintered the Democratic Party in New York, Morton pledged his support to Van Buren and the Barnburners. He was even asked to join Van Buren as vice-presidential candidate on a new ticket to be based "on the free territory principle." Morton demurred, suggesting that a candidate from the South or West would balance the new party. "I would certainly make any personal sacrifice which might be deemed useful in the establishment of the great principle of freedom," Morton wrote, "but my connection with the government presents an obstacle which I know not how to surmount."[73]

Although he remained at his post as collector, Morton campaigned openly for the Utica ticket of Van Buren and Henry Dodge of Wisconsin. "I must go for free territory and Van Buren, be the consequences what they may," he wrote to B. F. Butler. To Seth Whitmarsh, another old Antimason who had joined the ranks of the Democratic Party, Morton delivered the hard sell. "An honest and true Democrat could take but one side of the question — that *Democracy and slavery* were antipodes. . . . Judge my surprise and grief when I learned from you that you intended to support the extension of slavery into free territory!"[74] Although disappointed with the Free Soil Party convention's choice of Whig Charles Francis Adams as vice-presidential candidate (Morton called Adams "the greatest Iceberg in the Northern hemisphere"), Morton worked tirelessly, if quietly, for Van Buren's election.[75]

Van Buren, of course, lost the 1848 presidential election, both nationally and in Massachusetts.[76] But he did outpoll the Democratic candidate Lewis Cass, with at least 45 percent of the Free Soil vote coming from former Democrats.[77] For the first time, the Whig Party was a minority party in Massachusetts. This truth was not lost on the architects of the Free Soil–Democratic alliance that took control of Bay State politics in 1849, led by ex-Democrats such as Amasa Walker and ex-Whigs such as Charles Sumner (who had long preferred Jacksonian economic policies). Although Morton was enough of an old Jacksonian to oppose Sumner's Free Soil U.S. Senate bid on grounds that, except on the slavery issue, Sumner was an "ultra" and "impracicable," he had left the Democratic Party behind.[78] It seemed obvious to him and other antislavery (though not abolitionist) ex-Democrats that the Slave Power had reached all the way to Massachusetts. They could only hope to stop it — and to prioritize once again the old Democratic issues such as the secret ballot, regulation of banks and corporations, and cheap postage — with the help of other antislavery partisans, even their former opponents, including Charles Sumner.

Strikingly, the new political coalition that in the 1850s stood up to the Slave Power included Morton's entire constituency from the 1830s and 1840s. Marcus Morton and his unusual coterie of supporters — few of whom were abolitionists — were central to the new antislavery politics of the 1850s. These, along with the Garrisons, Walkers, and Parkers, helped bring on the Civil War and the end of slavery in North America.

↑

David Wilmot, the Proviso,
and the Congressional Movement
to Abolish Slavery

History has not been kind to David Wilmot. For half a century after he stood up in the House of Representatives to introduce the antislavery proviso that bears his name, contemporaries and historians awarded a rival the credit for authoring the measure.[1] Later, a fire destroyed all but a handful of his personal papers. Civil War historian Avery Craven minimized his contributions, calling him an "insignificant country lawyer from a backward corner of Pennsylvania."[2] Today Wilmot — more than perhaps any other antebellum political figure — is offered up by historians as a prime example of the ideology of "whiteness," which joined struggling northern whites with southern slaveholders in bonds of self-interest.[3] His antislavery has long been called into question as hypocritical, devoid of principle, self-serving, and most of all, racist. But recent historians have taken this analysis one step further. Wilmot's antislavery, some argue, was really a smokescreen designed to obscure other goals: keeping blacks out of the West and chipping away at their rights in the North. Put another way, the Free Soil goal of limiting slavery's expansion — embodied in the proviso — was really a proslavery gimmick that affirmed the right of whites both to hold slaves and to keep black people "quarantined" in the South.[4]

For the pivotal years 1846–54, David Wilmot became the personification of the political movement to halt the expansion of slavery. He serves as an emblem for good reason. As much as that of any other antebellum politician or ideologue, Wilmot's background and career exemplified the various ideological strands that, when braided together, became Free Soil. Like other up-and-coming Democratic activists, he absorbed a strong belief in producers' rights and opposition to the concentrating power of banks and monopolies. He supported land reform as a way to relieve economic inequality in the East and populate the West with property-owning families. As a result, he found himself targeted for political elimination by members of the national Democratic Party, especially slaveholders and their northern allies. The combination of his coming of age in rural Pennsylvania politics and his Washington experiences made this obscure first-term congressman the perfect vehicle for the nationalization of slavery restriction.

Instead of working to change the hearts of slaveholders — the preferred tactic of the abolitionist movement — Wilmot hoped to use legislation to stop slavery's expansion into new territories gained as a result of the war with Mexico, over which he believed Congress had complete control. But halting the spread of slavery was never Wilmot's ultimate goal; Wilmot clearly believed containment was the first step toward its eradication. In Wilmot's own words (rarely quoted by recent scholars), if slavery was barred from further expansion, "it will, at no distant day . . . insure the redemption of the Negro from his bondage in chains."[5] Although Wilmot was, unquestionably, what we today would label a white supremacist, he was adamant that no person, black or white, should be forced to live as a slave — uncompensated for labor and subjected to the whims and ownership of another. Wilmot himself would never have recognized the bond of whiteness that supposedly joined his interests to those of slaveholders; he believed slavery degraded both black and white laborers. These ideas about race, slavery, politics, and equality were forged at a moment of extraordinary political upheaval. To subsume them under the single rubric of whiteness minimizes the complexity of Free Soil's ideological and racial trajectory.

Social Origins: The Wilmot District

David Wilmot was born in 1814 to downwardly mobile Connecticut Yankees at the height of the New England land shortage.[6] His father, Randall Wilmot, moved first to the Catskills in Sullivan County, New York, and then to the new Pennsylvania county of Wayne in search of enough farmland to support his family. The Pennsylvania interior, long a matter of dispute between various states and Indian tribes, was still new to white settlement when the elder Wilmot walked there with his bride, Mary Grant, about 1805.[7] Proprietors from Connecticut, Pennsylvania, and New York had formed companies to settle the untamed lands of the Susquehanna region after extinguishing Indian titles in the late 1770s.

Thus, the northern tier's pattern of settlement was strikingly similar to that of the anti-rent districts and North Country of New York, complete with disputed titles, land-hungry settlers, and absentee landlords—elements that added to the anxieties felt by the men and women moving into the region. Restless settlers from three different areas held competing titles, often for the same land, leading to violent incidents that became known as the Yankee and Pennamite War. Settlers repeatedly resorted to "murders, arsons, battles, sieges, arrest and angry personal disputes . . . over the right of *jurisdiction* and the right of *soil*."[8] Finally, in 1782, the new U.S. Congress stepped in at the request of the states of Connecticut and Pennsylvania to settle once and for all the "Susquehanna troubles." In a decree that was finalized seventeen years later as the Compromise Law of 1799, Connecticut abandoned all claims to the area in favor of the state of Pennsylvania.

This compromise, however, did little for the "Half Share men" and "Wild Yankees," who had bought and improved land from the dispossessed Susquehanna company, and land battles continued to flare well into the 1820s. The Wilmots entered this sparsely populated and heavily disputed area, poor and hungry for a farm of their own.[9] The first mention of the family in Pennsylvania dates from 1812, when Randall Wilmot, listed as a "merchant," pledged money for the support of a Congregational preacher, who was to divide his time among three area churches and the outlying districts. To support his family, the elder Wilmot bought and sold several pieces of property within the Wayne County town of Bethany.[10] Randall Wilmot had some good years in Bethany, as his construction of a "mansion" in 1827 attests, before a series of failures and bankruptcies forced him to move first to Susquehanna County and then to Bozetta, Ohio.[11]

Despite his family's declining fortunes, young David Wilmot attended local schools and trained for the law in the office of a town attorney, a pattern common to members of Wilmot's political generation. Later, while apprenticing in the Wilkes-Barre office of Democratic lawyer George W. Woodward, Wilmot was said to have "dressed without taste," "read listlessly," and erred in his selection of the law as a vocation. Still, he managed to hold on to his job, and Woodward recommended Wilmot to the bar in August 1834.[12] While in Susquehanna County visiting his father, for whom he was assuming more and more financial responsibility, David Wilmot met a learned antislavery Quaker named Enoch Walker. Walker made his extensive private library available to Wilmot, who for the first time immersed himself in books. In later years Wilmot recalled how he was influenced especially by the works of William Penn and by Adam Smith's *Wealth of Nations*, although he never mentioned the vast numbers of antislavery tracts and books in Walker's collection.[13]

When choosing a place to begin his law practice, Wilmot passed over the established towns of Montrose, Bethany, and Wilkes-Barre and selected the sparsely populated county of Bradford, in the northeast corner of the state. In many ways, Bradford County resembled the stump-strewn towns Wilmot had lived in as a child. Political ambition probably had something to do with Wilmot's decision. Towanda, the rough county seat of Bradford in the heart of the northern tier, was ripe with political opportunity for a young Jacksonian.

The 12th Pennsylvania Congressional District (known throughout the Civil War era as the Wilmot District), included all of Bradford, Tioga, and Susquehanna counties in the northeast corner of the state. Rugged, densely wooded, and remote, the area was the last settled in Pennsylvania, and one local historian reported that "frontier" conditions persisted until the 1860s. The land was rocky and poor, especially when compared with the fertile soil of counties like Lancaster to the south. Unlike the bustling market towns downstate, northeast Pennsylvania had very little industry and even fewer banks. One pro-growth governor once remarked that the only industry "up there" was stealing timber — which was then made into shingles sold back to those from whom it had been filched.[14]

Predictably, the district was a bastion of Democratic electoral strength. In election after election, the voters of the 12th District voted overwhelmingly for the party of Jackson.[15] In 1824 Jackson rolled up 1,640 votes to John Quincy Adams's 31, and the county gave the Tennessean large majorities in 1828 and 1832 as well. Martin Van Buren managed to carry the 12th District with 56.6 percent during his loss to William Henry Harrison in 1840 (he won 49.9 percent statewide), and James Polk increased the Democratic share to 65.0 percent (50.6 percent statewide) in 1844.[16]

The reasons for the Democrats' dominance were both social and political. The people who settled the Susquehanna valley tended to be (or aspired to be) Jeffersonian yeomen and had left communities dominated by Federalists and their conservative descendants. This Jeffersonian-Jacksonian political orientation was buttressed by the actions of Pennsylvania's large, state-run canal companies in the 1830s and 1840s. Correspondents in local newspapers blamed the canal "monopolies" for keeping taxes high and benefiting residents of other regions and reserved special scorn for absentee "land sharks" and downstate politicians who voted for protective tariffs to aid the state's manufacturers.[17] One protariff politician cynically remarked that the only interest in protection in the northern tier "was protection from the officers of justice."[18] In this respect they closely resembled the hard-money,

David Wilmot and the Proviso

antibank radicals of New York's remote North Country, home of Democratic politicians Silas Wright and Preston King.

Wilmot quickly joined the wing of the Pennsylvania Democratic Party committed to then–vice president Martin Van Buren, authoring resolutions in May 1835 which claimed that the "slanders heaped upon [Van Buren] by his enemies have served only to endear him to the democratic party."[19] For slightly more than a year, Wilmot tried his hand at journalism, buying a share in and writing editorials for the *Towanda Banner and Democrat*. During his short tenure as a journalist, Wilmot turned out editorials supporting Van Buren's Independent Treasury ("the only safe and constitutional mode of collecting, keeping and disbursing the public revenue"); repeatedly denounced "Whig principles"; and touted Locofoco antibank positions.[20] His guiding light seems to have been William Leggett's *New York Evening Post*, from which he borrowed heavily. In one Leggett-inspired editorial, Wilmot argued that if the Whig Party defeated Van Buren's Independent Treasury, the laborer, the merchant, the farmer, and the mechanic would all be impoverished by diminished currency values: "The Whig party is the bank party in our country [and] . . . banks are the instruments of the most ruinous expansions and contractions in the currency—they have of late years, not once or twice only, but often and repeatedly, produced worse evils than any change to specie circulation could now produce, however suddenly effected."[21] In 1840, Towanda's population was a mere 715, with only 143 voters, and Wilmot rose quickly in local Democratic councils.[22]

Wilmot's religious and social affiliations also offer indications of his developing ideology. With each decision he made, he pledged his political, religious, and cultural allegiance to an antievangelical Jacksonianism and cemented his ties to the Van Buren wing of the Democratic Party. In 1841 Wilmot helped to charter Christ Church in Towanda, an Episcopal congregation, where he served as a vestryman.[23] Unlike the many evangelical Protestant denominations gaining converts in antebellum America, Episcopalian congregations such as Wilmot's were decidedly less associated with movements for benevolent reform such as temperance, women's rights, and abolitionism. Another reform movement embraced by the Northeast's evangelical Protestants was Antimasonry, a cause with significant political and religious dimensions. Antimasons ranged in their denunciations of the Masonic Order, with some calling its rituals satanic and others deriding its secrecy and foothold among the region's officeholders. Again placing himself on solid antievangelical ground, Wilmot joined Union Lodge No. 108 of Free and Accepted Masons in 1841, the same year he helped charter Christ

Church.[24] Wilmot's embrace of freemasonry can be viewed as primarily a political decision, since reform-minded Antimasonic candidates like Thaddeus Stevens consistently ran as Whigs against Democratic candidates throughout Pennsylvania.

As a Democratic stalwart, Wilmot believed reform movements like abolitionism diverted attention from the real issues of import, such as banking and monopolies, that threatened the nation's future. To many of Wilmot's neighbors and future constituents, slavery seemed distant and almost irrelevant. The institution was an extreme rarity in the Wilmot District—the area was settled by whites about the same time the Pennsylvania government decided gradually to abolish slavery in the state—and few African Americans lived there. Still, residents got a taste of the institution from the stream of fugitives fleeing north.[25] The rivers that cut through the thickly wooded region provided ideal routes for slaves escaping along the Underground Railroad, and the Carter house on Main Street and William Griffis's tavern in Towanda were well known in the community as havens for slaves making their way north along the banks of the Susquehanna.[26] In fact, Towanda's small black population was founded and continually supplemented by escaped slaves who stayed and took up residence in the remote region, far from the prying eyes and affidavits of slave catchers. One local historian remembered that "toward the end of the slave regime the fugitives came in such numbers that they became almost a nuisance, but in the main they made good citizens."[27]

By the 1830s, slavery had become an issue even in rural northeastern Pennsylvania. The steady trickle of fugitives through the northern tier coincided with the formation of societies dedicated to the immediate abolition of slavery. Abolitionist meetings took place in the Terrytown Lyceum in both 1830 and 1831, and the Bradford County and Wyalusing antislavery societies both date from the mid-1830s.[28]

An incident in February 1839 illustrated how antiabolitionist violence could erupt even in remote rural areas with few African American residents. That year the annual meeting of the Bradford County Antislavery Society erupted into a brawl after an abolitionist lecturer from Philadelphia was "disgracefully treated" by angry and disruptive townsfolk. Though details are scarce (local newspapers devoted little space to the incident), it is clear that the altercation spread into the streets outside the lyceum, where several people were hurt and property was damaged. At a crowded public meeting after the disturbance, Wilmot took a page from Leggett's political book and spoke out against the "fanatical" meeting while at the same time objecting to the violence perpetrated by the mob.[29] These events fit within a general northern pattern in the late 1830s and early 1840s where local elites fomented and often participated in antiabolitionist mob activity.[30]

Wilmot's political views on issues such as abolition, banking, territorial expansion, and race were very much in line with those of his future constituents. Many of them disliked slavery but also demonstrated hostility to the presence of organized abolitionism, with its associations of evangelical perfectionism and moral uplift. According to letters in the local press, the residents of the northern tier thought, at best, that the talk about sin and slavery was a distraction from the more important issues of the Independent Treasury, banks, and the abolition of imprisonment for debt.[31] And David Wilmot was successful in carving out popular positions on both slavery and abolition. His star was rising fast.

In 1843 Wilmot caught the attention of the *New York Globe*, which remarked on his "rich, full, melodious voice" and called him "the most eloquent man in Bradford County . . . almost slovenly in his dress and not over pious in his language." He won his party's nomination to Congress in 1844 and glided to victory that November, outpolling both presidential candidate James K. Polk and incumbent governor Francis R. Shunk.[32]

Portrait of a Northern Democrat

David Wilmot furnishes scholars with an archetypal portrait of a Democratic politician from the rural North at a time — the mid-1840s — when northern Jacksonians stood at an ideological and sectional crossroads. As did each of the other Democrats that plotted the proviso, Wilmot represented a district "passed over" by the revolutions in transportation, markets, and information exchange that transformed much of the northern states in the second quarter of the nineteenth century. More important, in each of these districts antislavery sentiment was on the rise, and Whig charges of Democratic acquiescence to southern slaveholders were potentially damaging to Democrats' political careers.[33] In each of the major issues he faced in Congress, then — from the tariff to the boundaries of Oregon Territory to land policy — Wilmot mirrored the changing views of his constituents.[34] A further examination of these views and the positions he staked out on major issues gives definition to the shifting ideologies of the northern Democratic electorate.

One issue Wilmot championed immediately upon arriving in Washington was land reform. Between 1844 and 1846 land reform activists flooded northern representatives' offices with petitions urging the distribution of public lands to settlers in the form of inalienable homesteads. Most of the appeals were extra editions of George Henry Evans's *Working Man's Advocate* printed as petitions, on which local land reformers collected signatures, clamoring for the "freedom of the public lands." The petitions were especially concentrated in the remote agricultural regions represented by the future proviso men in Congress. Wilmot's office was a favorite destination for the petitioners, and he dutifully presented scores of petitions full of signatures from Pennsylvanians demanding the public lands be set aside as homesteads for white northern farmers and their children.[35] Land reform was connected to antislavery; while northern Democrats could not agree on the particulars of the rivers and harbors bill or on internal improvements, many—including Wilmot—began to believe that the potential introduction of slavery into new, western territory could threaten the future for migrating northerners.[36]

Wilmot's ideas about land reform also appeared in his first speech on the House floor, on the issue of territorial expansion. He demanded that the United States recognize the Oregon Territory's most extreme northern boundary ($54°40'$), so even more American settlers could stake their claims in the West. The speech, which suggested that Oregon could be for northern immigrants what Texas was for southerners, placed him among the most enthusiastic of the Democracy's expansionists. In a legislative session where sectional tensions were beginning to percolate, Wilmot's speech also established him as a Democrat friendly to southern interests. Hoping to make the point explicitly, he told the House he was "no croaker against the South. . . . My home is in the North, yet, sir, I am not insensible to the claims of the South upon my affection and respect."[37]

Wilmot's most controversial votes during his first term had nothing to do with slavery or expansion. The tariff issue was paramount in the minds of Pennsylvanians, some of whom had taken a lead in developing the country's earliest industries and wanted to keep protective duties high. However, Wilmot's constituents scorned the nascent coal and iron barons, and by the mid-1840s many voters in the northern tier had concluded that protective tariffs were yet another example of "partial" legislation that funneled resources from poor farmers and artisans to downstate entrepreneurs and their financial backers.[38] Rejecting the protectionist argument that high duties benefited the nation as a whole, Wilmot claimed they helped create a privileged class of manufacturers while loggers, mechanics, and farmers were "fleeced on both sides" by the restrictive policy. The result of a continued protective tariff, Wilmot told the House, would be disastrous for mechanics and farmers, destroying their independence and driving them into wage-earning jobs in high-cost settings. He flatly denied that he was a "free-trade man" and claimed that he was in favor of protection — that is, protection for labor. "Your lords of the spindle . . . your Lawrences and Appletons," he said, "seek by every means in their power to depress American labor. . . . Sir, I demand protection for labor, against the cruel exactions of capital!"[39] Wilmot was the only member of the Pennsylvania delegation to vote for the Walker Tariff of 1846 (which replaced the protectionist tariff of 1842), despite specific instructions from the state legislature.

This overwhelming fear of a corrupting capitalist aristocracy — a hallmark of Jacksonian rhetoric in the 1830s — was easily transmuted during the next decade by northern Democrats such as Wilmot into suspicion about the privileges demanded and won by slaveholders. This was how future Free Soilers like Wilmot could manufacture a withering critique of slavery (a corrupt, antirepublican institution that divided men into servile dependents and quasi-aristocratic overlords) at the same time they exhibited an indifference bordering on contempt for the rights of blacks. "The negro race occupy enough of this fair continent," Wilmot declared in 1847. "Let us keep what remains for ourselves, and our children — for the emigrant that seeks our shores — for the poor man, that wealth shall oppress."[40] Privately, he put his feelings about slavery, black people, and slaveholders themselves in disturbingly psychosexual terms. "By God, sir," he told an associate, "men born and nursed by white women are not going to be ruled by men who were brought up on the milk of some damn Negro wench!"[41] For Wilmot, slavery was an insidious corruption that threatened both racial purity and democratic equality.

A Pivotal Term in Congress: 1846–1848

As he took the oath of office as a member of the 29th Congress, Representative Wilmot planned to be a loyal backer of the Polk administration and its southern supporters. But from the beginning of his term his politics and his district's proximity to New York placed him squarely within the wing of the Democratic Party loyal to Martin Van Buren. Most Van Burenites believed strongly that the ex-president had been betrayed by southerners in both 1840 and 1844. As has been demonstrated elsewhere in this study, northern Democrats also felt slighted over the annexation of Texas and shut out of Polk's choicest patronage appointments, which went to southerners and their northern allies like Buchanan. Western Democrats such as John Wentworth of Chicago were similarly furious with the president over his veto of the rivers and harbors bill and "capitulation" on Oregon.[42] The loyal Wilmot began to feel stung as well. His attempt to secure the Towanda postmastership for a close friend was rebuked by the president, who named a Buchanan ally instead. "I am fully determined to give no rest to the President until he does in some manner recognize the strong claims of my district," he wrote in a July 1846 letter that included references to the "southern" tariff and the expansion of slavery, as well as patronage concerns.[43] Such "betrayals" by the Polk administration over Texas, slavery, and appointments confirmed the Van Burenites' fears that the Democratic Party had been hijacked by an aristocracy of slaveholders and their doughfaced northern allies.[44]

This volatile partisan environment circumscribed Polk's request, on the last day of the first session of the 29th Congress, for $2 million to facilitate peace negotiations with Mexico and buy California and New Mexico, setting the stage for Wilmot's famous proviso. Almost from the moment of the introduction of the proviso, the "true motives" of its originators have been sought. Southern slaveholders, of course, viewed the measure as a duplicitous slap and a naked assault on their property rights. Historians have zeroed in on explanations as diverse as the tariff, federal patronage, revenge, political self-preservation, and most recently, racism.[45] While each interpretation offers a partial explanation, they all elide the basic fact that Wilmot and his allies introduced the proviso because of anxiety and disquiet over slavery and its expansion. This concern, of course, was wholly compatible with views on race most modern Americans find reprehensible. Yet for a growing group of northern, hard-money Democrats, an aristocratic and expansive Slave Power had replaced the Money Power as the biggest threat facing the party, the Union, and the republic. "We know something of the curse of slavery," said New York representative and Wilmot ally Bradford Wood. "[The question] is whether in the government of the country [the North] shall be borne down by the influence of your slaveholding aristocratic institution that have not in them the first element of Democracy."[46] Wood's New York colleague George Rathbun kept the focus on the question of the territories, where many proviso supporters hoped to make a stand against slavery's expansion. "They want it [the new territory] for slaves, because where slavery exists the slave power prevails," he told the other members of Congress.[47] For his part, Wilmot linked his concept of the

David Wilmot and the Proviso

proviso to the movement for land reform. "We take our stand upon the outposts of Freedom," he told one audience, "prepared to resist, and I trust, to resist to the death, the encroachments of unlawful and aggressive slavery. . . . May we not preserve the Free Soil of the country for the homes of freemen and their posterity?"[48]

Wilmot and his eight coconspirators, all but one of whom would soon leave the Democratic Party to become Free Soilers or Republicans, were taking the first steps to reflect the beliefs of their constituents, many of whom had long since grown tired of compromises with the South and slavery.[49] For example, Pennsylvania-born farmer and lawyer Sydney George Fisher employed feudal language to express his antislavery: "[Slaveholders] are essentially an aristocracy," he wrote in his diary, "a collection of landed proprietors surrounded by serfs, their property in slaves represented [as] the only sort of property that gives political power, and they are a small minority in population of the whole country. . . . On every democratic principle, therefore, the North should govern."[50] Throughout 1846–47, one can see dissident Democratic congressmen straining not only to reflect their (white) districts but to expand their antislavery constituency. One of the most common methods they employed was to demonstrate how the institution degraded Pennsylvanians and New Yorkers as much as Mississippians and Arkansans. In this light we can add meaning beyond mere racism to Wilmot's famous phrase "white man's proviso" and to his claim that the legislation "does not propose the abolition of slavery, either in States or in Territories, now or hereafter." The proviso's sole object and end, he said, was "to protect Free Soil from the unlawful and violent aggressions of slavery."[51]

In common with Lincoln, Wilmot never intended restriction to be the end of the movement against slavery. Wilmot repeatedly predicted that "slavery has within itself the seeds of its own dissolution. Keep it within given limits, let it remain where it now is, and in time it will wear itself out." Since slavery's existence could only be perpetuated by expansion, and because slave crops tended to exhaust the soil, Wilmot reasoned, "the planter . . . must abandon his worn-out land for new and virgin soil, or release his slaves."[52] Thus while Wilmot and his allies had the people of their remote, rural districts in mind when offering the proviso, they also expected the move to be the first, significant step toward eradicating slavery. Wilmot made this point unequivocally: limiting slavery would undoubtedly benefit white people, but it would also hasten emancipation.[53] In this particular belief Wilmot was essentially correct: the proviso *did* become a rallying point behind which thousands of northern voters—Democrats and Whigs—made their initial stand against an expansive slave South, and thus the antislavery constituency was vastly increased.

It would not be an exaggeration to say that on that day in August 1846 the supporters of the Wilmot Proviso commenced a new, congressional phase of the movement to halt slavery—a movement based not on moral suasion but on finding a *political* end to human bondage. This does not mean that Free Soil Democrats such as Wilmot possessed concrete plans for how slavery's ultimate end would occur, or what the freedpeople's place in a postemancipation American society would be. Yet the conspirators were carrying on the work of Whig antislavery congressmen John Quincy Adams (who led the fight to stop the gag rule, which Wilmot and most of his allies supported) and Joshua Giddings.[54] They also brought the issue of territorial expansion into direct conflict with the interests of slaveholders. This was the issue that brought northern white voters en masse into the antislavery movement. Wilmot and his proviso kept slavery at the center of American politics until the Civil War decided the fate of the peculiar institution.

In the immediate aftermath of the proviso's introduction, Wilmot and his allies were shocked to have provoked so little debate on the matter in the House. Perhaps this was due to the proviso's familiar language or to the fact that the measure's opponents viewed it less as a significant threat to their interests than as a political maneuver.[55] Even more surprising was the lack of attention the proviso provoked during the 1846 campaign. Northern newspapers mostly ignored it, instead focusing on the tariff and the war with Mexico. Because of his tariff vote (Pennsylvania was known as a protectionist state), Wilmot was particularly vulnerable. The incumbent was no longer a political novice, however, and he refused to apologize for his vote: "I stood by the rights and interests of the mass," he told fellow Pennsylvanians in September, "against the claims of the privileged few, by the cause of labor against the sordid aims of capital." The strategy worked in the 12th District, where small farmers and loggers knew that it was downstate industry that would benefit from higher tariffs. Wilmot won by a whisker, in an election where protectionist Whigs swept most of the state offices.[56]

When the 29th Congress returned for its second session in December 1846, Wilmot did not immediately reintroduce the proviso. President Polk summoned him to the White House and apparently convinced Wilmot that he did not intend to extend slavery and that the proviso belonged not in the appropriations bill but should manifest as a joint resolution.[57] Other antislavery Democrats, however, were dubious of Polk's insistence that slavery "has nothing to do" with the Mexican War.[58] Wilmot's Jacksonian ally Preston King stepped into the breach and reintroduced the proviso as an amendment to the president's appropriations bill (now a $3 million bill) in January 1847.

King's updated proviso stated that "there shall be neither slavery nor involuntary servitude in any territory on the continent of America which shall be hereafter acquired by, or annexed to, the United States." Thus there were significant differences between the proviso's August 1846 and January 1847 incarnations. Wilmot's 1846 measure would have prohibited the president from using the particular funds appropriated in the $2 Million Bill to acquire any Mexican territory where slavery would be permitted; King's version replaced this narrow language with a flat declaration that slavery would never exist in future territories, with no limit on time, space, or funds. From this point forward, the proviso asserted that Congress could (and likely would) act to halt the expansion of slavery on the continent.[59]

Wilmot rejoined the fray in February when he forcefully stood up for the proviso on the floor of the House. Distancing himself once again from the familiar charge of abolitionism, Wilmot claimed the proviso asked only for "the neutrality of this Government on the question of slavery. . . . Is there any complexion of Abolitionism in this, sir? I have stood up at home, and battled time and again against the Abolitionists of the North." Wilmot reiterated how northern Democrats had overwhelmingly supported Texas's annexation with slavery. "Shall further concessions be made by the North? Shall we give up free territory, the inheritance of free labor? . . . I ask not that slavery be abolished. I demand that the Government preserve the integrity of *free territory* against the aggressions of slavery — against its wrongful usurpations."[60]

This was the first extended explication of Wilmot's antislavery beliefs, which were shared by many of his fellow northern representatives and their constituents but sharply distinct from the perfectionist abolitionist movement. For these emerging Free Soilers, southern planters and their industrial allies — like the Money Power in the 1830s — had forced their views on the plain republicans of the North. "Sir," Wilmot pleaded, "there is no more to give up. . . . We have passed beyond the boundaries of slavery and reached free-soil. Who is willing to surrender it?" Speaking directly to his fellow free-state representatives, he asserted that "the laborer of the North claims your service; he demands that you stand firm to his interests and his rights; that you preserve the future homes of his children, on the distant shores of the Pacific, from the degradation and dishonor of negro servitude."[61] For emphasis, Wilmot repeated that he had "no squeamish sensitiveness upon the subject of slavery, nor morbid sympathy for the slave." The cause he pleaded was, in sharp contrast to that of congressional abolitionists such as Joshua Giddings, that of white northern workers and farmers. "I would preserve for free white labor a fair country, a rich inheritance, where the sons of toil, of my own race and own color, can live without disgrace," he said. "I stand for the inviolability of free territory; it shall remain free, so far as my voice or vote can aid in the preservation of its character."[62]

These statements make abundantly clear the fact that Wilmot was no racial egalitarian. For him, and for an overwhelming majority of his fellow northerners, white supremacy was both truth and fact. Wilmot's speech crystallizes in a few phrases the potent fusion of antislavery with racism that would so inspire the northern electorate — and inflame the slaveholders who controlled the South. In sharp contrast with August 1846, the proviso was a formidable threat. Still, none of his statements suggest that Wilmot condoned slavery in the South or wished for African Americans' perpetual (or even continued) enslavement. He decried abolitionists' calls for an immediate, even violent end to the slave system, but for Wilmot and an increasing number of northern commentators and voters, the slave system contained within it an entropy that might be exploited to bring about its demise. This assumption rested on the widespread belief that slavery needed to expand in order to thrive.

In every speech and letter Wilmot composed on the subject, he included a variation on the observation that slavery destroys not only its laborers but the land itself: "crop follows crop," he said, in Congress, "until the fertility of the soil is exhausted, [and] when the old fields are abandoned, new and virgin soil sought out, to be exhausted in the same manner and likewise abandoned . . . sterility follows its path."[63] Once the slave system was contained, however, Wilmot believed its days would be numbered. "Slavery has within itself the seeds of its own dissolution," he told a gathering of antislavery Democrats in 1847. "Keep it within given limits, let it remain where it now is, and in time it will wear itself out." Congressional restrictions, Wilmot reasoned, "if permitted to exert their legitimate influence, and not retarded in their operation by an extension of slave territory, will, *at no distant day*, put an end to slavery and its concomitant evils."[64] The application of the Wilmot Proviso to all territories on the continent where slavery had yet to exist would be a powerful first step toward its eradication. Borrowing a phrase from the politics of the twentieth century, Wilmot's proposed

Free Soil policy could properly be termed containment of slavery and the Slave Power. The House voted 115-106 to pass a bill that included the retooled proviso on February 15.[65]

Southern leaders could no longer sit idly by and hope support for the proviso would fizzle. Four days after the proviso passed the House for the second time, South Carolina senator John C. Calhoun introduced a series of competing "southern rights" resolutions on slavery in the territories meant to counteract the emerging Free Soil position. Congress, Calhoun said, "has no right to make any law, or do any act whatever," that would deprive a state of "its full and equal right in any territory of the United States, acquired or to be acquired." In addition, any law that would "deprive citizens of any of the States from emigrating, with their property, into any of the territories" would violate the Constitution and be "in derogation of that perfect equality which belongs to them as members of this Union."[66] The fundamental disagreement between Democrats Wilmot and Calhoun came down to whether territories were owned in common by the states—and therefore citizens of states could bring their property into them without restriction—or whether Congress had authority to determine the status of a territory, just as it did over the District of Columbia. Were the proviso allowed to become law, Calhoun told the Senate, the North would gain perpetual power over the South and prompt "political revolution, anarchy, civil war, and widespread disaster." The Senate approved Polk's $3 Million Bill with no mention of the proviso.[67]

Wilmot and his allies were faced with a daunting task. The Senate's version of the bill arrived in the House on the last day of the session. If it passed without amendment, Polk would have his funds and a free hand to set policy in the territories. Antislavery members again tried to add the proviso to the bill, but the administration's tireless lobbying paid off: six northern Democrats switched their votes, and six more did not show up to vote. Twenty-two northern Democrats voted with the South on March 3, 1847, but not one of them was part of Martin Van Buren's (or Wilmot's) wing of the party. As Leonard Richards points out in his most recent book, all but four of the turncoats were lame-duck congressmen serving out the final day of their terms; two had been defeated the previous fall by Free Soil candidates; and of the three New York congressmen, only one had even attempted to regain his party's nomination. William Woodworth, who had made a fortune from Cuban slaves, was defeated for renomination in 1846.[68] Polk got his money, but at a huge cost; the Free Soil revolt was in full swing.

With Congress adjourned and the 1848 presidential contest begun in earnest, Wilmot became a political star of the first order. While the original proviso had received little coverage in 1846, newspapers nationwide helped make it, in Calhoun's words, an "apple of discord" in 1847. Northern Democrats founded Wilmot Proviso Leagues, and Wilmot's name was "mentioned more frequently than the candidates for the Presidency," according to one partisan.[69] Wilmot proudly announced in his hometown paper that legislatures in every free state but two passed resolutions in favor of the proviso.[70] The South was similarly aroused, but in opposition to the measure. "The democratic party of Georgia will give support to no candidate for the Presidency of the United States who does not unconditionally, clearly and unequivocally, declare his opposition to the principles and provisions of the Wilmot Proviso," declared the state's convention in July 1847.[71]

For his part, Wilmot used his newfound celebrity to aid the schismatic Barnburner faction in neighboring New York state, powwowing with leaders like John Van Buren and Preston King about the rift in the state party. When the Barnburners gathered in Herkimer to formally declare their independence in October 1847, Wilmot delivered his most rousing speech to date in defense of his "namesake." "We stand on the defensive. . . . Shall the government of this Republic, by the extension of the Missouri Compromise into free territory, give legal existence to slavery? Shall it exert its power to overthrow the existing fundamental law of freedom, that now binds the soil, and establish and legalize slavery in its stead? . . . May we not preserve the Free Soil of the country for the homes of freemen and their posterity? These are the questions, and the only questions, involved in the Proviso."[72] Wilmot maintained that the South's "arrogant and insolent demand" for more slave territory was issued "in a tone of threatening defiance," with the assumption that the people of the North would yield to it. "Are we so tame, so servile, so degenerate, that we cannot maintain the rights of a Free Soil, and a free people? Where is the spirit of our fathers? Are we slaves, that knowing our rights, we *dare not* maintain them? I hold Free Soil as sacred as free men, and, so help me God!"[73]

Having begun with an attack on the "one idea" Slave Power, Wilmot then turned to those who "bring odium" upon Free Soil by seeing it as a movement "designed especially for the benefit of the black race." He conceded that emancipation would come sooner if the proviso was enacted, but he insisted that was not its primary purpose. Again combining white supremacy with antislavery into a potent political mixture, Wilmot (referring for the first time to the "white man's Proviso") asked

David Wilmot and the Proviso

whether that vast country, between the Rio Grande and the Pacific, shall be given up to the servile labor of the black, or be preserved for the free labor of the white man. . . . Let us stop this mad career of human slavery. The negro race already occupy enough of this fair continent; let us keep what remains for ourselves, and our children — for the poor man, that wealth shall oppress — for the free white laborer, who shall desire to hew him out a home of happiness and peace, on the distant shores of the mighty Pacific. Free laborers of the North! Down trodden free white men of the South! This is your cause, and the cause of your children![74]

Wilmot left the lectern to thunderous applause, a champion of a powerful new movement. In one speech, Wilmot characterized the essence and popularity of Free Soil. Following Ohio pioneer Thomas Morris, he adapted language from the bank war of the 1830s, with the " 'one-idea' slave power" substituting for the "monster bank."[75] Wilmot and the rest of the Democrats at Herkimer had hit upon a popular way to harness widespread northern resentment against the South and attack slavery without "succumbing" to abolitionism.

A Proviso Democrat: The 1848 Campaign

Although he certainly could have done so, David Wilmot did not continue to take his fame and celebrity on the road in an attempt to build on his national reputation. Instead, he remained in Washington for the duration of the 30th Congress, which met from December 1847 until August 1848. Wilmot did make brief trips outside the capital, to the state party convention in Harrisburg where James Buchanan torpedoed a resolution endorsing the proviso, for example, and to return home after the sudden death of his twelve-year-old son. But Wilmot spent most of his time in the House, attempting to persuade his fellow members to keep slavery out of the territories. In the opening months of the 30th Congress, Wilmot temporarily abandoned his strategy of attaching amendments to revenue bills and introduced a tax designed to bleed both capitalists and slaveholders. Ostensibly a direct tax on capital property to help finance the war in Mexico, Wilmot's scheme attracted the special ire of slaveholders, who saw this "Wilmot Proviso No. 2" as an attempt to tax "heavily the slaves of the South." Responding to attacks by slaveholders, Wilmot feigned surprise: "I do not know why a few thousand capitalists of the South, who hold a certain species of property,

𝕲o it, ye 𝕮ripples! 𝕽a~a~up!

WILMOT, THE WIZARD.

FIGURE 6

"Wilmot, the Wizard" (1848). Embellishing a satirical poem in the short-lived, proslavery humor magazine The John-Donkey, *this illustration of the portly Wilmot astride a flying beast was played for laughs. The drawing represents the height of the Free Soil threat in American politics, when Wilmot's "monster" proviso possessed the capacity to "swallow the South at a gulp."*

should be exempt from taxation," he said. "My object was to call upon capital generally . . . wherever found, to bear its just proportion of the burdens of the government."[76]

Although he fully supported the breakaway Barnburner movement in New York and the campaign for Free Soil, Wilmot opted to remain a "Proviso Democrat" during the 1848 campaign. In Pennsylvania, he admitted to Salmon P. Chase, "little interest is taken in the question of slavery extension, out of my own district." He believed that Pennsylvanians had been deceived by his nemesis James Buchanan, Polk's secretary of state, who used his control of the state's press and patronage networks to keep the state's newspapers silent or in opposition to the proviso movement. With the papers fully in Buchanan's control, Wilmot told Chase that a third party movement in his home state would have to depend mainly on Whigs for support, depriving the Free Soil movement of its popular edge.[77]

As the Free Soil Party prepared to meet in Buffalo in August 1848 to nominate Wilmot's hero Martin Van Buren for president, Wilmot chose to remain in the House to fight, once again, a legislative battle over slavery extension. Southern senators from both parties had passed a complex territorial bill that included the so-called Clayton Compromise, which provided for a territorial government for Oregon without slavery but left the status of California and New Mexico up to the courts. Wilmot led the forces in the lower chamber that defeated the compromise (which, ironically, if passed might have aided Van Buren's campaign by pulling votes away from the surging Whigs) by successfully adding language to the bill extending the provisions of Jefferson's 1787 Northwest Ordinance to the western territories.

The day after the bill passed in the House on its way back to the Senate, Wilmot delivered a speech on the floor he may have originally intended for the Free Soil convention in Buffalo, outlining in clear language his arguments for the legality—and necessity—of slavery restriction. His first topic was the concept of popular sovereignty, a doctrine touted by Senator Lewis Cass, the presidential candidate of Wilmot's own party. Calling popular sovereignty, which would allow settlers in territories to decide for either freedom or slavery, a "novel and most extraordinary doctrine," Wilmot strongly asserted the responsibility of Congress to decide the fate of the future states, since "territories possess no inherent political sovereignty." Since the time of the Northwest Ordinance, he said, *Congress* had exercised "full and exclusive" sovereignty over the territories, ranging from decisions over the right of suffrage, distribution of public lands, and the manner of the selection of jurors. "Will any man tell me why it is, that we may regulate the questions of suffrage and eligibility to office in a territory, and not the question of slavery? Is slavery of higher regard than these? . . . Does slavery dictate its own laws, and define its own limits? Is there no power to stop its progress—to stay its advances—to arrest the curse and desolation of its march?"[78]

Wilmot's next target was his own party, especially northerners such as Cass and Buchanan who aspired to the presidency. "A northern democratic statesman, however exalted . . . must qualify himself as a candidate for the Presidency by written pledges to the South—must purge himself of the taint and leprosy of freedom, and receive the stamp that marks him as the genuine candidate of the slave power." The mission of the Democratic Party, he insisted, could never be to "take upon its broad shoulders the institution of slavery, and carry it over upon lands now free." "The gallant and true men who fought the battle of popular rights against privilege and monopoly— who aided in crushing the monster bank, and wresting from the grasp of eastern capital the hard earnings of labor, will never fight the battles of slavery propagandism." Again investing the rhetoric of antislavery with an older brand derived from the pen of William Leggett, Wilmot insisted that since southern capital had "a thousand millions of dollars invested in slaves," the current struggle, like the bank war in the 1830s, was best viewed as one between "capital and labor."[79]

Finally, Wilmot refined his democratic critique of the institution developed in 1846–47 still further, clearly reaching back to an older, republican ideal of yeoman independence. When confronted with slavery, he said, in a passage that was clearly autobiographical, an ordinary white man "feel[s] a sense of humiliation when he looks up to the vast distances between himself and the lordly planter, in the shadow of whose aristocratic possessions he lives as an inferior, if not a dependent." Living in the midst of a social system made up of "lords and vassals," he said, one can only rarely hope to rise to the condition of the former, meaning he must inevitably "sink to a level with the latter."[80] Not only, then, was slavery restriction essential for the continued independence of ordinary white citizens—Wilmot claimed it was essential for the survival of freedom as well, in all of the Americas. "Our northern boundary," he asserted, "never moves except to recede. . . . Extend slavery to the Pacific, and it forthwith takes up its march to the South . . . from [Mexico's] northern boundary to the Isthmus of Panama. . . . Slavery will riot in the extent of its possessions and power; and then will grow up at the south the mightiest oligarchy that the world ever saw."[81]

Once again Wilmot was attempting to fashion a political coalition based on a new brand of legislative antislavery in the House of Representatives. By linking slaveholders with capitalists he hoped to demonstrate that slavery degraded whites as well as blacks, Pennsylvanians as well as Kentuckians. With the Free Soil convention gaining attention in the background, the U.S. Senate quietly accepted Wilmot's version of the territorial bill on August 13. The session over, Wilmot returned to his district, to campaign for Van Buren and his own reelection — but as a Proviso Democrat, not a member of the Free Soil Party.

Filling some of the gaps in Wilmot's political biography clearly helps to delineate the early story of Free Soil in both the remote East and the U.S. Congress. Beyond Wilmot's racism — a point where much recent historical analysis has ceased — lay the seeds of the third party system and the irrevocable conflicts of the Civil War era.

CHAPTER SIX

↑

The Cincinnati Clique,
True Democracy, and the Ohio Origins
of the Free Soil Party

While Jacksonian antislavery sprouted and thrived in such remote areas of the Northeast as the Catskills and eastern New Hampshire, a handful of political abolitionists in southwestern Ohio marshaled the various local realignments into a national Free Soil movement in the late 1840s. This group of political abolitionists, which included Jacksonian antislavery pioneer (and ex-Democratic senator) Thomas Morris, abolitionist editor Gamaliel Bailey, and future secretary of the treasury Salmon P. Chase, was instrumental in recognizing and exploiting the political appeal of Jacksonian antislavery. More than any other members of the developing northern coalition, these Ohioans arranged and then officiated at the marriage between Jacksonian egalitarianism and antislavery that produced the Free Soil Party.

Among the leaders of this "Ohio movement" only Morris was a bona fide radical Jacksonian in the 1830s. Both Bailey and Chase came out of political traditions that were distinctly anti-Democratic. But as numerous historians have pointed out (often with a hint of puzzlement), political abolitionists like Bailey and Chase wholeheartedly embraced Democratic issues and ideology and became more committed to these positions as their involvement in the antislavery struggle increased. By the mid-1840s each was — on issues other than slavery — a devout hard-money Democrat. Some scholars have linked this tendency toward Jacksonianism to a unique Ohio or western strain of abolitionism. Others have simply noted the trajectory without offering an interpretation.[1]

There may in fact be no single explanation; still, this trend's importance in antebellum politics merits a good-faith attempt. One rationale is intellectual. At the foundation of the Jacksonian antislavery arguments formulated by Morris and Leggett lay deep-seated notions of democratic egalitarianism.

Both of these early heretics came to the antislavery point of view via careers built on attacking "aristocratic inequalities," whether grounded in unequal access to capital, unfair privileges granted by governments, the existence of monopolies, or the high price of postage. Thomas Morris provided a powerful personal and political link between Jacksonian antislavery ideas and the Cincinnatians' attempts to broaden their movement. Amid their endeavor to expand the antislavery movement beyond the small cadre of Yankee-born, Whiggish, and reform-minded abolitionists (concentrated on the Western Reserve), Thomas Morris and his Democratic supporters in southern Ohio provided the most available pool of new votes. As they reached out to potential supporters outside their own political traditions, Bailey, Chase, and their allies began to see that issues such as slavery expansion and hard money, to cite one example, were linked.

Bailey was perhaps the strongest Liberty Party advocate of cooperation with the major parties, and he repeatedly underscored this point in the *Philanthropist.* "God help the poor slave, if he is doomed to wait for his freedom, till the Liberty party has literally become the majority party of the country," Bailey wrote.[2] The Cincinnatians, as third party partisans, were used to clashing with the antislavery Whigs of the Western Reserve on this point. The Whigs of northern Ohio were convinced that their party was the best instrument for antislavery political action; as a result, most antislavery sympathizers in that region voted Whig. Things were far different, however, in the southern part of the state.

Southern Ohio, like Kentucky, was populated by resettled Pennsylvanians, Virginians, and Carolinians — a far cry from the Yankee evangelicals on the Western Reserve. Adding to this distinctly nonevangelical mix were the thousands of German and Irish immigrants who arrived in Cincinnati, the West's largest city, every year.[3] As small-scale farmers, artisans, and immigrants, many of the residents of southern Ohio, old and new, supported the political principles of the Democratic Party. Although large numbers of them held viciously antiblack views, many had consciously chosen to live in an area where slavery was legally banned. There was little love for the *institution* of slavery in southern Ohio. It was to these nominal Democrats, then, that coalition-minded antislavery partisans such as Bailey naturally turned in the 1840s.

Chase's own position on coalition quickly evolved in Bailey's direction. Within two years of abandoning the Whig Party, he insisted that the principles of the Democratic Party were in "exact harmony with the principles of Liberty men." From here it was but a small step toward urging a union with the "True Democracy"—Chase's name for a Jackson party purged of its proslavery elements.[4]

Drawing upon Jacksonian antislavery arguments and tirelessly working for a union with like-minded northerners—often to the chagrin of their fellow political abolitionists—southern Ohio's Liberty leaders paved the way for the national Free Soil movement. The story of how this clique, located on the physical border between slavery and freedom, fashioned this national coalition begins with the defeated Thomas Morris's return to Ohio.

Morris's Return

Thomas Morris's Senate term expired on March 4, 1839. Written out of the Ohio Democratic Party the previous year for his abolitionist views, Morris returned home with little hope of a future in politics. But the ex-senator had become something of a hero to Ohio's small yet growing number of political abolitionists, especially in the Democratic southwestern corner of the state. One of Cincinnati's more literate antislavery partisans lamented Morris's forced retirement in verse:

> The heart and lip are dumb!
>   And the Southern taunt is tamely met
> Our kneeling day is come!
>   Freedom's bright Star hath set!
> The recreant West hath kneeled
>   To the footstool of the South;
> And the voice of her own free son is sealed,
>   The gag is in *her* mouth.[5]

Morris's ouster robbed the Senate of its most stalwart antislavery voice. But his return to Ohio had a lasting and powerful impact on antislavery politics in the Old Northwest and the nation. His potent blend of Jacksonian and antislavery politics was not lost on Gamaliel Bailey, the editor of Ohio's first abolitionist newspaper, the *Philanthropist*, who was then searching for ways to strengthen his movement's meager appeal. Together Morris and Bailey helped originate a western brand of antislavery politics, dedicated to attracting a wider variety of adherents by cooperating with the established parties. Morris, Bailey, and other converts to this western style of abolitionist politics (most notably Salmon P. Chase) gradually overwhelmed the Liberty Party's more immediatist eastern wing. Then, sensing that the various political crises of the 1840s had opened a window of opportunity for a broader antislavery union, the Ohio Liberty leaders brought about their long-planned union between antislavery and Jacksonian politics. It was under the wing of what Bailey and Chase called "True Democracy" that the Jacksonian antislavery of William Leggett, George Henry Evans, and Thomas Morris connected with the sectional politics that were convulsing the northern states.

Just days after his retirement, Thomas Morris spoke at a public meeting in Cincinnati to defend his course in the Senate and denounce the state's new fugitive slave law, passed at the urging of two "ambassadors" from the Kentucky legislature. The speech was a resounding success. Enthusiastic former constituents filled the courthouse to hear Morris insist that "Ohio, under the Federal Constitution, was not bound to deliver up runaway slaves."[6] Gamaliel Bailey exhaustively covered the meeting and printed Morris's speech in the *Philanthropist*, even though "a majority of the Abolitionists in the city knew nothing of the meeting till it was over." What elicited Bailey's interest was not the substance of Morris's comments — attacks on the Servile Bill and speeches vindicating abolitionists were common fare in the *Philanthropist*'s columns. What was different about this courthouse meeting was its audience. "Be it remembered," Bailey wrote, "Abolitionists were but a small portion of the meeting. The great applause came chiefly from citizens uncommitted to Abolition — most of them Democrats."[7]

Morris's ability to appeal directly to antislavery Democrats was exactly what Bailey was looking for. In fact, Bailey had been searching for ways to broaden the appeal of political abolitionism since 1837 — a time when most abolitionists insisted that *any* involvement in politics would diminish the movement's moral appeal.[8]

Gamaliel Bailey and Political Abolitionism

Gamaliel Bailey came to the abolitionist movement in Ohio from a background strikingly different from that of former slaveholder James Birney, Yankee Joshua Giddings, or evangelical Theodore Weld. Bailey had grown up in southern New Jersey, a world away from New England and its swath of western migration. Unlike most other abolitionist leaders, who came from Congregationalist, Quaker, Unitarian, or Baptist backgrounds, Bailey was raised a Methodist. In the lower North, Bailey's Methodist Protestant church (headquartered in Baltimore) had strong southern ties.

As had his father, Bailey trained as a physician. He worked as ship's surgeon aboard a China trader in 1830, but life at sea did not agree with the young doctor. Much of Bailey's time onboard was spent tending to the ship's numerous cholera victims. The epidemic that raged through Canton and dotted the harbor with floating bodies filled Bailey with horror. It also precipitated a religious conversion. He returned home in the summer of 1830 committed to act on his newfound faith.

Bailey gladly traded saw and scalpel for the journalist's pen in 1831. A schism within the Methodist Episcopal Church led to the founding of the *Methodist Protestant* in Baltimore, and Bailey jumped at the chance to combine religious and literary pursuits. The new Methodist Protestant Church was founded by Methodist Episcopal dissenters (mostly laymen and itinerant preachers such as Bailey's father) who wanted representation in the church's annual and general conferences. The new church removed all distinctions between itinerant and local preachers, gave equal representation to lay members, and abolished all hierarchical offices.[9]

Bailey quickly rose to become the editor of the *Methodist Protestant*. Although church policy kept him from discussing domestic politics, Bailey articulated the new church's democratic principles and extended them to advocate egalitarianism, European liberalism, and Christian benevolence. In one article reflecting on a host of European reform movements, Bailey illustrated his belief that Christianity formed the basis of democratic progress. "The despotism of kings and the tyranny of Satan," Bailey wrote, "are alike sinking beneath the predominating influence of political freedom and the genius of christianity. . . . [The people] are learning . . . to assert the infallible principle of the equality of man." He shunned alcohol and chastised those who were intemperate. More important, his Methodism and his exposure to slavery in Baltimore made him a strong proponent of the Colonization movement.[10]

Bailey's conversion to immediate abolitionism came in 1834, after he had left the *Methodist Protestant* to join his family in Cincinnati. Soon after arriving in Ohio, where he once again hoped to build a medical practice, Bailey began to lecture on physiology at Lane Theological Seminary. There he participated in the famous Lane Debate orchestrated by abolitionist Theodore Weld, weighing the merits of Colonization and immediatism in the battle against slavery. Weld's revivalist techniques worked wonders on Bailey and the other participants, who concluded the debate with a near-unanimous endorsement of immediate abolition. The next year, Bailey helped found the immediatist Cincinnati Antislavery Society.[11]

Close affiliation with abolitionists in a city only a river's width from a slave state hindered Bailey's fledgling medical career. He therefore struggled to combine his antislavery sentiments with his literary expertise. An opportunity presented itself in early 1836 when former Kentucky slaveholder James Birney moved his paper, the *New Richmond Philanthropist,* to Cincinnati as the organ of the local antislavery society. Birney was more of an agitator than an editor, however, and by September Bailey was almost entirely responsible for the paper.[12]

Bailey was in a unique position among abolitionists in the late 1830s. Far from the eastern controversies engulfing the followers of William Lloyd Garrison and the Tappans (which led to the breakup of the American Antislavery Society), he was free to develop a third course of political action.[13] In the *Philanthropist* and in meetings of the Ohio Antislavery Society (of which he was secretary), Bailey made Thomas Morris's concept of a Slave Power conspiracy the political centerpiece. He also championed an interpretation of the U.S. Constitution that fell somewhere between Garrison's condemnation of it as a pact with Satan and Alvan Stewart's assertion that it was an antislavery document. To Bailey, the Constitution supported slavery in several instances but clearly defined it as a *local* institution that depended for its existence on state law. Thus, Congress had the means to limit and retard its development.[14] Also inherent in Bailey's developing view of political antislavery was the belief that slavery threatened northern whites as well as southern blacks. The idea was to steer clear of divisive infighting and attract the widest possible number of abolitionists to the cause. It was a technique that would prove valuable in the 1840s.[15]

Bailey began his abolitionist career opposed to organized political action, but he was swimming against a strong current. After 1836, abolitionists throughout the North were moving toward forming a political organization. Bailey, however, was convinced that an independent antislavery party would expose the movement as impotent and tiny. "We are utterly opposed to every measure that looks toward a separate political organization," Bailey wrote in the spring of 1838. "The cause of antislavery belongs to all parties and sects. . . . All that can safely be done in a political way is to be done by questioning candidates."[16]

During the election of 1837 Bailey had urged the readers of the *Philanthropist* not to vote at all, since none of the candidates had responded favorably to a questionnaire devised by the Ohio Antislavery Society. The election of 1838, however, was a different matter. Thomas Morris's Senate term was due to expire, and Bailey hoped a Democratic state legislature would return him to Washington. In addition, several Democratic candidates had suggested in questionnaires that they favored a repeal of the state's "black laws," which denied free blacks access to courts and schools and attempted to bar them from settling in Ohio. Since the Whigs would replace Morris with another (presumably less fervently antislavery) senator and had remained silent on the subject of the black laws, Bailey used the *Philanthropist* to aid the Jacksonians.[17]

Bailey exploited the issue of Whig governor Joseph Vance's arrest and extradition of abolitionist John B. Mahan to Kentucky (on a charge that he aided the escape of a slave) to smear the Whigs as trucklers to slaveholders. He printed extra copies of the *Philanthropist* and distributed them with leading Democratic papers to increase his usual readership. These tactics seemed to work: the Democrats swept the election. Vance, elected in 1837 with a 6,000-vote majority, was beaten the following year by more than 5,000, and the Jacksonians won control of both houses of the state legislature. Bailey (as well as most eastern abolitionists papers) gave full credit for the reversal to the antislavery vote. He advised Birney to "tell our friends in New York that Ohio Abolitionists know how to *vote*, if not give money. They have stuck to their text in a most logical style, and preached a sermon to politicians that will never be forgotten."[18]

Bailey's elation did not last long. First, Whig leaders from the Western Reserve accused the *Philanthropist* of shilling for the Democrats, and the paper lost significant Whig support. Then the Democratic legislature that Bailey helped to elect dropped Morris and strengthened the odious black laws by passing a stronger fugitive slave bill at the request of the Kentucky legislature. Furious with the Democrats' betrayal, Bailey began to rethink the arguments for a strong, inclusive independent party to oppose the Slave Power.[19]

In 1839 the American Antislavery Society met in Albany, New York, and passed a resolution calling for separate political action.[20] The resolution struck Bailey as ridiculous. It prohibited abolitionists from voting for any presidential candidate unless he declared himself in favor of the immediate abolition of slavery, an act Bailey believed was entirely beyond the office's Constitutional powers. Instead of relying on this "absurd" test, Bailey claimed he felt comfortable voting for any presidential or congressional candidate in favor of immediate abolition in the District of Columbia or opposed to the gag rule in Congress. Bailey was already at odds with the political abolitionists in the East.[21]

This conflict only worsened after the national Liberty Party convention formally nominated Bailey's old partner James G. Birney for president. Bailey grudgingly placed Birney's name above the *Philanthropist*'s masthead while continuing to argue that no political party founded solely on opposition to slavery could ever succeed electorally.[22] As an alternative, Bailey stuck with his proposal for the "gradual formation of a *political party*, the distinctive feature of which shall be, *Liberalism* in opposition to *Servile-ism*. Its doctrines will be those of our Declaration of Independence."[23]

Bailey's vision for this "liberal" party came further into focus at a statewide abolitionist meeting at Hamilton (just north of Cincinnati) in September 1840. From the convention's resolutions committee, Bailey and Morris endorsed a ticket of Birney electors while simultaneously blocking all attempts to commit the party to congressional and legislative races. Thus they urged at least tacit cooperation with other parties. Adding to this strategy, Bailey instructed abolitionists to vote for antislavery candidates from the major parties "whenever possible."[24]

After Birney's miserable showing in the presidential election of 1840 — he won fewer than 7,000 votes nationwide — Bailey guided the Ohio Liberty Party toward a path different from that of its eastern counterparts.[25] He realized that any future success depended on luring support from the thousands of antislavery voters who had cast their ballots for Van Buren and Harrison in 1840. In 1840 and 1841 Bailey and Morris added two provisions to the state's political antislavery creed: a determination to support nonabolitionist candidates and an avowal not to act politically to abolish slavery in the South. Thus political abolitionism in Ohio had three distinct factions by 1841: Bailey and Morris's Liberty Party, a collection of political abolitionists committed to cooperation with antislavery Democrats and Whigs; antislavery Whigs concentrated in the Western Reserve; and abolitionists hoping for an organization resembling New York's and Massachusetts' Liberty organizations. These three versions of political antislavery would compete in the state throughout the 1840s.

Antislavery Unionism

Bailey and Morris's antislavery was profoundly influenced by the politics and society of southern Ohio and, specifically, Cincinnati. The West's most important city and a cultural crossroads between North, South, East, and West, Cincinnati was home to large populations of both pro- and antislavery voters. It was a world apart from the Yankee-settled Western Reserve in the northeastern part of the state, which was a center of antislavery Whiggery. As numerous studies have shown, the men and women who settled in the lower Northwest often held profoundly virulent antiblack views directed most forcefully against the area's large population of free blacks. They cared little more for white abolitionists.[26]

Within this political atmosphere Gamaliel Bailey resolved to build a broad-based antislavery party. He viewed the area's Scotch-Irish farmers, artisans, and laborers as the constituency for this new, "True Democratic" party. Numerous editorials in the *Philanthropist* were devoted to wooing this particular group of voters, nominal Democrats who increasingly disapproved of the party's subservience to the Slave Power.[27]

But Cincinnati's workers were, on the whole, not yet ready to join the antislavery movement. In fact, the depression of the early 1840s and an Ohio supreme court ruling which held that slaves brought into the state were automatically free, fanned *anti*abolitionist flames in Cincinnati. Fueled by proslavery rhetoric that the ruling would cost the city much of its lucrative trade with the South, mobs in 1841 attacked black businesses and homes, stormed the offices of the *Philanthropist*, and threw Bailey's presses into the Ohio River. Bailey, however, remained steadfast in his determination to remain active "under the very shadow of slavery" and was able quickly to raise the $850 needed to restart the paper.[28]

Bailey acquired a national reputation as a dauntless abolitionist as a result of the riot, and he used his newfound celebrity to reach a wider audience and broaden the appeal of the struggling Liberty Party. He also began to provide details about what he had meant when he spoke of a party based on "equal rights principles." It took shape as an antislavery party unmistakably Jacksonian in outlook.[29]

This was a bold strategy for a leader of a movement that, at the time, counted on former Whigs for the bulk of its votes. Yet Bailey's views on political economy and state's rights were strikingly Democratic. As did any good hard-money Jacksonian, Bailey opposed monopolies, banks, and protective tariffs he believed benefited only one class of society. Some of Bailey's Democratic views can be traced to his religious background. The schism within the Methodist Episcopal Church that caused Bailey's family to join the dissident Methodist Protestants was over the former's inequality among members and rigid hierarchy. From his days at the *Methodist Protestant* Bailey claimed that special privileges granted to one person or class fostered incurable divisions in society.[30] Morris undoubtedly had an effect on Bailey's antimonopolism as well. Monopolies were something of an obsession with Morris, and Bailey published many of his antimonopoly diatribes in the *Philanthropist*.[31]

Despite his Jacksonian leanings, Bailey began the 1840 campaign believing with northern Whigs that their party was more likely than the Democrats' to become an instrument for antislavery action. But he confided to Birney that same year that, although he opposed Van Buren's reelection, "I confess, I am more, far more of a *real* Democrat in my notions of public policy, than a Whig; if I *incline* then to favor somewhat Gen'l Harrison [the Whig candidate who had not yet refused to abolish slavery in the District of Columbia], it is in the face of my political partialities. . . . This is queer, is it not?"[32] Bailey knew that to reach beyond the small ranks of Liberty voters, the party had to appeal to Democrats, since antislavery Whigs tended to remain loyal to their party, which had sent antislavery lawyer Joshua Giddings to Congress from the Western Reserve in 1838. Remembering the large number of Cincinnati's artisans and mechanics who joined the Ohio Antislavery Society during the previous decade, Bailey took the *Philanthropist* on a decidedly prolabor tack in the early 1840s.

First, Bailey followed Thomas Morris's lead by explicitly linking slaveholders to the exploitative factory system, calling slavery "a monopoly in the bodies and souls of nearly three million laborers."[33] He repeatedly referred to slaveholders as capitalists and in 1844 defined slavery as a system that "degrades labor—which makes it a mere tool of capital—strips it of all political consequence."[34]

One radical correspondent, Eli Nichols of Loydsville, took up the arguments of George Henry Evans by urging abolitionists to aid northern workers in their struggle against capitalism. Bailey went far beyond defense of free labor in his attacks on the Slave Power; his paper was critical of the North's class inequalities as well.[35] Bailey's strategy did not win him the support of the eastern abolitionist establishment; Gerrit Smith went so far as to call "Ohio abolitionism" a "sham" for caring more for white laborers than for enslaved blacks. But the dialogue in the *Philanthropist* was more than a cynical attempt to win the support of white workers. As the decade wore on, Bailey stepped up his efforts to make the Liberty Party a True Democratic party, one that combined antislavery and Morris's concept of "equal rights and impartial justice."[36]

To accomplish this, Bailey had to convince Ohio's Democrats that it was in their interest to support an antislavery party. Thus, in editorials attacking the discriminatory black laws, Bailey argued that they unfairly punished whites as well as blacks by making it illegal to aid in the escape of a fugitive. Finally, he appealed to Democrats who sensed that the party violated its own core principles by espousing equal rights for whites and not blacks. Abolitionists, according to this reasoning, were the "true" Democrats, since they applied Jacksonian doctrine to "all mankind, irrespectively of sex, color, class or condition."[37]

Third Party Politics

After the 1840 election debacle the Cincinnati wing of the Ohio Liberty Party recognized the futility of nominating abolitionists such as Birney on single-issue platforms. They reacted with dismay to news that an 1841 Liberty convention in New York had renominated Birney for the 1844 election, even though the delegates also replaced Thomas Earle with Thomas Morris in the vice-presidential slot. Two new recruits to Bailey's group — anticapitalist educator Samuel Lewis and Salmon P. Chase, a onetime Whig lawyer who had often pleaded the cases of fugitive slaves — took the lead in a semisecret plan to replace the aristocratic Birney with a more electable candidate.[38] The names most often mentioned by Chase and Lewis in 1841 were New York's Whig governor William H. Seward and the venerable John Quincy Adams, neither of whom had ever joined the Liberty Party. Bailey quietly kept the Liberty nominees off the *Philanthropist*'s masthead and printed the occasional positive article about Seward.[39]

The next phase of Chase's plan was to call a national Liberty convention formally to replace Birney. Chase, Bailey, Morris, Lewis, and Leicester King helped orchestrate a call for the convention at a state meeting in Columbus in January 1843. Chase's increasingly public campaign to replace Birney angered many Liberty partisans, who still viewed him as a Johnny-come-lately bent on diluting the abolitionist movement. Compounding this distrust was the complete failure of Chase's scheme: Seward, Adams, and William Jay all flatly refused to be considered for the Liberty nomination.[40]

Meanwhile, Liberty success in Ohio had forced a showdown between third party men and the state's antislavery Whigs. After Birney's miserable showing in 1840 (he polled only 903 votes in Ohio), the Liberty Party received more than 5,500 votes for gubernatorial candidate Leicester King in 1842 and more than 6,500 in the 1843 state elections. Fearing that increased Liberty support would benefit the Democrats, Whig leaders intensified their efforts to weaken the third party.[41]

Bailey, now firmly committed to the idea of a third party (as opposed to mere cooperation with Whigs and Democrats), began to emphasize differences between the Liberty and Whig parties. This tactic, inevitably, led the *Philanthropist* to focus on the Whigs' links to eastern capital and the hated

Money Power. In 1843 Bailey, Chase, and Lewis supported and secured passage of resolutions endorsing specie currency, opposing protective tariffs, and demanding equal rights for immigrants—all decidedly anti-Whig proposals. Not surprisingly, Whig papers accused the Cincinnati clique of collusion with the Democrats; one labeled the *Philanthropist* "the most . . . entirely locofoco paper we ever saw, in the proposed garb of Christian morals." Bailey replied, "We should blush, if our radicalism did not go far beyond 'Loco Focoism.' It consists in the principle of 'equal and exact justice' to all men." The next step for Bailey, Chase, and the rest of the clique was to transform the Liberty Party into the nation's True Democratic party.[42]

Immediately after the 1844 election (where Birney's nationwide vote was an improved but still anemic 62,000), Birney's friends again brought his name forward as standard-bearer.[43] This time, however, the Cincinnati clique was ready. Not only had Birney proven himself an exceedingly poor candidate; his political views on issues other than slavery had veered toward the reactionary. Birney had always opposed the principles of Jacksonianism, but in 1844 he began to blame an "excess of democracy" for the nation's moral failings. To the dismay of many Liberty supporters, he openly attacked universal manhood suffrage in his letter accepting the presidential nomination in 1844 and continued to do so throughout the campaign.[44] Bailey's group had failed to unseat Birney before the 1844 election but stood ready to block his nomination for 1848. Bailey made it abundantly clear that "if by the action of certain cliques and influences, Mr. Birney be placed in such a relation to our cause . . . we should feel ourselves entirely free from all obligation to the party."[45]

Not all of Ohio's Liberty leaders welcomed Chase and Bailey's pronouncements. Birney's son William particularly resented the efforts to broaden the party's appeal (as well as the public disloyalty displayed toward his father). "[Chase, Lewis, and Bailey] belong to the temporising, bargain and sale class of politicians, and are frequently hazarding our cause by their recommendation of petty demagogical tricks to gain a largely increased and floating vote," the younger Birney wrote to his father. "Friday night, Mr. Chase had the wildness to propose a change of our party name from 'Liberty' to 'True Democrat.' . . . My private opinion is that Chase only awaits a favorable opportunity to go into the Loco ranks."[46]

This last claim was overstated, but Chase, Bailey, and Lewis did aim to manufacture a new True Democratic party if they could not convince other Liberty partisans to become one. In the spring of 1845 Chase drafted a call for the Southern and Western Convention of the Friends of Constitutional

Liberty. From the start, this was to be a broader gathering than the Liberty Party's usual base of support. Chase's call urged every southerner and northerner who believed that "Republicanism can be maintained, only, by eternal and uncompromising war against the . . . Slave Power" to assemble to use "all Constitutional and honorable means, to effect the extinction of Slavery in their respective States, and its reduction to its Constitutional limits in the United States."[47]

The convention's "Address," expertly written by Chase, further rankled antislavery Whigs and Liberty men. The original draft declared the mission of the Liberty Party "synonymous" with that of the True Democracy. More than a few Whigs and abolitionists viewed the draft as an attempt to form a coalition with the Democratic Party. Birney, who presided over the convention, referred the address to a committee that struck the offending passage, as well as another labeling the Liberty Party the "True Democracy of the United States." Still, the final address, delivered to 2,000 delegates from each midwestern state and territory as well as western Virginia, Pennsylvania, Kentucky, Rhode Island, New York, and Massachusetts, made Chase's sympathies clear: "Our reverence for Democratic principles is the precise measure of our detestation of those who are permitted to shape the action of the Democratic party. . . . That party only, which adopts in good faith the principles of the Declaration of Independence and directs its most decisive action against slavery, is the True Democratic party of the United States."[48]

Not content with an endorsement of (often unfulfilled) Democratic principles, Chase concluded with a partisan attack on Whiggery. Any concessions the Whigs gave to antislavery would be reluctantly conceded, he said. "Its natural position is conservative. . . . Its natural line of action is to maintain things as they are. Its natural bond of union is regard for interests rather than for rights."[49] Eastern abolitionists, as well as antislavery Whigs like Giddings and Seward, were infuriated by Chase's remarks. Western Reserve Liberty adherent Q. F. Atkins flatly accused Chase of ignoring his committee's explicit instructions to expunge offensive passages of "awful squinting" to Democrats, while Seward calmly explained that the Democratic Party "was . . . is, and must be, the slavery party," while the Whigs, as its permanent antagonist, "must be, always . . . an antislavery party *more or less.*"[50]

The convention ended with a call for a "union of all sincere friends of Liberty and Free Labor" upon the grounds of a divorce of the national government from slavery and a promise to use "all proper and constitutional modes to discourage and discontinue the system of work without wages."[51]

The events of 1845, however, pushed Chase and the Cincinnati clique even further toward the Democracy's Van Buren wing. Through Samuel Medary, Van Buren's Ohio mouthpiece, the coalitionists learned the extent of the New York Barnburners' antipathy for the Polk administration and its southern supporters. In 1844 Medary even attended the Ohio Liberty Convention, where, according to Chase's lieutenant G. W. Ellis, he treated the Cincinnati group with respect and voiced his contempt for Calhoun and his southern followers. "Look out for a revolution next year in the Democratic ranks," Ellis alerted Chase, "they must abandon the south or loose [sic] the north."[52]

Chase tried to reach out to Ohio's Van Buren Democrats, but most of them were fearful of too close an alliance with abolitionists.[53] Just as Chase was beginning to feel discouraged, however, John P. Hale announced his opposition to annexation and touched off New Hampshire's antislavery revolution.[54] Always plotting to expand Liberty's appeal, Chase watched the emergence of the New Hampshire Independent Democrats with glee. He quickly introduced himself to Hale and shared his plans for a Democratic-Liberty amalgamation. "It seems quite useless to have two organizations, contending for the same objects," Chase wrote. "I am well persuaded moreover that the Liberty party can accomplish little as such, except indirectly." Only a True Democratic party, combining antislavery and Jacksonian ideals, could win the hearts and minds of the American people, he argued.[55]

With New Hampshire as a model, Chase and his group became convinced that the Democratic Party was the political alter ego of their own Liberty Party: the egalitarian, antimonopoly principles of the radical Democrats meshed easily with the Cincinnatians' constitutional, moderate antislavery. "I think that the political views of the Democrats are in the main sound," Chase wrote the Whig Giddings in August 1846. "I have sometimes thought that if all the antislavery men whose opinions are Democratic should act with the party in this state they might change its character wholly." Later in the same letter, Chase illuminated his views even more explicitly: he could not attend a Whig antislavery conference in Columbus or support its platform because "I do not concur in Whig views of public policy either as an antislavery man or as simply a citizen." He explained that he opposed any government support for corporate banking, a rechartering of the defunct Bank of the United States, or a protective tariff.[56]

Salmon P. Chase and True Democracy

The introduction of the Wilmot Proviso in August 1846 seemed to validate Chase's controversial strategy for the Liberty Party. Not only was the proviso hatched, introduced, and sustained by northern Democrats, but its core reasoning was indebted to Thomas Morris's speeches and Chase's own legal arguments in 1837 in defense of a fugitive slave named Matilda.[57] The Free Soil Democrats' break with the southern wing of the party only strengthened Chase's resolve to forge a coalition.[58]

After the Wilmot debates and the schism within the Democratic Party, the paramount objective for Chase became a national, multiparty antislavery union. Ironically, his Liberty colleagues, afraid that their principles would be irrevocably diluted, became his staunchest opponents. Conservative Liberty men wanted to stay the old course, hold a convention, and quickly nominate candidates. Increasingly, New Hampshire's U.S. senator-elect John P. Hale was mentioned as Birney's successor for the top nomination.[59] In New York, William Goodell and Gerrit Smith supported transforming the Liberty Party into a radical, multireform movement and even attracted the support of Jacksonian antislavery pioneer George Henry Evans by endorsing free homesteads. This group formally broke with the main Liberty Party and formed the Liberty League at Macedon Lock, New York, in June 1847.[60]

While Chase and Bailey supported many of the Macedonians' principles, they knew the new league would have extremely limited electoral appeal. Bailey, who in January began publishing a new paper called the *National Era* in Washington, D.C., hoped to attract dissidents from the major parties to the Liberty cause by nominating Hale for the presidency. Only Hale, wrote Bailey beginning in mid-1846, could reasonably hope to "receive the suffrages of every true lover of freedom in the country, be he Whig, Democrat, or Liberty man."[61]

Chase, however, opposed having the Liberty Party nominate Hale in 1847, for fear that the candidate would be forever stigmatized as an abolitionist. He hoped to delay any nominations until the spring of 1848; by that time, he reasoned, both major parties could be ready to burst their sectional seams. Better to let Hale gain prominence as an independent antislavery leader in the U.S. Senate before burdening him with the Liberty Party albatross.[62]

The coalitionists lost this particular battle at the 1847 Liberty convention in Buffalo. The party easily nominated Hale for president over Gerrit Smith. But the Ohioans made their mark at the convention in other ways. Chase's platform bore the unmistakable mark of the Cincinnati clique, not the eastern Liberty establishment. In fact, its chief plank borrowed directly from Gamaliel Bailey's 1839 editorials on political action in the *Philanthropist*. It demanded that Congress repeal the District of Columbia's Slave Code and the 1793 Fugitive Slave Law, prohibit slavery in the territories, and "array the powers of the general government, on the side of liberty and free labor." Ohio coalitionist Leicester King was selected as the vice-presidential nominee.[63]

One historian of the Liberty Party characterized the 1847 Buffalo convention as the end of old-fashioned political abolitionism.[64] Instead of clinging to one idea, the Cincinnati-inspired platform called for attainable and constitutional legislative action on the vital issues of the day. It also appealed to a far wider electorate than had previous Liberty platforms. While backing away from the original demand of immediate abolition, the party now urged slavery's abolition "by the constitutional acts of the federal and state governments." To many abolitionists, this introduction of Jacksonian states' rights doctrine was an expedient dilution of moral principle; to the Cincinnati clique, it was a realistic way to bring about the first step in slavery's extinction.

Buffalo

Between the two national Buffalo conventions—Liberty in October 1847 and Free Soil in August 1848—northern antislavery sentiment increased dramatically. The actions of the major parties played a large role in this explosion: both the Whigs and the Democrats nominated presidential candidates unacceptable to even mildly antislavery partisans. The Whigs' Zachary Taylor was a Louisianan and a slaveholder, and the Democrats' Lewis Cass was a popular sovereignty westerner who had long courted southern support. Meanwhile, the Wilmot Proviso controversy and the end of the Mexican War had focused the debate on the immediate future of the territories (and, indirectly, land distribution) and away from the evangelical and moral arguments of old-guard Liberty adherents. The Ohioans used these changes to argue that the time had come to unite at least their own faction of Liberty men with recalcitrant northern Whigs and Democrats.

Coalition with Ohio's Democratic Party became closer to reality after the Jacksonians suddenly reversed course and adopted the Wilmot Proviso in early 1848. Meeting in convention in January, the state party resolved that it was their "duty" as Democrats to "prevent [slavery's] increase, to mitigate, and finally to eradicate the evil."[65] Despite favoring Cass for the presidency, this Democratic state convention came closer to endorsing antislavery than any in the Northwest. Nonpartisan "Proviso meetings," involving both Whigs and Democrats, convened across the state in 1847 and early 1848 and paved the way for coalition. Finally, Chase scheduled a massive Ohio "Free Territory" convention to demonstrate unity and issue a nonpartisan call for a national Free Soil convention for 1848.[66] Chase's call rhetorically reached far beyond the usual Liberty constituency: "We ask no man to leave his party or surrender his party views. . . . Let all come who prefer free territory to slave territory and are resolved to act and vote accordingly. If candidates have been already nominated who represent our principles, let us approve them; if not, let us ourselves form a ticket we can support."[67]

Chase's document, signed by 3,000 Ohio voters in thirty counties, was specifically tailored for Democrats and Whigs dissatisfied with their parties' nominations. When the convention met in June, Chase meticulously organized a steering committee comprised of Democrats and Whigs. The 1,000 delegates to the meeting heard speeches by Chase, Lewis, and others, who carefully praised each star in the constellation of political antislavery: Wilmot, Hale, and the New York Barnburners as well as Whigs John G. Palfry, Henry Wilson, John McLean, and Giddings.[68] Most significant, however, was Chase's series of resolutions, which would be recycled in August as the Free Soil Party's platform. The Free Territory convention represented the culmination of Chase's evolving program of coalitionist, Jacksonian antislavery and a complete break with Liberty Party practice. In addition to hardmoney concerns and tariff reform, Chase added a demand for free and inalienable homesteads, borrowing a page from George Henry Evans's book. More importantly, he made the notion of free farms a formal "corollary" to Free Soil. Far from being a mere dilution of the old one idea, Chase had brought various strains of antislavery together and charted a new and, he hoped, politically viable course.[69]

The Buffalo Free Soil Convention has been well mined by American historians. Scholars usually conclude that the cacophonous meeting formed the beginning of a new antislavery movement, one that climaxed with the election of Abraham Lincoln and the Republican Party in 1860. But the convention also represents the culmination (and maturation) of a particularly *Jacksonian* brand of antislavery. Of course, Liberty men and Conscience Whigs were present and played prominent roles at the convention. It is important to note, however, that the two other major groups attending were Free Soil Democrats (men such as Amos Tuck, David Wilmot, and Marcus

Morton) and New York Barnburners, distinct entities but both Jacksonian in origin. Likewise, the most potent presidential candidates—Hale and Van Buren—were also Jacksonian Democrats, and the author of the Free Soil platform (Salmon P. Chase) was a confirmed hard-money Jacksonian on every issue but his abolitionism. Conscience Whigs such as Charles Francis Adams and John Palfry fully understood this; their faction had the hardest time swallowing the platform and the party's eventual nominee.

Hale was the candidate who best united the various Free Soil factions. New Hampshire Whigs trusted him from experience; he was well known among the Massachusetts delegates; the Liberty Party had already nominated him; and he still possessed many Democratic friends. If the 20,000 delegates assembled under the gigantic tent had cast a vote at the start of the convention, Hale might well have been the Free Soil presidential candidate by acclamation. But the convention's real decisions were made by a select Committee of Conferees, made up of equal numbers of Democrats, Liberty men, and Whigs, which met next door to the big tent at Buffalo's Universalist church.[70]

Even among these party leaders, Hale was "strongly predominant and seemingly irresistible," according to the convention's official reporter. But it soon became clear that the New York Barnburners cared more about their candidate, Van Buren, than their platform, and that Liberty leaders cared far more about the platform than their (still reluctant) candidate. After a short discussion, the two sides agreed the ex-president would run on a "thorough Liberty platform" demanding that the federal government separate itself from all responsibility for slavery's existence or continuance.[71]

The platform was mostly the work of Chase, who was aided by Van Buren lieutenants B. F. Butler and Preston King. Most of it was a rehashing of Chase's Free Territory resolutions, with calls for free homesteads and a tariff for revenue only. Yet despite the addition of a call for internal improvements (to placate western Democrats and Whigs), the platform was a thoroughly Jacksonian document. More precisely, it was a culmination of the ideas developed in the 1830s by Morris, Leggett, and George Henry Evans, reborn as a mature Free Soil ideology. Each of the pioneers was represented by a specific plank in Chase's platform.

> We accept the issue which the Slave Power has forced upon us, and to their demand for more Slave States and more Slave Territory, our calm but final answer is, No more Slave States and no more Slave Territory. [Morris]

It is the Duty of the Federal Government to Relieve itself from all Responsibility for the Existence or Continuance of Slavery wherever that Government Possess Constitutional Power to Legislate on that Subject, and is thus Responsible for its Existence. [Leggett]

The Free Grant to Actual Settlers, in consideration of the expenses they incur in making settlements in the wilderness . . . and of the public benefits resulting therefrom, of reasonable portions of the public lands, under suitable limitations, is a wise and just measure of public policy, which will promote . . . the interest of all the States of this Union. [Evans] [72]

When the platform was read aloud to the crowd in the tent, Charles Francis Adams reported, "every sentence, every paragraph was cheered into its legal existence." [73]

Many historians have judged Joshua Leavitt's Buffalo pronouncement that the Liberty Party was "not dead, but TRANSLATED" as naive at best and cynical at worst. [74] The usual indictment is that in order to win more votes, the antislavery movement ignobly sacrificed black equality as its central goal. While it is certainly true that slavery restriction was substituted for direct abolition and that the Free Soil Party platform ignored the issues of racism and fugitive slaves, the Free Soil Party represented the culmination of Morris, Bailey, and Chase's goal to found a True Democratic party. With the national Democratic party firmly in the hands of its southern wing, Free Soilers were able to create an entirely new antislavery party with distinctly Jacksonian accents. To the dismay of many former Whigs, these Democratic overtones extended most obviously to the party's presidential candidate, Martin Van Buren. With the creation of the True Democratic Party, the antislavery movement was transformed. But instead of weakening the political abolitionist movement by truckling to northern racists (as some historians have charged), Chase and his Free Soil allies placed it on an entirely different course — one with considerably more political appeal than Birney's Liberty Party.

CHAPTER SEVEN

Free Soil, Free Labor, Free Speech, and Free Men

The Election of 1848

One of the most enthusiastic of the 20,000 delegates to descend on Buffalo for the Free Soil Convention was Walt Whitman, who no doubt reveled in the sweaty, multitudinous throng of the main tent and the joyous antislavery singalongs led by the famous Hutchinson family. The convention — which at times resembled a P. T. Barnum circus, an outdoor revival meeting, and a torchlit Workingmen's rally such as those Whitman attended with his father in the 1820s — was a physical manifestation of the democracy he had written about in the *Eagle* and his private notebooks. The year 1848 was an eventful one for Whitman. In January he had been fired from the *Eagle* by its Hunker owner for refusing to rethink his antislavery views. He spent much of the spring in New Orleans, writing for the *Crescent* and waiting for a new chance to become an influential New York editor like his hero William Cullen Bryant. The day after the Barnburners bolted the Democratic convention in Baltimore, Whitman resigned from the *Crescent* to join the Free Soil cause. The *New York Advertiser* announced his return to the city on June 28 and described the graying scribe as "large as life, but quite as vain, and more radical than ever."[1]

As a bona fide Barnburner martyr, Whitman was easily chosen to be a delegate to the Buffalo convention on August 5, about the same time he agreed to edit a new Free Soil paper in Brooklyn to compete with the Hunker *Eagle*. In the first issue of his new *Brooklyn Freeman*, published September 9, 1848, Whitman promised to "oppose, under all circumstances, the addition to the Union, in the future, of a single inch of *slave land*, whether in the form of state or territory." He also devoted considerable space in that first issue to an editorial on the views of Thomas Jefferson, whom, in a feverish attempt to reconcile his antislavery and Democratic ideologies, Whitman reimagined as an abolitionist. "How he hated slavery!" Whitman wrote of the slaveholding sage of Monticello. "He was, in the literal sense of the world, an *abolitionist*; and properly and usefully so, because he was a southerner, and the evil lay at his own door." More even than for David Wilmot, who frequently called his proviso "Jefferson's Proviso," Whitman's mythical Jefferson was the font for the antislavery flood the would-be poet saw sweeping across the northern states in the late summer of 1848.[2]

Like many Free Soil papers published in the weeks after the Buffalo meeting, Whitman's exuded confidence that its candidates and cause would emerge triumphant at the ballot box. The enthusiastic and successful union of antislavery forces forged in Buffalo, he believed, ensured that containment of slavery would be the central issue in the 1848 campaign. Yet the weeks immediately following the Buffalo convention were undoubtedly the high point of the new Free Soil Party's existence. Free Soilers of every political stripe issued predictions of the party's inevitable electoral triumph throughout August and September. This optimism may seem grandiose and unrealistic today, judging from the election's final results, but in the early weeks of the campaign, both northern Whigs and Democrats were thrown on the defensive. Support for the Wilmot Proviso continued to unify antislavery advocates from every party; enthusiastic Free Soil "ratification" meetings sprouted from Ohio to New Hampshire; and in the *National Era*, Gamaliel Bailey reported that northerners were flocking to the cause by the thousands.[3]

In Cincinnati on August 25, a Free Soil meeting organized by former Democrats and Liberty men brought out 1,000 people to cheer for Van Buren and "Free Soil, Free Labor, Free Speech and Free Men." That same week the Liberty Party's candidate John P. Hale officially withdrew from the race and pledged his "hearty, energetic, and unanimous support" for the ticket of Van Buren and Adams.[4] Salmon P. Chase, campaigning in Ohio's Western Reserve, predicted a regional Free Soil sweep in excess of 13,000 votes, enough to gain all the state's electoral votes.[5] Shrewd politicians from both major parties predicted that the new party might well take New York, Massachusetts, and Vermont as well as Ohio.[6]

In Brooklyn, Whitman's luck took a turn for the worse. The same night he published the first issue of his new paper, a fire broke out on Fulton Street that destroyed nearly twenty downtown acres — including the *Freeman*'s office on Orange Street. The fire might as well have been an omen for the Free Soil Party's prospects in the fall campaign. As Whitman went door-to-door seeking financial support to restart his paper, problems emerged that threatened the new party's potential electoral strength. First and most damaging was the co-optation by the major parties of the Free Soilers' main issue: slavery restriction. The Wilmot Proviso was immensely popular across the North, and the Free Soil Party was the only party to endorse it. Whigs and Democrats, however, were quick to co-opt the issue as their own, even if it meant broadcasting markedly different messages to voters in the North and South. Ohio Whig Tom Corwin, for example, crisscrossed his state promising that, if elected, Zachary Taylor would never veto the proviso. Democrats emphasized Lewis Cass's northern pioneer background to distance him from his prosouthern pronouncements. "[Cass] is as strongly opposed to the further extension of slavery as we are," trumpeted the *Cleveland Plain Dealer*.[7] Chicago editor "Long John" Wentworth went so far as to hoist Cass's name above the masthead while still running daily Free Soil editorials.[8] Despite an energetic and surprisingly cooperative alliance between antislavery Democrats, Whigs, and Liberty men, the major parties' tactics sapped more Free Soil votes with every passing day. "Suppose the mists which the arts of politicians have raised to obscure the positions of Generals Taylor and Cass could be this hour dispelled," wrote an increasingly desperate Bailey from Washington. "[If] the People could see them in their true light as the pledged guardians of the Slave Interest and the opponents of the policy of Slavery Restriction," he continued, "we do not believe that either of them could carry a single free state."[9]

Another structural defect in the Free Soil edifice was its presidential candidate. While Van Buren was the overwhelming choice of Barnburners, radical Democrats, and even Chase's camp (who thought the former president could win the most votes), Free Soil Whigs had trouble stomaching the Little Magician. One paper in the Northwest made the Whig distaste for Van Buren abundantly clear: "The members of the [Buffalo] Convention know full well that the Whig party is the true antislavery party. . . . To ask a Whig to vote for Martin Van Buren is an insult."[10] In Ohio, at least, Hale or McLean would likely have polled far more votes than Van Buren. From Washington, Gamaliel Bailey urged opponents of slavery to ignore the candidate's past record and focus on his latest incarnation. "Van Buren was subservient to the Slave Power in 1836, you say — well, he is not, like Gen. Cass, a vassal to it, or like Gen. Taylor, its embodiment in 1848," Bailey wrote. "On the contrary, he is its open, direct antagonist."[11]

Other key northern Democrats of Van Buren's generation were unusually tepid toward the Free Soil Party, even if they were declared supporters of the Wilmot Proviso. Marcus Morton, while endorsing Van Buren, declined to

FIGURE 7

"The Modern Colossus" (1848).

This cartoon shows Free Soil candidate Martin Van Buren's
difficulty bridging the gap between the Free Soil (here called Whig-Abolition)
and Democratic party platforms. As abolitionist icon Abby Fulsom beckons,
Van Buren attempts to stretch over Salt River, a symbol of political ruin,
without "splitting asunder." (Library of Congress)

campaign actively for the party, citing certain retribution for his Democratic
subordinates in the Boston Customs House.[12] Former Kitchen Cabinet fix-
ture Francis Blair initially supported the Free Soil ticket and, citing an 1845
letter, suggested Andrew Jackson, were he alive, would throw his support to
its presidential candidate as well. "I cannot hope to be alive and witness the
acclamation with which the people of the United States will call Mr. Van
Buren to the Presidency at the expiration of Mr. Polk's term," Jackson had
written just before his death. Still, while admitting his heart was with Van
Buren, Blair later reversed course and voted for Cass.[13] Other old Jacksonians such as Thomas Hart Benton (who favored the proviso) and George
Bancroft (who did not) also remained with the Democrats.[14]

The Campaign

Despite problems stemming from the Free Soil Party's lack of a national political organization, its partisans conducted an energetic campaign. David
Wilmot, fresh from his October reelection to Congress, stumped across New
York state. Joshua Giddings, who finally abandoned the Whig Party after
years of agonized loyalty, canvassed the counties of southern Ohio, while
Chase toured Gidding's Western Reserve. By far the most effective Free Soil
campaign speaker, however, was "Prince John" Van Buren. The candidate's
son enthusiastically took up the Buffalo convention's plank that invited
him to "stump the United States generally."[15] Between August and November, the younger Van Buren delivered at least thirty major addresses in
New York, Ohio, Pennsylvania, and all the New England states. He was
especially effective with urban working-class audiences. In his speeches he
took Jacksonian antislavery arguments to new rhetorical heights, excoriating
the slave conspirators, ridiculing compromising doughfaces and meddlesome Whigs, and above all, emphasizing the degrading influence of slavery
on free labor.[16]

Scholars have commented frequently about the Free Soilers' use of racist
antislavery arguments, especially those made by former Barnburners like
Van Buren, to win support in 1848.[17] But while Free Soilers (and especially
Barnburners) were often filled with racial prejudice — and trumpeted these
views on the campaign trail — the Jacksonian antislavery arguments used in
the campaign were more than simple pandering to northern racism. As
Richard Sewell has observed, the Barnburners' primary concern was for
whites; yet at the same time they believed that slavery encouraged sloth,
degraded free labor, and, as had the national bank, favored an aristocratic
elite. These evils were far more pressing to them than the potential presence
in the territories of people they viewed as "inferior."[18]

If, for example, Van Buren and the Free Soilers had stopped with the
Wilmot Proviso and declared that its necessity was based simply on the need
to reserve western lands for white people, the party would have represented
a clear step backward from the Liberty Party. But the Free Soil Party was
indebted to a far wider constellation of antislavery arguments than the
creation of a lily-white West. As its platform and the stories of its creators
proved, the Free Soil Party was about more than the sum of racist parts.
Central to this "new" direction for political antislavery was the platform's
call for free farms.[19]

John Van Buren often stressed the new party's plank calling for free homesteads in his appeals to workingmen and freeholders, reminding them that reserving the public lands for settlers kept them out of the hands of speculators and land monopolists, as well as slaveholders. Most northerners were familiar with the notion of the free grant. In 1846 George Henry Evans had printed a popular pamphlet (called *Vote Yourself a Farm*) that spurred a massive petition drive from New York, Massachusetts, Ohio, and Pennsylvania.[20] But he also repeatedly said that "to buy and sell human beings . . . is revolting not only to a freeman and a democrat, but to a philanthropist and a christian."[21]

Free Blacks and Free Soil

The 1848 campaign forced the North's free blacks to make a difficult decision: whether to support the Free Soil Party. On one hand, Free Soilers had backed away from the black community's demands for racial equality and the abolition of slavery everywhere. Yet several black abolitionists had attended the Buffalo convention (including Frederick Douglass, Henry Bibb, Samuel Ward, Henry Highland Garnet, and Charles Remond), and Douglass and Bibb had addressed the meeting from the main stage. Both were, for the most part, received warmly.[22] Certainly, there was no black participation at the major parties' conventions. During the campaign, however, the Free Soilers neglected to solicit the support of free blacks. In the *North Star*, Douglass initially declared his preference for abolitionist candidate Gerrit Smith but later endorsed Van Buren because he believed the ex-president had a better chance to win. Ward refused to endorse Free Soil, arguing that Barnburners by any name intended to "rob black men of their rights."[23]

A small group of black leaders who billed themselves as the National Negro Convention met in Cleveland in September 1848 to formulate a unified set of views. Douglass was elected chair of the meeting, which stopped short of endorsing Free Soil candidates. Instead, they passed resolutions recognizing the goal of the Free Soilers to "increase the interest now felt in behalf of the downtrodden and oppressed" and stating that "while we heartily engage in recommending to our people the Free Soil movement, and the support of the Buffalo convention . . . we claim and are determined to maintain the higher standard and the more liberal views which have heretofore characterized us as abolitionists."[24] Free blacks understood that the Free Soil Party had backed away from some of their most deeply held demands, while at the same time holding out a potential for larger success. Most gave it qualified support.

George Henry Evans, another potentially effective Free Soil publicist, refused to join the new party in 1848. Despite Free Soilers' endorsement of his concept of free homesteads (by far the largest organization to do so), Evans urged supporters to vote instead for Gerrit Smith. He called Smith and his Liberty League the "true" Free Soil party: "those who first used that term, not as a bait, a lure, a cheat, a gull-trap, but as an honest expression of a great idea."[25] Many of Evans's former followers in upstate New York disagreed. In Delaware County, for example, tenant leaders like Dr. Jonathan Allaben forged Free Soil coalitions with county Barnburners in 1847–48. Allaben chaired the county's Jeffersonian League and Free Soil Club, which held rallies for Van Buren and gubernatorial candidate John Dix as early as June 1848.[26] As one Delaware anti-renter recalled, "the Free-Soilers carried everything before them" in the coming election.[27]

The Results

On election day, Van Buren failed to win a single state, although his candidacy cost Cass New York and Taylor Ohio. Taylor eked out a narrow victory built on his success in the South, in which he won eight of fifteen slave states and increased the Whig proportion in the section by 10 percent over 1844. Taylor also carried the northern states of New York, Massachusetts, and Pennsylvania. Cass swept the Old Northwest and won the other seven slave states, but Van Buren finished ahead of him in New York, Vermont, and Massachusetts. Cass's dismal showing in the Empire State, in fact, cost him the election; the difference between Cass's and Taylor's votes was 140,000, approximately equal to Van Buren's New York total.[28]

Although organizational weakness and a lack of campaign money hampered the Free Soil effort, the election results illustrate a striking political realignment within the North's Democratic Party. Analysis of the towns, counties, and states that produced a significant Free Soil vote suggests that a lion's share of third party supporters were former Democrats. The election of 1848, then, was more than a political campaign; it was a watershed for northern politics, representing party realignments at local, state, and national levels. The coalitions built in 1848 paved the way for the anti-Nebraska Republican coalition in 1854.[29]

New York's returns indicate the most substantial and long-standing political shifts. Van Buren received more than 42 percent of his 291,804 votes in his home state and won pluralities in St. Lawrence, Herkimer, Oswego, Wayne, Delaware, Chemung, Cortland, Madison, Onondaga, and Lewis

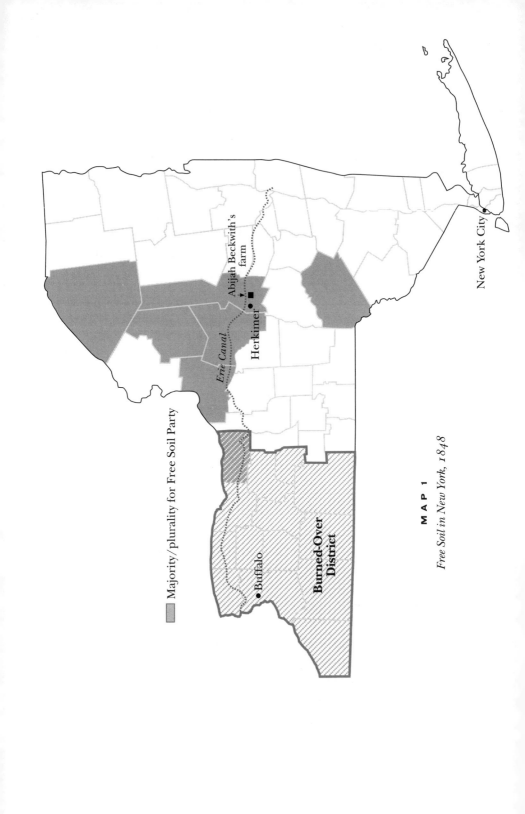

MAP 1

Free Soil in New York, 1848

Majority/plurality for Free Soil Party

New York City

Abijah Beckwith's farm

Herkimer

Erie Canal

Buffalo

Burned-Over District

counties. Democratic votes declined 24 percent from their 1844 levels; the Whig percentage remained unchanged. Binding these Free Soil counties together was their previously strong support for Democratic candidates. Except for Cortland County in the Finger Lakes region, Democrat James K. Polk, a Tennessee slaveholder, had carried every one of the Van Buren counties four years earlier.[30]

Nor were a majority of these counties in areas with strong Liberty Party traditions. The Liberty Party won only slightly more than 3 percent of the statewide vote in 1844, while the Free Soil Party polled 27 percent in 1848. Only Madison County (home of Liberty League candidate Gerrit Smith) and neighboring Cortland gave more than 10 percent of their 1844 totals to Liberty candidate James G. Birney. St. Lawrence, Herkimer, Wayne, and Delaware counties had given just 4 percent, 8 percent, 7 percent, and 3 percent, respectively, of their votes to Birney.[31]

Geographically, New York's Free Soil vote does not correspond to the Burned-Over District and Greater New England maps usually trotted out by scholars to show the sources of antislavery votes.[32] Instead of an east-west nexus paralleling the Erie Canal, the Free Soil counties better correspond to a north-south line drawn through the middle of the state (see map 1). This north-south line connects the St. Lawrence River with the southern tip of the Catskill Mountains, extending into the northern tier of Pennsylvania. Thus not simply ex-Democrats voted for Van Buren in 1848 but, rather, a particular kind of former Jacksonian. As discussed above, Democrats from remote rural regions (like Preston King of St. Lawrence, Abijah Beckwith of Herkimer, and Jonathan Allaben of Delaware) were more likely to enter free-soil coalitions. These were the same regions that had led the charge against banks and government-financed internal improvements in the 1830s and early 1840s.[33]

Shifts in Democratic vote percentages from 1844–48 against those in the Liberty–Free Soil vote percentages over the same years show an extremely strong inverse correlation ($-.938$) between Democratic and Free Soil voters.[34] (A coefficient of -1.00 would indicate a perfect negative relationship between variables, suggesting that all Free Soil votes came from Democrats; a perfect $+1.00$ would be impossible, since this coefficient is measuring a loss of votes in one column and a gain in another.)[35] This not only suggests that a striking number of Free Soil voters were former Democrats but that antislavery Whigs had refused to support Van Buren.[36] Also telling is the strength with which these former Jacksonian, Free Soil counties entered the Republican Party. In 1844, for example, St. Lawrence County voters (who gave Van Buren a resounding 56 percent in 1848) chose Polk over Clay 54 percent to 41 percent. Twelve years later, the county gave 75 percent to John C. Frémont, and in 1860 Abraham Lincoln won 74 percent of the county's votes. In anti-rent Delaware County, the results were similar. In 1844 Polk won 56 percent; sixteen years later the former Jacksonian stronghold gave Lincoln 60 percent of the vote.[37] Between the start of the anti-rent movement and Van Buren's candidacy in 1848, a sizable number of New York's radical Democrats had become Free Soilers; in the 1850s almost all of them entered the Republican Party.

Democrats and Free Soil

Nationally, the correlation between former Jacksonians and Free Soilers was also quite strong, though not as definitive as the shift in New York. A correlation measuring Democratic votes in 1844–48 and Liberty and Free Soil votes in 1844–48 in the eighty-two counties where Van Buren polled more than 20 percent showed a coefficient of −.664. When the same correlation was done comparing Whig and Free Soil votes, the resulting coefficient was a statistically insignificant −.122.[38]

When the eleven counties in Ohio (all in the Whiggish northeast corner of the state; see map 2) that polled more than 20 percent for Van Buren are factored out, the coefficient of correlation jumps to −.836.[39] In Ohio, state-level politics helped to thwart Chase's optimistic predictions for Free Soil success. The Free Soil Party ran no state ticket but was assumed to hold the balance of power in the state because of the large number of potential antislavery voters on the Western Reserve and in and around Cincinnati. Observers throughout the North expected Whig gubernatorial candidate Seabury Ford, who held mild antislavery views, to win easily over the avowedly proslavery Democrat J. B. Weller.[40] Though neither man actively courted the Free Soil vote, Ohio's Free Soil papers generally praised Ford. When the election was over, however, the expected Whig landslide failed to materialize; in fact, Ford barely eked out a 300-vote victory from nearly 300,000 cast.[41]

Apparently Ford, who never formally endorsed the Wilmot Proviso, had not given Free Soil Democrats enough reasons to overlook his probank, high-tariff economic positions, and they stuck with Weller. The results of the state election precipitated a national Whig panic. Whig politicians and orators crisscrossed the state, urging antislavery supporters to stick with Taylor. According to Bailey, "Powerful efforts are being made [by such antislavery

MAP 2

Free Soil in Ohio, 1848

Whigs as Seward and Horace Greeley] to break down the Free Soil movement in Ohio . . . [by] appealing with weeping and wailing and lamentation
to the Buckeyes to come to the help of 'Old Zach.'"[42] The effect of this
internecine strife was to reinforce traditional party allegiances. Despite Gidding's's heroic delivery of the Western Reserve for Van Buren (the correlation between Whigs and Free Soilers was −.964, showing a very strong
match), the net effect of the Free Soil election in Ohio was to deliver the
state to Cass.[43]

Chase and the Cincinnati clique were only able to muster about 9.1

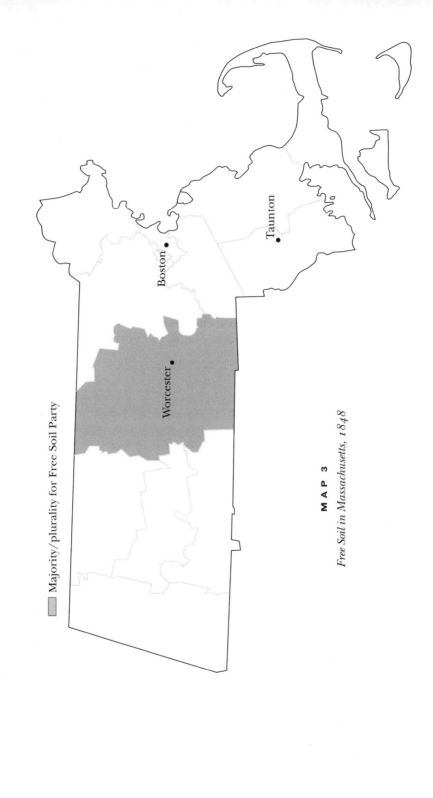

Majority/plurality for Free Soil Party

Boston

Taunton

Worcester

MAP 3

Free Soil in Massachusetts, 1848

percent of the vote in their home county of Hamilton. Jacob Brinkerhoff's Richland County polled barely 3.5 percent for Van Buren (although turnout plummeted by 40 percent), and the late Thomas Morris's home county of Clermont only mustered 7.4 percent for Free Soil.[44] These counties remained heavily Democratic. Still, Chase engineered a Senate seat for himself in early 1849, adding to the state's Free Soil congressional delegation composed of Representatives Joseph Root and Giddings.

The results in Massachusetts were mixed. Despite the addition of important antislavery Democrats like Marcus Morton, Amasa Walker, and Amos Phelps to the state's Free Soil coalition, a majority of the party's votes appear to have come from Conscience Whigs. The correlation coefficient between the change in Whig votes between 1844 and 1848 and the change in Liberty–Free Soil votes is a significant −.769, while the Democrat–Free Soil coefficient is an insignificant −.375.[45] But other evidence suggests Democrats played a more significant role. For example, between the 1844 and 1848 gubernatorial votes, the Democrats lost 16, the Whigs lost 2, and the Free Soil Party gained 17 percent from the previous Liberty totals. Comparisons of the 1844 and 1848 presidential tallies reveal a similar trend (Democrats: −13 percent; Whigs: −6 percent; Free Soil: +19 percent).[46] These findings back up Marcus Morton's repeated complaints that Conscience Whigs dominated the Massachusetts Free Soil organization. "Nearly all the committees and candidates have been taken from the whig section of the party," Morton told B. V. French in 1850, "[yet] a majority of the Free-soil party are democrats. [Henry] Wilson . . . asserted that in '48 30,000 of the 40,000 Free-soil votes came from democrats. Shall one-quarter control three quarters?"[47]

In 1848 Free Soilers won their only Bay State plurality in Worcester County (see map 3), where Conscience Whigs and Jacksonian workers united to support Van Buren and Phillips and to send Charles Allen, the grandson of Sam Adams, to Congress. Twelve years later, Worcester voters polled 76 percent for Frémont and 70 percent for Lincoln.[48] Both major parties were disrupted by the Free Soil campaign, and the weak Democratic Party never recovered. The second party system in Massachusetts completely collapsed immediately following the 1848 election.

In New Hampshire, one of the birthplaces of Free Soil coalition making, the regular Democrats were able to retain control of the state. In eastern Carroll County, Van Buren won almost 21 percent of the vote, his highest total in the state (see map 4). Van Buren hurt Taylor more than Cass in New Hampshire; the correlation coefficient between Whig and Free Soil voters is

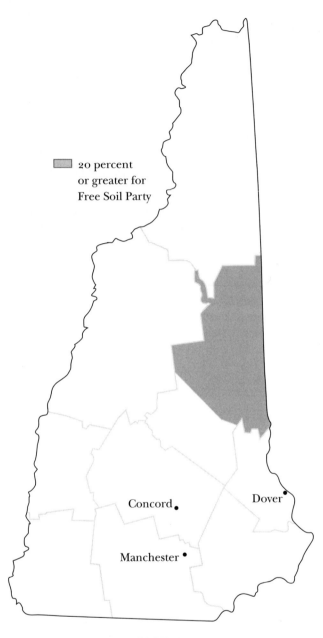

20 percent
or greater for
Free Soil Party

Concord.

Dover.

Manchester.

MAP 4
Free Soil in New Hampshire, 1848

−.668, while the Democrat–Free Soil coefficient is −.485.[49] Still, Hale's Independent Democracy continued to gather strength, while George G. Fogg's *Independent Democrat* editorialized for Free Soil, free homesteads, and an end to the expansion of slavery. After the 1852 election of favorite son Franklin Pierce to the presidency, three antislavery factions emerged in the state: Hale's Independent Democrats, Whigs, and Know-Nothings. All three factions nominated identical tickets in 1854–55, and by the next fall New Hampshire's political realignment was completed. In 1856 New Hampshire joined the Republican column, and it tenaciously remained Republican for the rest of the century and beyond.[50]

Excepting Wilmot's district, Free Soil was much less of a key issue in Pennsylvania than in New York, Ohio, Massachusetts, and New Hampshire.[51] Whigs, many of whom had endorsed the Wilmot Proviso, were successful in reviving the issue of the free-trade Walker Tariff in the Keystone State, which had cost every congressional Democrat save Wilmot his seat in 1846.[52] This was enough to overcome the formidable Democratic organization headed by James Buchanan. The Free Soil votes in the Wilmot district's counties of Bradford, Potter, and Tioga came overwhelmingly from Democrats but made little difference in the statewide race (see map 5).[53]

In Vermont, Van Buren received 29 percent of the vote, his highest percentage in the nation. In this Whig stronghold, Van Buren's candidacy seems to have dampened what could have been a full-scale political revolution in the state. Antislavery Whig governor William Slade backed the Free Soil Party, but most of the ticket's support came from the state's Democrats. The coefficient of correlation between Democratic and Free Soil voting is a strong −.847.[54] Democrats also lost more votes than Whigs from the 1844 election.[55] In May 1849 the state's Democrats and Free Soilers formed the Free Democracy, based on a moratorium on new slave states, cheap postage, free education, and free homesteads.[56]

In the Midwest, the Free Soil Party was most successful in northeast Illinois and southeast Wisconsin (see map 6). Here Free Soilers mixed their antiextensionist arguments with support of their plank for federal improvements. The improvements plank was definitely overlooked in rural New York or eastern cities. Wisconsin was a new state in 1848, and it is inconclusive as to whether Illinois Free Soil votes came more from Democrats or Whigs. What is clear, however, is that Free Soil totals would have been much larger had popular editor and congressman "Long John" Wentworth of Chicago gone beyond his endorsement of the Wilmot Proviso and supported the Free Soil Party.[57]

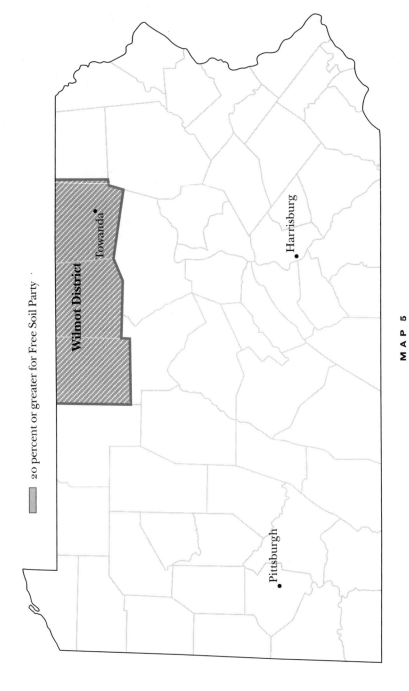

20 percent or greater for Free Soil Party

Wilmot District

Towanda

Harrisburg

Pittsburgh

M A P 5

Free Soil in Pennsylvania, 1848

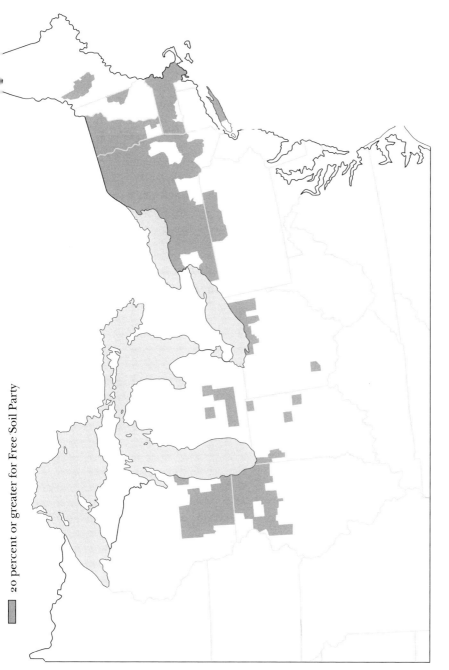

■ 20 percent or greater for Free Soil Party

M A P 6

Election of 1848: Free Soil Vote by Counties

(*Sources: Burnham,* Presidential Ballots; *Rayback,* Free Soil)

The Evolution of Jacksonian Antislavery

Jacksonian antislavery had evolved from the isolated grumblings of a small group of dissidents into a powerful ideology and movement. By 1848, Jacksonian arguments against slavery had provoked political convulsions in nearly every northern state and, at the same time, taken the existing antislavery movement in new, uncharted directions. By the end of the Civil War, the political power (as well as the severe limits) of these Free Soil arguments would be clear. Not until after secession would the twin goals of Free Soil — emancipation and the Homestead Act — be enacted. Yet while Democrats who became Republicans generally supported both measures by 1862–63, it was often as far as they were willing to go. Racial equality, though embraced by a few Free Soilers, was still anathema to many ex-Democrats; similarly, the 1862 Homestead Act was not tailored to unemployed workers and freed slaves, the way George Henry Evans had urged back in the 1840s. If the Free Soilers had lived up to their most lofty pronouncements, the post–Civil War era might well have been altogether different.

↑

Free Soilers, Republicans, and the Third Party System, 1848–1854

Even though the results of the 1848 election were disappointing for Free Soilers, supporters throughout the North remained optimistic — even giddy — about the future of their movement. "With our righteous cause the free soil men are invincible," wrote Preston King, who won another term in Congress, this time as a Free Soiler. "The late election is only the Bunker Hill of the moral & political revolution which can terminate only in success to the side of freedom."[1] The new party had disrupted the party system, affected the outcome of a presidential canvass, elected twelve members to Congress, and gained the balance of power in several state capitols, including Ohio and Massachusetts. Moreover, Free Soilers had every reason to believe they had momentum on their side. They viewed their ideology as destined to prevail; once the rest of the electorate of the free states came around to the idea that the expansion of slavery threatened northerners, the Constitution, and even the Union itself, the party could not help but gain in influence and stature.

Even anti–Free Soil satirists accepted the idea of the electoral genies contained in the Wilmot Proviso and the Buffalo bottles. A short-lived humor magazine *The John-Donkey* published a poem titled "Wilmot, the Wizard" that poked fun at the congressman but spoke with awe of the proviso's popular power:

> For straightway he did introduce
> A monster weird and spunkey,
> With hair like fire, a head like a goose,
> And ears like a huge John-donkey. . . .

He swallowed the South at a gulp, with all
Its niggers and other people;
He took down a church by way of *bonne bouche,*
And tickled its nose with the steeple.[2]

A crude illustration accompanying the doggerel (see fig. 6) shows the portly congressman riding his dragonlike "monster," ready to trample those who favored popular sovereignty, Whiggery, or any other solution to the territorial problem.

Yet despite all the Free Soilers' thunder, the fact remained that third parties had an extremely poor track record over the course of the nation's political history. Most had been absorbed into one of the major parties or had merely evaporated for lack of electoral success. Between 1848 and 1854, the year the Kansas-Nebraska Act reawakened the antiextensionist movement and flooded it with new allies, the future of the political movement initiated by Leggett and brought to the public's attention by men like David Wilmot and Salmon Chase was profoundly uncertain. During those pivotal six years, in which a seemingly endless series of cataclysmic events stunned, numbed, and, finally, provoked the American public, Free Soilers scrambled to keep their party intact and their message coherent. For two years after the 1848 election, Free Soilers debated whether or not to form temporary coalitions with regular Democrats. In this concluding chapter I will briefly examine three of these coalitions—in Ohio, Massachusetts, and New York—and assess their mixed records. I will then turn to the new challenges that faced the movement in the aftermath of the Compromise of 1850, which attempted to settle the question of slavery in the territories once and for all. Many northerners, including Martin Van Buren, chose to accept the compromise as a flawed but politically necessary expedient to end a careening sectional crisis. But one measure of the compromise—the South's long-demanded Fugitive Slave Act, which compelled northerners actively to assist in the return of runaway slaves—propelled still more men and women into the Free Soil camp. By 1854 the stage was set for a permanent political realignment with the birth of a new party based on Free Soil goals and principles.

Free Soil–Democratic Coalitions

Two opposing strategic views emerged from the 1848 election, each enunciated by an Ohio Free Soiler, one from the Whig antislavery tradition and

A MODERN DEMOCRAT.
MOTTO:
EVERY THING TO EVERYBODY.

FIGURE 8

"A Modern Democrat" (1850s). This rendering by an Iowa cartoonist depicts the difficulties a split northern Democratic Party faced after the Compromise of 1850. The Janus-faced center figure has one foot on either side of a fence; one hand helps a runaway slave, while the other yanks a chained slave by the neck. To make the hypocrisy of the party more explicit, the artist depicted the figure with a whisky bottle in his "proslavery" pocket (and a stereotypical "Irish"-featured face on this side), while in his "antislavery" pocket he holds a signed teetotaler's pledge. (Huntington Library, San Marino, Calif.)

another from the Jacksonian. Joshua Giddings, a social reformer and evangelical congressman from the Western Reserve, had bolted the Whig Party as soon as it nominated slaveholder Zachary Taylor for president. After Taylor's victory, Giddings insisted that the Free Soil Party remain independent of the other parties so as to "*correct public opinion,* not . . . control political action." On the opposite side stood Salmon P. Chase, who urged immediate

Conclusion   **183**

union at both the state and national levels with northern Democrats. His Buffalo platform was, after all, a potent combination of traditional Democratic programs and free-soil ideas that would have made William Leggett proud. Applying the Jacksonians' "cardinal doctrine of equal rights" to slavery containment was, as Chase had argued since 1844, a logical step for the northern Democracy. Coalitions with willing Democrats were, for Chase, the surest path to achieving antislavery goals.[3]

Chase wasted no time making his plan a reality in Ohio, leaving the Giddings faction to lick its wounds in silence. With Free Soil legislators holding the balance of power in the legislature, Chase took advantage of a dispute over district boundaries to secure for himself a choice political plum: a seat in the U.S. Senate. In a breathtaking example of backroom maneuvering, Chase traded Free Soil support for Democratic control in the state's lower house for the Jacksonians' support of Chase for the Senate seat and the repeal of Ohio's repressive black laws.[4] Ohio Free Soilers even adopted Chase's preferred name—Free Democrats—in 1849 and in county after county broke bread with regular Democratic organizations.

A Bay State Coalition

Eyeing with envy the tangible successes of fusion with Democrats in Ohio, Free Soil organizations in other states attempted to mimic Chase's model throughout the North in 1849. In Wisconsin Free Soilers and Democrats met in March to issue a series of Jacksonian resolutions and plan for a formal alliance in the fall elections, but Democrats loyal to Lewis Cass double-crossed the Free Soilers and engineered a slate of antiproviso candidates. Wisconsin's Free Soil Party virtually ceased to exist.[5] In New Hampshire and Maine, Democrats and Free Soilers continued to work together, sending Amos Tuck back to Congress and Hannibal Hamlin to the U.S. Senate for a second term. A temporary coalition in Connecticut resulted in three new antislavery congressional representatives and a majority in the state house.

Yet it was a combination of Free Soilers and Democrats from Massachusetts that became the envy of antislavery parties across the North. After the 1848 election—with prosouthern Cotton Whigs in firm control of the party and the state house and slaveholding Whig Zachary Taylor in the White House—Free Soilers and Democrats spoke frequently about uniting on a platform of equal rights. Only by uniting with Bay State Democrats, declared ardent coalitionist Amasa Walker, would Free Soilers be able to defeat the twin aristocracies personified by the northern Money Power and the southern Slave Power. "We are bound to regard the interests of the not-over-paid laborer of the North, as truly as those of the entirely unpaid laborer of the South," he told his fifty-two fellow Free Soil legislators in April 1849. The best way to achieve this, he said, was to meld with the state's Democrats.[6] Walker was joined in this project by the similarly coalition-minded "Natick Cobbler" Henry Wilson and Harvard-educated Free Soiler Charles Sumner. Like his political mentor Salmon Chase, Sumner kept company with Whigs but personally held hard-money Jacksonian beliefs on a broad range of issues. The ambitious Sumner also hoped to follow Chase's path into national politics, a journey that for both men began with Free Soil–Democratic coalitions.

Massachusetts Democrats made the task easier when they adopted a strong slate of antislavery resolutions at their 1849 convention. They were met more than halfway by the Free Soilers, who tapped Sumner to compose a party platform that relied heavily on Jacksonian programs such as cheap postage, free homesteads, and election reform—issues that were lifted straight from former governor Marcus Morton's old gubernatorial addresses. Still, no formal coalition was struck in time for the 1849 elections, in which the Whigs swept the statewide offices.

While the Whig Party in Massachusetts withstood the flirtations between the state's Free Soilers and Democrats in 1849, it could not survive the buffetings caused by the Compromise of 1850. Conceived and shepherded through the Congress by Whig statesman Henry Clay, the compromise attempted to resolve issues as disparate as the boundaries of Texas, the status of the territories of California and New Mexico, the legality of the slave trade in the District of Columbia, and the necessity of a strong fugitive slave law. The compromise gained a significant supporter when the Bay State's own Whig senator, the "godlike" Daniel Webster, famously rose in the Senate on March 7, 1850, to urge northerners not to "taunt or reproach" the South with further antislavery measures. Until the "Seventh of March" speech, Webster had publicly supported the Wilmot Proviso. Generations of Americans would be forced to memorize the oration for its lofty pro-Union rhetoric, but it yoked the Massachusetts Whig Party forevermore to the compromise and its most divisive provision, the Fugitive Slave Law. Almost immediately Free Soilers with Whig backgrounds abandoned their previous opposition to a formal union with Massachusetts's Democracy. In a stunning reversal of a decade of Whig electoral dominance, Democrats and Free Soilers combined to win a majority of seats in the state legislature in the 1850 elections and, since no statewide candidates won a clear majority, the power to choose the next governor, lieutenant governor, and U.S. senator.

When the time came to divvy up the offices, antislavery Democrat George Boutwell was elected governor while Sumner, like his mentor in Ohio, was sent to the U.S. Senate as a Free Soiler. "Laus Deo!" an ecstatic Chase wrote to his new partner in the Senate. "Now I feel as if I had a brother colleague — one with whom I shall sympathize and be able fully to act."[7] Although the Democratic–Free Soil union was always a difficult one, it continued to bear political fruit in the year ahead. Free Soilers and Democrats joined to regulate the state's banks and corporations, introduce a secret ballot for elections, and place Harvard College under more state control. For the moment, however, a strong personal liberty law to thwart the Fugitive Slave Act was blocked by prosouthern Democrats.[8]

Yet the compromise precipitated the conversion to antislavery of one the Bay State's most doughfaced Jacksonian politicians. Like many of the free-soil dissidents referred to in earlier chapters, Robert Rantoul Jr. of Essex County was a steadfast hard-money Democrat during the 1830s; yet during the 1840s he eschewed the Van Buren wing of the party and became a key northern supporter of proslavery stalwarts like John C. Calhoun and President John Tyler. True, he had developed a close friendship with John Greenleaf Whittier while rooming with the abolitionist poet during the 1835 session of the Massachusetts legislature, and he had long defended abolitionists' rights of petition and speech. But when the chance came to bolt the party and support the Wilmot Proviso in 1846 and the Free Soil ticket in 1848, Rantoul remained an antiproviso Cass Democrat. Sounding suspiciously like Martin Van Buren in the 1820s, Rantoul continued to insist (somewhat absurdly) that slavery had nothing to do with the 1848 election — the real issue was the free-trade Walker Tariff.[9]

But the combination of the Fugitive Slave Act, which forced northerners for the first time to deal directly with slavery on their own streets, and Massachusetts's unique three party system after 1849 precipitated a dramatic transformation. In 1850 the former doughface suddenly emerged as one of the North's leading antislavery Democrats. Once Rantoul accepted that slavery was an issue — that slaveholders were, indeed, a threat to northern workers and farmers on a par with New England's textile barons — it became for him the only issue, swallowing up all others in a matter of days or weeks. Rantoul excoriated the Fugitive Slave Act (and the compromise in general) as an attempt by aristocratic southerners to dictate policy to the rest of the country and to make northerners confront what he believed was, once, a strictly southern concern. "Is one third of the white people of the

United States to dictate to the other two thirds," he asked in a speech in Lynn in April 1851 "and call their submission 'peace'?"[10]

Soon after this speech criticizing the compromise, Rantoul unexpectedly became a defense attorney for Thomas Sims, an accused fugitive, in a trial that received significant national attention. Although Rantoul failed in his effort to stop federal authorities from returning Sims to slavery, his performance at the trial ingratiated him to Essex County's Free Soilers, and they nominated him as their candidate for Congress. With the backing of both Free Soilers and the county's regular Democrats, he won handily. Surprisingly, during the last months of his life — he died suddenly in August 1852 — Rantoul became a proponent of rapid abolition, declaring that there would be no "finality" for the slavery issue other than universal emancipation.[11] But his reasoning continued to be that of a radical, hard-money, and states' rights Jacksonian. "The man who thinks he is a democrat," he told the local Democratic district convention a month before his death, "and seeks to produce that state of society which builds up great accumulations of property in a few hands . . . who dares to sacrifice liberty (whether in the person of his white brother, or his colored brother, I care not) who is willing to sacrifice or endanger liberty because it will make a tenth of a cent's difference in the price of cotton goods, is no democrat."[12] Using reasoning similar to William Leggett's a decade and a half earlier, in his conversion Rantoul exemplified Jacksonian antislavery in the postcompromise era. For Rantoul, southern slaveholders, previously his closest political allies, had with the compromise renounced the essential principles of the Democratic Party. They had used their power as slaveholders to stomp on the liberties of slaves and their power in Washington to stomp on the liberties of northerners.

A New York Reunion

The desertion of Jacksonian stalwarts like Rantoul from the Democratic Party presaged the success of the Republican coalition half a decade later. But events in New York during the same years told a different story. Free Soilers in the Empire State, primarily former Democrats, craved less a coalition with their old party than a full-scale reunion. Given their recent successes as electoral spoilers, they assumed they would not have to sacrifice their antislavery principles if a reconciliation should occur. While Ohio and Massachusetts defectors most often considered their 1848 break with the party of Jackson to be final, many Barnburners-turned-Free-Soilers could not resist the urge to return to the Democratic Party many of them had helped to found. William Cullen Bryant, who had broken with his Jacksonian brethren over slavery and expansion as far back as 1840, was a telling example. The 1848 election, he bragged, "so disturbed the composition of the democratic party of the north, that it will compel it to reorganize with the principle of free soil in its creed as a settled doctrine."[13] With the Slave Power's hold on· the party supposedly broken, many New York Free Soilers reasoned, the Democratic Party, at least in the North, had been redeemed.

As in 1847, a generational rift seemed to separate older Free Soilers who craved reunion and younger ones who wanted to continue to function as a separate party. Henry S. Randall, speaking for what he called the "class of young, able and educated men who have led in the Free-Soil movement," wrote to Martin Van Buren to urge that the new party remain independent. "[Free Soilers] will, *if led boldly on*, become the dominant party throughout the West. I give my vote to go the full length."[14] Yet the ex-president, at age sixty-five, was ready to return to the Democratic fold. His son John at first tried to stake out intergenerational middle ground but ended up siding with his father on the matter. "We expect," he told Free Soilers at Utica in 1849, "to make the democratic party of this state the great anti-slavery party of this state, and through it to make the democratic party of the United States the great anti-slavery party of the United States. Those who do not contemplate this result will do well to get out of the way."[15]

With leaders of both factions hoping for quick reconciliation, Free Soilers and Hunkers gathered separately but concurrently in Rome, New York, in August 1849. The Hunkers passed resolutions calling slavery an evil and opposing its extension into free territory, but the Free Soilers insisted they add provisions detailing Congress's authority to interfere with slavery — an implied endorsement of the Wilmot Proviso. When Hunkers William Marcy and Horatio Seymour balked, hopes for a quick reunion were scuttled. The next month the Hunkers nominated their own ticket but authorized the state committee to replace four of the candidates with Free Soilers should the latter group acquiesce and withdraw their previous ultimatum. They did. More radical antislavery stalwarts like Abijah Beckwith could not believe the new party would so quickly compromise on basic Free Soil principles like the Wilmot Proviso. Compromiser John Van Buren tried to soften the blow: "We are asked to compromise our principles," he said, but "the day of compromise is past. . . . We will unite with our late antagonists, and will hold them as we hold the rest of mankind — enemies in war, in peace, friends."[16] Voters were not assuaged. Whigs defeated every fusion candidate but one in the fall elections. Still, the taste of reconciliation remained in the air.

Even Preston King, the single Free Soiler elected to Congress from New York, supported a rapprochement with the regular Democratic Party. Nine-tenths of northern Democratic congressmen, he wrote in the *National Era*, were ready to back the intentions of the Wilmot Proviso — "if not, I should not desire this union [with Democrats]."[17] Three days later, antislavery editor Gamaliel Bailey chose to look on the bright side. Since Free Soil luminaries like King and abolitionist Henry B. Stanton were among those urging a reunion with the Democrats, the enterprise should be given the benefit of the doubt. "They meant well," he wrote to the suspicious Joshua Giddings. "Why cast them off and denounce them?" Besides, he concluded to his ex-Whig correspondent, "the essential principle of Democracy, is direct antagonism to slavery. . . . He is no Democrat who would compromise with the oppressors of the human race."[18] Not all observers saw the impending reunion as a capitulation. Southern commentators and conservative Hunkers like editor James Gordon Bennett viewed the New York rapprochement as a complete and "dangerous" surrender to the Free Soilers' "amalgamationist views."[19]

After favoring a reunion in 1849, King suddenly reversed course, deciding that Free Soilers had bargained away too much in their attempts at reunification. In increasingly panicked letters to Azariah Flagg, in the winter of 1849–50 King tried to head off a final pact.[20] But it was too late. Predicting "cloudiness" for those intent on preserving the proviso as the party's "cornerstone," King admitted he and his fellow radicals had viewed the overtures of the Hunkers through rose-colored glasses. "The democratic party cannot in my opinion live without known and fixed principles," he wrote to John Bigelow of the *Evening Post*. He feared the party, which had just nominated Hunker Horatio Seymour for governor over Barnburner James Wadsworth, would quickly become "a mere combination to put men in office without regard to their principles, [making] it precisely what we have always charged the whig party to be."[21]

Once again a national issue — the Compromise of 1850 — intruded upon New York and precipitated a wholesale reshuffling of the composition of the factions of the state's Democratic Party. Instead of Barnburners and Hunkers, in 1850 the party split into pro-compromise Hards and less doctrinaire Softs, with former Barnburners included in both new groups (though clustered overwhelmingly in the latter). When one Hard introduced a resolution offering congratulations on the recent compromise at the joint Democratic Party convention, John Van Buren vigorously protested; after he was shouted down, the measure passed with only twenty "nays" heard in opposition. Yet instead of walking out with chins held high (as had happened three years earlier), former Free Soilers instead kicked the floor and muttered under their breath. In the dark year of 1850, when faced with a choice over keeping faith with the proviso or returning to a united Democratic Party, the once proud Barnburners chose the latter. Preston King's longtime ally Jabez D. Hammond wrote that he was "sick, sick, sick of this vain political world"; one year later David Dudley Field's "cornerstone" resolution from 1847 declaring uncompromising opposition to more slave states was quietly removed from the masthead of the *Albany Atlas*.[22]

From Compromise to Kansas

The months following the introduction of the Compromise of 1850 were dark ones for Free Soil politicians like Preston King. He was powerless to derail the reunion with the New York Hunkers, a coalition he himself had championed during the previous year. As the compromise measures wended their way through Congress, King watched impotently as mass "Union" meetings supplanted rallies that earlier that year had gathered to support Free Soil. When in Washington, King continued to board with David Wilmot at Mrs. Scott's rooming house, but increasingly he spent his free time at the home of Gamaliel and Margaret Bailey, dining and conversing about the day's events. Each Saturday evening when Congress was in session the Baileys held an informal salon for the city's Free Soilers. In addition to King and Wilmot, the gatherings typically included Senators John P. Hale, Salmon P. Chase, and Charles Sumner and Congressmen Joshua Giddings, Hannibal Hamlin, Henry Wilson, William Slade, Horace Mann, and Robert Rantoul Jr. Other frequent guests were those who, if not Free Soilers themselves, "were tending in that direction," such as Thomas Hart Benton, William Seward, Thaddeus Stevens, and Horace Greeley. Visiting abolitionists including Joshua Leavitt, Henry Ward Beecher, Moncure Conway, and John Greenleaf Whittier often joined in for evenings of conversation, coffee drinking (the Baileys were teetotalers), and "blind man's bluff."[23] Many Free Soilers later recalled that the evenings at the Baileys' lightened their moods during the months that Clay's Compromise snaked its way through Congress, serving "to unite and strengthen all who participated in them . . . cheering the resolute and determining in opinion the timid."[24] The social scene at the Baileys' was vital in keeping Free Soilers from various backgrounds talking and planning their next move.

After six long years of full-bore agitation on the slavery issue, both politicians and voters showed signs of fatigue. Exhausted Americans in both North and South were ready to declare a metaphoric cease-fire and, for the moment at least, accept the tenets of the Compromise of 1850. Endorsing this view, Hunker Democrat William Marcy wrote in his diary how he believed that, with the compromise safely passed, "the agitating & dangerous questions were settled," even if he felt compelled to add that they may not have been concluded in "the best possible way." Without the lifeblood of constant agitation to nourish its ranks, the Free Soil movement languished in the years between the compromise and the Kansas-Nebraska Act.[25]

Free Soilers such as Chase who still hoped to manufacture a large-scale coalition with the Democratic Party were despondent when the party of Jackson nominated New Hampshire doughface Franklin Pierce for president on the forty-ninth ballot at its 1852 convention. In contrast to the carnivalesque atmosphere at Buffalo four short years earlier, the 1852 Free Soil convention in Pittsburgh was a grim affair. Mutual distrust ruled between those who continued to favor coalition with Democrats and those intent on purifying the party of all but the most proven political abolitionists. Coalitionists carried the day on most points. Henry Wilson chaired the convention, and the delegates voted to change their name from Free Soil to Free Democratic. Finally, New Hampshire senator John P. Hale was selected as the presidential nominee on the first ballot. Although Hale was a former Jacksonian, his nomination pleased most noncoalitionists as well, since he had been the candidate of the Liberty Party in 1847. For vice president, the convention tapped a westerner known for his diatribes against the compromise in Congress, former Whig George W. Julian.[26] Coalitionists did not, however, control the resolutions committee, which was chaired by Joshua Giddings and was packed with abolitionists like Gerrit Smith. The 1852 Free Soil platform was a far cry from the "big tent" of 1848. In addition to the usual planks calling for the divorce of the federal government from slavery, new ones forbade cooperation, under any circumstances, with Whigs or Democrats and called slavery "a sin against God and a crime against man."[27]

When the 1852 votes were counted, the Free Democrats were pummeled in every quarter, even where they had done well four years before. With the exhausted David Wilmot in retirement, voters in Pennsylvania's 12th Congressional District voted overwhelmingly for Pierce, who cleverly managed *not* to offend either northern Democrats or southern fire-eaters during the campaign. In New York, Martin Van Buren supported Pierce whole-heartedly, while Preston King surprised his fellow Free Democrats by railing against his former party's platform but sparing its candidate. The few votes Hale received in New York state were from a determined coterie of ex-Liberty men. In all, he won just 156,000 votes, and the only Free Democrat elected to Congress was Gerrit Smith. At the state level, the party's collapse was also evident: in no northern state did the spoiler party of 1848 win enough seats to hold the balance of power.

Mass Defections, 1854–1856

For fourteen months after the 1852 election, Free Soil — as a movement, an ideology, and a party — was practically moribund. Then on January 4, 1854, the diminutive Illinois senator Stephen A. Douglas introduced a bill to organize the territories of the Louisiana Purchase from north of 36°30′ all the way to the Canadian border. Despite the Missouri Compromise's un-equivocal ban on slavery there, Douglas's bill granted the residents of the territory's future states the ability to decide for themselves whether to allow slavery. Douglas was no mere doughface, however. As Michael Morrison's recent analysis of the Kansas-Nebraska Act points out, Douglas was a leader of a growing group within the Democratic Party, centered in the Old North-west, that valued both geographic expansion (a concept that harkened back to Jefferson) and internal improvements (a policy long championed by Whigs and Hunkers). Douglas hoped to use the Kansas-Nebraska Act, as Van Buren had used Andrew Jackson's candidacy in the 1820s, to revive and restore order to the Democratic Party. At the same time, he saw the act's potential to assure his own wealth — any railroad that crossed the new terri-tory would likely terminate near his vast holdings south of Chicago — and, with the southern support it virtually guaranteed, ensure his future political success.

Douglas's brand of popular sovereignty, then, emerged in 1854 as the side of the Democratic coin opposite Free Soil. Both came out of Jackson-ian antipathy for centralized authority and aristocracy in any form. Yet while Free Soilers, based in the eastern states at the center of this study, chan-neled these ideas into a position opposing slaveholders' expansion, Doug-las's allies, strongest in the Midwest, fashioned their opposition to con-centrated power into popular sovereignty. Similarly, adherents to both ideologies claimed theirs carried Democratic principles to their logical con-clusion. By replicating Jefferson's Northwest Ordinance, in which Congress

outlawed slavery in a territory, Free Soilers claimed to be the true Democrats. Their opponents countercharged that Free Soilers were bent on
strengthening the federal government against the rights and liberties of the
residents of a territory who, in a republican society, had the right to choose
their own way of life.

Not surprisingly, both sides also clung to the same 1830s-vintage Jacksonian rhetoric. Both Free Soilers and popular sovereignty advocates invari-
ably accused their opponents of being "aristocrats" and "federalists." For
Iowa's Augustus Dodge, "never was there a question which revived more
thoroughly the distinctive differences between federalism and democracy,
States' rights and consolidation, than does the 'Nebraska-Kansas' bill."[28]
Conversely, Free Soilers saw Kansas-Nebraska and popular sovereignty as
but the latest example in a long series of attempts to place the government
and its people in the service of conspiring and antidemocratic slaveholders.
Just days after Douglas introduced his bill, Free Soilers Salmon Chase and
Joshua Giddings (with help from Charles Sumner and Gerrit Smith) composed an influential pamphlet titled *Appeal of the Independent Democrats in
Congress to the People of the United States.* Published in Gamaliel Bailey's *National Era* on January 24, the day after the introduction of the final Kansas-
Nebraska bill, the appeal convincingly grafted older Free Soil arguments to
the issues of the day. The authors indicted Douglas's bill on several levels: as
"a gross violation of a sacred pledge; as a criminal betrayal of precious
rights; as part and parcel of an atrocious plot to exclude from a vast unoc-
cupied region immigrants from the Old World and free laborers from our
own States, and convert it into a dreary region of despotism, inhabited by
masters and slaves."[29]

Chase later referred to the *Appeal* as the "*most valuable* of my works";
certainly it was the most effective piece of political propaganda he ever
produced. More than any other document, it crystallized precisely why Free
Soilers so opposed Douglas and his arguments for the Kansas-Nebraska bill.
By knuckling under to slave state senators' demands for the outright repeal
of the Missouri Compromise, Douglas had disturbed an agreement that had
been "canonized in the hearts of the American people" for the preceding
thirty years. The bill also cut directly to the heart of the restrictionist ideas
Free Soilers traced all the way back to Jefferson's Northwest Ordinance.
Finally, it made explicit the ideological differences dividing the two northern wings of the Democratic Party into Free Soil and Popular Sovereignty
camps. Whereas Douglas claimed his bill left the issue of slavery extension
up to "the people" (who, Jacksonians continued to believe, could only be

wrong if deceived), Free Soilers saw only a crass bargain with aristocrats who would bypass democracy to infect millions of acres with the stain of slavery.[30]

In the weeks after Douglas's bill was introduced, stunned Free Soilers — joined by antislavery Democrats and Whigs — focused on the repeal of the Missouri Compromise as a symbol of a newly energized Slave Power's rapacious disregard for legality and fairness. Gone were the days of John C. Calhoun's defensiveness on the issue; his successors were aggressive in the extreme. "It was understood at the time the Missouri compact passed," wrote farmer and Free Soiler Abijah Beckwith in the *Albany Atlas*, "that the South dictated the terms, and they had the best of the bargain . . . [but] it produced quiet and was ratified by the passage of solemn law." Now slaveholders were plainly using "bad faith . . . to try and prevent the future benefit of the North" long expected to derive from the compact. The result, as Beckwith noted, was once again a radicalization of northern antislavery attitudes. Not only was compromise with the Slave Power unwise; it was, history had proven, impossible.[31] One Ohio Democrat who later served as a Republican congressman summed up the bitterness and surprise caused by this latest "broken promise": "We have submitted to slavery long enough, and must not stand it any longer. . . . I am done catching negroes for the South."[32]

It was not just Douglas's bill that convinced many Democrats, including several New York Free Soilers who had drifted back to the party of Jackson after 1848, that the age of compromise was gone forever. The Pierce administration's decision to make the bill a "test of Democratic orthodoxy" was also a powerful factor. Even with the full weight of the administration behind it, northern Democratic congressmen split down the middle on the bill, with forty-four voting in favor and forty-three voting against.[33] Democrats' refusal to tolerate even minor differences of opinion over Kansas-Nebraska forced many longtime Jacksonians out of the party for good. With the exception of old-line Barnburners like Martin Van Buren and Azariah C. Flagg, most of the leading 1840s dissidents, such as William Cullen Bryant, David Dudley Field, David Wilmot, and Preston King, left the Democracy almost immediately after the Kansas-Nebraska Act became law. King led more than 100 New York Jacksonians out of their party as soon as the state convention voted down an anti-Nebraska plank in September 1854. For this group, the brief reunion with the state's Hunkers was the aberration in what was otherwise an unbroken antislavery allegiance after 1847. The year 1854 was, in many ways, a continuation of the free-soil revolt that had begun seven years earlier.[34]

For these defectors and the thousands that followed them in 1855–56, the violence in Kansas Territory after Douglas's bill dramatized how significantly the Pierce administration was in thrall to the Slave Power. One Illinois editor who called himself a "Democrat of the Jeffersonian, Jacksonian stamp" moved to Kansas to halt what he described as the imposition of aristocracy there by both slaveholders and rich abolitionists from New England. "We come not, then, as the peculiar advocate of any section," Josiah Miller wrote in his new *Kansas Free State*. "We disavow all connection with Emigrant Aid Companies. . . . We intend [to] advocate the freedom of white men, as well as that of negroes."[35] For Miller and his readers—who tended to oppose the abolitionist leanings of the *Herald of Freedom* as well as the proslavery bombast of the *Squatter Sovereign*—allowing slaveholders to move into Kansas permanently tilted the playing field in favor of wealthy tyrants from both the North and the South. One *Free State* correspondent wrote that he read the paper because it condemned oppression of all sorts, "not only of the slaveholder toward the slave, but of the *capitalist* towards the *poor man*."[36]

In each northern state, ex-Democrats were key members of the widening anti-Nebraska movement. In Michigan a party of "Free Democrats" nominated the "Free Soil Cass Man" Kingsley Bingham for governor almost a week before a similar gathering in Ripon, Wisconsin, first used the name "Republican" for their new party of restrictionists. It was in New York, however, that the largest defections came, in torchlit parades, from the old Barnburner strongholds upstate. Abijah Beckwith's Herkimer County, which had voted for Van Buren in 1848 and then given Pierce and the Democrats a 1,000-vote majority in 1852, awarded Republican candidate John C. Frémont 63 percent of the vote in 1856. Frémont won Preston King's home of St. Lawrence County with an astonishing 75 percent of the votes cast there. More than 7,700 voters chose him over James Buchanan in what had been one of the North's most dependable Democratic strongholds. As Eric Foner points out, in the sixteen New York counties where Van Buren ran either first or second in 1848, Republican majorities totaled more than 56,000.[37]

In *Free Soil, Free Labor, Free Men*, Foner rightly suggests that ex-Democrats' influence in the early Republican Party far exceeded their numbers, which he estimates at about 25 percent of their membership. In a nation where people were often born into political parties the way they were born into religions, it was easier for ex-Democrats to vote for Republicans with Jacksonian backgrounds. To succeed, Republicans needed both Democratic candidates and voters. Foner estimates that eleven of the twenty-six Republican congressmen elected in 1858 were ex-Jacksonians, as were half of Republican state candidates between 1855 and 1861.[38] After all, unlike the Whigs—who after 1854 had no party—Democrats who voted Republican did so by choice. Both the state and national Republican platforms from 1854–56 were remarkable in their similarities to those drafted by the Free Soil and Free Democratic parties in 1848 and 1852. Congressional containment of slavery, an end to new slave states or slave territory, abolition in the District of Columbia, and the repeal of the Fugitive Slave Law were, first and foremost, Free Soil planks.[39]

Part of the genius of the early Republican Party was its ability to avoid the pitfalls experienced by earlier unions of antislavery Whigs and Jacksonians. The Republicans' early state platforms are notable for their conspicuous avoidance of any issue besides slavery. Michigan's anti-Nebraskans, for example, explicitly stated in their 1854 platform that they were "postponing and suspending all differences with regard to political or administrative policy."[40] This was especially critical since, as noted in this study, so many of the Democratic defectors in the 1840s and 1850s were hard-money radicals. The only way to smooth the way for party harmony (while keeping the Republicans competitive in protectionist states like Pennsylvania and pro-railroad states like Illinois) was to focus obsessively on the issue of slavery containment.[41] This is not to say former Jacksonian radicals abandoned their strong hard-money economic views. In March 1860 William Cullen Bryant presciently worried that there was a "conspiracy . . . to pervert the Republican party to the purposes of the owners of coal and iron mines." At the same time, many of the ex–hard money Democrats pushed for the nomination of like-minded Salmon Chase at the 1860 Republican convention. Such activity not only added weight to Chase's long-shot candidacy but also advanced another goal for many ex-Jacksonians: sabotaging ex-Whig William Seward's chances to capture the nomination.[42]

Ex-Democrats who appear in this study figured prominently in the nomination and election of Republican standard-bearer Abraham Lincoln. When Lincoln won the new party's 1860 nomination on the third ballot at the Chicago convention, David Wilmot presided. Former Jacksonians were extremely pleased with the resulting ticket, which included one of their own, Hannibal Hamlin, as the candidate for vice president.[43] Walt Whitman, who in 1855 had shed his partisan editor's persona for that of the poet, had by the fall of 1860 already embarked on what would become a special five-year relationship with the new Republican nominee: "Lincoln is particularly my man," he wrote to Horace Traubel. "[He] particularly belongs to me; yes, and by the same token, I am Lincoln's man. We are afloat in the same stream, — we are rooted in the same ground."[44] Finally, Abijah Beckwith, the elderly farmer and Free Soil "hotspur" who did not expect to live much beyond the 1848 election, was chosen — at age seventy-six — to serve as one of Lincoln's New York electors. The card with which he cast his presidential ballot in the Electoral College on December 4, 1860, remains glued to the final page of the handwritten autobiography Beckwith began for his grandson and namesake in 1847, at the height of the Barnburner revolt.[45]

For the hundreds of thousands of Jacksonian Democrats who turned against slavery in the 1830s, 1840s, and 1850s, the Democratic Party they had once embraced had become, in the words of another old Barnburner, a "tool of the slaveholding oligarchy." They had developed arguments against slavery that owed little to the evangelical morality of abolitionists and substantially widened the antislavery movement, illustrating how the enslavement of any human being threatened Americans white and black. They had brought to the new Republican Party a die-hard Jacksonian unionism that ensured a large number would view the South's secession claims as treasonous. And they had linked the issue of slavery with the issue of land distribution and reform, which allowed one antislavery Democratic paper in territorial Kansas to announce its intention to "advocate the freedom of white men, as well as that of negroes." This appeal, it is important to note, was made on behalf of both black and white Americans, at the expense of an aristocracy of slaveholders and not in the herrenvolk terms recently identified with antislavery Democrats.[46] "To occupy its present ground," wrote Preston King in 1858, "the democratic party has changed its members, its principles, its purposes, its character. Everything but its name is changed." It was thus the job of a new party, stocked with former Democrats and opponents of slavery from all parties, to enact the twin goals of free soil after the southern states had left the union: the Homestead Act and emancipation. These mainstays of the Republican ideology were instrumental to bringing an end to slavery in the United States.[47]

What would the history of the postbellum United States have been if, as one early proponent had envisioned, inalienable homesteads on the public lands had been granted to every head of household — Indian, black, and white? Certainly 1830s Jacksonian dissident George Henry Evans's concept of freedom — a definition that was, significantly, shared by the 4 million freedpeople — differed mightily from the liberal, middle-class description offered by free laborites and even most abolitionists: self-ownership.[48] As Eric Foner asked a quarter-century ago, "Did not freedom suggest more than simply the end of slavery, perhaps even a right on the part of blacks to the land they had cleared and tilled?" Evans and many of his fellow Jacksonian opponents of aristocracy, land monopoly, and slavery saw yeoman farming and inalienable landownership as the true opposites of servitude. Self-ownership, for them, offered little more than a chance to be exploited by bosses, landlords, or capitalists unless it was supplemented by the benefits and natural rights conferred by landownership. A truly democratic and egalitarian future depended on it. "The black as well as the white must, in my opinion, have his right to *land* restored to him before he can be free," Evans wrote to abolitionist Gerrit Smith in 1844. If each head of household were granted enough land to support a family, he continued, "there would be no fear of Indian wars, our standing army might be abolished, and our peaceful example would prevail in other nations." Evans's utopian vision of a West populated by free people and landowners of all races was not one that was shared by most members of the free-soil coalition. Yet neither did the democratic and egalitarian ideas that gave birth to Jacksonian antislavery preclude a future where equality of condition was as much of a concern as equality of opportunity.[49]

Table 1

Massachusetts Gubernatorial Returns, 1828–1843 (percentage)

	Democrat (Morton)	National Republican/ Whig	Anti-mason	Working-men	Liberty	Scattered	Morton's change
1828	12.89	81.53	0.00	0.00	0.00	5.58	—
1829	19.50	71.63	0.00	0.00	0.00	8.87	6.61
1830	30.61	65.52	0.00	0.00	0.00	3.87	11.11
1831	25.96	65.19	0.00	0.00	0.00	8.85	−4.65
1831	20.55	53.92	25.01	0.00	0.00	0.52	−5.42
1832	23.66	52.85	22.97	0.00	0.00	0.51	3.12
1833	24.84	40.32	29.30	5.55	0.00	0.00	1.18
1834	24.81	57.72	13.91	3.35	0.00	0.22	−0.03
1835	38.87	57.86	2.93	0.00	0.00	0.34	14.06
1836	45.91	53.78	0.00	0.00	0.00	0.30	7.05
1837	39.38	60.28	0.00	0.00	0.00	0.34	−6.54
1838	44.49	54.97	0.00	0.00	0.00	0.54	5.11
1839	50.00	49.70	0.00	0.00	0.00	0.30	5.51
1840	43.33	55.68	0.00	0.00	0.85	0.14	−6.67
1841	46.25	50.40	0.00	0.00	3.14	0.21	2.92
1842	47.88	46.56	0.00	0.00	5.41	0.15	1.63
1843	44.72	47.74	0.00	0.00	7.34	0.20	−3.16

Source: Official Returns: Massachusetts State Archives.

Table 2
New York County Returns, Ranked by 1848 Free Soil Vote Percentage

| County | 1848 Free Soil vote | Change in vote by party, 1844–48 | | |
		Free Soil*	Democrat	Whig
St. Lawrence	58.46	54.26	−47.93	−6.32
Herkimer	55.60	47.83	−45.64	−2.18
Oswego	47.75	38.30	−36.29	−2.00
Wayne	46.17	39.59	−37.42	−2.17
Delaware	44.80	42.06	−44.31	2.25
Chemung	44.78	42.42	−42.69	0.27
Cayuga	43.00	39.41	−38.60	−0.82
Fulton	40.61	38.34	−40.25	1.91
Cortland	39.96	29.69	−24.57	−5.12
Madison	39.86	25.03	−22.43	−2.60
Onondaga	39.37	34.18	−31.14	−3.03
Lewis	38.71	34.73	−29.57	−5.16
Tompkins	38.45	34.49	−30.75	−3.73
Jefferson	37.57	31.91	−29.06	−2.85
Yates	37.39	32.66	−26.78	−5.88
Monroe	37.15	33.82	−32.09	−1.73
Steuben	36.42	34.02	−34.53	0.50
Orleans	34.81	29.49	−26.53	−2.96
Ontario	34.60	29.58	−25.99	−3.59
Oneida	33.84	26.62	−24.04	−2.58
Allegany	33.82	28.36	−24.71	−3.65
Niagara	33.69	28.54	−22.14	−6.40
Seneca	32.97	30.50	−22.02	−8.48
Greene	32.74	32.28	−29.28	−3.00
Livingston	31.72	28.58	−27.34	−1.24
Wyoming	30.83	22.49	−14.80	−7.68
Suffolk	30.46	30.22	−34.82	4.60
Franklin	28.13	25.15	−18.06	−7.09
Montgomery	27.80	26.44	−30.73	4.29
Clinton	26.49	17.47	−17.08	−0.40
Washington	26.48	22.56	−22.11	−0.45
Columbia	25.77	25.65	−26.02	0.37
Ulster	25.57	25.44	−27.72	2.27
Rensselaer	24.87	23.38	−23.60	0.22
Essex	23.67	20.66	−20.97	0.31
Cattaraugus	23.03	14.73	−14.77	0.04
Warren	22.59	18.95	−20.83	1.89
Genessee	22.28	17.32	−12.51	−4.81
Chautauqua	21.13	17.76	−11.87	−5.90

County	1848 Free Soil vote	Change in vote by party, 1844–48		
		Free Soil*	Democrat	Whig
Otsego	20.65	16.97	−15.65	−1.32
Chenango	19.47	16.76	−16.25	−0.51
Tioga	18.81	16.87	−15.52	−1.36
Putnam	18.64	18.64	−19.18	0.53
Albany	18.07	17.19	−19.26	2.07
Erie	17.78	14.43	−15.73	1.30
Queens	17.59	17.59	−23.17	5.58
Westchester	17.50	17.28	−22.48	5.21
Saratoga	17.41	16.07	−17.48	1.41
Orange	16.34	15.97	−17.09	1.12
Sullivan	14.99	14.18	−14.43	0.25
Broome	14.97	12.96	−10.10	−2.85
Schenectady	13.91	13.03	−14.58	1.55
Dutchess	13.27	12.94	−16.69	3.75
Rockland	11.91	11.87	−20.58	8.71
Schoharie	11.18	9.50	−9.24	−0.26
New York	9.92	9.70	−16.06	6.35
Kings	6.62	5.84	−10.49	4.65
Richmond	5.91	5.86	−9.00	3.14

Source: Burnham, *Presidential Ballots*, 632–47.

Note: Coefficient of correlation between change in percentage Democratic vote, 1844–48, and change in percentage Liberty/Free Soil vote, 1844–48: −.9379. Coefficient of correlation between change in percentage Whig vote, 1844–48, and change in percentage Liberty/Free Soil vote, 1844–48: −.4357.

*Liberty and Free Soil parties

Table 3

New Hampshire County Returns, Ranked by 1848 Free Soil Vote Percentage

| County | 1848 Free Soil vote | Change in vote by party, 1844–1848 | | |
		Free Soil*	Democrat	Whig
Carroll	20.84	12.46	−4.11	−8.35
Cheshire	19.28	11.80	0.97	−12.77
Merrimack	16.46	6.05	1.22	−7.28
Grafton	15.57	6.86	1.39	−8.25
Sullivan	14.67	5.57	1.81	−7.38
Hillsborough	14.24	6.18	−0.62	−5.57
Rockingham	12.81	4.94	−2.17	−2.77
Coös	12.65	6.72	−0.88	−5.83
Belknap	12.31	3.49	4.74	−8.23
Strafford	12.16	3.57	−0.12	−3.45

Source: Burnham, *Presidential Ballots*, 624–27.

Note: Coefficient of correlation between change in percentage Democratic vote, 1844–48, and change in percentage Liberty/Free Soil vote, 1844–48: −.4849. Coefficient of correlation between change in percentage Whig vote, 1844–48, and change in percentage Liberty/Free Soil vote, 1844–48: −.6676.

*Liberty and Free Soil parties

Table 4

Massachusetts County Returns, Ranked by 1848 Free Soil Vote Percentage

| County | 1848 Free Soil vote | Change in vote by party, 1844–1848 | | |
		Free Soil*	Democrat	Whig
Worcester	43.39	32.13	−13.35	−18.78
Plymouth	37.06	27.67	−17.22	−10.45
Norfolk	32.98	24.43	−18.41	−6.03
Franklin	30.92	22.78	−10.42	−12.36
Bristol	28.77	22.59	−25.01	2.42
Essex	27.50	15.46	−7.95	−7.51
Middlesex	26.35	17.93	−14.55	−3.38
Nantucket	22.98	18.48	−13.15	−5.32
Berkshire	20.69	15.65	−17.03	1.38
Hampden	16.78	10.74	−8.16	−2.58
Dukes	16.07	11.94	−17.50	5.56
Barnstable	15.48	9.14	−11.71	2.57
Suffolk	15.01	11.36	−11.06	−0.30

Source: Burnham, *Presidential Ballots*, 511–13.

Note: Coefficient of correlation between change in percentage Democratic vote, 1844–48, and change in percentage Free Soil vote, 1844–48: −.3749. Coefficient of correlation between change in percentage Whig vote, 1844–48, and change in percentage Free Soil vote, 1844–48: −.7687.

*Liberty and Free Soil parties

Table 5

Pennsylvania County Returns, Ranked by 1848 Free Soil Vote Percentage

County	1848 Free Soil vote	Change in vote by party, 1844–1848 Free Soil*	Democrat	Whig
Tioga	28.49	27.81	−28.13	0.32
Potter	26.33	20.40	−15.96	−4.44
Bradford	25.64	24.73	−24.75	0.02
Mercer	15.32	3.95	−10.12	−11.23
Crawford	11.30	9.03	−5.35	−3.67
Beaver	10.03	4.51	1.20	−5.72
Wayne	7.11	6.53	−6.65	0.13
Susquehanna	6.38	4.36	−4.40	0.04
Warren	6.26	5.44	−5.55	0.11
Erie	6.09	4.84	−1.98	−2.86
Venango	5.94	3.24	−1.52	−1.72
Washington	5.72	2.08	−2.14	0.06
Indiana	4.91	2.76	−1.71	−1.05
Allegheny	4.46	1.41	−2.57	1.16
Chester	4.29	3.39	−1.97	−1.42
Elk	4.08	0.30	7.95	−8.25
Butler	3.51	0.51	−1.37	0.86
Armstrong	3.28	2.19	−7.60	5.42
McKean	2.73	2.73	−3.41	0.68
Montgomery	2.30	1.81	−3.72	1.81
Luzerne	2.27	1.84	−7.61	5.77
Delaware	2.20	1.78	−0.61	−1.17
Wyoming	2.07	2.01	−2.62	0.61
Philadelphia	1.64	1.10	−4.38	3.28
Bucks	1.53	1.26	−1.50	0.24
Westmoreland	1.44	0.53	−2.92	2.39
Greene	1.33	0.86	−1.22	0.36
Clearfield	1.18	1.18	−1.80	0.62
Fayette	1.11	0.55	−2.24	1.69
Jefferson	1.00	0.62	−2.82	2.20
Clarion	1.00	0.74	−7.56	6.83
Lancaster	0.92	0.80	−2.07	1.28
Mifflin	0.82	0.53	0.40	−0.93
Adams	0.57	0.44	−1.58	1.14
Dauphin	0.57	0.29	−4.50	4.21
Huntingdon	0.55	0.55	3.70	−4.26
Union	0.52	0.13	−4.11	4.19
Northampton	0.51	0.51	−1.68	1.17
Columbia	0.51	0.49	−6.26	5.77

County	1848 Free Soil vote	Change in vote by party, 1844–1848		
		Free Soil*	Democrat	Whig
Somerset	0.50	0.34	−0.91	0.57
Cambria	0.46	0.36	−0.27	−0.09
Schuylkill	0.42	0.37	−15.06	14.69
Cumberland	0.39	0.31	−1.15	0.85
Berks	0.35	0.33	−3.54	3.21
Pike	0.29	0.29	−5.10	4.81
Lycoming	0.21	−0.20	−3.55	3.75
Northumberland	0.20	0.02	−5.13	5.11
Monroe	0.13	0.08	−3.48	3.39
Perry	0.13	0.13	−4.96	2.31
Centre	0.09	−0.07	1.90	−1.82
Juniata	0.06	0.06	−3.53	3.47
Franklin	0.06	−0.02	−6.09	6.11
Clinton	0.05	0.05	−1.15	1.10
Lehigh	0.05	0.05	−0.64	0.59
Lebanon	0.04	0.04	−2.14	2.10
York	0.04	0.03	−2.93	2.90
Carbon	0.04	0.04	4.86	−4.90
Bedford	0.02	−0.06	1.14	−1.08

Source: Burnham, *Presidential Ballots*, 704–21.

Note: Coefficient of correlation between change in percentage Democratic vote, 1844–48, and change in percentage Liberty/Free Soil vote, 1844–48: −.7953. Coefficient of correlation between change in percentage Whig vote, 1844–48, and change in percentage Liberty/Free Soil vote, 1844–48: −.2423.

*Liberty and Free Soil parties

Table 6

Ohio County Returns, Ranked by 1848 Free Soil Vote Percentage

| County | 1848 Free Soil vote | Change in vote by party, 1844–1848 | | |
		Free Soil*	Democrat	Whig
Ashtabula	55.20	44.56	−2.60	−41.96
Geauga	43.35	36.90	−1.40	−35.49
Lorrain	43.25	32.05	−3.04	−29.01
Cuyahoga	38.50	33.32	−4.45	−28.87
Trumbull	38.50	29.41	−7.45	−21.95
Lake	37.71	33.86	−1.99	−31.87
Medina	25.10	19.85	−3.90	−15.94
Portage	24.79	19.91	2.34	−22.25
Clinton	23.79	18.14	−1.03	−17.11
Summit	22.20	18.58	−2.37	−16.21
Erie	22.05	19.71	−12.95	−6.76
Huron	19.06	16.21	−5.65	−10.56
Greene	16.37	13.16	−3.21	−9.94
Columbiana	15.88	12.94	−0.59	−12.35
Williams	15.52	15.52	−2.17	−13.35
Harrison	14.42	9.53	0.11	−9.64
Lucas	11.59	11.01	−0.35	−10.65
Meigs	11.53	9.71	−0.58	−9.13
Seneca	11.12	10.11	−3.18	−6.94
Ross	2.96	1.41	−1.84	0.43
Carroll	10.80	6.72	−2.56	−4.16
Washington	10.33	6.59	1.34	−7.93
Knox	10.10	7.94	0.55	−8.49
Ottawa	9.66	7.79	1.33	−9.12
Jefferson	9.23	7.26	−2.44	−4.82
Guernsey	9.11	5.21	−0.35	−4.86
Hamilton	9.09	7.29	−4.89	−2.40
Logan	8.98	5.57	0.16	−5.73
Champaign	8.88	7.98	−0.57	−7.42
Stark	8.84	7.69	0.07	−7.76
Belmont	8.82	5.82	1.06	−6.88
Athens	8.71	2.75	2.50	−5.25
Union	8.65	6.82	−0.70	−6.12
Brown	8.52	5.47	−0.80	−4.67
Monroe	8.46	5.51	0.14	−5.65
Warren	8.39	6.59	0.68	−7.27
Preble	7.97	6.16	−0.99	−5.17
Licking	7.95	4.81	−1.54	−3.26
Clermont	7.43	4.98	−9.15	−10.51
Highland	7.31	4.73	−1.37	−3.36
Delaware	7.23	4.71	−0.62	−4.09
Butler	6.48	5.43	−1.33	−4.09
Adams	6.23	3.28	−0.87	−2.41

County	1848 Free Soil vote	Change in vote by party, 1844–1848		
		Free Soil*	Democrat	Whig
Morgan	6.18	4.65	−1.38	−3.28
Miami	5.87	3.26	1.14	−4.40
Fayette	5.74	2.43	2.11	−4.54
Sandusky	5.65	5.11	−2.54	−2.57
Clark	5.09	3.92	2.20	−6.11
Montgomery	5.02	3.75	−1.29	−2.47
Franklin	4.36	3.06	1.38	−4.44
Hardin	4.07	3.48	−0.64	−2.84
Madison	3.77	3.36	0.08	−3.43
Richland	3.45	2.23	−2.79	0.56
Gallia	3.39	2.13	−0.19	−1.94
Crawford	3.31	3.04	2.69	−5.73
Wayne	3.25	2.11	0.68	−2.79
Henry	3.20	3.20	4.24	−7.45
Coshoton	3.13	1.71	1.41	−3.12
Tuscarawas	3.05	2.36	1.13	−3.49
Pickaway	3.03	2.79	0.37	−0.72
Muskingum	2.84	1.38	1.09	−2.46
Lawrence	2.70	2.53	1.44	−3.97
Darke	2.58	1.70	−0.13	−1.56
Marion	2.45	−0.49	3.60	−3.10
Jackson	2.33	1.67	−1.52	−0.15
Shelby	2.25	0.99	1.81	−2.80
Wood	2.21	2.12	−1.22	−0.90
Pike	1.85	0.88	0.32	−1.20
Mercer	1.57	1.25	−2.51	1.26
Holmes	1.33	1.18	−1.23	0.04
Hocking	1.05	0.94	−3.24	2.29
Hancock	0.87	0.77	1.28	−2.05
Fairfield	0.70	0.46	−0.09	−0.37
Perry	0.51	0.43	−0.51	0.07
Scioto	0.42	0.42	−1.24	0.82
Putnam	0.29	0.11	0.41	−0.53
Allen	0.11	−0.38	2.04	−1.66
Paulding	0.00	0.00	−1.41	1.41
Van Wert	0.00	0.00	0.00	0.00

Source: Burnham, *Presidential Ballots*, 676–97.

Note: Coefficient of correlation between change in percentage Democratic vote, 1844–48, and change in percentage Liberty/Free Soil vote, 1844–48: −.4332. Coefficient of correlation between change in percentage Whig vote, 1844–48, and change in percentage Liberty/Free Soil vote, 1844–48: −.9637.

*Liberty and Free Soil parties

Table 7

*Counties Polling in Excess of 20 Percent of Votes for Free Soil Party, 1848,
Ranked by Free Soil Percentage*

County	1848 Free Soil vote	Change in vote by party, 1844–1848		
		Free Soil*	Democrat	Whig
Lake, Ill.	58.65	47.13	−30.49	−16.64
St. Lawrence, N.Y.	58.46	54.26	−47.93	−6.32
Herkimer, N.Y.	55.60	47.83	−45.64	−2.18
Ashtabula, Ohio	55.20	44.56	−2.60	−41.96
McHenry, Ill.	48.91	42.92	−30.55	−12.37
Oswego, N.Y.	47.75	38.30	−36.29	−2.00
Wayne, N.Y.	46.17	39.59	−37.42	−2.17
Bureau, Ill.	45.35	27.73	−17.22	−10.51
Delaware, N.Y.	44.80	42.06	−44.31	2.25
Chemung, N.Y.	44.78	42.42	−42.69	0.27
Worcester, Mass.	43.39	32.13	−13.35	−18.78
Geauga, Ohio	43.35	36.90	−1.40	−35.49
Lorrain, Ohio	43.25	32.05	−3.04	−29.01
Kane, Ill.	43.14	28.85	−23.35	−5.50
Cayuga, N.Y.	43.00	39.41	−38.60	−0.82
Kendall, Ill.	41.84	27.32	−20.43	−6.90
De Kalb, Ill.	41.70	16.26	−10.47	−5.80
Fulton, N.Y.	40.61	38.34	−40.25	1.91
Putnam, Ill.	40.03	−3.80	−13.08	16.89
Cortland, N.Y.	39.96	29.69	−24.57	−5.12
Madison, N.Y.	39.86	25.03	−22.43	−2.60
Onondaga, N.Y.	39.37	34.18	−31.14	−3.03
Cook, Ill.	38.90	29.75	−28.04	−0.97
Lewis, N.Y.	38.71	34.73	−29.57	−5.16
Cuyahoga, Ohio	38.50	33.32	−4.45	−28.87
Trumbull, Ohio	38.50	29.41	−7.45	−21.95
Tompkins, N.Y.	38.45	34.49	−30.75	−3.73
Lake, Ohio	37.71	33.86	−1.99	−31.87
Jefferson, N.Y.	37.57	31.91	−29.06	−2.85
Yates, N.Y.	37.39	32.66	−26.78	−5.88
Monroe, N.Y.	37.15	33.82	−32.09	−1.73
Plymouth, Mass.	37.06	27.67	−17.22	−10.45
Du Page, Ill.	36.54	20.76	−8.04	−12.72
Steuben, N.Y.	36.42	34.02	−34.53	0.50
Boone, Ill.	35.74	28.76	−16.52	−12.24
Orleans, N.Y.	34.81	29.49	−26.53	−2.96
Ontario, N.Y.	34.60	29.58	−25.99	−3.59

| County | 1848 Free Soil vote | Change in vote by party, 1844–1848 | | |
		Free Soil*	Democrat	Whig
Oneida, N.Y.	33.84	26.62	−24.04	−2.58
Allegany, N.Y.	33.82	28.36	−24.71	−3.65
Niagara, N.Y.	33.69	28.54	−22.14	−6.40
Norfolk, Mass.	32.98	24.43	−18.41	−6.03
Seneca, N.Y.	32.97	30.50	−22.02	−8.48
Greene, N.Y.	32.74	32.28	−29.28	−3.00
Ionia, Mich.	32.58	32.51	−3.96	−21.88
Livingston, N.Y.	31.72	28.58	−27.34	−1.24
Jasper, Ind.	31.68	31.65	−9.24	−19.87
Franklin, Mass.	30.92	22.78	−10.42	−12.36
Wyoming, N.Y.	30.83	22.49	−14.80	−7.68
Tioga, Pa.	28.49	27.81	−28.13	0.32
Franklin, N.Y.	28.13	25.15	−18.06	−7.09
Montgomery, N.Y.	27.80	26.44	−30.73	4.29
Essex, Mass.	27.50	15.46	−7.95	−7.51
Grant, Ind.	27.47	7.22	4.20	−11.41
Randolph, Ind.	26.92	15.68	−3.53	−12.15
Clinton, N.Y.	26.49	17.47	−17.08	−0.40
Washington, N.Y.	26.48	22.56	−22.11	−0.45
Middlesex, Mass.	26.35	17.93	−14.55	−3.38
Potter, Pa.	26.33	20.40	−15.96	−4.44
Ogle, Ill.	26.22	17.37	−5.22	−12.15
Franklin, Maine	25.90	13.39	−5.59	−7.80
Columbia, N.Y.	25.77	25.65	−26.02	0.37
Bradford, Pa.	25.64	24.73	−24.75	0.02
Ulster, N.Y.	25.57	25.44	−27.72	2.27
Medina, Ohio	25.10	19.85	−3.90	−15.94
Rensselaer, N.Y.	24.87	23.38	−23.60	0.22
Portage, Ohio	24.79	19.91	2.34	−22.25
Clinton, Ohio	23.79	18.14	−1.03	−17.11
Essex, N.Y.	23.67	20.66	−20.97	0.31
Allegan, Mich.	23.17	23.15	−6.89	−14.55
Cattaraugus, N.Y.	23.03	14.73	−14.77	0.04
Nantucket, Mass.	22.98	18.48	−13.15	−5.32
Warren, N.Y.	22.59	18.95	−20.83	1.89
Steuben, Ind.	22.53	16.29	−4.14	−12.15
Genessee, N.Y.	22.28	17.32	−12.51	−4.81
Summit, Ohio	22.20	18.58	−2.37	−16.21
Ingham, Mich.	22.18	22.13	−1.81	−15.43
Erie, Ohio	22.05	19.71	−12.95	−6.76
Chautauqua, N.Y.	21.13	17.76	−11.87	−5.90

County	1848 Free Soil vote	Change in vote by party, 1844–1848		
		Free Soil*	Democrat	Whig
Carroll, N.H.	20.84	12.46	−4.11	−8.35
Kalamazoo, Mich.	20.75	7.19	−3.77	−3.43
Berkshire, Mass.	20.69	15.65	−17.03	1.38
Otsego, N.Y.	20.65	16.97	−15.65	−1.32
Knox, Ill.	20.40	10.25	−5.98	−4.28

Source: Burnham, *Presidential Ballots*.

Note: Coefficient of correlation between change in percentage Democratic vote, 1844–48, and change in percentage Liberty/Free Soil vote, 1844–48: −.63656. Coefficient of correlation between change in percentage Whig vote, 1844–48, and change in percentage Liberty/Free Soil vote, 1844–48: −.19949. Coefficient of correlation between change in percentage Democratic vote, 1844–48, and change in percentage Liberty/Free Soil vote, 1844–48 (Ohio data removed): −.83308. Coefficient of correlation between change in percentage Whig vote, 1844–48, and change in percentage Liberty/Free Soil vote, 1844–48 (Ohio data removed): −.05495.

*Liberty and Free Soil parties

NOTES

Abbreviations

Columbia	Columbia University, New York, N.Y.
CU	Cornell University, Karl A. Kroch Library, Ithaca, N.Y.
Dartmouth	Dartmouth University Library, Hanover, N.H.
LC	Library of Congress, Washington, D.C.
MHS	Massachusetts Historical Society, Boston
MML	Marcus Morton Letterbooks, Massachusetts Historical Society, Boston
MSH	Official Election Returns, 1824–60, Massachusetts State House, Boston
NA	National Archives, Washington, D.C.
NHHS	New Hampshire Historical Society, Concord
NYPL	New York Public Library, New York, N.Y.
NYSL	New York State Library, Albany

Introduction

1. *Congressional Globe*, 29th Cong., 1st sess., 1211.

2. Ibid., 1211–13.

3. Wilmot outlined his version of the origins of the proviso in a speech made in Albany, N.Y., October 27, 1847, and referred all queries to the published speech, the third of three nearly identical speeches delivered during the fall campaign. See *Herkimer Convention*, 10–15.

4. Ibid., 12.

5. The same device had been used in Congress just two days earlier (and with little southern opposition) when the House had provided for a territorial government in Oregon, complete with the words, "neither slavery nor involuntary servitude shall ever exist in said territory, except for the punishment of crimes." It is quite possible that a copy of the Oregon free-soil amendment was still sitting on each member's desk on the afternoon of August 8, 1846.

6. *New York Herald*, Aug. 11, 1846.

7. Just moments after the first vote in the House, southern floor leaders rounded up 21 more votes against the bill, but they remained 6 votes short of victory (81-75). In the final House vote taken on the appropriations bill including the proviso, it passed easily, 87-64. See *Congressional Globe*, 29th Cong., 1st sess., 1217–18. The Kentucky Whigs were Henry Grider and William P. Thomasson.

8. Morton to George Bancroft, Dec. 26, 1845, Bancroft Papers, MHS.

9. Morton to M. Eddy, *Niles' Weekly Register*, 5th ser. Dec. 1, 1838, 222.

10. On Democratic racism, see Saxton, *Rise and Fall of the White Republic*, 127–65;

on the virulent racism of one Jacksonian constituency, see Roediger, *Wages of Whiteness*. The recent highly critical interpretations of Jacksonians and race are predicated on Richard H. Brown, "Missouri Crisis," and Richards, "Jacksonians and Slavery." See also Baker, *Affairs of Party*.

11. Schlesinger, *Age of Jackson*, 471, 433.

12. For an excellent historiographical overview, see Feller, "Brother in Arms."

13. Charles G. Sellers Jr., "Andrew Jackson versus the Historians"; Formisano, "Toward a Reorientation of Jacksonian Politics"; Richards, "Jacksonians and Slavery."

14. Saxton, *Rise and Fall of the White Republic*, 127–65; Roediger, *Wages of Whiteness*. Such critiques suffer from a common tendency to conflate Jacksonian Democracy and the Democratic Party. Jacksonian Democracy, a varied and national movement, sought to use democratic power to fortify against an array of political and social forces (aristocracies, monopolies, conspiracies, paper money, banks, centralized power, and corrupt statesmen) that, inevitably, threatened to take it away. The Democratic Party, on the other hand, was a professional organization that used money, people, and ideas to win votes. For a different view, see Wilentz, "Slavery, Antislavery, and Jacksonian Democracy."

15. James Brewer Stewart, *Holy Warriors*; Kraditor, *Means and Ends in American Abolitionism*; Walters, *Antislavery Appeal*; Reinhard O. Johnson, "Liberty Party in New England."

16. See, for example, the comments of Philip C. Barbour of Virginia, Nathaniel Macon of North Carolina, and William Smith of South Carolina, in *Annals of Congress*, 15th Cong., 2d sess., Feb. 15, 1819, 1188; 16th Cong., 1st sess., Jan. 20, 26, 1820, 227–28, 268–69. Thanks to Sean Wilentz for sharing his draft of "Missouri Crisis Revisited." On the Missouri Crisis, see Richard H. Brown, "Missouri Crisis."

17. Van Buren to Thomas Ritchie, Jan. 13, 1827, Van Buren Papers, LC.

18. By the 1840s, northerners and southerners agreed that slavery had to expand in order to survive. See Barney, *Road to Secession*, xiv–xv, 71, 171.

19. Thanks to Michael A. Morrison for helping me to develop this idea. See his *Slavery and the American West*; Major L. Wilson, *Space, Time, and Freedom*; Kohl, *Politics of Individualism*. As David Brion Davis has pointed out, for many Americans the opposite of slavery was not liberty, but equality.

20. Meyers, *Jacksonian Persuasion*.

21. *Congressional Globe*, 25th Cong., 3d sess., appendix, 175.

22. Jackson's farewell address, for example, referred to "the planter, the farmer, the mechanic, and the laborer" as "the bone and sinew of the country; men who love liberty and desire nothing but equal rights and equal laws." See Richardson, *Compilation*.

23. Sedgwick, *Thoughts on the Proposed Annexation of Texas*, 36.

24. Schlesinger, *Age of Jackson*, 406–8. See also Calhoun to Orestes Brownson, Oct. 31, 1841, in Brownson, *Orestes Brownson's Early Life*, 302.

25. *Democratic Review* 13 (July 1843): 27.

26. Byrdsall to Calhoun, Feb. 22, 1847, in Boucher and Brooks, *Correspondence Addressed to Calhoun*, 368.

27. Major L. Wilson, *Space, Time, and Freedom*; Michael A. Morrison, *Slavery and the American West*; Kohl, *Politics of Individualism*. In his incarnation as a poet, not a free-soil editor, Walt Whitman famously wrote, "Do I contradict myself? Very well then. . . . I contradict myself; I am large. . . . I contain multitudes" (*Leaves of Grass*, 55).

28. See Rayback, "Martin Van Buren's Desire for Revenge," for an overview.

29. Beckwith, "Autobiographical Record," CU, 15.

30. Ibid., 34.

31. John P. Hale, for example, became a Free Soiler after attending a marathon of church services in both his own Episcopal and the more egalitarian Freewill Baptist church. See below, Chapter 3.

32. Beckwith, "Autobiographical Record," CU, 43–44.

33. Compared with neighboring Oneida County, home of the growing market and canal town of Utica, Herkimer was less affluent, its population was stagnant, and its down-county markets were less accessible. Between 1830 and 1850, Herkimer County's population increased by 6.2 percent (the county had actually *lost* population between 1840 and 1845), while Oneida's population rose by 28.4 percent. The state as a whole, including New York City, grew by 38.2 percent over the same period. The value of the average home in Herkimer was $536, compared with $705 in Oneida; only 34 percent of the county's land was listed as "improved," compared with 60 percent in Oneida. See Hough, *Census of the State of New York*, xxiv, 234, 242–43. Only eleven people in the county listed their occupation as "banker" or "bank officer," compared with thirty-eight in Oneida.

34. The largest denominations in Herkimer, judging by the census enumeration of "usual number attending" each church, were Methodists (29 percent) and Baptists and Freewill Baptists (17 percent), followed by Presbyterians (9 percent). Oneida's were Methodists (22 percent), Catholics (17 percent), Presbyterians (13 percent), and Congregationalists (12 percent). Between 1836 and 1844, the Democratic tallies in presidential elections were 72 percent, 58 percent, and 56 percent; in 1848 the Free Soil Party won the county with 56 percent, while the Whig totals from 1844 declined by just 400 votes. See Burnham, *Presidential Ballots*, 636.

35. Foner, *Free Soil*. As even a casual reading of this work will reveal, I am deeply indebted to this book and its author. In the decade following the publication of Foner's book, several historians published studies examining the Free Soil Party and its effects on the American political scene. Most of these works, however, focus entirely on national politics and limit their scope to the party's brief existence. As a result the radical roots and abundant ambiguities of free soil have been elided. See Rayback, *Free Soil*; Blue, *Free Soilers*; Mayfield, *Rehearsal for Republicanism*. Dated, but still useful, is Theodore Clarke Smith, *Liberty and Free Soil Parties*. Sewell, *Ballots for Freedom*, remains the best scholarly work on free-soil and antislavery politics, despite its broad survey of the entire range of antislavery politics.

36. *Herkimer Convention*, 14.

37. Foner, *Nothing but Freedom*, 6.

38. Robinson, *Address to the Voters*, 11. See also Richards, *Slave Power*.

39. Lincoln to Anson G. Henry, Nov. 19, 1858, in Basler, *Collected Works of Abraham Lincoln*, 3:339.

Chapter One

1. Silas Wright, quoted in Richards, *"Gentlemen of Property and Standing,"* 92. On the gag rule, see Miller, *Arguing about Slavery*, 210–26; Richards, *Life and Times*, 115–25. On antiabolitionist mobs, see Richards, *"Gentlemen of Property and Standing"*; Grimsted, *American Mobbing*.

2. Schlesinger, *Age of Jackson*, 426. See also Wilentz, "Jacksonian Abolitionist."

3. "Naval Court Martial: Trial of Midshipman William Leggett," *New York Evening Post*, July 8, 24, 1835. According to John Quincy Adams, who was present at the trial, "the tone and character of the defense, so called . . . consisting of a continual invective upon his commander, ought not to have passed without reprehension and rebuke." See also Schlesinger, *Age of Jackson*, 186.

4. "A Voice from the Forecastle," undated review in Amasa Walker scrapbooks, Walker Papers, MHS.

5. Proctor, "William Leggett." See also Wilentz, "Jacksonian Abolitionist."

6. Ibid., 242; William Cullen Bryant, "Reminiscences of the 'Evening Post,' " in Bigelow, *William Cullen Bryant*, 326–27.

7. Hone, *Diary* 1:240; Hofstadter, "William Leggett," 586–94; Meyers, *Jacksonian Persuasion*, 185–93.

8. *New York Evening Post*, Mar. 23, 1835; Leggett, *Political Writings*, 1:243–47.

9. *New York Evening Post*, Dec. 1834; Leggett, *Political Writings*, 1:103; Lawrence H. White, *Democratick Editorials*, 80.

10. Rifkin, "William Leggett," 48.

11. The best account of the July Days riots remains Richards, *"Gentlemen of Property and Standing,"* 113–22, 150–55; see also Kerber, "Abolitionists and Amalgamators."

12. *New York Evening Post*, July 8, 1834; Leggett, *Political Writings*, 1:28–31; Lawrence H. White, *Democratick Editorials*, 192. Antiadministration editors James Watson Webb and William Leete Stone had helped precipitate the riots by spreading amalgamation rumors and publishing the time and location of an abolitionist meeting. Stone, for example, urged "friends of the UNION and of the SOUTH" to attend, while Webb announced that the "fanatics" were gathering to "have their zeal inflamed by the doctrines of abolition and amalgamation." See *New York Commercial Advertiser*, July 4, 1834; *New York Courier and Enquirer*, July 4, 8, 9, 10, 1834. Webb had caned Leggett in 1833 after Leggett spat on him. See Richard Brown, "James Watson Webb."

13. *New York Evening Post*, Sept. 9, 1835; Lawrence H. White, *Democratick Editorials*, 209.

14. Leggett, *Political Writings*, 2:10.

15. *New York Evening Post*, Sept. 3, 4, 1835; Leggett, *Political Writings*, 2:50–55.

16. Whittier, *Old Portraits and Modern Sketches*, 197.

17. *New York Evening Post*, Sept. 7, 1835; *Plaindealer*, Mar. 4, 1837; Leggett, *Political Writings*, 2:63, 237.

18. See, for example, Byrdsall, *History of the Locofoco*. Leggett was, from the start, a leading light of the Locofocos, although he never formally joined the party.

19. In his otherwise excellent study of antislavery constitutionalism, William M. Wiecek completely overlooked Leggett's contribution to what he labeled "moderate constitutional antislavery." The fact remains, however, that Leggett's constitutional arguments, coming out of a Jeffersonian-Jacksonian reverence for the Constitution, anticipated the arguments of political abolitionists Alvan Stewart and James Birney by about two years. See Wiecek, *Sources of Antislavery Constitutionalism*, 17, 202–28.

20. The term "strict construction" is usually associated with Thomas Jefferson's "Kentucky Resolutions" affirming states' rights.

21. Article I, Section 8, for example, refers only to "the migration or importation of such persons as any of the States now existing shall think proper to admit"; Article IV, Section 2, refers to "person[s] held to service or labor in one State."

22. *Plaindealer*, Feb. 25, 1837; Leggett, *Political Writings*, 2:232–36.

23. *Plaindealer*, Feb. 25, 1837.

24. On Bailey and Chase, see Chapter 7, below. On Stewart, see Wiecek, *Sources of Antislavery Constitutionalism*, 205, 218, 254–57, 265–66. On Chase and the Constitution, see Foner, *Free Soil*, 73–77.

25. *Plaindealer*, Feb. 25, 1837; Leggett, *Political Writings*, 2:227–32.

26. *Plaindealer*, Dec. 3, 24, 1837.

27. Ibid., Dec. 24, 1837. For Evans's defense of the Turner rebellion, see *Working Man's Advocate*, Sept. 24, Oct. 1, 8, 15, 1831.

28. *Plaindealer*, Feb. 11, 1837.

29. Ibid., Feb. 25, July 29, 1837; Leggett, *Political Writings*, 2:327–30.

30. Leggett, *Political Writings*, 2:77–78.

31. *New York Evening Post*, Sept. 29, Oct. 27, 31, 1838; Alger, *Life of Edwin Forrest*, 1:348–50; Mushkat, *Tammany*, 176–80.

32. Leggett to Sherrod Williams et al., Oct. 13, 1838, in *New York Evening Post*, Oct. 22, 1838; See also ibid., Oct. 20, 31, Nov. 10, 1838.

33. Leggett to (Theodore Sedgwick Jr.?), Oct. 24, 1838, printed in Leggett, *Political Writings*, 2:335–36.

34. Alger, *Life of Edwin Forrest*, 1:373–75; Schlesinger, *Age of Jackson*, 260.

35. Whittier, *Works*, 4:22; *Democratic Review* 6 (Nov. 1839): 430.

36. Details on Evans's early life are sketchy. On the Evans family, see Evans, *Autobiography of a Shaker*, 2–14. On Evans's life, see *Autobiography of a Shaker*; Masquerier, *Sociology*, 93–99, 204–7; Hugins, *Jacksonian Democracy and the Working Class*, 85–88, 91–94; Malone, *Dictionary of American Biography*, 6:201–2; Bradshaw, "George Henry Evans."

37. Bradshaw, "George Henry Evans," 184.

38. Ibid. Evans first appears in Longworth's *New York City Directory* in 1828.

39. On Frances Wright, see Eckhardt, *Fanny Wright*.

40. *Working Man's Advocate*, Oct. 31, 1829.

41. Zahler, *Eastern Workingmen and National Land Policy*, 16–27. The history of the Workingmen's movement is best told in Wilentz, *Chants Democratic*, esp. 172–216.

42. Wilentz, *Chants Democratic*, 208–16. See also Hugins, *Jacksonian Democracy and the Working Class*, 24–35.

43. *Working Man's Advocate*, Apr. 3, 17, 1830.

44. Ibid., Jan. 29, 1831. On Johnson, see Schlesinger, *Age of Jackson*, 140–42.

45. *Working Man's Advocate*, Mar. 24, 1832.

46. Wilentz, *Chants Democratic*, 214. On Jackson's veto message, see Meyers, *Jacksonian Persuasion*, 16–32.

47. See *Richmond Whig*, Aug. 29, Sept. 3, 1831, quoted in Foner, *Nat Turner*, 14–23.

48. *Working Man's Advocate*, Sept. 3, 1831.

49. *Virginia Herald*, Sept. 3, 1831.

50. John Floyd to Governor James Hamilton of South Carolina, Nov. 19, 1831, Floyd Papers, LC.

51. *New York Journal of Commerce* quoted in the *Liberator*, Sept. 10, 1831.

52. *Albany Argus*, Sept. 22, 1831.

53. *New York Courier and Enquirer*, Oct. 3, 1831.

54. *Liberator*, Sept. 3, 1831.

55. William Lloyd Garrison to Laroy Sutherland, Sept. 8, 1831. Reprinted in Foner, *Nat Turner*, 83.

56. Ibid. On Garrison, see James Brewer Stewart, *Holy Warriors*.

57. *Working Man's Advocate*, Sept. 24, 1831.

58. Ibid.

59. Ibid.

60. See, for example, ibid., Sept. 24, Oct. 1, 8, 15, 1831.

61. Ibid., Oct. 1, 1831; emphasis in original.

62. Ibid., Oct. 15, 1831.

63. Ibid.

64. Ibid., Oct. 1, 1831.

65. Roediger, *Wages of Whiteness*, 65–92; Ignatiev, *How the Irish Became White*. Most issues Evans covered did not pertain to "black" slavery, but to what Evans termed "white" slavery—the subjugation of white labor by an emerging capitalist system of labor relations.

66. *Radical*, Mar. 1841. "The black as well as the white must, in my opinion, have his right to the land restored to him before he can be free," Evans wrote to Gerrit Smith. Until homesteads on the public lands were available to all heads of households, emancipation would only "give the landless black the privilege of changing masters" (Evans to Smith, printed in *Working Man's Advocate*, July 6, 1844).

67. Fitzhugh, *Sociology for the South*, 86; *Charleston Mercury*, Mar. 17, 1860.

68. Smith to J. K. Ingalls, editor of the *Landmark*, Aug. 15, 1848, in Broadside 1614, NYSL; see also Bronstein, *Land Reform and Working-Class Experience*, 93–94.

69. Beckwith, "Autobiographical Record," CU, 39, 42.

70. Commons et al., *Documentary History of American Industrial Society*, 305–7.

71. Salmon P. Chase, quoted in Morris, *Life of Thomas Morris*, xi; Brisbane, *Eulogium on the Life and Character of the Late Thomas Morris*, 4.

72. *Congressional Globe*, 25th Cong., 3d sess., 175; emphasis in original.

73. On the master symbol of the bank, see Meyers, *Jacksonian Persuasion*, 10, 254–55.

74. Morris, *Life of Thomas Morris*, 15. On Morris's early life, see ibid., 9–22; Swing, "Thomas Morris." For a more scholarly account of Morris's career, see Neuenschwander, "Senator Thomas Morris."

75. Morris, *Life of Thomas Morris*, 20.

76. Ibid., 20–21. Smith's political career ended in disgrace after he was implicated in Aaron Burr's southwestern scheme. He resigned from the Senate in 1807 and moved to Bayou Sara, Louisiana, where he died in poverty.

77. Ibid., 24. Later, Morris said that for this specification, the gentleman "deserved a marble monument."

78. Swing, "Thomas Morris," 354; Morris, *Life of Thomas Morris*, 25.

79. Morris, *Life of Thomas Morris*, 32–58. Quotation on 32.

80. Ibid., 33. On the history of early Ohio, see William T. Utter, *Frontier State*.

81. Morris, *Life of Thomas Morris*, 60; Stevens, *Early Jackson Party in Ohio*, 99–100; Neuenschwander, "Senator Thomas Morris," 127, 137 n. 9; Dorn, "Samuel Medary." Jackson paraphrased one of Medary's editorials in his famous bank veto message.

82. Neuenschwander, "Senator Thomas Morris," 127.

83. Morris, *Life of Thomas Morris*, 61–62.

84. *Washington Globe*, Dec. 20, 1832, quoted in Neuenschwander, "Senator Thomas Morris," 127.

85. Swing, "Thomas Morris," 355; Neuenschwander, "Senator Thomas Morris," 128.

86. Thomas Morris to Jonathan D. Morris, Nov. 30, 1833, Jan. 1, 1834, in Morris, *Life of Thomas Morris*, 346, 351.

87. *Congressional Globe*, 24th Cong., 1st sess., 150.

88. Ibid., 77.

89. Sewell, *Ballots for Freedom*, 8.

90. *Congressional Globe*, 24th Cong., 1st sess., 77.

91. Thomas Morris to Jonathan D. Morris, Nov. 30, Dec. 17, 22, 1833, in Morris, *Life of Thomas Morris*, 345–49.

92. *Congressional Globe*, 24th Cong., 1st sess., Mar. 3, Apr. 8, 1836.

93. *Register of Debates in Congress*, 12:1168–70.

94. On the early use of the Slave Power conspiracy, see Richards, *Slave Power*, 2–4, 17–21.

95. Richards, *Life and Times*, 175–79.

96. On the Cincinnati antiabolitionist riot of July 1836, see Richards, *"Gentlemen of Property and Standing,"* 92–100. On Birney, see Fladeland, *Birney*.

97. Neuenschwander, "Senator Thomas Morris," 131. The minutes of the meeting were published in Birney's *Philanthropist*, Dec. 9, 1836.

98. *Philanthropist*, Dec. 9, 1836.

99. Thomas Morris to A. Campbell, Nov. 13, 1837, quoted in Neuenschwander, "Senator Thomas Morris," 131.

100. *Congressional Globe*, 25th Cong., 2d sess., 67.

101. Thomas Morris to T. J. Buchanan, John Brough, and David Tod, Dec. 11, 1838, in Morris, *Life of Thomas Morris*, 192–94.

102. Thomas Morris to Samuel Medary, Dec. 26, 1838, in Morris, *Life of Thomas Morris*, 202.

103. Thomas Morris to ?, Jan. 15, 1839, in Morris, *Life of Thomas Morris*, 176–82.

104. *Congressional Globe*, 25th Cong., 3d sess., 177.

105. Ibid., appendix, 167–75.

Chapter Two

1. Martin Van Buren to Thomas Ritchie, Jan. 13, 1827, Van Buren Papers, LC.

2. Butler, *Martin Van Buren*, 19; DeAlva Stanwood Alexander, *Political History of the State of New York*, 1–3.

3. Forty-two percent of Van Buren's 291,804 votes were cast in New York; see Burnham, *Presidential Ballots*. Van Buren won pluralities in St. Lawrence, Herkimer, Oswego, Wayne, Delaware, Chemung, Corland, Madison, Onondaga, and Lewis counties. See also Thomas B. Alexander, "Dimensions of Voter Partisan Constancy."

4. In his excellent recent book *Young America*, Widmer describes the "electrifying" effect Leggett's writings and career had on young New York Democrats. Bryant wrote that "his most ardent admirers — his peculiar *party*, we may say — were chiefly found among *the young men* of his native city; because it was chiefly to the unsophisticated and uncorrupted mind of generous youth, that his mind addressed itself" (9).

5. *New York Evening Post*, June 13, July 20, Aug. 16, 1836.

6. Theodore I had called Thomas Jefferson "the greatest rascal and traitor in the United States" (Schlesinger, *Age of Jackson*, 154).

7. On Theodore Sedgwick II, see Godwin, *Biography of William Cullen Bryant*, 184. On Catherine Maria Sedgwick, see Kelley, *Power of Her Sympathy*.

8. Sedgwick to Martin Van Buren, Feb. 1, 1834, Sedgwick Papers, MHS; Pierce, *Letters of Charles Sumner*, 2:172; Schlesinger, *Age of Jackson*, 187–88.

9. It was Sedgwick, not Leggett, who was at the paper's helm in October 1834 when the radical wing of the Democratic Party, inspired by Leggett, broke away from the regular, Tammany group wing. The radicals adopted the name Locofocos after Tammany stalwarts left the hall and shut off the lights, leaving them to light candles with the new self-igniting friction matches called locofocos. Before the meeting adjourned, the Locofocos decided to name a separate ticket and their own platform. Sedgwick steadfastly supported the Locofoco or Equal Rights Party. See *New York Evening Post*, Nov. 9, 1834.

10. Theodore Sedgwick Jr. to Theodore Sedgwick Sr., Oct. 10, 1833, Sedgwick Papers, MHS.

11. Richards, *Slave Power*, 141–44.

12. *New York Evening Post*, Feb. 20, 1840. Unlike many Democrats, Sedgwick here meant free blacks as well as free whites: "Who doubts that the free blacks are worse off than the slaves? The one race is oppressed morally, but their physical comforts are in the main cared for. It is in the interest of the masters that they should be well fed and well housed. The other is oppressed both physically and morally—they are degraded and overwhelmed with prejudice—no matter whether deserved or undeserved, the result is the same" (Sedgwick, *Thoughts on the Proposed Annexation of Texas*, 43).

13. Sedgwick, *Thoughts on the Proposed Annexation of Texas*, 13, 36.

14. The term "hard money" refers to people who prefer a specie-based economy rather than one reliant on paper bank notes. In addition to preferring coin over unstable paper notes, hard-money Democrats tended to oppose chartered monopolies and corporations, embrace free trade, and distrust banks.

15. Ellis, *Landlords and Farmers*, 160, 184–89; John H. Thompson, *Geography of New York State*, 106–10; Summerhill, "Farmer's Republic," 144.

16. Hough, *Census of the State of New York*.

17. St. Lawrence County, the state's largest geographically but chronically underpopulated, contained just 27,595 people in 1825. The population more than doubled to 62,354 by 1845. See ibid., xxiv.

18. Ibid., 445.

19. Muller, "Preston King," 124. Although hatred of monetary losses due to discounts and "irredeemable shinplaster" caused antibank radicals like King to see the dangers of the proposed banking system (which Whigs would never admit), they never were able to propose an alternative program to meet the needs of a dynamic economic community. Antibank prejudice and sound banking views rarely met in the same person.

20. Gunn, *Decline of Authority*. On the Bucktails, see Garraty, *Silas Wright*; Donald B. Cole, *Martin Van Buren*, chap. 2; Niven, *Martin Van Buren*. See also Larson, *Internal Improvement*.

21. Larson, *Internal Improvement*, 77–78.

22. Wright to Azariah Flagg, Aug. 29, 1827, Flagg Papers, Columbia.

23. *St. Lawrence Republican*, esp. June, July 1834. I do not mean to indicate that hard-money Democrats were "anticapitalist," a misleading term for the Jacksonian era. Their main objection was to privilege and favoritism, not to entrepreneurialism or even speculation.

24. Ibid., July 22, 29, 1834. On King, see Muller, "Preston King."

25. Donovan, *Barnburners*, 23–25. Hoffman's Herkimer neighbor and friend Abijah Mann led a U.S. Congress committee to Philadelphia to investigate Biddle's Bank of the United States. Finding the door barred, he recruited Jacksonian laborers from the area to "excavate" under the "monster's" wall. Once inside, Mann looked through the bank's records to report personally to Jackson the names of congressmen given credit by the bank. See U.S. Congress, *Biographical Dictionary*, 1285; Muller, "Preston King," 342.

26. This group of legislators also opposed *every* new bank that requested a

legislative charter during the 1835–36 session. Even when a new bank charter passed, King would propose an amendment requiring paper bills to exceed $20 or limit interest rates to 5 or 6 percent, since larger rates "produced an excessive profit at the expense of the debtor." See *Journal of the New York Assembly* (1835–36), 1099–1120; Muller, "Preston King," 123. Under free banking, a prospective banker had only to meet a handful of regulatory prerequisites and was free to open a bank anywhere. The bank's capital was invested in state or federal bonds that were lodged with the state's comptroller, from whom the bank received the banknotes it circulated. If a bank failed to redeem its banknotes into specie, the comptroller began bankruptcy proceedings and sold the bonds to pay back noteholders. See Bodenhorn, *History of Banking in Antebellum America*, 39, 83; Bray Hammond, "Free Banking and Corporations."

27. *Radical*, no. 1 [Jan.?], 1841. On Evans and land reform, see Bronstein, *Land Reform and Working-Class Experience*, esp. 52–111; Zahler, *Eastern Workingmen and National Land Policy*. On Evans's early life, see Evans, *Autobiography of a Shaker*, 2–14. On Evans's life, see Masquerier, *Sociology*, 93–99, 204–7; Walter Hugins, *Jacksonian Democracy and the Working Class*, 85–88, 91–94; Bradshaw, "George Henry Evans."

28. *Anti-Renter*, Jan. 31, Feb. 14, 28, Apr. 4, June 6, 1846; National Reform petitions to Congress in the Center for Legislative Archives, Committee on Public Lands, 29th Congress, folder HR29A-G17.2, NA.

29. There has been a welcome resurgence in scholarly interest in the anti-rent wars in the past several years. Reeve Huston's excellent *Land and Freedom* is the best book on the subject in more than fifty years, and Charles W. McCurdy's *Anti-Rent Era* thoroughly covers the pivotal legal ramifications of the uprising.

30. *Working Man's Advocate*, July 6, 1844. See also Evans's *People's Rights*, July 24, 1844. Not all proponents of land reform shared Evans's racial views. Philadelphia land reformer John Campbell left the movement to publish the racist journal *NegroMania*. See Bronstein, *Land Reform and Working-Class Experience*, 91–92.

31. Smith to J. K. Ingalls, editor of the *Landmark*, Aug. 15, 1848, in Broadside 1614, NYSL.

32. Reeve Huston, *Land and Freedom*, 166–67.

33. Compiled from lists of anti-renters who supported the NRA or helped collect funds for the *Anti-Renter* and through a list published in the newspaper. See *Anti-Renter*, Jan. 17, Feb. 14, June 6, 1846. These names were then checked against lists of those participating in the Whig and Democratic conventions in the years 1840–44.

34. *Albany Patriot*, July 1, 1846.

35. Ibid., Oct. 21, 1846; *Anti-Renter*, Oct. 31, 1846; *Albany Atlas*, Oct. 28, 1846. See also Christman, *Tin Horns and Calico*, 272.

36. Donovan, *Barnburners*.

37. The two-thirds rule had been in effect during the first two Democratic nominating conventions, in 1832 and 1835, but in 1840 a majority rule was used. There was thus no precedent established for the 1844 meeting. On the convention, see Paul, *Rift in the Democracy*; for an excellent discussion of the use of the two-thirds rule, see Richards, *Slave Power*, 112–15.

38. Wadsworth to Van Buren, June 1, 1844, and Calhoun to Richard Pakenham, Apr. 18, 1844, in Calhoun, *Papers of John C. Calhoun*, 18:273–78; O'Sullivan to Van Buren, May 29, 1844, Van Buren Papers, LC.

39. Lemuel Stetson to Azariah C. Flagg, Dec. 31, 1844, Flagg Papers, NYPL.

40. "Secret Circular" reprinted in Godwin, *Biography of William Cullen Bryant*, 1:416–17.

41. Donovan, *Barnburners*, 59.

42. Stetson to Flagg, Jan. 25, 1845, Flagg Papers, NYPL; Richards, *Slave Power*, 144–45; Garraty, *Silas Wright*, 287–329. In "Van Buren, Democracy, and the Partisan Politics of Texas Annexation," Michael Morrison disputes the Barnburners' reasoning, pointing out that Polk actually won more votes in the Northeast than Van Buren had in 1840. This fact, however, does not diminish the near-panic among Barnburners that Democratic candidates had nearly been sunk by the Texas "mill stone." See John M. Niles to Gideon Welles, Jan. 12, 1845, Welles Papers, Huntington Library, San Marino, Calif.; Wright to Polk, Dec. 20, 1844, Polk Papers, LC; Wright to Van Buren, Apr. 21, 1844, Van Buren Papers, LC.

43. Seventy-eight percent of northern Democrats voted to kill the gag, 19 percent more than had voted against it in the opening days of the preceding Congress. Of the New York delegation (often second only to New Hampshire among northern states supporting the gag) eighteen of twenty Democrats joined northern Whigs to defeat the gag rule. See Richards, *Slave Power*, 146.

44. King to Flagg, Dec. 21, 1844, Flagg Papers, NYPL.

45. For a detailed breakdown of the vote, see Richards, *Slave Power*, 148.

46. Polk agreed to split the Oregon Territory with Great Britain at the forty-ninth parallel, rather than provoke a war.

47. Dix to Flagg, May 15, 1846, Flagg Papers, NYPL; Van Buren to Bancroft, Feb. 15, 1845, Bancroft Papers, MHS.

48. Welles to Van Buren, July 28, 1846, Van Buren Papers, LC.

49. *Brooklyn Eagle*, Feb. 3, 1847.

50. "Sit" is antebellum printers' slang for "situation." Quotation from Whitman, *Specimen Days*, 242.

51. *Brooklyn Eagle*, Dec. 21, 1846.

52. Quaife, *Diary of James K. Polk*, 2:304–5.

53. *Congressional Globe*, 29th Cong., 2d sess., 114.

54. See Preston King and Simeon Smith papers, St. Lawrence University Library, Canton, N.Y., which deal at great length with family members moving to Wisconsin.

55. Dix to Flagg, Aug. 30, 1847, Flagg Papers, NYPL.

56. *Albany Evening Atlas*, Oct. 2, 1847. See also *New York Evening Post*, Oct. 3–8, 1847; Field, *Life of David Dudley Field*, 115. Field's Syracuse resolution was displayed for several years at the head of the lead column in the Barnburner *Albany Atlas*. Hunkers preferred to table the resolution to avoid voting it down and appearing "doughfaced."

57. *Albany Argus*, Oct. 17, 1847. Doolittle was referring to Azariah C. Flagg, who was dumped as the party's candidate for comptroller for the first time since 1824.

58. *Brooklyn Eagle,* Apr. 22, 1847.

59. *Albany Atlas,* Oct. 9, 1847. See early drafts of Van Buren's call in box 18, Tilden Papers, NYPL.

60. Flagg to John A. Dix, Oct. 19, 1847, Flagg Papers, Columbia. See also Martin Van Buren to Flagg, Oct. 13, 1847, Van Buren Papers, LC.

61. *St. Lawrence Republican,* Oct. 15, 1847; Flagg to Dix, Oct. 19, 1847, Flagg Papers, Columbia; Flagg to Van Buren, Oct. 12, 1847, and Van Buren to Flagg, Oct. 13, 1847, Van Buren Papers, LC.

62. Beckwith, "Autobiographical Record," CU, 8.

63. Ibid., 14–15.

64. Ibid., 28, 30, 39.

65. *Brooklyn Eagle,* Apr. 27, 1847.

66. David Wilmot to Martin Van Buren, Oct. 6, 1847, Van Buren Papers, LC; Van Buren to the editor of the *Wilkes-Barre Republican Farmer,* Oct. 20, 1847, quoted in *Niles' Weekly Register,* Nov. 13, 1847.

67. Most old guard Barnburners, who hoped to recapture the state's Democratic machinery by "regular" means, skipped the meeting.

68. Chase to Charles Sumner, Dec. 2, 1847, in Chase, "Letters of Salmon P. Chase," 2:124–25; "Speech of Mr. Wilmot," reported in Gardiner, *Great Issue,* 57.

69. *Herkimer Convention,* 7–9.

70. *St. Lawrence Republican,* Nov. 11, 1847.

71. Flagg to John A. Dix, Nov. 22, 1847, Flagg Papers, Columbia; *St. Lawrence Republican,* Nov. 11, 1847.

72. *Brooklyn Eagle,* Nov. 4, 1847.

73. Ibid., Nov. 3, 1847.

74. Michael A. Morrison, *Slavery and the American West,* 85; for southern Democratic opinion, see Thomas Ritchie's editorial "The Disorganizers in New York," *Richmond Enquirer,* Oct. 25, 1847.

75. On Hale and the "Independent Democracy" of New Hampshire, see Chapter 3, below.

76. Welles to Azariah C. Flagg, Feb. 4, 1848, and Dix to Flagg, Feb. 3, 1848, Flagg Papers, Columbia. For an excellent overview and critique of the revenge theory, see Rayback, "Martin Van Buren's Desire for Revenge."

77. Welles to Flagg, Feb. 4, 1848, Flagg Papers, Columbia.

78. Gardiner, *Great Issue,* 95.

79. Quoted in Denis Tilden Lynch, *Epoch and a Man,* 510.

80. On the trajectory of Van Buren's views on slavery, see Major L. Wilson, *Presidency of Martin Van Buren;* Feller, "Brother in Arms," 64–65.

81. "Address of the Democratic Members of the Legislature of the State of New York," in Bigelow, *Writings and Speeches of Samuel J. Tilden,* 2:546–49, 565–66. The address was first printed in the *Albany Evening Atlas,* Apr. 14, 1848.

82. Ibid., 569.

83. Ibid., 573.

84. John Van Buren to Martin Van Buren, Apr. 20, 30, 1848, and Martin Van Buren to John Van Buren, May 3, 1848, Van Buren Papers, LC.

85. Gardiner, *Great Issue*, 100.

86. "Proceedings of the Democratic National Convention," May 24, in the *Washington Daily Union*, May 26, 1848, quoted in Michael A. Morrison, *Slavery and the American West*, 134–35.

87. Woodford, *Lewis Cass*, 253; Gardiner, *Great Issue*, 101.

88. Porter and Johnson, *National Party Platforms*, 11.

89. Samuel J. Tilden, "To the Democratic-Republican Electors of the State of New York," printed in Gardiner, *Great Issue*, 101–7; see also the *Albany Evening Atlas*, June 2, 1848.

90. Van Buren to Francis P. Blair, June 22, 1848, Van Buren Papers, LC.

91. "Reply of Mr. Van Buren," printed in Gardiner, *Great Issue*, 111–17; B. McFarland, President of Tippecanoe Mass Meeting, to Samuel Young, President of the Utica Convention, June 22, 1848, printed in *Proceedings of the Utica Convention*. An informal ballot gave Van Buren 69 votes, former lieutenant governor Addison Gardiner 14, and Dix 2. John Van Buren and others cast their votes for Gardiner to prevent charges that they were forcing delegates to vote for the former president. See John Van Buren to Martin Van Buren, June 26, 1848, Van Buren Papers, LC.

Chapter Three

1. Tuck, *Autobiographical Memoirs*, 70.

2. John P. Hale to Lucy Hale, Jan. 4, 7, 1845, Hale Papers, NHHS. New Hampshire voters had solidly backed annexationist James K. Polk in 1844, and the state's Democratic legislature had recently passed nine resolutions instructing the state's representatives to work for "reannexation." The eighth of these stated that "we believe with Mr. Clay, 'that the reannexation of Texas will add more free than slave states to the Union, and that it would be unwise to refuse a permanent acquisition . . . on account of a temporary institution' " (*New Hampshire House Journal*, Nov. sess. [1844], 346–56).

3. The measure, requiring simple majorities in both houses of Congress, passed the House of Representatives by a vote of 120-98 on January 25, 1845. See *Congressional Globe*, 28th Cong., 2d sess., 194.

4. Hale descended from a long line of Harvard-educated ministers and jurists. His grandfather Samuel was a prominent New Hampshire Tory. On Hale's early life, see Sewell, *John P. Hale and the Politics of Abolition*, 2–3. Sewell's is an excellent and valuable biography.

5. Ibid., 3–8.

6. James Perham to Hale, Jan. 2, 1828, and Henry Y. Simpson to Hale, Feb. 2, 1834, Hale Papers, NHHS. For Democratic politics in New Hampshire before the Civil War, see Donald B. Cole, *Jacksonian Democracy in New Hampshire*.

7. Hale to E. W. Toppan, Feb. 14, 1840, Hale Papers, NHHS; *Dover Gazette*, Mar. 18, 1843.

8. *Congressional Globe*, 34th Cong., 1st sess., 1476. For Hale's votes during the first session of the 28th Congress, see *Congressional Globe*, 28th Cong., 1st sess., 99, 102–3, 592, 691. See also Sewell, *John P. Hale and the Politics of Abolition*, 36–51.

9. John P. Hale to Lucy Hale, Dec. 3, 1843, Hale Papers, NHHS.

10. Ibid., Dec. 21, 1843; *Congressional Globe*, 28 Cong., 1st sess., 4. Fifty-nine percent of northern congressmen voted to repeal the gag in 1843.

11. *Hill's Patriot*, Dec. 14, 1843; *Newport Argus and Spectator*, Jan. 12, 1844; *Dover Gazette*, Jan. 6, 1844; *Exeter News-Letter*, Jan. 8, 1844; *New Hampshire Patriot*, Dec. 28, 1843; William Claggett to Hale, Jan. 3, 1844; John H. Wiggins to Hale, Jan. 5, 1844; C. L. McCurdy to Hale, Dec. 26, 1843; and Samuel Downing to Hale, Jan. 4, 1844, Hale Papers, NHHS.

12. *Congressional Globe*, 28th Cong., 2d sess., 7. Seventy-eight percent of northern Democrats joined northern Whigs to defeat the gag rule in December 1844, an increase of 19 percent over the previous year's vote. Many of these swing votes came from supporters of Martin Van Buren, angry that their candidate had been dumped in favor of Polk, who felt less beholden to the South.

13. John P. Hale to Lucy Hale, Jan. 7, 1845, Hale Papers, NHHS. Sewell and Cole date Hale's final decision to oppose the joint resolution as January 10, the day he attempted to introduce a proviso to the legislation that would divide Texas into free and slave halves. But Hale had already made his decision at least three days earlier, before his attempt to "test" the New Hampshire legislature's eighth resolution. See *Congressional Globe*, 28th Cong., 2d sess., 120; Sewell, *John P. Hale and the Politics of Abolition*, 50–51; Donald B. Cole, *Jacksonian Democracy in New Hampshire*, 218.

14. See Sedgwick to Hale, Jan. 19, 28, 1845, Hale Papers, Dartmouth; John P. Hale to Lucy Hale, Jan. 22, Feb. 5, 7, Hale Papers, NHHS.

15. Franklin Pierce to Hale, Jan. 24, 1845, Hale Papers, Dartmouth.

16. Donald B. Cole, "Presidential Election of 1832," 34.

17. Hill was a member of Jackson's "kitchen cabinet," and Woodbury served as secretary of the navy (1831–34) and treasury (1834–41).

18. Hale to E. W. Toppan, Feb. 14, 1840, Hale Papers, NHHS. In the early 1840s, New Hampshire's legislature passed an *un*limited liability law for corporations, and the Railroad Act of 1840 prohibited railroads from acquiring land through the use of eminent domain. It also stipulated that farmers could remove tracks from their land if they were not satisfied with their compensation. As a result, only 57 miles of track were laid in New Hampshire between 1840 and 1845, as opposed to 249 miles in Massachusetts and 100 in Connecticut. See Kirkland, *Men, Cities, and Transportation*, 275–84; Donald B. Cole, *Jacksonian Democracy in New Hampshire*, 185–215.

19. In 1790 there were fewer than 500 African Americans in the state. The 1830 census showed just over 600, out of a population of 270,000. See *Abstract of the Returns of the Fifth Census*, 4, 48.

20. New Hampshire congressman (and later senator) Charles G. Atherton reintroduced the expired gag at the beginning of the third session of the 25th Congress, tellingly illustrating that the ban on abolitionist petitions was not simply a southern affair. See *Congressional Globe*, 25th Cong., 3d sess., 24–25, 27–28. Atherton also helped enact a more drastic gag rule during the next Congress, which made it a standing rule for Congress to even receive a petition regarding slavery. See *Congressional Globe*, 26th Cong., 1st sess., 150–51.

21. *New Hampshire Senate Journal,* June sess. (1836), 30–31; Sewell, *John P. Hale and the Politics of Abolition,* 30.

22. *Dover Gazette,* Aug. 25, 1835; *Herald of Freedom,* Aug. 22, 1845; Sewell, *John P. Hale and the Politics of Abolition,* 32.

23. On Freewill Baptism and its effects on Democratic and antislavery politics, see below.

24. John P. Hale to Lucy Hale, Dec. 22, 1844, Hale Papers, NHHS.

25. Sewell, *John P. Hale and the Politics of Abolition,* 33.

26. Parkman to Hale, Dec. ?, 1843, Hale Papers, NHHS.

27. Ibid.

28. Bean, "Social Views of the Free Will Baptists"; Sewell, *John P. Hale and the Politics of Abolition,* 34. The ban lasted from 1835 to 1846.

29. "A Frank Constituent" to Hale, Nov. 23, 1843, Hale Papers, NHHS. On issues other than slavery, the constituent said he was in full agreement with the "radical Democracy."

30. Myers, "Beginning of Antislavery Agencies," 8–10; Reinhard O. Johnson, "Liberty Party in New England," 278. On the *Herald of Freedom* and its editor, see Robert Adams, "Nathaniel Peabody Rogers."

31. James Birney received an embarrassing 126 votes in New Hampshire in 1840. The party did better in its gubernatorial races: after nominating the popular Daniel Hoit, Liberty numbers rose to 1,273 in March 1841, and to 3,402 in the 1843 race. See *Dover Gazette,* Mar. 18, 1843; Reinhard O. Johnson, "Liberty Party in New England," 282–85.

32. Hale, *Letter to the Democratic Republican Electors,* 4–7.

33. John Brown to Hale, Feb. 1, 1845, Hale Papers, NHHS; Tuck, *Autobiographical Memoirs,* 75.

34. Hayes, *Reminiscence,* 10–17.

35. Pierce to Hale, Jan. 24, 1845, Hale Papers, Dartmouth; *New Hampshire Patriot,* Jan. 16, 1845. See also Levi Woodbury to Pierce, Jan. 11, 1845, Pierce Papers, NHHS.

36. John P. Hale to Lucy Hale, Jan. 11, 1845, Hale Papers, NHHS.

37. In addition to New Hampshire, Hale received supportive letters from Boston; Oneida, Westchester, New York, and Herkimer counties in New York; and Maine. Hale's letters of support came mostly from towns in Strafford, Carroll, Rockingham, and Merrimack counties.

38. S. B. Parsons to Hale, Jan. 27, 29, 1845, Hale Papers, NHHS.

39. Amos Tuck to Hale, Jan. 15, 1845, Hale Papers, NHHS.

40. N. P. Cram to Hale, Jan. 18, 1845, and Jacob Ela to Hale, Jan. 15, 1845, Hale Papers, NHHS.

41. James Peverly to Hale, Jan. 13, 1845, Hale Papers, NHHS.

42. *History of Coös County;* Center, "History of the Town of Colebrook"; Donald B. Cole, "Presidential Election of 1832," 40.

43. *Democracy and Patriotism,* bound between Mar. 1 and 8, 1845, issues of the *Dover Gazette* at NHHS; S. B. Parsons to Hale, Feb. 18, 1845, Hale Papers, NHHS.

44. Proceedings of the convention in *Dover Gazette,* Feb. 22, 1845; Sewell, *John P.*

Hale and the Politics of Abolition, 58. John Woodbury was not related to New Hampshire party boss Levi Woodbury.

45. John Brown to Hale, Feb. 1, 17, 1845, Hale Papers, NHHS; meeting reported in *Dover Gazette*, Feb. 15, 1845. For Ossippee's support of Hale's course on the gag rule, see Brown to Hale, Feb. 6, 1844, Hale Papers, NHHS.

46. N. F. Barnes to Hale, Feb. 14, 1845, Hale Papers, NHHS.

47. *Proceedings of a Democratic Meeting at Rochester*, Mar. 1, 1845, printed in pamphlet form before March 8, 1845, issue of *Dover Gazette*, NHHS.

48. See *Democracy and Patriotism*, bound between Mar. 1 and 8, 1845, issues of the *Dover Gazette* at NHHS.

49. Hayes, *Reminiscence*, 10–17; Tuck, *Autobiographical Memoirs*, 62.

50. Hayes, *Reminiscence*, 32–35.

51. *Manchester Independent Democrat*, May 14, 1845; Hayes, *Reminiscence*, 35–37.

52. *New York Tribune*, Feb. 13, 1845.

53. *Liberator*, Jan. 24, 1845. Garrison called Hale's letter a "miracle of political independence and uprightness" and later declared that he "was *very* anxious to do something that should secure John P. Hale's election." This "something" was convincing the Massachusetts Antislavery Society to send four agents into New Hampshire to work for Hale. See Sewell, *John P. Hale and the Politics of Abolition*, 64; Whittier, *Complete Poetical Works*, 293. Whittier wrote to Hale that he "would rather be the author of that letter than the President of the United States. . . . It is one of the boldest and noblest words ever spoken for Liberty" (Whittier to Hale, Jan. 24, 1845, printed in Pickard, *Life and Letters of John Greenleaf Whittier*, 1:306–7).

54. The Independent Democratic and regular Democratic tickets were identical, except Hale's name was substituted for Woodbury's in the former. Under New Hampshire's winner-take-all system, Woodbury needed a majority of the top vote getters on the other tickets to win the seat.

55. Tuck to Hale, Mar. 14, 1845, Hale Papers, NHHS.

56. For example, some newspapers reported that Hale's name replaced that of Sawyer, the Whig congressional candidate, on several ballots. Sawyer ran 1,758 votes behind gubernatorial candidate Anthony Colby and 729 behind his closest ticket-mate, suggesting that between 729 and 1,758 voters preferred another candidate.

57. By using the larger Whig number and examining the spring election returns in the *New Hampshire Patriot*, Mar. 20, 1845, I have been able to account for approximately 6,500 (93 percent) of Hale's votes:

Democrat: Steele (gov.) 23,298; Moulton 24,068; Johnson 24,011; Norris 23,765; Woodbury 21,913;

Whig: Colby (gov.) 15,591; Goodwin 14,692; Nesmith 14,690; Edwards 14,562; Sawyer 13,833;

Liberty: Hoit (gov.) 5,464; Porter 5,272; Moore 4,968; Perkins 4,554; Cilley 4,503;

Independent Democrat: Hale 7,053;

Scattering: 1,536.

58. William Claggett to Hale, Mar. 27, 1845, Hale Papers, NHHS; Hayes, *Reminiscence*, 40; Tuck, *Autobiographical Memoirs*, 75.

59. Robert C. Wetmore, "Prospectus for Publishing a Paper, to be called 'The Independent Democrat'" (Manchester, N.H., Apr. 1, 1845), located in run of the *Independent Democrat*, NHHS.

60. This can partially be explained by the loss of Hale's leading campaign issue: when President Tyler signed the joint resolution for annexing Texas to the United States on March 1, annexation was no longer a subject for debate.

61. Tuck to Hale, Apr. 17, 1845, Hale Papers, NHHS; *Boston Post*, Apr. 22, 1845, printed in the *Liberator*, May 9, 1845.

62. *Liberator*, May 9, 1845. Hale's biographer Richard Sewell concluded that his "antislavery convictions became stronger, more clearly defined, and more central to his political philosophy" during the three-year period between his *Letter* and the Free Soil Campaign in 1848. See Sewell, *John P. Hale and the Politics of Abolition*, 87. I argue, however, that as early as the spring of 1845 Hale was already committed to antislavery. He was not yet a political abolitionist (like Thomas Morris or Gamaliel Bailey), a label he earned when he accepted the Liberty Party's presidential nomination in 1847.

63. *Dover Gazette*, Apr. 12, 1845.

64. Hayes, *Reminiscence*, 41–42.

65. Ibid.

66. Fogg to Hale, June 13, 1845, Hale Papers, NHHS.

67. According to the *Independent Democrat*, Sept. 25, 1845, Woodbury received 18,010 votes, the Whig candidate Goodwin received 10,155, and Hale received 8,355, with 121 scattering, leaving the Democrat 621 votes short of a majority. The paper reported "the largest meetings ever held" in Hale strongholds like Deerfield, Goffstown, and Moultonborough on the banks of Lake Winnipesaukee; see ibid., Aug., Sept. 1845. One of Hale's rhetorical staples was revealing that northern congressmen called New Hampshire the South Carolina of the North.

68. Ibid., Dec. 4, 1845. Hale's support in traditionally Whig towns was lower in the November runoff, but he continued gaining from Liberty and, especially, Democratic areas. See *New Hampshire Patriot*, Mar. 18, 1846.

69. *Independent Democrat*, Dec. 4, 1845.

70. Augustus Harris to Hale, Feb. 27, 1845; S. B. Parsons to Hale, Apr. 27, May 30, 1845; John Brown to Hale, Feb. 1, 17, Nov. 5, 1845, all in Hale Papers, NHHS. On New Hampshire politics in the 1830s, see Donald B. Cole, "Presidential Election of 1832," 32–50.

71. Following Donald B. Cole, I am using Margery D. Howarth's division of New Hampshire's 209 towns into seven geographic regions. The regions are (from east to west) the seacoast, the southeast uplands, the Merrimack Valley, the southwest uplands, the Connecticut River Valley, and (in the north) the lake district and the White Mountains. See Howarth, *New Hampshire*.

72. Donald B. Cole, "Presidential Election of 1832," 32; see above for Hale's course on the federal gag.

73. Barron, *Those Who Stayed Behind.*

74. Cook, *Ossippee,* 157; *Statistical View of the United States,* 7th Census (compendium), 272–77, 373.

75. New England Freewill Baptism should not be confused with the southern Free Will Baptists, a denomination that arose in the 1720s out of the general Baptist movement in North Carolina. See Davidson, *Early History of Free Will Baptists.*

76. Bordin, "Sect to Denomination Process," 77–78; Davidson, *Early History of Free Will Baptists,* 35–37.

77. Randall (b. 1749) followed the common New Light pattern of questioning established Congregational doctrine and placed special emphasis on the "freedom of the will." One church chronicler wrote how Freewill Baptism "spoke to the experiences of the [northern] frontier rather than talk down to them with abstruse doctrine . . . [emphasizing] redemption as a matter of free will among people." This, of course, was anathema to Congregationals, Orthodox Methodists, and even many Baptists. See Cook, *Ossippee,* 175; Burgess and Ward, *Free Baptist Cyclopedia; Freewill Baptist Bicentennial Papers.*

78. I. D. Stewart, *History of the Free Will Baptists,* 450. The vast majority, however, still lived in eastern New Hampshire and western Maine.

79. With few exceptions (Freewill Baptist preachers foremost among them) New Hampshire's clergy condemned abolitionism. For example, in 1841 the Church Committee of Dartmouth College threatened to excommunicate one antislavery preacher for having "lost sight of social distinctions, the necessity & lawfulness of rule & restraint, & the wholesome regulation of the word & Providence of God by which alone society is preserved." See Sewell, *John P. Hale and the Politics of Abolition,* 31.

80. Donald B. Cole, "Presidential Election of 1832," 40–44. In Jacksonian Coös County, for example, 79 percent of the vote went to Jackson in 1832, and only 36 percent of the churches were Congregational. In Cheshire, where 60 percent of the churches were Congregational, Clay won 64 percent of the vote.

81. Cook, *Ossippee,* 161.

82. *Independent Democrat,* Apr. 9, Mar. 26, 1845.

83. Bean, "Social Views of the Free Will Baptists"; Burgess and Ward, *Free Baptist Cyclopedia,* 20.

84. *New Hampshire House Journal,* June sess. (1835), 16, and November sess. (1836), 187; *Independent Democrat,* Mar. 26, 1846. The charter was denied until Hale was elected Speaker of the Lower House in 1846.

85. Weld said that the "antislavery record of the Freewill Baptists . . . is a trail of light" (Burgess and Ward, *Free Baptist Cyclopedia*), 21.

86. *Morning Star,* Apr. 14, 1841.

87. See, for example, John P. Hale to Lucy Hale, Sept. 2, 1839, Apr. 27, 1840, Oct. 12, 1842, Hale Papers, NHHS.

88. The best source for the solidification of the alliance in 1845/early 1846 is Sewell, *John P. Hale and the Politics of Abolition,* 76–78. Democratic and Independent Democratic sources are all but silent on the subject; Sewell uses Whig correspondence to flesh out the political outlines.

89. Tuck to Hale and D. S. Palmer to Hale, Feb. 2, 1846, Hale Papers, NHHS. The reason for the secrecy was the legitimate fear that if they were exposed, Woodbury would easily win his majority.

90. The technique of holding simultaneous conventions would, of course, be repeated in New York in 1847.

91. Williams, the Democrat, received 26,914 votes (3,600 more than in 1845); Colby, the Whig, garnered 17,704; and Berry, the Liberty-Independent Democrat, doubled Hoit's 1845 showing with 10,406. The empty congressional seat would not be filled until after the next general election.

92. When the legislature convened in June, the Senate had 4 Democrats, 0 Whigs, 2 Independent Democrats, and 6 vacancies; the House had 122 Democrats, 102 Whigs, 22 Independent Democrats, and 14 Liberty men. See *Independent Democrat*, Mar. 26, 1845; Peverly to Hale, Mar. 15, 1846, Hale Papers, NHHS.

93. Whittier, *Writings*, 3:117.

94. *New Hampshire House Journal*, June sess. (1846), 73.

95. Ibid., 74–75.

96. Ibid., 238, 377–78, 407; Sewell, *John P. Hale and the Politics of Abolition*, 83–84; *Speech of John P. Hale, Upon the Slavery Resolutions, in the House of Representatives, June 25, 1846* (Concord, 1846), NHHS; *Laws of the State of New Hampshire*, 295.

97. Several tiffs contributed to the resentment between the parties. Independents and Liberty men were angered by Whig papers' claims that the 1846 election was a "Whig triumph," and abolitionists never warmed to Governor Colby. See *New Hampshire Sentinel*, Mar. 1846, quoted in Reinhard O. Johnson, "Liberty Party in New England," 311–12.

98. The party officially opposed the further extension of slavery at a meeting in the state house yard in October. See *New Hampshire Patriot*, Oct. 22, 1846.

99. *Granite Freeman*, June 17, 1846; *Emancipator*, Sept. 16, 1846; Tuck to John L. Carleton, Sept. 16, 1846, Tuck Papers, NHHS; Tuck, *Autobiographical Memoirs*, 76. The official fusion of the two organizations was gradual, but it culminated in early 1847 with the merger of the *Independent Democrat* and *Granite Freeman* into the *Independent Democrat and Freeman*, edited by former Democrat George G. Fogg.

100. On Morris, see Chapter 1, above.

101. Hale spoke freely on topics such as Oregon and delivered withering criticisms of the war in Mexico. See *Congressional Globe*, 30th Cong., 1st sess., 160, 804, 810.

102. On Chase and the formation of the national Free Soil coalition, see Chapter 6, below.

103. Hayes, *Reminiscence*, 37–39.

104. Tuck, *Autobiographical Memoirs*, 70–72. Further personalizing his attack, Tuck fumed that Wendell Phillips "never seemed more confounded or more bitter than when slavery disappeared."

Chapter Four

1. *Boston Atlas*, Oct. 24, 1838. On the dominance of the conservative National Republican and Whig parties in state politics, see Sheidley, *Sectional Nationalism*.

The best overview of antebellum state politics in Massachusetts remains Formisano, *Transformation of Political Culture*.

2. Morton wrote to John C. Calhoun on December 8, 1828, that "this aristocracy, ever changing in numbers but steady in its purpose, has the much greater proportion of our political existence controuled [*sic*] the government of the states" (MML).

3. For example, in numerous private and public letters, Morton had termed slavery a "sin" or a "curse" and "the most portentous evil which a righteous God ever inflicted upon a nation." As a member of the U.S. Congress he also voted against extending slavery and opposed the admission of Texas into the Union as a slave state. See Morton to Morton Eddy, Sept. 28, 1837, in *Niles' Weekly Register*, no. 55 (1837), 222; Morton to Gardiner B. Perry, Sept. 23, 1835, MML.

4. See the *Boston Post*, Dec. 17, 1845.

5. Both antebellum politicians and contemporary historians made (and make) significant distinctions between antislavery and abolitionism. The former refers to opposition to slavery to any degree and for any reason, while the latter refers to a specific and identifiable group that after 1830 agitated for immediate emancipation of all slaves.

6. Littlefield, "Governor Marcus Morton"; Morton to Bancroft, Sept. 1, 1841, Bancroft Papers, MHS.

7. Henry F. Howe, *Salt Rivers of the Massachusetts Shore*, 270–81.

8. Bancroft, "Political Portraits." See also Littlefield, "Governor Marcus Morton," 78, 81; Malone, *Dictionary of American Biography*, 13, 259.

9. Bancroft, "Political Portraits," 385; Littlefield, "Governor Marcus Morton," 80.

10. Darling, *Political Changes in Massachusetts*, 28. In addition to Morton, Massachusetts political figures such as John Bolles, B. F. Hallett, Samuel Gridley Howe, and Horace Mann were also Brown graduates.

11. Bancroft, "Political Portraits," 385; Morton to Calhoun, Feb. 19, 1843, MML.

12. Morton quickly built a "large and lucrative practice" in Bristol County by, as one contemporary recalled, "appear[ing] in every case which was tried" (Littlefield, "Governor Marcus Morton," 82).

13. Morton to Eddy, Sept. 28, 1837, in *Niles' Weekly Register*, no. 55 (1837), 222. For Morton's opposition to the admission of Missouri as a slave state, see *Annals of Congress*, 15th Cong., 2d sess., 33:1214–15; 15th Cong., 2d sess., 34:1274; 16th Cong., 1st sess., 36:1572, 1587; 16th Cong., 2d sess., 37:944, 1116, 1146, 1209.

14. Morton to Eddy, Sept. 28, 1837, in *Niles' Weekly Register*, no. 55 (1837), 222.

15. Morton to George Bancroft, Dec. 26, 1845, Bancroft Papers, MHS.

16. Bancroft, "Political Portraits," 387.

17. James L. Huston, *Securing the Fruits of Labor*, 6–11.

18. Morton to Calhoun, Dec. 8, 1828, MML.

19. Darling, *Political Changes in Massachusetts*, is still the most thorough source for the history of the antebellum Democratic Party in Massachusetts. See 40–84 for the formation of the Jacksonian coalition in the state.

20. Ibid., 53–55.

21. *Statesman,* Apr. 4, 1828.

22. Darling, *Political Changes in Massachusetts,* 58.

23. Morton to Calhoun, Jan. 6, 1829, MML.

24. Ibid. Two years later Morton confessed that "the President himself, always was personally unpopular, in this State. There are some points in his character which our people do not and never will like" (ibid., Mar. 10, 1831).

25. Of course, Calhoun was not concerned about racial minorities, but minority groups (such as slaveholders) or views (that slavery was a positive good).

26. Morton to Calhoun, Feb. 13, 1834, MML.

27. Ibid., Mar. 7, 1829. Calhoun, of course, was well known vehemently to oppose protective tariffs as damaging to southern planters.

28. Jackson's public break with Calhoun was precipitated by the nullification controversy (Calhoun had joined with South Carolinians wishing to "nullify" a federal tariff); the Eaton affair (where Calhoun's wife Floride had publicly snubbed Peggy Eaton, the young wife of Secretary of War John H. Eaton); and Jackson's censure for actions in Florida in 1818 (it was disclosed that Calhoun had secretly denounced Jackson's actions there). See Schlesinger, *Age of Jackson,* 54–56.

29. The correspondence between Calhoun and Jackson relating to Calhoun's responsibility for the Monroe administration's censure in 1818 was published in the *Boston Statesman* and numerous other papers on February 26, 1831. On the Eaton affair, see Marszalek, *Petticoat Affair.* On nullification, see Freehling, *Prelude to Civil War.* See also Schlesinger, *Age of Jackson,* 54–56; Niven, *John C. Calhoun and the Price of Union,* 175.

30. Instead of writing Calhoun an average of six letters a year, as he had from 1829 to 1831, Morton left a three-year gap between March 10, 1831, and February 13, 1834. After the latter date, Morton's next (and last) letter to Calhoun is dated February 20, 1843 (MML).

31. Morton to Calhoun, Feb. 13, 1834, MML.

32. Ibid., Mar. 7, Apr. 18, 1830; Darling, *Political Changes in Massachusetts,* 44, 81.

33. See Calhoun's *Exposition and Protest* printed in Lence, *Union and Liberty.*

34. Morton to George Bancroft, Dec. 18, 1834, and to G. B. Perry, Sept. 23, 1835, MML; see also Darling, *Political Changes in Massachusetts,* 81–83.

35. *Register of Debates in Congress,* 2:1579–80.

36. Horace Binney to ?, printed in Binney, *Life of Horace Binney,* 82; Emerson, *Journals,* July 30, 1835, 517.

37. More radical, "immediatist" abolitionists eschewed suffrage. See James Brewer Stewart, *Holy Warriors,* 35–50, 59–60.

38. Morton to G. B. Perry, Sept. 23, 1835, MML.

39. *Boston Atlas,* Aug. 25, 1835. On the Faneuil Hall meeting and the Boston mob, see Richards, *"Gentlemen of Property and Standing,"* 58–64.

40. *Emancipator,* Dec. 1, 1847. The *Daily Advocate* was edited by the newly minted Jacksonian (and former Antimason) B. F. Hallett, who for a brief time in the mid-1830s dabbled in antislavery politics.

41. See Appendix, Table 1, for Massachusetts gubernatorial returns for the years Morton was the Democratic candidate.

42. Morton to M. Eddy, Sept. 28, 1837, printed in the *Boston Advocate*, Nov. 8, 1837, and the national *Niles' Weekly Register*, no. 55 (1837), 222.

43. Morton to Bancroft, Dec. 7, 1837, MML.

44. Ibid.; Morton to Eddy, Sept. 28, 1837, printed in the *Boston Advocate*, Nov. 8, 1837, and the national *Niles' Weekly Register*, no. 55 (1837), 222.

45. David Wilmot, one of the better-known antislavery Democrats, always placed his opposition to slavery in racial terms, claiming he wished to "preserve for free white labor a fair country, a rich inheritance," in the West. See Wilmot's speech in *Herkimer Convention*, 10.

46. Darling, *Political Changes in Massachusetts*, 241.

47. Bancroft, "Political Portraits," 392–93; Littlefield, "Governor Marcus Morton," 91; Darling, *Political Changes in Massachusetts*, 215–20. Massachusetts law required the death penalty for murder, treason, rape, arson, burglary, and highway robbery.

48. Quotation in *Refutation of the Charge of Abolitionism*, 4; Darling, *Political Changes in Massachusetts*, 251. Even Morton's lieutenant governor was a Whig, leaving him at the head of what Arthur B. Darling called "a hostile government."

49. Bancroft, "Political Portraits."

50. Darling, *Political Changes in Massachusetts*, 273, 281.

51. Quoted in Reinhard O. Johnson, "Liberty Party in New England," 250.

52. These peculiar winner-take-all election rules helped the National Republicans and Whigs hold on to the state legislature and senate in much stronger numbers than their votes reflected (1828–43).

53. Darling, *Political Changes in Massachusetts*, 292; Reinhard O. Johnson, "Liberty Party in New England," 251. The *Liberator* claimed that a few of the Liberty representatives ignored the plan and voted entirely for Democrats, but there is little evidence to support Garrison's claim. See *Liberator*, Mar. 17, 1843.

54. Morton to Whittier, Dec. 20, 1842, quoted in the *Emancipator*, Dec. 31, 1845.

55. Arthur B. Darling concluded that in the 1842 election, the Liberty Party drew votes primarily from ex-Whigs. See Darling, *Political Changes in Massachusetts*, 290–92. But analysis of the entire 1840s, especially past 1844, when the Liberty Party rose to its greatest electoral strength in Massachusetts, indicates that the lion's share came from disgruntled Democrats. See Reinhard O. Johnson, "Liberty Party in New England," 127–69. Edward Magdol came to a similar conclusion for the Liberty Party as a whole in *Antislavery Rank and File*, 146–48.

56. Morton to Atherton, Feb. 18, 1845, MML; emphasis Morton's.

57. Morton to Bancroft, July 3, 1845, MML.

58. Ibid., Jan. 13, 1845.

59. Morton to C. G. Atherton, Feb. 21, 1845, Feb. 18, 1846; Morton to Cave Johnson, June 23, 1845, MML. See also Morton to R. J. Walker and to Bancroft, summer 1845, MML.

60. Morton to Johnson, July 2, 1845, MML.

61. "Extract," [?] to Morton, n.d. [1845], MML. While it is fairly certain that

Worth was, in fact, an abolitionist, he remained a strong Democrat and Free Soil (Van Buren) supporter. See Morton to Benjamin Tappan, Apr. 21, 1846, MML.

62. *Boston Post*, Dec. 17, 1845. In a letter to George Bancroft, B. F. Hallett asked, "With his letters to Whittier and Eddy . . . showing the closest communion with abolitionism, from '37 to '44, can the President send in his name to the Senate with consistency?" (Hallett to Bancroft, Sept. 23, 1845, Bancroft Papers, MHS). On the imbroglio, see also I. H. Wright to Bancroft, Mar. 21, 1845, and Chauncy Clarke to Bancroft, Mar. 25, 1845, Bancroft Papers, MHS.

63. Morton to Bancroft, Dec. 26, 1845, MHS; emphasis Morton's. See also Morton to Eddy, Feb. 21, 1846, MML.

64. On the Slave Power conspiracy, see Leonard Richards's brilliant *Slave Power*; on the origin of the term "Slave Power," see above, Chapter 1.

65. Morton to Fairfield, Jan. 26, 1846; Morton to Niles, Feb. 12, 1846; Morton to Atherton, Feb. 21, 1846; Morton to Tappan, Apr. 21, 1846, MML. On Benjamin Tappan's antislavery, see Feller, "Brother in Arms."

66. On defense pamphlets, see Freeman, *Affairs of Honor*, 113, 116–21.

67. *Refutation of the Charge of Abolitionism*, 14.

68. *Emancipator*, Dec. 31, 1845.

69. *Refutation of the Charge of Abolitionism*, 21.

70. Morton to Bancroft, Feb. 27, 1847, Bancroft Papers, MHS.

71. "Remarks by Amasa Walker, Esq., in the late Democratic State Convention," n.d., in Amasa Walker scrapbooks, Walker Papers, MHS.

72. Morton to Dix, Mar. 2, 1848, MML.

73. J. Oakley to Morton, quoted in Morton to A. C. Flagg, June 17, 1848, MML.

74. Morton to Whitmarsh, Aug. 9, 21, 1848, MML.

75. Morton to John Van Buren, Oct. 4, 1848; see also Morton to Chittenden, Aug. 24, 1848; to Willis, Aug. 24, 1848; to Chapin, Aug. 31, 1848; to Tillinghast, Sept. 19, 1848; and to Mason, Sept. 20, 1848, all in MML.

76. In the 1848 elections in Massachusetts, among Democrats, Lewis Cass received 35,281 votes (26 percent) in the presidential contest, and Caleb Cushing garnered 25,323 votes (20 percent) in the gubernatorial race. Among Whigs, Zachary Taylor (pres.) won 61,972 votes (46 percent); George Briggs (gov.), 61,640 (50 percent). Among Free Soilers, Martin Van Buren (pres.) had 38,307 votes (28 percent); Stephen C. Phillips (gov.), 36,011 (29 percent) (MSH).

77. Sewell, *Ballots for Freedom*, 219.

78. Morton to Frederick Robinson, Nov. 22, 1850, MML.

Chapter Five

1. Within a month of the proviso's introduction, Jacob Brinkerhoff of Ohio claimed that he, not Wilmot, was the measure's true author and that Wilmot was a mere front man. Wilmot's own account does not necessarily contradict this. Despite dueling claims by both Brinkerhoff's and Wilmot's partisans, the measure was almost certainly a work of cooperation. For Brinkerhoff's version, see Hamlin, *Life*

and Times of Hannibal Hamlin, 156–57; Henry Wilson, *Rise and Fall of the Slave Power,* 2:16. For an excellent account of the historiography of the proviso, see Foner, "Wilmot Proviso Revisited."

2. Quotation from Craven, *Coming of the Civil War,* 221.

3. See Ignatiev, *How the Irish Became White.*

4. See esp. Saxton, *Rise and Fall of the White Republic,* 153–54; Roediger, *Wages of Whiteness,* esp. 43–95.

5. *Herkimer Convention,* 14.

6. The state of Connecticut claimed what is today Pennsylvania's northern tier (a strip of land with the same latitude as Connecticut, beginning just west of Dutchess County, New York, and extending ad infinitum into the interior) before ceding the land to the United States.

7. When the Wayne County seat was laid out on May 16, 1800, the stakes for the courthouse were driven "in a virgin forest, at a point where the ground sloped gently in every direction except to the northwest" (Alfred Mathews, *History of Wayne, Pike, and Monroe Counties,* 8). Building materials for the new town had to be brought from Philadelphia via Easton, over roads thick with tree stumps.

8. Heverly, *History of the Towandas,* 11.

9. Ibid., 11–14.

10. Going, *Wilmot,* 5.

11. Ibid., 5, 10.

12. Ibid., 9.

13. Ibid., 12; DuBois and Mathews, *Galusha Grow,* 44. There were many tracts by Quaker abolitionists in Walker's library, but Wilmot remembered the collection for its books on "political institutions." For insight on how the *Wealth of Nations* was read in the early republic, see Merrill, "Anticapitalist Origins of the United States." Echoes of Smith can be found in Wilmot's speech against the Tariff of 1846. See below.

14. *Pennsylvanian,* July 24, 1846. The governor, David R. Porter, was heavily invested in iron and railroads.

15. Burnham, *Presidential Ballots,* 7–8, 34–35, 706, 718.

According to Burnham, *Presidential Ballots,* Democratic electoral percentages in Pennsylvania's 12th Congressional District, for presidential ballots (1836–52), were as follows:

1836, 56.7 percent; 1840, 56.4 percent; 1844, 65 percent; 1848, 37.9 percent (Free Soil election); 1852, 55.5 percent.

16. Ibid., 704–5; Craft, *History of Bradford County,* 195.

17. *Bradford Porter,* Oct. 23, 1844; *Bradford Reporter,* July 22, 1846; *Carbondale Democrat* quoted in *Bradford Reporter,* July 29, 1846. While both parties in Pennsylvania supported high tariffs to protect the state's growing industry and manufacturing centers, the small farmers of the northern tier adamantly opposed protective tariffs. See Craven, *Coming of the Civil War,* 224.

18. *Pennsylvanian,* July 26, 1846. The quote was attributed to former governor Porter.

19. *Towanda Northern Banner,* May 21, 1835.

20. *Towanda Banner and Democrat*, Nov. 26, 1839, Mar. 28, May 23, 1840.

21. Ibid., May 23, 1840.

22. Heverly, *History of the Towandas*, 4.

23. Craft, *History of Bradford County*, 195.

24. Ibid., 194. Union Lodge No. 108 had ceased meeting from 1832 to 1839, during the height of Antimasonry. If the lodge were active, Wilmot might have joined earlier. On freemasonry, see Goodman, *Towards a Christian Republic*.

25. The 1790 *Census of the United States* reports only 3 slaves living in the part of Luzerne County that would become Tioga, Potter, and Bradford counties, out of a population of 2,606. The 1820 census lists 53 free blacks and no slaves. By 1850, the census reported 301 "colored" people. The number increased only slightly, to 320, in 1860. See U.S. Bureau of the Census, *7th Census* and *8th Census* (compendiums).

26. Dayton, "Underground Railroad." On the Underground Railroad, see Gara, *Liberty Line*.

27. Dayton, "Underground Railroad," 146.

28. Craft, *History of Bradford County*, 194.

29. Ibid. See also records of the Bradford County Antislavery Society at the Bradford County Historical Society, Towanda, Pa.

30. See Richards, *"Gentlemen of Property and Standing."*

31. See, for example, *Bradford Reporter*, Oct. 23, 1844, July 22, 1846.

32. *New York Globe*, 1843, in Going, *Wilmot*, 35–36. Wilmot carried the district by almost 3,000 votes (54.6 percent), earning 500 more than Shunk and 700 more than Polk. See *Bradford Reporter*, Nov. 20, 27, 1844. The main issue of the campaign was the high protective tariff of 1842, popular in Pennsylvania but not in the remote northern tier, where farming and timber cutting were virtually the only occupations.

33. Foner, "Wilmot Proviso Revisited," 275. Martin Van Buren, for example, had written in 1845 how Democratic support for a war viewed by northern voters as one waged for the extension of slavery would amount to "political suicide" ("Van Buren–Bancroft Correspondence," 439).

34. *Bradford Reporter*, fall 1844, spring 1845.

35. National Reform Association petitions in folder HR29A-G17.2, Collection of House Records, NA. Wilmot presented petitions from Armstrong, Fayette, Allegheny, Bradford, and Luzerne counties during the 29th Congress. Wilmot's successor in Congress, Galusha A. Grow, would later be known as the "Father of the Homestead Act" for his efforts to bring about land reform.

36. See Fehrenbacher, *Chicago Giant*, 69, 74, for a western congressman's linking of land reform and the principles of slavery restriction.

37. *Congressional Globe*, 29th Cong., 1st sess., appendix, 184–88. Wilmot said, "Without these harbors Oregon is comparatively worthless; with them, Oregon is worth a war. These surrendered, let New York and Boston be surrendered with them; these lost, all would be lost." At one time, historians attributed the Wilmot Proviso to the resentment felt by western Democrats over the Polk administration's broken promise to press as hard for all of Oregon as for the admission of Texas. See

Persinger, "'Bargain of 1844,'" 1:189–95. But this thesis did not explain why eastern Democrats like Wilmot and future key proviso supporters Preston King and George Rathbun also took radical all-Oregon stands.

38. The 1842 tariff was enacted to protect the nation's fledgling manufactures and industry, and Pennsylvania's coal and iron industries (as well as some workers) were benefiting handily under the shield from foreign competition. As a result of this success, the state legislature in Harrisburg adopted resolutions instructing the Pennsylvania senators and representatives in Washington to resist any revision of the protective tariff. See *Pennsylvania Senate Journal* (1846), 1:58; *Pennsylvania House Journal* (1846), 1:184–85; *Harrisburg Telegraph,* Jan. 28, Feb. 11, 1846; Eiselen, *Rise of Pennsylvania Protectionism,* 188.

39. *Congressional Globe,* 29th Cong., 1st sess., appendix, 767–71. The House easily passed the Walker tariff and sent the measure to a deadlocked Senate. Trapped between the interests of his home state of Pennsylvania and those of his administration, Vice President Alexander Dallas was forced to cast the tie-breaking vote in favor of the new lower tariff.

40. *Albany Atlas,* Nov. 9, 1847.

41. Quoted in Going, *Wilmot,* 174–75 n.

42. *Congressional Globe,* 29th Cong., 1st sess., 205–6. See also Fehrenbacher, *Chicago Giant,* 70; Chaplain W. Morrison, *Democratic Politics and Sectionalism;* Rayback, "Martin Van Buren's Desire for Revenge"; Foner, "Wilmot Proviso Revisited."

43. Wilmot to Victor E. Piollet, July 4, 1846, Bradford County Historical Society, Towanda, Pa.

44. See, for example, Feller, "Brother in Arms."

45. Stenberg, "Motivation of the Wilmot Proviso"; Craven, *Coming of the Civil War,* 224; Chaplain W. Morrison, *Democratic Politics and Sectionalism,* 15, 179–80 n; Foner, "Wilmot Proviso Revisited."

46. *Congressional Globe,* 29th Cong., 2d sess., appendix, 345.

47. Ibid., 180.

48. *Elmira Gazette,* Nov. 4, 1847. Wilmot submitted scores of petitions in the 1840s from northerners hoping to "free the public lands" for settlers in the form of inalienable homesteads.

49. Paul Dillingham (Vt.); Hannibal Hamlin (Maine); Jacob Brinkerhoff (Ohio); Preston King, Martin Grover, George Rathbun, and Timothy Jenkins (N.Y.). James Thompson of Pennsylvania was present for the early discussions of the proviso, abandoned it in 1847, and remained a lifelong Democrat.

50. Fisher, "Diary," June 11, 1848.

51. *Herkimer Convention,* 13.

52. Ibid., 14.

53. Ibid.

54. Miller, *Arguing about Slavery.*

55. Thanks to Frederick J. Blue for this suggestion and for sharing his work in progress on David Wilmot. For more on Wilmot, see his forthcoming *From Left to Right: Varieties of Antislavery Political Leadership.*

56. Wilmot to Chauncy Guthrie, Theodore Leonard, and others, Sept. 18, 1846, in Going, *Wilmot*, 152, 154–55.

57. Chaplain W. Morrison, *Democratic Politics and Sectionalism*, 27. For Wilmot's version of events, see *Congressional Globe*, 30 Cong., 2d sess., appendix, 139.

58. Quaife, *Diary of James K. Polk*, 2:306–8.

59. *Congressional Globe*, 30 Cong., 2d sess., 96. For King's reintroduction of the proviso, see above, Chapter 2.

60. *Congressional Globe*, 29th Cong., 2d sess., appendix, 352–55; Going, *Wilmot*, 165–67.

61. Going, *Wilmot*, 175–76.

62. Ibid.

63. Ibid., 180.

64. *Herkimer Convention*, 14; emphasis mine.

65. *Congressional Globe*, 29th Cong., 2d sess., 303, 352. Thanks again to Frederick J. Blue, who discusses this concept in his chapter on Wilmot in his forthcoming *From Left to Right: Varieties of Antislavery Political Leadership*.

66. *Congressional Globe*, 29th Cong., 2d sess., 455; Chaplain W. Morrison, *Democratic Politics and Sectionalism*, 34–35.

67. *Congressional Globe*, 29th Cong., 2d sess., 453–55.

68. Richards, *Slave Power*, 153–54; U.S. Congress, *Biographical Dictionary* (1957).

69. *Nineteenth Century*, quoted in Going, *Wilmot*, 230. The *Articles of the Union of the Indiana David Wilmot Proviso League* sought a reshuffling of parties, dedicating their organization to "those who love their country more than party." See Going, *Wilmot*, 230.

70. *Bradford Reporter*, Sept. 12, 1847.

71. Going, *Wilmot*, 232.

72. *Herkimer Convention*, 13.

73. Ibid.

74. Ibid., 14.

75. Wilmot, however, never advocated black suffrage like Morris.

76. *Congressional Globe*, 30th Cong., 1st sess., 304.

77. Wilmot to Chase, May 29, 1848, quoted in Going, *Wilmot*, 321.

78. *Congressional Globe*, 30th Cong., 1st sess., appendix, 1076; Going, *Wilmot*, 663–64.

79. Going, *Wilmot*, 673.

80. Ibid., 676.

81. Ibid., 671, 679.

Chapter Six

1. Volpe, *Forlorn Hope of Freedom*, 109, 116–17; Blue, *Chase*, 50–53. In his *Salmon P. Chase: A Biography*, John Niven ascribes Chase's swing toward Jacksonian views as a combination of the "practical and the ideal" (88). In *Gamaliel Bailey and Antislavery Union*, Stanley Harrold links Bailey's Jacksonian swing to his "border state

perspective" and his interest in worldwide reform movements such as the Anti–Corn Law League; see ix, xii–xiii, 22–23, 85–88.

2. *Cincinnati Weekly Herald and Philanthropist*, Apr. 29, 1846.

3. Chaddock, *Ohio before 1850*, 31–37, 42–43.

4. Chase to Giddings, Feb. 4, 1843, quoted in Volpe, *Forlorn Hope of Freedom*, 116; *Philanthropist*, Aug. 16, 1843.

5. "To the Hon. Thomas Morris," printed in Morris, *Life of Thomas Morris*, 203.

6. *Philanthropist*, May 15, 1839.

7. Ibid.

8. Ibid., May 12, 1837; Harrold, *Gamaliel Bailey*, 18.

9. Donald G. Mathews, *Slavery and Methodism*, vii, 207; Harrold, *Gamaliel Bailey*, 5.

10. Harrold, *Gamaliel Bailey*, 6–9; *Methodist Protestant*, Mar. 11, 1831, quoted in ibid., 8.

11. Harrold, *Gamaliel Bailey*, 17.

12. Ibid., 18–24.

13. On the split in the American Antislavery Society, see Walters, *Antislavery Appeal*, 11–13; Sewell, *Ballots for Freedom*, 75; James Brewer Stewart, *Holy Warriors*, 88–96. Garrisonians, of course, opposed all political action, relying solely on moral suasion to transform public opinion. The other wing, led by people like Joshua Leavitt and Lewis Tappan, favored combating the single issue of slavery in the political realm. Of course, this latter group also disagreed amongst themselves on whether to accomplish this end through third party action or within the Whig Party.

14. *Philanthropist*, Oct. 14, 1836, May 22, 1838; Bailey to James G. Birney, May 24, 1838, in Dumond, *Letters of James Gillespie Birney*, 1:457. See also Wiecek, *Sources of Antislavery Constitutionalism*, 202–28.

15. *Philanthropist*, Nov. 12, 1839, June 16, 1841.

16. Ibid., Mar. 27, 1838.

17. Ibid., Sept., Oct. 1838; Harrold, *Gamaliel Bailey*, 28–29.

18. Theodore Clarke Smith, *Liberty and Free Soil Parties*, 30–31; Bailey to Birney, Oct. 28, 1838, in Dumond, *Letters of James Gillespie Birney*, 1:473.

19. Morris was thrown over for his response to a Democratic questionnaire that sought to determine the extent of his abolitionist views. The historical record does not show who made the determination that Morris's views were too extreme to warrant his reelection. See Morris to T. J. Buchanan, John Brough, and David Tod, Dec. 11, 1838, in Morris, *Life of Thomas Morris*, 192–93; Chapter 1, above.

20. *Emancipator*, Aug. 8, 1839; Rayback, "Liberty Party Leaders of Ohio," 166.

21. *Philanthropist*, Oct. 8, 1839; Theodore Clarke Smith, *Liberty and Free Soil Parties*, 35.

22. *Philanthropist*, Apr. 21, July 7, 1840.

23. Ibid., Apr. 30, 1839.

24. Ibid., Sept. 8, 1840.

25. Burnham, *Presidential Ballots*, 246–48. Birney polled 6,225 of nearly 2.5 million votes cast (.002 percent).

26. Litwack, *North of Slavery*; Dykstra, *Bright Radical Star*; Richards, *"Gentlemen of Property and Standing."*

27. See, for example, *Philanthropist*, Sept. 25, 1838, June 16, 1841.

28. Harrold, *Gamaliel Bailey*, 42–43; Richards, *"Gentlemen of Property and Standing,"* 156–66. Most of the money came from eastern antislavery organizations and individuals, including Lewis Tappan, William Jay, John G. Whittier, and Gerrit Smith, who sent $20 for Cincinnati's free blacks and $10 for the *Philanthropist*.

29. Harrold, *Gamaliel Bailey*, 45; *Philanthropist*, Apr. 30, Nov. 11, Dec. 31, 1839, July 21, 1840, Jan. 6, Apr. 29, 1841.

30. Harrold, *Gamaliel Bailey*, 8–9, 46–47. On Protestantism and morality, see Walters, *Antislavery Appeal*, 37–53.

31. *Philanthropist*, Feb. 5, 1839, Oct. 28, 1840, Feb. 17, Nov. 10, 1841.

32. Bailey to James G. Birney, Feb. 21, 1840, in Dumond, *Letters of James Gillespie Birney*, 1:532.

33. *Philanthropist*, May 19, 1840.

34. Ibid., Feb. 28, 1844.

35. Nichols to Bailey, May 6, 1840, in *Philanthropist*, May 19, 1840. See also ibid., Nov. 4, 1840, Nov. 10, 17, 1841.

36. Smith to Bailey, Sept. 13, 1842, in *Philanthropist*, Oct. 15, 1842; letter from Hon. Thomas Morris, Jan. 15, 1839, in ibid., Feb. 5, 1839.

37. *Philanthropist*, May 19, 1840, Sept. 1, 1841, June 15, 1842.

38. Birney, a slaveholder turned abolitionist, was an imperious and stiff candidate and had little electoral appeal beyond Liberty Party stalwarts. He had also, by the early 1840s, begun to voice his misgivings toward democracy and universal manhood suffrage, to the dismay of many of his friends and supporters. See, for example, Birney to Joshua Leavitt et al., Jan. 10, 1842, in Dumond, *Letters of James Gillespie Birney*, 2:645–56; Fladeland, *Birney*, 215–16.

39. Chase to Lewis Tappan, Sept. 15, 1842, Chase Papers, LC; Rayback, "Liberty Party Leaders of Ohio," 171; *Philanthropist*, Oct. 1, 1842. Chase only joined the Liberty Party in May 1841, after losing reelection to the Cincinnati city council, where he served as a Whig, the previous month. See Blue, *Chase*, 45; Niven, *Chase*, 58–61. On Chase's decision to join the Liberty Party, see Niven, *Chase*, 62–67.

40. Rayback, "Liberty Party Leaders of Ohio," 172.

41. Bailey to Birney, Nov. 16, 1842, in Dumond, *Letters of James Gillespie Birney*, 2:709; Theodore Clarke Smith, *Liberty and Free Soil Parties*, 57; Harrold, *Gamaliel Bailey*, 51.

42. For editorials linking the Whig Party to the Money Power, see *Philanthropist*, Aug. 27, 1842, Mar. 1, 1843; Harrold, *Gamaliel Bailey*, 53. Quotations in *Philanthropist*, Dec. 23, 1842, Nov. 8, 1843.

43. Joshua Leavitt to Birney, Dec. 18, 1844, in Dumond, *Letters of James Gillespie Birney*, 2:889–90; Theodore Clarke Smith, *Liberty and Free Soil Parties*, 79–80. Birney's totals were undoubtedly worsened by the Garland forgery, a letter released by Michigan Whigs that suggested Birney was in league with the Democrats of that state.

44. James G. Birney to Joshua Leavitt et al., Jan. 10, 1842; Theodore Weld to Birney, Jan. 22, 1842; Seth M. Gates to Birney, Jan. 24, 1842; Bailey to Birney, Mar. 31, 1843, all in Dumond, *Letters of James Gillespie Birney*, 2:645–56, 665, 674, 726–28. See also Fladeland, *Birney*, 215–16; Harrold, *Gamaliel Bailey*, 64.

45. *Cincinnati Weekly Herald and Philanthropist*, Dec. 25, 1844.

46. William Birney to James G. Birney, Nov. 25, 1844, in Dumond, *Letters of James Gillespie Birney*, 2:887.

47. *Cincinnati Weekly Herald and Philanthropist*, Apr. 23, 1845. A draft of the call can be found in the Chase Papers, LC, dated Apr. 19, 1845.

48. "Address of the Southern and Western Liberty Convention," in Chase and Cleveland, *Anti-Slavery Addresses*, 104–6.

49. Ibid.

50. Atkins to Chase, June 25, 1845, also quoted in Volpe, *Forlorn Hope of Freedom*, 117; Seward to Chase, Aug. 4, 1845, Chase Papers, LC.

51. *Cincinnati Weekly Herald and Philanthropist*, June 25, 1845.

52. G. W. Ellis to Chase, Feb. 15, 1844, Chase Papers, LC.

53. An exception was the maverick Democrat Jacob Brinkerhoff, who was elected to Congress from Mansfield, Ohio, in 1842. He was the first Democratic opponent of slavery in Congress since Morris's expulsion in 1839. See Weisenburger, *Passing of the Frontier*, 444–45. On Brinkerhoff's role in the introduction of the Wilmot Proviso, see Chapter 5, above.

54. Chase to Jacob Brinkerhoff, Feb. 25, 1845, Chase Papers, LC. On Hale and New Hampshire, see Chapter 3, above.

55. Chase to Hale, June 30, 1845, Hale Papers, NHHS.

56. Chase to Giddings, Aug. 15, 1846, Chase Papers, LC.

57. In his 1837 defense of the fugitive slave Matilda, a light-skinned African American woman whom Birney had hired as a housekeeper, Chase argued that slavery was a creation of local law only and could not exist outside the jurisdiction that had licensed it. Furthermore, slavery could not exist in Ohio because of Jefferson's Northwest Ordinance. These arguments (Chase's first foray into the antislavery cause) were, of course, built on ideas promulgated by Thomas Morris (most directly in his April 13, 1836, Senate speech) and James G. Birney in the early issues of the *Philanthropist*. See *Register of Debates in Congress*, 12:1168–70. Even though Chase lost the case (and was ridiculed for his arguments), it eventually became the Constitutional basis of the Republican Party's program. See Fladeland, *Birney*, 148–49; Niven, *Chase*, 50–54; Foner, *Free Soil*, 75.

58. On the Barnburner revolt and 1847 split in the New York Democracy, see Chapter 2, above.

59. Birney suffered a paralytic stroke after falling from a horse in August 1845 and was no longer a candidate.

60. The Liberty League, too, had radical Democratic predilections, including the elimination of legalized monopolies, free homesteads, and the establishment of free trade. See Sewell, *Ballots for Freedom*, 117–21.

61. *Cincinnati Weekly Herald and Philanthropist*, July 22, Oct. 7, 1846; *National Era*, May 27, 1847.

62. Chase to Hale, June 15, 1848, Hale Papers, NHHS; *Cincinnati Weekly Herald*, July 22, 1846; Niven, *Chase*, 102.

63. *Cincinnati Weekly Herald*, Nov. 3, 1847, quoted in *National Era*, Nov. 8, 1847.

64. Rayback, "Liberty Party Leaders of Ohio," 165–78.

65. *True Democrat*, Jan. 14, 1848, quoted in Theodore Clarke Smith, *Liberty and Free Soil Parties*, 121.

66. The convention was planned to issue simultaneous calls for the Buffalo convention with the Barnburner meeting at Utica. See above, Chapter 2.

67. *National Era*, May 25, 1848.

68. Ibid., June 29, 30, July 6, 1848; Theodore Clarke Smith, *Liberty and Free Soil Parties*, 130.

69. *Addresses and Proceedings of the Free Territory Convention of Ohio*; Theodore Clarke Smith, *Liberty and Free Soil Parties*, 130; Henry Wilson, *Rise and Fall of the Slave Power*, 2:142.

70. Other estimates put the number of delegates and spectators at 30,000. See Theodore Clarke Smith, *Liberty and Free Soil Parties*, 139.

71. Dyer, *Great Senators*, 95; Henry B. Stanton to Hale, Aug. 20, 1848, and Joshua Leavitt to Hale, Aug. 22, 1848, Hale Papers, NHHS; Sewell, *Ballots for Freedom*, 157; Theodore Clarke Smith, *Liberty and Free Soil Parties*, 139.

72. "Free Soil Party Platform," in Wilentz, *Major Problems in the Early Republic*, 549–51.

73. Adams quoted in Sewell, *Ballots for Freedom*, 157.

74. See, for example, Foner, "Racial Attitudes," 328–29. Richard Sewell is a notable exception; see *Ballots for Freedom*, 152–69.

Chapter Seven

1. *New York Advertiser* quoted in Erkkila, *Whitman the Political Poet*, 52.

2. *Brooklyn Freeman*, Sept. 9, 1848.

3. *National Era*, Aug. 31, 1848; Sumner to Chase, July 7, 1848, Chase Papers, LC. See also George G. Fogg to John P. Hale, Aug. 21, 1848, Hale Papers, NHHS. Hale predicted that Van Buren would win New York and enough smaller states to throw the election into the House of Representatives.

4. Hale to Samuel Lewis, Aug. 28, 1848, in *National Era*, Sept. 7, 1848.

5. Chase to Martin Van Buren, Aug. 21, 1848, Van Buren Papers, LC. Theodore C. Smith reported that there were, on average, two Free Soil meetings per day on the reserve between August 10 and November 9, 1848. See Theodore Clarke Smith, *Liberty and Free Soil Parties*, 143.

6. Theodore Clarke Smith, *Liberty and Free Soil Parties*, 143–47; Sewell, *Ballots for Freedom*, 165.

7. *Cleveland Plain Dealer*, June 7, 1848; Sewell, *Ballots for Freedom*, 167.

8. Fehrenbacher, *Chicago Giant*, 80–85; Blue, *Free Soilers*, 111.

9. *National Era*, Oct. 12, 1848.

10. *Detroit Advertiser*, Aug. 4, 1848, quoted in Theodore Clarke Smith, *Liberty and Free Soil Parties*, 149.

11. *National Era*, Aug. 24, 31, 1848.

12. Morton to D. D. Field, June 17, 1848, MML; see Chapter 4, above.

13. Jackson to Blair, Jan. 24, 1845, in Blair-Lee Papers, Princeton University, Princeton, N.J.; William Ernest Smith, *Blair Family in Politics*, 1:239–40.

14. Benton, *Thirty Years' View*, 2:723; Nye, *George Bancroft*, 177.

15. Dyer, *Phonographic Report*, 27–28.

16. Rayback, "American Workingman and the Antislavery Crusade." For more on John Van Buren and his role in the Barnburner revolt in New York, see Chapter 2, above.

17. Foner, "Racial Attitudes"; Blue, *Free Soilers*, 129; Bilotta, *Race and the Rise of the Republican Party*, 92, 96–97, 101.

18. Sewell, *Ballots for Freedom*, 173–75; *Albany Atlas*, Apr. 28, 1848; Gardiner, *Great Issue*, 52–55.

19. Chase had included a homestead plank in the Ohio Free Territory Convention in June 1848. See Chapter 6, above. Barnburners had been educated about the political appeal of the free grant in the mid-1840s. See Chapter 2, above. Martin Van Buren officially endorsed the homestead plank in a letter to National Reformer and anti-renter Alvan Earl Bovay three weeks before the Buffalo convention. See Van Buren to Bovay, July 20, 1848, quoted in *Albany Atlas*, July 26, 1848.

20. *Vote Yourself a Farm*, pamphlet printed in Commons et al., *Documentary History of American Industrial Society*, 305–7. For land reform petitions, see folder HR29A-G17.2, Collection of House Records, NA. The petitions were often forwarded to congressmen who had endorsed the Wilmot Proviso. Galusha Grow, Wilmot's successor in Congress, became known as the Father of the Homestead Act for his efforts to enact land reform.

21. *Albany Atlas*, Feb. 29, Apr. 28, Nov. 21, 1848. See Van Buren's speech in *Herkimer Convention*; Gardiner, *Great Issue*, 49–55.

22. Dyer, *Phonographic Report*, 4, 21. Dyer reported that at least one delegate complained about the presence of blacks at the convention and at the lectern.

23. Blue, *Free Soilers*, 118–19; Douglass, *Life and Writings*, 367–69. Ward quoted in Blue, *Free Soilers*, 119.

24. Resolutions quoted in Blue, *Free Soilers*, 120–21.

25. *Young America*, Sept. 28, 1848.

26. *Delaware Gazette*, June 28, Oct. 4, 1848. As a symbol of the new political alignment in Delaware County, Allaben served on the same Free Soil committee with Col. John Edgerton, a relative of the deputy who accompanied Osman Steele to the Moses Earle farm the day Steele was murdered.

27. H. J. Munger, "Reminiscences of the Anti-Rent Rebellion," New York State Historical Association, Cooperstown, 10.

28. Burnham, *Presidential Ballots*; Rayback, *Free Soil*, 253–57, 294–97.

29. On the Free Soil Party's financial troubles in New York, Massachusetts, and Ohio, see B. F. Butler to Martin Van Buren, Oct. 3, 1848, Van Buren Papers, LC; A. Jewett to Chase, Oct. 24, 1848, Chase Papers, LC. For discussions of the origins of Free Soil votes, see Thomas B. Alexander, "Dimensions of Voter Partisan Con-

stancy," 96, 104–5; Rayback, *Free Soil*, 281–87; Sewell, *Ballots for Freedom*, 168–69; Blue, *Free Soilers*, 143–45.

30. See Appendix, Table 2. New York's voting totals were Cass, 114,320 (25 percent); Taylor, 218,603 (48 percent); Van Buren, 123,128 (27 percent).

31. Burnham, *Presidential Ballots*, 632.

32. See, for example, Sewell, *Ballots for Freedom*, 167; Blue, *Free Soilers*, 149; Mayfield, *Rehearsal for Republicanism*, 123.

33. See Chapter 2, above.

34. See Appendix, Table 2.

35. In general, coefficients of correlation between +.50 and −.50 are statistically insignificant. On statistical methods, see Dollar and Jensen, *Historian's Guide to Statistics*.

36. John Mayfield found a correlation of +.83 when comparing Taylor's to Clay's 1844 totals (a strong finding), and one of +.89 with Winfield Scott's in 1852, indicating strong cohesiveness within the Whig vote in New York state. See Mayfield, *Rehearsal for Republicanism*, 194.

37. Burnham, *Presidential Ballots*, 642, 634.

38. See Appendix, Table 2.

39. Ibid.

40. Weller's largest claim to fame was his introduction of a measure censuring Joshua Giddings for presenting antislavery resolutions to Congress. See *Journal of the House of Representatives*, 27th Cong., 2d sess., 571.

41. Price, "Election of 1848 in Ohio," 289; Theodore Clarke Smith, *Liberty and Free Soil Parties*, 153.

42. *National Era*, Oct. 26, 1848.

43. The state totals were Cass, 154,775; Taylor, 138,360; Van Buren, 35,354. See Price, "Election of 1848 in Ohio," 300; Theodore Clarke Smith, *Liberty and Free Soil Parties* 154.

44. See Appendix, Table 6.

45. See Appendix, Table 4.

46. Presidential/gubernatorial results for 1848 were Cass/Cushing (Dem.), 26.0 percent/20.4 percent; Taylor/Briggs (Whig), 45.7 percent/49.7 percent; Van Buren/Phillips (Free Soil), 28.3 percent/29.0 percent (MSH). Turnout was the highest since 1844; more than 18,000 votes were added to the 1847 totals.

47. Morton to French, Nov. 22, 1850, MML.

48. Burnham, *Presidential Ballots*, 512. On Worcester politics and society before the Civil War, see Brooke, *Heart of the Commonwealth*.

49. See Appendix, Table 3.

50. *Independent Democrat and Freeman*, Nov. 23, 1848, Nov. 6, 1856, Nov. 8, 1860; Burnham, *Presidential Ballots*, 624–25; Sewell, *Ballots for Freedom*, 271.

51. Wilmot to Chase, May 29, 1848, Chase Papers, LC.

52. See Chapter 5, above.

53. The coefficient of correlation between the changes in Democratic and Liberty–Free Soil votes, 1844–48, was −.796. The Whig–Free Soil coefficient was an insignificant −.242.

54. Rayback, *Free Soil*, 284; Sewell, *Ballots for Freedom*, 216; Blue, *Free Soilers*, 146.

55. Vermont Democrats, −14.5 percent; Vermont Whigs, −6.5 percent; Vermont Free Soilers, +21 percent. See Burnham, *Presidential Ballots*, 512.

56. *National Era*, June 7, 1849; Sewell, *Ballots for Freedom*, 216.

57. See Appendix, Table 7; Blue, *Free Soilers*, 111.

Conclusion

1. King to Charles Sumner, Dec. 25, 1848, King Papers, St. Lawrence University Library, Canton, N.Y.

2. *John-Donkey*, Jan. 8, 1848.

3. Giddings to Chase, May 6, 1849, Chase Papers, LC; Chase to George Reber, June 19, 1849. See also Sewell, *Ballots for Freedom*, 202–30; Mayfield, *Rehearsal for Republicanism*, 126–47.

4. *National Era*, Mar. 1, 1849.

5. McManus, *Political Abolitionism in Wisconsin*, 48–53, 55–65.

6. *Boston Daily Republican*, Apr. 23, 1849, in Walker Papers, MHS. Walker was president of the New England Antislavery Convention in 1835. See clipping in box 2, vol. 3, Walker Papers, MHS.

7. Chase to Sumner, Apr. 28, 1851, Sumner Papers, quoted in Sewell, *Ballots for Freedom*, 223. John Greenleaf Whittier titled his poem celebrating the 13th Amendment "Laus Deo."

8. Sewell, *Ballots for Freedom*, 218–23.

9. Bulkley, "Democrat and Slavery," 228.

10. Hamilton, *Memoirs*, 732.

11. Ibid., 833.

12. Ibid., 841. See also Bulkley, "Democrat and Slavery," 236–37.

13. *New York Evening Post*, Nov. 8, 1848.

14. Randall to Van Buren, Dec. 18, 1848, Van Buren Papers, LC. See also Preston King to Charles Sumner, Dec. 6, 1848, King Papers, Ogdensburg Public Library, Ogdensburg, N.Y.

15. *New York Evening Post*, Sept. 15, 1849. On the older generation's willingness to forgo antislavery for reconciliation, see Arphaxed Loomis to John Bigelow, Dec. 13, 1848, Bigelow Papers, NYPL.

16. Quoted in Donovan, *Barnburners*, 114.

17. *National Era*, Sept. 24, 1849.

18. Bailey to Giddings, Sept. 29, 1849, quoted in Harrold, *Gamaliel Bailey*, 146.

19. Bennett's *New York Herald* quoted in Sewell, *Ballots for Freedom*, 227. See also Muller, "Preston King," 492–94.

20. See King to Flagg, December 1849–March 1850, Flagg Papers, Columbia.

21. King to Bigelow, Aug. 24, 1850, King Papers, Ogdensburg Public Library, Ogdensburg, N.Y.

22. Hammond to Gerrit Smith, Aug. 29, 1850, quoted in Sewell, *Ballots for Freedom*, 228; Mayfield, *Rehearsal for Republicanism*, 158–59.

23. George Julian quoted in Harrold, *Gamaliel Bailey*, 134; Greenwood, "American Salon."

24. Hannibal Hamlin to Grace Greenwood, printed in Hamlin, *Life and Times of Hannibal Hamlin*, 277.

25. Marcy quoted in Michael A. Morrison, *Slavery and the American West*, 128. Morrison's brilliant chapter on popular sovereignty and the origins of the Kansas-Nebraska Act have greatly influenced this author; see ibid., 126–56.

26. Julian, *Political Recollections*, provides an excellent account of the 1852 Free Soil convention. See also Mayfield, *Rehearsal for Republicanism*, 178–79; Blue, *Free Soilers*, 239–48.

27. Mayfield, *Rehearsal for Republicanism*, 180. For good measure, Giddings's committee also called for immediate recognition of the government of Haiti, a plank laudable for its antiracism but in 1852 guaranteed to alienate most voters.

28. Dodge quoted in Michael A. Morrison, *Slavery and the American West*, 143.

29. *National Era*, Jan. 24, 1854.

30. Chase, "Diary and Correspondence," 263; Foner, *Free Soil*, 95.

31. Undated clippings from *Albany Atlas* and *Mohawk Courier* in Beckwith, "Autobiographical Record," CU. The author hand-dated the clippings as "Feby. 1854."

32. Joseph P. Smith, quoted in Foner, *Free Soil*, 157.

33. The *Washington Union*, the Pierce administration's organ, used this phrase demanding Democratic adherence to Douglas's amended bill on January 24, 1854. In New York, where free-soil Democracy was still strongest, twelve of twenty-one Democratic congressmen voted against the bill. See *National Era*, June 1, 1854.

34. *New York Evening Post*, Sept. 8, 1854.

35. *Kansas Free State*, Jan. 3, Oct. 29, 1855.

36. Samuel A. Johnson, *Battle Cry of Freedom*, 79.

37. Foner, *Free Soil*, 163–64.

38. Ibid., 165.

39. Sewell, *Ballots for Freedom*, 261. See also Gamaliel Bailey's editorial in *National Era*, Sept. 28, 1854.

40. Foner, *Free Soil*, 170.

41. Leading Democratic-Republicans with strong hard-money backgrounds included Wilmot, Hannibal Hamlin, Chase, Kinsley Bingham, and Preston King.

42. Foner, *Free Soil*, 181–83. Delegates such as Gideon Welles, Francis and Montgomery Blair, James Wadsworth, and Bryant lobbied hard against Seward in Chicago.

43. Of the five leading candidates for the vice presidency, only one (Cassius Clay) was a former Whig. See Foner, *Free Soil*, 182.

44. Whitman to Horace Traubel, quoted in Aaron, *Unwritten War*, 70.

45. Beckwith, "Autobiographical Record," CU, 137, 73. The younger Abijah later moved with his father to Michigan, where his grandfather had deeded him forty acres he received "for services rendered in the war of 1812." Another grandson served as a colonel in the 121st New York Infantry in the Civil War.

46. *New York Tribune*, July 25, 1856, quoted in Foner, *Free Soil*; *Kansas Free State*, Oct. 29, 1855.

47. King to Welles, Sept. 16, 1858, Welles Papers, Huntington Library, San Marino, Calif.; Foner, *Free Soil*, 178.

48. The final version of the Homestead Act, of course, reflected a similar liberal view of landownership and benefited middle-class farmers and not the unemployed eastern workers that formed the core of Evans's vision of the western homesteader.

49. Foner, *Nothing but Freedom*, 6; Jamie Bronstein, *Land Reform and Working-Class Experience*, 92–94; *People's Rights and Working Man's Advocate*, July 6, 1844; *Working Man's Advocate*, Aug. 17, 1844.

Manuscript Collections

Albany, New York
  New York State Library
    Anti-Rent Collection
    Goldsbrow Banyar Papers
    Benjamin F. Butler Papers
    Azariah C. Flagg Papers
    Samuel A. Law Papers
    William L. Marcy Papers
    Van Rensselaer Manor Papers
Boston, Massachusetts
  Massachusetts Historical Society
    Charles Francis Adams Papers
    George Bancroft Papers
    Marcus Morton Letterbooks
    Sedgwick Family Papers
    Amasa Walker Papers
  Massachusetts State House
    Official Election Returns, 1824–60
Canton, New York
  St. Lawrence County Historical Association
    Silas Wright Papers
  St. Lawrence University Library
    Preston King Papers
    Simeon Smith Papers
Concord, New Hampshire
  New Hampshire Historical Society
    George C. Fogg Papers
    John P. Hale Papers
    Franklin Pierce Papers
    Amos Tuck Papers
Cooperstown, New York
  New York State Historical Association
    Henry Christman Papers
    H. J. Munger, "Reminiscences of the Anti-Rent Rebellion"
Delhi, New York
  Delaware County Historical Society
    Edgerton Collection
    Matthew Griffin Diary

Thirteen Good Reasons why no Honest WHIG should vote the "Equal Rights" or Anti-Rent Ticket. 1845. Broadside in Political Clippings from the Mid-1800s to 1897.

Hanover, New Hampshire
  Dartmouth University Library
    John P. Hale Papers
Ithaca, New York
  Cornell University, Karl A. Kroch Library
    George W. Smith Papers
      Abijah Beckwith, "Autobiographical Record, 1847–75"
Madison, Wisconsin
  James R. Doolittle Papers
New York, New York
  Columbia University
    John A. Dix Papers
    Azariah C. Flagg Papers
  New-York Historical Society
    John A. King Papers
  New York Public Library
    John Bigelow Papers
    Azariah C. Flagg Papers
    Samuel J. Tilden Papers
    Gideon Welles Papers
Ogdensburg, New York
  Ogdensburg Public Library
    Preston King Papers
Princeton, New Jersey
  Princeton University, Firestone Library
    Blair-Lee Papers
    Butler Family Papers
    Silas Wright–Benjamin F. Butler Correspondence
San Marino, California
  Huntington Library
    Francis Lieber Papers
    Gideon Welles Papers
Syracuse, New York
  Syracuse University Library
    Gerrit Smith Papers
Towanda, Pennsylvania
  Bradford County Historical Society
    David Wilmot Papers
Washington, D.C.
  Library of Congress
    James G. Birney Papers
    Benjamin F. Butler Papers

John C. Calhoun Papers
Salmon P. Chase Papers
John Floyd Papers
Giddings-Julian Papers
Horace Greeley Papers
James K. Polk Papers
Martin Van Buren Papers
Wadsworth Family Papers
National Archives
Collection of House Records, 24th–37th Congs. (1835–62)

Newspapers

Albany Argus
Albany Atlas
Albany Freeholder
Albany Patriot
Anti-Renter (Albany, N.Y.)
Boston Advocate
Boston Atlas
Boston Post
Boston Statesman
Bradford (Pa.) Porter
Bradford (Pa.) Reporter
Brooklyn Eagle
Brooklyn Freeman
Charleston Mercury
Cincinnati Weekly Herald and Philanthropist
Delaware Gazette (Delaware County, N.Y.)
Democratic Review
Dover (N.H.) Gazette and Strafford Advertiser
Elmira (N.Y.) Gazette
Emancipator
Equal Rights Advocate (Columbia County, N.Y.)
Harrisburg Telegraph
Independent Democrat (Concord, N.H.)
The John-Donkey
Landmark
Liberator
The Man
Morning Star (Dover, N.H.)
National Era
New Hampshire Patriot
New York Commercial Advertiser
New York Courier and Enquirer

New York Evening Post
New York Herald
New York Tribune
Niles' Weekly Register
Ohio Statesman
People's Rights
Plaindealer
Radical
Richmond Enquirer
St. Lawrence (N.Y.) Republican
Subterranean
Towanda (Pa.) Banner and Democrat
U.S. Magazine and Democratic Review
Virginia Herald (Fredericksburg)
Voice of the People
Working Man's Advocate
Young America

Published and Unpublished Works

Aaron, Daniel. *The Unwritten War: American Writers and the Civil War.* New York: Knopf, 1973.

Abel, Annie Heloise, and Frank J. Klineburg. *A Side-Light on Anglo-American Relations, 1839–1858.* Lancaster, Pa.: Lancaster Press, 1927.

Abstract of the Returns of the Fifth Census. Washington, D.C.: United States Census Office, 1831.

Adams, John Quincy. *Memoirs.* Philadelphia: Lippincott, 1877.

Adams, Robert. "Nathaniel Peabody Rogers: 1794–1846." *New England Quarterly* 21 (September 1947): 365–76.

Addresses and Proceedings of the State Independent Free Territory Convention of the People of Ohio. Cincinnati: Herald Office, 1848.

The Address of the Southern and Western Liberty Convention, held at Cincinnati, to the People of the US. . . . New York: William Harned, 1845.

Alexander, DeAlva Stanwood. *A Political History of the State of New York.* New York: Henry Holt, 1906.

Alexander, Thomas B. "The Dimensions of Voter Partisan Constancy in Presidential Elections from 1840–1860." In *Essays on American Antebellum Politics, 1840–1860,* edited by Stephen E. Maizlish and John J. Kushma, 70–121. College Station: Texas A&M University Press, 1982.

———. "Harbinger of the Collapse of the Second Two-Party System: The Free Soil Party of 1848." In *A Crisis of Republicanism: American Politics in the Civil War Era,* edited by Lloyd E. Ambrosius. Lincoln: University of Nebraska Press, 1990.

———. *Sectional Stress and Party Strength: A Study of Roll Call Voting Patterns in the United States House of Representatives, 1836–1860.* Nashville: Vanderbilt University Press, 1967.

Alger, William Rounseville. *Life of Edwin Forrest*. Philadelphia: Lippincott, 1877.

Allen, George. *An Appeal to the People of Massachusetts, on the Texas Question*. Cambridge, Mass.: Metcalf, 1844.

Anderson, Russell H. "New York Agriculture Meets the West, 1830–1850." *Wisconsin Magazine of History* 16 (September 1932): 163–98.

Annals of Congress. 15th Cong., 2d sess.–16th Cong., 2d sess. 1819–21.

An Anti-Slavery Man. *Zachary Taylor, Lewis Cass, and Martin Van Buren Compared; or, Slavery Extension and Free Soil*. Boston: Bela Marsh, 1848.

Ashworth, John. *"Agrarians" and "Aristocrats": Party Political Ideology in the U.S. 1837–1846*. New York: Cambridge University Press, 1987.

———. *Slavery, Capitalism, and Politics in the Antebellum Republic*. Vol. 1, *Commerce and Compromise, 1820–1850*. Cambridge: Cambridge University Press, 1996.

Baker, Jean H. *Affairs of Party: The Political Culture of Northern Democrats in the Mid-19th Century*. Ithaca: Cornell University Press, 1983.

Bancroft, George. *History of the United States*. 10 vols. Boston: Little, 1974.

———. "Political Portraits with Pen and Pencil, No. XXVII: Marcus Morton of Massachusetts." *United States Magazine and Democratic Review* 9 (October 1841): 383–95.

Barnes, Gilbert H. *The Antislavery Impulse, 1830–1844*. New York: D. Appleton-Century, 1933.

Barney, William. *The Road to Secession: A New Perspective on the Old South*. New York: Praeger, 1972.

Barron, Hal S. *Those Who Stayed Behind: Rural Society in Nineteenth Century New England*. New York: Cambridge University Press, 1984.

Basler, Roy P., ed. *The Collected Works of Abraham Lincoln*. New Brunswick, N.J.: Rutgers University Press, 1953.

Bauer, K. Jack. *The Mexican War, 1846–1848*. New York: Macmillan, 1974.

Beale, Howard K., ed. *Diary of Gideon Welles*. New York: Norton, 1960.

Bean, Raymond J. "Social Views of the Free Will Baptists." In *The Freewill Baptist Bicentennial Papers, 1780–1980*. N.p.: New Hampshire Historical Society, 1980.

Beckner, Steven K. "Leggett: 19th Century Libertarian." *Revson* 8 (1977): 32–34.

Benson, Lee. *The Concept of Jacksonian Democracy: New York as a Test Case*. Princeton: Princeton University Press, 1961.

Benton, Thomas Hart. *Thirty Years' View*. New York: Appleton, 1854.

Berwanger, Eugene H. *The Frontier against Slavery: Western Anti-Negro Prejudice and the Slavery Extension Controversy*. Urbana: University of Illinois Press, 1967.

Bigelow, John. *Retrospections of an Active Life*. New York: Baker and Taylor, 1909.

———. *William Cullen Bryant*. New York, 1880.

———, ed. *Writings and Speeches of Samuel J. Tilden*. New York: Harper and Bros., 1885.

Bilotta, James D. *Race and the Rise of the Republican Party, 1848–1865*. New York: P. Lang, 1992.

Binney, Charles C. *Life of Horace Binney*. Philadelphia: Lippincott, 1903.

Bishop, Morris, ed. "The Journeys of Samuel J. Parker." *New York History* 45 (April 1964): 145–54.

Blanchard, Michael D. "The Politics of Abolition in Northampton." *Historical Journal of Massachusetts* 19 (Summer 1991): 175–96.

Blau, Joseph L. *Social Theories of Jacksonian Democracy.* New York: Hunter, 1947.

Blue, Frederick J. *The Free Soilers: Third Party Politics, 1848–1854.* Urbana: University of Illinois Press, 1973.

———. *Salmon P. Chase: A Life in Politics.* Kent, Ohio: Kent State University Press, 1987.

Bodenhorn, Howard. *History of Banking in Antebellum America: Financial Markets and Economic Development in an Era of Nation-Building.* New York: Cambridge University Press, 2000.

Bogue, Allan. *From Prairie to Corn Belt.* Chicago: University of Chicago Press, 1963.

Bordin, Ruth. "The Sect to Denomination Process in America: The Freewill Baptist Experience." *Church History* 34 (March 1965): 77–94.

Boucher, Chauncey S., and Robert P. Brooks, eds. *Correspondence Addressed to John C. Calhoun, 1837–1849.* Washington, D.C.: U.S. Government Printing Office, 1930.

Boughton, Smith A. *Autobiographical Sketch.* N.p. Typescript in Henry Christman Papers, New York State Historical Association, Cooperstown.

Bradshaw, James Stanford. "George Henry Evans." In *Dictionary of Literary Biography,* edited by Perry J. Ashley, vol. 43, *American Newspaper Journalists, 1690–1872,* 184–88. Detroit: Gale Research, 1985.

Brauer, Kinley. *Cotton versus Conscience: Massachusetts Whig Politics and Southwestern Expansion, 1843–1848.* Lexington: University of Kentucky Press, 1967.

Brisbane, W. H. *An Eulogium on the Life and Character of the Late Thomas Morris.* Cincinnati, 1845.

Bronstein, Jamie L. *Land Reform and Working-Class Experience in Britain and the United States, 1800–1862.* Stanford: Stanford University Press, 1999.

Brooke, John L. *The Heart of the Commonwealth: Social and Political Culture in Worcester, Mass., 1713–1861.* New York: Cambridge University Press, 1989.

Brown, Jeffrey P., and Andrew R. L. Cayton. *The Pursuit of Public Power: Political Culture in Ohio, 1787–1861.* Kent, Ohio: Kent State University Press, 1994.

Brown, Richard. "James Watson Webb." In *Dictionary of Literary Biography,* edited by Perry J. Ashley, vol. 43, *American Newspaper Journalists, 1690–1872,* 456–59. Detroit: Gale Research, 1985.

Brown, Richard H. "The Missouri Crisis: Slavery and the Politics of Jacksonianism." *South Atlantic Quarterly* 65 (1966): 55–72.

Brown, Richard Maxwell. "Back Country Rebellions and the Homestead Ethic in America, 1740–1790." In *Tradition, Conflict, and Modernization: Perspectives on the American Revolution,* edited by Richard Maxwell Brown and Don E. Fehrenbacher, 73–102. New York: Academic Press, 1977.

Brownson, Henry F. *Orestes A. Brownson's Early Life, from 1803–1844.* Detroit: Brownson, 1898.

Bulkley, Robert D., Jr. "A Democrat and Slavery: Robert Rantoul, Jr." *Essex Institute Historical Collections* 110 (July 1974): 216–38.

Burgess, G. A., and J. T. Ward, eds. *The Free Baptist Cyclopedia.* Chicago: Women's Temperance Publication Association, 1888.

Burnham, Walter Dean. *Presidential Ballots, 1836–1892.* Baltimore: Johns Hopkins University Press, 1955.

Butler, William Allan. *Martin Van Buren: Lawyer, Statesman, and Man.* New York: Appleton, 1862.

Byrdsall, Fitzwilliam. *History of the Locofoco, or, Equal Rights Party.* New York: B. Franklin, 1842.

Calendar of the Gerrit Smith Papers in the Syracuse University Library. 2 vols. Albany: Historical Records Survey, New York State, 1941.

Calhoun, John C. *The Papers of John C. Calhoun.* 22 vols. Edited by Robert L. Meriwether, W. Edwin Hemphill, and Clyde N. Wilson. Columbia: University of South Carolina Press, 1959–95.

Carleton, William G. "Political Aspects of the Van Buren Era." *South Atlantic Historical Quarterly* 50 (April 1951): 167–85.

Carwedine, Richard. *Evangelicals and Politics in Antebellum America.* New Haven: Yale University Press, 1993.

Center, Gilbert S. "A History of the Town of Colebrook, New Hampshire." M.A. thesis, University of New Hampshire, 1950.

Chaddock, Robert E. *Ohio before 1850: A Study of the Early Influences of Pennsylvanian and Southern Population in Ohio.* New York: Longmans, Green, 1908.

Chase, Salmon P. *Address before a Free Soil Convention.* Cincinnati, 1848.

———. "Letters of Salmon P. Chase." In *Annual Report of the American Historical Association.* 1902.

———. *People's Convention: To the People of Ohio.* Cincinnati, 1848.

Chase, Salmon Portland, and Charles Dexter Cleveland. *Anti-Slavery Addresses of 1844 and 1845.* New York: Negro Universities Press, 1969.

Christman, Henry. *Tin Horns and Calico: A Decisive Episode in the Emergence of Democracy.* New York: Henry Holt, 1945.

Cole, Donald B. *Jacksonian Democracy in New Hampshire, 1800–1851.* Cambridge, Mass.: Harvard University Press, 1970.

———. *Martin Van Buren and the American Political System.* Princeton: Princeton University Press, 1984.

———. "The Presidential Election of 1832 in New Hampshire." *Historical New Hampshire* 21 (December 1966): 32–50.

Cole, G. Glyndon. *Historical Materials Relating to Northern New York.* Canton, N.Y.: North Country Reference and Research Resources Council, 1968.

Commons, John R., Ulrich B. Philips, Eugene A. Gilmore, Helen L. Sumner, and John B. Andrews, eds. *A Documentary History of American Industrial Society,* vol. 7, *Labor Movement, 1840–60.* Cleveland, Ohio: Arthur H. Clark, 1910.

Congressional Globe. 24th Cong., 1st sess.–37th Cong., 2d sess. 1835–63.

Conklin, Henry. *Through "Poverty's Vale": A Hardscrabble Boyhood in Upstate New York, 1832–1862.* Syracuse: Syracuse University Press, 1981.

Cook, Edward M., Jr. *Ossippee, New Hampshire, 1785–1985: A History.* Portsmouth, N.H.: Peter E. Randall, 1989.

Craft, David. *History of Bradford County, Pennsylvania, 1770–1878*. Towanda, Pa., 1878.

Craven, Avery. *The Coming of the Civil War*. New York: Scribner, 1942.

Crippen, Lee F. *Simon Cameron, Ante-Bellum Years*. Oxford, Ohio: Mississippi Valley Press, 1942.

Cross, Whitney. *The Burned-Over District: The Social and Intellectual History of Enthusiastic Religion in Western New York, 1800–1850*. Ithaca: Cornell University Press, 1950.

Crouthamel, James L. *James Watson Webb: A Biography*. Middletown, Conn.: Wesleyan University Press, 1969.

Darling, Arthur B. *Political Changes in Massachusetts, 1824–1848*. New Haven: Yale University Press, 1925.

———. "Workingmen's Party in Massachusetts." *American Historical Review* 29 (October 1923): 81–86.

Davidson, William Franklin. *An Early History of the Free Will Baptists: 1727–1830*. Nashville, Tenn.: Vanderbilt University Press, 1974.

Davis, David Brion. *The Slave Power Conspiracy and the Paranoid Style*. Baton Rouge: Louisiana State University Press, 1969.

Dayton, Mrs. George A. "The Underground Railroad and Its Stations in Bradford County." *The Settler* (1924), 142–48.

Debow, J. D. *The Seventh Census of the United States, 1850*. Washington, D.C.: Robert Armstrong, 1853.

Declaration of the Free Soil Association of the District of Columbia. Washington, D.C.: Buell and Blanchard, 1848.

Degler, Carl. "The Locofocos: Urban 'Agrarians.' " *Journal of Economic History* 16 (1956): 322–33.

DeVoto, Bernard. *The Year of Decision: 1846*. Boston: Little, Brown, 1943.

Devyr, Thomas Ainge ["A Land Reformer," pseud.]. *The Homestead and the Union*. Williamsburgh, N.Y.: the author, 1860.

Devyr, Thomas Ainge. *The Odd Book of the Nineteenth Century*. Greenpoint, N.Y.: the author, 1882.

———. *Our Natural Rights: A Pamphlet for the People, by One of Themselves. Dedicated, by permission, to Wm. Sharman Crawford, Esq., M.P.* Belfast: John Tate, 1836.

Dix, John A. *Memoirs*. Compiled by Morgan Dix. New York: Harper and Bros., 1883.

Dollar, Charles M., and Richard H. Jensen. *Historian's Guide to Statistics: Quantitative Analysis and Historical Research*. New York: Holt, Rinehart, and Winston, 1971.

Donovan, Herbert D. A. *The Barnburners*. New York: New York University Press, 1925.

Doolittle, James R. "Negro Question: Slavery and Reconstruction — Doolittle Correspondence." *Publications of the Southern Historical Association* 11 (January 1907).

Dorn, Helen P. "Samual Medary — Journalist and Politician, 1801–1864." *Ohio State Archaeological and Historical Quarterly* 53 (January 1944): 15.

Douglass, Frederick. *Life and Writings of Frederick Douglass*. Edited by Philip S. Foner. New York: New York International Publishers, 1950.

DuBois, James T., and Gertrude S. Mathews. *Galusha Grow, Father of the Homestead Law*. Boston: Houghton Mifflin, 1917.

Dumond, Dwight L. *Antislavery Origins of the Civil War in the United States*. Ann Arbor: University of Michigan Press, 1959.

——, ed. *Letters of James Gillespie Birney, 1831–1857*. 2 vols. American Historical Association. New York: Appleton, 1938.

Dyer, Oliver. *Great Senators of the United States Forty Years Ago*. New York: R. Bonner's Sons, 1889.

——. *Phonographic Report of the Proceedings of the National Free Soil Convention*. Buffalo: G. H. Derby, 1848.

Dykstra, Robert R. *Bright Radical Star: Black Freedom and White Supremacy on the Hawkeye Frontier*. Cambridge, Mass.: Harvard University Press, 1993.

Eckhardt, Celia Morris. *Fanny Wright: Rebel in America*. Cambridge: Cambridge University Press, 1984.

Eighteenth Ward Jeffersonian League. *The Free Soil Question, and its Importance to the Voters of the Free States, in Address of the 18th Ward Jeffersonian League, New York*. New York: Wm. C. Bryant and Co., 1848.

Eiselen, Malcolm Rogers. *The Rise of Pennsylvania Protectionism*. Philadelphia: University of Pennsylvania Press, 1932.

Ellis, David M. *Landlords and Farmers in the Hudson-Mohawk Region, 1790–1850*. Ithaca: Cornell University Press, 1946.

Emerson, Ralph Waldo. *Journals of Ralph Waldo Emerson, 1820–1872*. Edited by Edward Waldo Emerson and Waldo Emerson Forbes. Boston: Houghton Mifflin, 1910.

Erkkila, Betsy. *Whitman the Political Poet*. New York: Oxford University Press, 1989.

Ershkowitz, Herbert, and William G. Shade. "Consensus or Conflict?: Political Behavior in the State Legislatures during the Jacksonian Era." *Journal of American History* 58 (December 1971): 591–621.

Evans, Frederick William. *Autobiography of a Shaker*. New York: American News Co., 1888.

Fehrenbacher, Don E. *Chicago Giant: A Biography of "Long John" Wentworth*. Madison, Wis.: American History Research Center, 1957.

Feller, Daniel. "A Brother in Arms: Benjamin Tappan and the Antislavery Democracy." *Journal of American History* 88 (June 2001): 48–74.

——. *The Jacksonian Promise: America, 1815–1840*. Baltimore: Johns Hopkins University Press, 1995.

Field, Henry M. *The Life of David Dudley Field*. New York: Charles Scribner's Sons, 1898.

Filler, Louis. *The Crusade against Slavery: 1830–1860*. New York: Harper and Row, 1960.

Fisher, Sydney George. "Diary." *Pennsylvania Magazine of History and Biography* 86 (January 1962): 68–98.

Fitzhugh, George. *Sociology for the South*. New York: Burt Franklin, 1965.

Fladeland, Betty. *James Gillespie Birney: Slaveholder to Abolitionist.* Ithaca: Cornell University Press, 1955.

Fogel, Robert. *Without Consent or Contract: The Rise and Fall of American Slavery.* New York: Norton, 1989.

Foner, Eric. *Free Soil, Free Labor, Free Men: The Ideology of the Republican Party before the Civil War.* New York: Oxford University Press, 1970.

———. *Nat Turner.* Englewood Cliffs, N.J.: Prentice Hall, 1971.

———. *Nothing but Freedom: Emancipation and Its Legacy.* Baton Rouge: Louisiana State University Press, 1984.

———. "Politics and Prejudice: The Free Soil Party and the Negro, 1849–1852." *Journal of Negro History* 50 (October 1965): 239–56.

———. "Racial Attitudes of the New York Free Soilers." *New York History* 46 (October 1965): 311–29.

———. "The Wilmot Proviso Revisited." *Journal of American History* 56 (September 1969): 262–79.

Foote, Henry S. *A Casket of Reminiscences.* Washington, D.C.: Chronicle Publishing, 1874.

Ford, Lacy K. "Inventing the Concurrent Majority: Madison, Calhoun, and the Problem of Majoritarianism in American Politics." *Journal of Southern History* 60 (1994): 19–58.

Formisano, Ronald P. *The Birth of Mass Political Parties: Michigan, 1827–1861.* Princeton: Princeton University Press, 1971.

———. "Toward a Reorientation of Jacksonian Politics: A Review of the Literature, 1959–1975." *Journal of American History* 63 (June 1976): 42–65.

———. *The Transformation of Political Culture: Massachusetts Parties, 1790s–1840s.* New York: Oxford University Press, 1983.

Frederickson, George M. *The Arrogance of Race: Historical Perspectives on Slavery, Racism, and Social Inequality.* Middletown, Conn.: Wesleyan University Press, 1988.

Freehling, William W. *Prelude to Civil War: The Nullification Controversy in South Carolina, 1816–1836.* New York: Harper and Row, 1966.

———. *The Road to Disunion: Secessionists at Bay, 1776–1854.* New York: Oxford University Press, 1990.

Freeman, Joanne B. *Affairs of Honor: National Politics in the New Republic.* New Haven: Yale University Press, 2001.

The Free Soil Minstrel. New York: Martyn and Ely, 1848.

Free Soil Songs for the People. Boston: Wright's Steam Press, 1848.

The Freewill Baptist Bicentennial Papers, 1780–1980. N.p.: New Hampshire Historical Society, 1980.

Friedman, Lawrence J. *Gregarious Saints: Self and Community in American Abolitionism, 1830–1870.* New York: Cambridge University Press, 1982.

Gara, Larry. *The Liberty Line: The Legend of the Underground Railroad.* Lexington: University of Kentucky Press, 1961.

———. "Slavery and the Slave Power: A Crucial Distinction." *Civil War History* 15 (March 1969): 4–18.

Gardiner, O. C. *The Great Issue; or, the Three Presidential Candidates.* New York: Wm. C. Bryant and Co., 1848.

Garraty, John. *Silas Wright.* New York: Columbia University Press, 1949.

Gates, Paul Wallace. *The Farmer's Age: Agriculture, 1815–1860.* New York: Holt, Rhinehart, and Winston, 1960.

Gattell, Frank Otto. *John Gorham Palfry and the New England Conscience.* Cambridge, Mass.: Harvard University Press, 1963.

Gienapp, William E. *The Origins of the Republican Party, 1852–1856.* New York: Oxford University Press, 1987.

Gillet, Ransom Hooker. *Life and Times of Silas Wright.* Albany: Argus, 1874.

Godwin, Parke, ed. *A Biography of William Cullen Bryant, with Extracts from his Private Correspondence.* New York: Appleton, 1883.

——. *The Life and Writings of William Cullen Bryant.* New York: Appleton, 1884.

Going, Charles Buxton. *David Wilmot, Free Soiler: A Biography of the Great Advocate of the Wilmot Proviso.* New York: Appleton, 1924.

Goodman, Paul. *Of One Blood: Abolitionism and the Origins of Racial Equality.* Berkeley: University of California Press, 1998.

——. *Towards a Christian Republic: Antimasonry and the Great Transition in New England, 1826–1836.* New York: Oxford University Press, 1988.

Gorn, Elliot J. *The Manly Art: Bare-Knuckle Prize Fighting in America.* Ithaca: Cornell University Press, 1986.

Gould, Jay. *History of Delaware County, and the Border Wars of New York.* Roxbury, N.Y.: Keeny and Gould, 1856.

Graebner, Norman. *Empire on the Pacific: A Study of American Continental Expansion.* New York: Ronald Press, 1955.

Grant, Philip, Jr. "The Bank Controversy and New Hampshire Politics, 1834–35." *Historical New Hampshire* 23 (January 1968): 19–35.

Greenberg, Kenneth S. *Masters and Statesmen: The Political Culture of American Slavery.* Baltimore: Johns Hopkins University Press, 1985.

Greenwood, Grace. "An American Salon." *Cosmopolitan* 8 (1890): 438–47.

Grimsted, David. *American Mobbing, 1828–1861: Toward Civil War.* New York: Oxford University Press, 1998.

Gunn, L. Ray. *The Decline of Authority: Public Economic Policy and Political Development in New York State, 1800–1860.* Ithaca: Cornell University Press, 1988.

Hale, John P. *Letter to the Democratic Republican Electors of New Hampshire.* Washington, D.C.: Blair and Rives, 1845.

Hamilton, Luther, ed. *Memoirs, Speeches, and Writings of Robert J. Rantoul, Jr.* Boston: John P. Jewett and Co., 1854.

Hamlin, Charles E. *The Life and Times of Hannibal Hamlin.* Cambridge, Mass.: Harvard University Press, 1899.

Hammond, Bray. "Free Banking and Corporations: The New York Free Banking Act of 1838." *Journal of Political Economy* 44 (April 1936): 184–90.

Hammond, Jabez D. *The History of Political Parties in the State of New York.* Albany: Van Benthuysen, 1842.

Harlow, Ralph Volney. *Gerrit Smith: Philanthropist and Reformer*. New York: Henry Holt, 1939.

Harrold, Stanley. "Forging an Antislavery Instrument: Gamaliel Bailey and the Foundation of the Ohio Liberty Party." *Old Northwest* 2 (Spring 1976): 371–87.

———. *Gamaliel Bailey and Antislavery Union*. Kent, Ohio: Kent State University Press, 1986.

Hatch, Nathan O. *The Democratization of American Christianity*. New Haven: Yale University Press, 1989.

Haydon, Roger, ed. *Upstate Travels: British Views of 19th Century New York*. Syracuse: Syracuse University Press, 1982.

Hayes, John L. *A Reminiscence of the Free-Soil Movement in New Hampshire, 1845*. Cambridge, Mass.: J. Wilson and Son, 1885.

Helton, Leonard L. "George Henry Evans: Anti-Monopolist." M.A. thesis, University of Tennessee, 1952.

Herkimer Convention: The Voice of New York! Albany, N.Y., 1847.

Heverly, C. F. *History of the Towandas, 1770–1886*. Towanda, Pa.: Reporter-Journal Printing, 1886.

Hietala, Thomas R. *Manifest Design: Anxious Aggrandizement in Late Jacksonian America*. Ithaca: Cornell University Press, 1985.

History of Coös County, New Hampshire. Somerswirth: New Hampshire Publishing, 1972.

Hoag, Enoch. *The Slave Power; or, the Spirit of Our Fathers Contrasted with the Spirit of their Sons*. Boston: Damrell and Moore's Steam Power Press, 1848.

Hofstadter, Richard. "William Leggett: Spokesman of Jacksonian Democracy." *Political Science Quarterly* 58 (December 1943): 581–94.

Holt, Michael F. *Forging a Majority: The Formation of the Republican Party in Pittsburgh, 1848–1860*. New Haven: Yale University Press, 1969.

———. *The Political Crisis of the 1850s*. New York: Wiley, 1978.

———. *The Political Culture of the American Whigs*. Chicago: University of Chicago Press, 1979.

———. *Political Parties and American Political Development: From the Age of Jackson to the Age of Lincoln*. Baton Rouge: Louisiana State University Press, 1981.

———. *The Rise and Fall of the American Whig Party: Jacksonian Politics and the Onset of the Civil War*. New York: Oxford University Press, 1999.

Hone, Philip. *Diary of Philip Hone*. Edited by Allan Nevins. New York: Dodd, 1927.

Horsman, Reginald. *Race and Manifest Destiny: The Origins of American Racial Anglo-Saxonism*. Cambridge, Mass: Harvard University Press, 1981.

Hough, Franklin B. *Census of the State of New York for 1855*. Albany: Van Benthuysen, 1857.

———. *History of St. Lawrence and Franklin Counties, NY*. Albany: Little and Co., 1853.

Howarth, Margery D. *New Hampshire: A Study of its Cities and Towns*. . . . Concord: New Hampshire Foundation, 1936.

Howe, Daniel Walker. "The Evangelical Movement and the Political Culture in the North during the Second Party System." *Journal of American History* 77 (March 1991): 1216–39.

Howe, Henry F. *Salt Rivers of the Massachusetts Shore.* New York: Rinehart, 1951.

Hugins, Walter E. *Jacksonian Democracy and the Working Class: A Study of the New York Workingmen's Movement.* Stanford: Stanford University Press, 1960.

Huston, James L. *Securing the Fruits of Labor: The American Concept of Wealth Distribution, 1765–1900.* Baton Rouge: Louisiana State University Press, 1998.

Huston, Reeve. *Land and Freedom: Rural Society, Popular Protest, and Party Politics in Antebellum New York.* Oxford: Oxford University Press, 2000.

Ignatiev, Noel. *How the Irish Became White.* New York: Routledge, 1995.

Ilisevich, Robert D. *Galusha A. Grow: The People's Candidate.* Pittsburgh: University of Pittsburgh Press, 1989.

Jameson, J. Franklin, ed. "Correspondence of John C. Calhoun." In *American Historical Association Annual Report for 1899.* 1900.

Jarvis, Russell. *Facts and Arguments Against the Election of General Cass, Respectfully Addressed to the Whigs and Democrats of the Free States, by an Anti-Abolitionist.* New York: R. Craighead, 1848.

Jentz, John B. "The Antislavery Constituency in Jacksonian New York City." *Civil War History* 27 (June 1981): 101–22.

———. "Artisans, Evangelicals, and the City: A Social History of Abolition and Labor Reform in Jacksonian New York." Ph.D. diss., City University of New York, 1977.

Johnson, Paul E. "The Modernization of Mayo Greenleaf Patch: Land, Family, and Marginality in New England, 1766–1818." *New England Quarterly* 55 (December 1982): 488–516.

———. *Sam Patch: The Famous Jumper.* New York: Hill and Wang, 2003.

Johnson, Paul E., and Sean Wilentz. *The Kingdom of Matthias.* New York: Oxford University Press, 1994.

Johnson, Reinhard O. "The Liberty Party in Massachusetts, 1840–1848: Antislavery Third Party Politics in the Bay State." *Civil War History* 28 (September 1982): 237–65.

———. "The Liberty Party in New England, 1840–1848: The Forgotten Abolitionists." Ph.D. diss., Syracuse University Press, 1976.

Johnson, Samuel A. *The Battle Cry of Freedom: The New England Emigrant Aid Company in the Kansas Crusade.* Lawrence: University of Kansas Press, 1954.

Journal of the New York Assembly. Albany, N.Y.: Van Benthuysen, 1948.

Julian, George W. *Political Recollections, 1840–1872.* Chicago: Jansen, McClurg and Co., 1884.

Kelley, Mary. *The Power of Her Sympathy: The Autobiography and Journal of Catherine Maria Sedgwick.* Boston: Massachusetts Historical Society, 1993.

Kerber, Linda K. "Abolitionists and Amalgamators: The New York City Race Riots of 1834." *New York History* 48 (January 1967): 28–39.

King, Preston. *Oration Delivered at Canton . . . July 4, 1848.* Ogdensburg, N.Y., 1848.

Kirkland, Edward C. *Men, Cities, and Transportation: A Study in New England History.* Cambridge, Mass.: Harvard University Press, 1948.

Klammer, Martin. *Whitman, Slavery, and the Emergence of Leaves of Grass.* University Park: Pennsylvania State University Press, 1995.

Knupfer, Peter B. *The Union As It Is: Constitutional Unionism and Sectional Compromise, 1787–1861.* Chapel Hill: University of North Carolina Press, 1991.

Kohl, Lawrence F. *The Politics of Individualism: Parties and the American Character in the Jacksonian Era.* New York: Oxford University Press, 1989.

Kraditor, Aileen S. *Means and Ends in American Abolitionism: Garrison and His Critics on Strategy and Tactics.* New York: Pantheon, 1967.

Kraut, Alan M. *Crusaders and Compromisers: Essays on the Relationship of the Antislavery Struggle to the Antebellum Party System.* Westport, Conn.: Greenwood Press, 1983.

Landon, Harry F. "Silas Wright as Governor." *New York History* 15 (July 1934): 302–9.

Larson, John Lauritz. *Internal Improvement: National Public Works and the Promise of Popular Government in the Early United States.* Chapel Hill: University of North Carolina Press, 2001.

Laurie, Bruce. *Working People of Philadelphia, 1800–1850.* Philadelphia: University of Pennsylvania Press, 1980.

Laws of the State of New Hampshire, Passed June Session, 1846. Concord, 1846.

Leggett, William. *A Collection of the Political Writings of William Leggett.* Edited by Theodore Sedgwick Jr. New York: Taylor and Dodd, 1840.

——. *Tales and Sketches. By a Country Schoolmaster.* New York: J. and J. Harper, 1829.

Lence, Ross M., ed. *Union and Liberty: The Political Philosophy of John C. Calhoun.* Indianapolis: Liberty Fund, 1992.

Lewis, William G. W. *Biography of Samuel Lewis: First Superintendent of Common Schools for the State of Ohio.* Cincinnati: R. P. Thompson, 1857.

Liesler, Jacob. *Letters to the People of Pennsylvania on the Political Principles of the Free Soil Party.* Philadelphia, 1848.

Littlefield, Nathan W. "Governor Marcus Morton: An Address Delivered Jan. 13, 1905." *Collections of the Old Colony Historical Society* 7 (1909): 75–92.

Litwack, Leon. *North of Slavery: The Negro in the Free States, 1790–1860.* Chicago: University of Chicago Press, 1961.

Lowden, Lucy. "The Granite State for Lincoln." *Historical New Hampshire* 25 (March 1970): 3–23.

Lowell, James Russell. *The Bigelow Papers.* Boston: Ticknor, 1853.

Lynch, Denis Tilden. *An Epoch and a Man: Martin Van Buren and His Times.* New York: Liveright, 1929.

Lynch, William O. "Antislavery Tendencies of the Democratic Party in the Northwest, 1848–50." *Mississippi Valley Historical Review* 11 (December 1924): 319–31.

Magdol, Edward. *The Antislavery Rank and File: A Social Profile of the Abolitionists' Constituency.* New York: Greenwood Press, 1986.

Maizlish, Stephen E. *The Triumph of Sectionalism: The Transformation of Ohio Politics, 1844–1856.* Kent, Ohio: Kent State University Press, 1983.

Maizlish, Stephen E., and John J. Kushma, eds. *Essays on American Antebellum Politics, 1840–1860.* College Station: Texas A&M University Press, 1982.

Malone, Dumas, ed. *Dictionary of American Biography.* New York: Scribner, 1934.

Mandel, Bernard. *Labor, Free and Slave: Workingmen and the Anti-Slavery Movement in the United States.* New York: Associated Authors, 1955.

Mann, Horace. *Horace Mann's Letters on the Extension of Slavery into California and New Mexico; and on the Duty of Congress to Provide the Trial by Jury for Alleged Fugitive Slaves.* Washington, D.C.: Buell and Blanchard, 1850.

Marszalek, John F. *The Petticoat Affair: Manners, Mutiny, and Sex in Andrew Jackson's White House.* Baton Rouge: Louisiana State University Press, 1998.

Masquerier, Lewis. *Sociology, or, the Reconstruction of Society, Government, and Property.* Westport, Conn.: Greenwood Press, 1970.

Mathews, Alfred. *History of Wayne, Pike, and Monroe Counties* [Pa.]. Philadelphia: R. T. Peck and Co., 1886.

Mathews, Donald G. *Slavery and Methodism: A Chapter in American Morality, 1780–1845.* Princeton: Princeton University Press, 1965.

Mayfield, John. *Rehearsal for Republicanism: Free Soil and the Politics of Antislavery.* Port Washington, N.Y.: National University Publications, 1980.

Mayham, Albert C. *The Anti-Rent War on Blenheim Hill: An Episode of the 40's.* Jefferson, N.Y.: Frederick L. Frazee, 1906.

McClure, Alexander. *Colonel Alexander K. McClure's Recollections of Half a Century.* Salem, Mass.: Salem Press, 1902.

McCormick, Richard P. *The Second American Party System: Party Formation in the Jacksonian Era.* Chapel Hill: University of North Carolina Press, 1968.

McCoy, Drew R. *The Elusive Republic: Political Economy in Jeffersonian America.* Chapel Hill: University of North Carolina Press, 1980.

McCurdy, Charles W. *The Anti-Rent Era in New York Law and Politics, 1839–1865.* Chapel Hill: University of North Carolina Press, 2001.

McManus, Michael J. *Political Abolitionism in Wisconsin, 1840–1861.* Kent, Ohio: Kent State University Press, 1998.

McPherson, James M. *Battlecry of Freedom: The Civil War Era.* New York: Oxford University Press, 1988.

———. "The Fight against the Gag Rule: Joshua Leavitt and Antislavery Insurgency in the Whig Party, 1839–1842." *Journal of Negro History* 48 (July 1963): 177–95.

Merk, Frederick. *Slavery and the Annexation of Texas.* New York: Knopf, 1972.

Merrill, Michael. "The Anticapitalist Origins of the United States." *Review* 13 (September 1990): 465–97.

Meyers, Marvin. *The Jacksonian Persuasion: Politics and Belief.* Palo Alto: Stanford University Press, 1957.

Miller, William Lee. *Arguing about Slavery: The Great Battle in the United States Congress.* New York: Knopf, 1995.

Mintz, Max M. "The Political Ideas of Martin Van Buren." *New York History* 30 (October 1949): 442–48.

Monroe, John D. *The Anti-Rent War in Delaware County, New York.* Kortright, N.Y.: the author, 1940.

Morris, Benjamin Franklin, ed. *The Life of Thomas Morris: Pioneer and Long a Legislator of Ohio, and U.S. Senator from 1833–1839.* Cincinnati: Moore, Wilstach, Keys and Overend, 1856.

Morrison, Chaplain W. *Democratic Politics and Sectionalism: The Wilmot Proviso Controversy.* Chapel Hill: University of North Carolina Press, 1967.

Morrison, Michael A. *Slavery and the American West: The Eclipse of Manifest Destiny and the Coming of the Civil War.* Chapel Hill: University of North Carolina Press, 1997.

———. "Martin Van Buren, Democracy, and the Partisan Politics of Texas Annexation." *Journal of Southern History* 61 (November 1995): 695–724.

Murdock, William D. C. *Address on the Free Soil Question: "QU'Y-A-T-IL?"* Georgetown: J. F. and J. A. Crow, 1848.

Muller, Ernest Paul. "Preston King: A Political Biography." Ph.D. diss., Columbia University, 1957.

Murphy, Teresa A. *Ten Hours Labor: Religion, Reform, and Gender in Early New England.* Ithaca: Cornell University Press, 1992.

Mushkat, Jerome. *Tammany: The Evolution of a Political Machine.* Syracuse: Syracuse University Press, 1971.

Myers, John L. "The Beginning of Antislavery Agencies in New Hampshire, 1832–1835." *Historical New Hampshire* 25 (September 1970): 3–25.

Neuenschwander, John A. "Senator Thomas Morris: Antagonist of the South, 1836–1839." *Cincinnati Historical Society Bulletin* 32 (June 1974): 123–39.

New Hampshire House Journal.

New Hampshire Senate Journal.

New Jersey Free-Soil Convention. *New Jersey Free-Soil Convention, held at Trenton, on the 16th of September, 1848.* New Brunswick, N.J.: Times Press, 1848.

New York State. *Report on the Census of 1855.* Albany: Van Benthuysen, 1856.

New York State Assembly Documents, No. 189. Albany: Van Benthuysen, 1844.

Nichols, Roy F. *The Democratic Machine, 1850–1854.* New York: Columbia University Press, 1923.

———. *Franklin Pierce: Young Hickory of the Granite Hills.* Philadelphia: University of Pennsylvania Press, 1958.

Niven, John. *Gideon Welles: Lincoln's Secretary of the Navy.* New York: Oxford University Press, 1973.

———. *John C. Calhoun and the Price of Union: A Biography.* New York: Oxford University Press, 1988.

———. *Martin Van Buren: The Romantic Age of American Politics.* New York: Oxford University Press, 1983.

———. *Salmon P. Chase: A Biography.* New York: Oxford University Press, 1995.

Nye, Russell B. *Fettered Freedom: Civil Liberties and the Slavery Controversy.* East Lansing: Michigan State University Press, 1949.

———. *George Bancroft: Brahmin Rebel.* New York: Knopf, 1944.

O'Connor, Thomas J. *Lords of the Loom: The Cotton Whigs and the Coming of the Civil War.* New York: Scribner, 1968.

Parker, Wilmond W. "The Migration from Vermont to Northern New York." *New York History* 15 (June 1934): 398–406.

Paul, James C. N. *Rift in the Democracy.* Philadelphia: University of Pennsylvania Press, 1951.

Pease, William H., and Jane H. Pease. "Anti-Slavery Ambivalence: Immediatism, Expediency, Race." *American Quarterly* 17 (1965): 682–95.

Pencak, William, and Conrad Wright, eds. *New York and the Rise of American Capitalism: Economic Development and the Social and Political History of an American State.* New York: New York Historical Society, 1989.

Pendleton, Eldridge H. "The New York Anti-Rent Controversy, 1830–1860." Ph.D. diss., University of Virginia, 1974.

Perkins, Dexter. "John Quincy Adams." In *The American Secretaries of State and Their Diplomacy*, edited by Samuel Flagg Bemis, 4:3–114. New York: Cooper Square Publishers, 1963.

Perry, Lewis, and Michael Fellman, eds. *Antislavery Reconsidered: New Perspectives on the Abolitionists.* Baton Rouge: Louisiana State University Press, 1979.

Persinger, Clark E. "The 'Bargain of 1844' as the Origin of the Wilmot Proviso." In *Annual Report of the American Historical Association for the Year 1911.* 1913.

Pessen, Edward. *Most Uncommon Jacksonians: Radical Leaders of the Early Labor Movement.* Albany: State University of New York Press, 1967.

Pickard, Samuel T. *Life and Letters of John Greenleaf Whittier.* 2 vols. Boston, 1894.

Pierce, E. L., ed. *Memoir and Letters of Charles Sumner.* Boston: Roberts Brothers, 1877–93.

Polk, James K. *Polk: The Diary of a President.* Edited by Allan Nevins. London: Longman's, 1929.

Porter, Kirk H., and Donald B. Johnson, eds. *National Party Platforms, 1840–1960.* Urbana: University of Illinois Press, 1961.

Potter, David M. *The Impending Crisis, 1848–1861.* New York: Harper and Row, 1976.

Price, Erwin H. "The Election of 1848 in Ohio." *Ohio Archaeological and Historical Quarterly* 36 (January 1927): 188–311.

Proceedings of the National Liberty Convention Held at Buffalo, NY, June 14th and 15th, 1848. . . . Utica, N.Y.: S. W. Green, 1848.

Proceedings of the Utica Convention for the Nomination of the President of the United States Held at Utica, NY, June 22, 1848. Albany, 1848.

Proctor, Page S. "William Leggett (1801–1839): Journalist and Literator." *Papers of the Bibliographical Society of America* 44 (1950): 239–53.

Quaife, Milo Milton, ed. *The Diary of James K. Polk during His Presidency, 1845–1849.* Chicago: A. C. McClurg, 1910.

Ratcliffe, Donald J. *The Politics of Long Division: The Birth of the Second Party System in Ohio, 1818–1828.* Columbus: Ohio State University Press.

Rawley, James A. *Race and Politics: "Bleeding Kansas" and the Coming of the Civil War.* Philadelphia: Lippincott, 1969.

Rayback, Joseph G. "The American Workingman and the Antislavery Crusade." *Journal of Economic History* 3 (1943): 152–63.

———. *Free Soil: The Election of 1848.* Lexington: University of Kentucky Press, 1970.

———. "The Liberty Party Leaders of Ohio: Exponents of Antislavery Coalition." *Ohio Archaeological and Historical Quarterly* 57 (January 1948): 165–78.

———. "Martin Van Buren's Desire for Revenge in the Campaign of 1848." *Mississippi Valley Historical Review* 40 (March 1954): 707–16.

A Refutation of the Charge of Abolitionism . . . Against the Hon. Marcus Morton. Boston: French's Press, 1845.

Register of Debates in Congress. 18 vols. Washington, D.C.: Gales and Seaton, 1824–37.

Remini, Robert V. *Andrew Jackson and the Course of American Diplomacy, 1833–1845.* New York: Harper and Row, 1984.

Resolutions of the Legislature of Michigan, in favor of the Prohibition of Slavery Within any Territory of the United States now or Hereafter to be Acquired. Washington, D.C.: Tippin and Streeper, 1849.

Reunion of the Free-Soilers of 1848. Boston: Albert J. Wright, 1877.

Rezneck, Samuel. "Social History of an American Depression, 1837–1843." *American Historical Review* 40 (July 1935): 662–87.

Richards, Leonard L. *"Gentlemen of Property and Standing": Anti-Abolition Mobs in Jacksonian America.* New York: Oxford University Press, 1970.

———. "The Jacksonians and Slavery." In *Antislavery Reconsidered: New Perspectives on the Abolitionists,* edited by Lewis Perry and Michael Fellman, 99–118. Baton Rouge: Louisiana State University Press, 1979.

———. *The Life and Times of Congressman John Quincy Adams.* New York: Oxford University Press, 1986.

———. *The Slave Power: The Free North and Southern Domination, 1780–1860.* Baton Rouge: Louisiana State University Press, 2000.

Richardson, James D., ed. *A Compilation of the Messages and Papers of the Presidents.* New York: Bureau of National Literature, 1897.

Riddle, A. G. "Recollections of the 47th General Assembly of Ohio, 1847–48." *Magazine of Western History* 6 (1875): 341–51.

Rifkin, Lester Harvey. "William Leggett: Journalist-Philosopher of American Democracy in New York." *New York History* 32 (January 1951): 45–60.

Robbins, Roy. *Our Landed Heritage: The Public Domain, 1776–1970.* Lincoln: University of Nebraska Press, 1976.

Robinson, Frederick. *Address to the Voters of the Fifth Congressional District.* N.p.: Massachusetts Historical Society, [1862].

Roediger, David R. *The Wages of Whiteness: Race and the Making of the American Working Class.* New York: Verso, 1991.

Roth, Randolph A. *The Democratic Dilemma: Religion, Reform, and the Social Order in the Connecticut River Valley of Vermont, 1791–1850.* Cambridge: Cambridge University Press, 1987.

Ryan, Mary P. *The Cradle of the Middle Class: The Family in Oneida County, New York, 1790–1865*. New York: Cambridge University Press, 1981.

Saxton, Alexander. *The Rise and Fall of the White Republic: Class, Politics, and Mass Culture in Nineteenth Century America*. New York: Verso, 1990.

Schlesinger, Arthur, Jr. *The Age of Jackson*. Boston: Little, Brown, 1945.

——, ed. *The History of American Presidential Elections*. New York: Chelsea House, 1971.

Scroggins, Mark. *Hannibal: The Life of Abraham Lincoln's First Vice President*. Lanham, Md.: University Press of America, 1994.

Sedgwick, Theodore, Jr. *Thoughts on the Proposed Annexation of Texas to the United States*. New York: Wm. C. Bryant and Co., 1844.

Sellers, Charles G, Jr. "Andrew Jackson versus the Historians." *Mississippi Valley Historical Review* 44 (March 1958): 615–34.

——. *James K. Polk: Continentalist, 1843–1846*. Princeton: Princeton University Press, 1966.

——. *The Market Revolution: Jacksonian America, 1815–1846*. New York: Oxford University Press, 1991.

Sellers, James L. "James R. Doolittle." *Wisconsin Magazine of History* 17 (December 1933): 168–78.

Sewell, Richard H. *Ballots for Freedom: Antislavery Politics in the United States, 1837–1860*. New York: Oxford University Press, 1976.

——. *A House Divided: Sectionalism and Civil War, 1848–1865*. Baltimore: Johns Hopkins University Press, 1988.

——. *John P. Hale and the Politics of Abolition*. Cambridge, Mass.: Harvard University Press, 1965.

Sheidley, Harlow W. *Sectional Nationalism: Massachusetts Conservative Leaders and the Transformation of America, 1815–1836*. Boston: Northeastern University Press, 1998.

Silbey, Joel. *The American Political Nation, 1838–1893*. Stanford: Stanford University Press, 1991.

——. *The Shrine of Party: Congressional Voting Behavior, 1841–1852*. Pittsburgh: University of Pittsburgh Press, 1967.

Smith, Gerrit. *Speeches of Gerrit Smith in Congress*. New York: Mason Bros., 1855.

Smith, Norman W. "The 'Amhearst Bubble': Wildcat Banking in Early Nineteenth Century New Hampshire." *Historical New Hampshire* 20 (March 1965): 27–40.

——. "A Mature Frontier: The New Hampshire Economy, 1790–1850." *Historical New Hampshire* 24 (September 1969): 3–19.

Smith, Theodore Clarke. *The Liberty and Free Soil Parties of the Old Northwest*. New York: Longmans, Green, 1897.

Smith, William Ernest. *The Francis Preston Blair Family in Politics*. New York: Macmillan, 1933.

Snyder, Charles McCool. *The Jacksonian Heritage in Pennsylvania Politics, 1833–1848*. Harrisburg: Pennsylvania Historical and Museum Commission, 1958.

Stanton, Henry Brewster. *Random Recollections*. New York: Harper and Bros., 1887.

Statistical View of the United States. Washington, D.C.: A. O. P. Nicholson, 1854.

Stenberg, Richard R. "The Motivation of the Wilmot Proviso." *Mississippi Valley Historical Review* 18 (March 1932): 535–41.

Stevens, Henry R. *The Early Jackson Party in Ohio.* Durham, N.C.: Duke University Press, 1957.

Stewart, I. D. *The History of the Free Will Baptists for Half a Century.* Dover, N.H.: Freewill Baptist Print Establishment, 1862.

Stewart, James Brewer. *Holy Warriors: The Abolitionists and American Society.* New York: Hill and Wang, 1976.

Stokes, Melvyn, ed. *The Market Revolution in America.* Charlottesville: University of Virginia Press, 1996.

Summerhill, Thomas. "The Farmer's Republic: Agrarian Protest and the Capitalist Transformation of Upstate New York, 1840–1890." Ph.D. diss., University of California, San Diego, 1993.

Swing, James B. "Thomas Morris." *Ohio Archaeological and Historical Society Publications* 10 (1902): 352–60.

Tappan, Lewis. *The Life of Arthur Tappan.* New York: Hurd and Houghton, 1870.

Temin, Peter. *The Jacksonian Economy.* New York: Norton, 1969.

Thompson, John H. *Geography of New York State.* Syracuse: Syracuse University Press, 1966.

Thompson, Joseph P. *The Duties of the Christian Citizen: A Discourse.* New York: S. W. Benedict, 1848.

Townshend, N. S. "Comments Upon Mr. Riddle's Paper." *Magazine of Western History* 6 (1875): 623–28.

Tuck, Amos. *Autobiographical Memoirs of Amos Tuck.* N.p.: New Hampshire Historical Society, 1902.

Turner, Lorenzo D. "Walt Whitman and the Negro." *Chicago Jewish Forum* 15 (September 1956): 5–11.

U.S. Congress. *Biographical Dictionary of the United States Congress, 1774–1989.* Washington, D.C.: U.S. Government Printing Office, 1989.

Utter, William T. *The Frontier State, 1803–1825.* Columbus: Ohio State University Press, 1942.

Van Buren, Martin. "Autobiography, J. C. Fitzpatrick, ed. American Historical Association." In *Annual Report of the American Historical Association for the Year 1918.* 1918.

"Van Buren–Bancroft Correspondence, 1830–1845." *Proceedings of the Massachusetts Historical Society* 42 (June 1909): 381–442.

Voegeli, V. Jacques. *Free but Not Equal: The Midwest and the Negro during the Civil War.* Chicago: University of Chicago Press, 1967.

Volpe, Vernon L. *Forlorn Hope of Freedom: The Liberty Party in the Old Northwest, 1838–1848.* Kent, Ohio: Kent State University Press, 1990.

Walters, Ronald G. *The Antislavery Appeal: American Abolitionism after 1830.* New York: Norton, 1984.

Watson, Harry L. *Liberty and Power: The Politics of Jacksonian America.* New York: Hill and Wang, 1990.

Weisenburger, Francis P. *The Passing of the Frontier, 1825–1850*. Columbus: Ohio State Archaeological and Historical Society, 1941.

Welles, Gideon. *Diary*. Edited by Howard K. Beale. New York: Norton, 1960.

Whig Almanac, 1839–1848. New York: New York Tribune, 1868.

White, Lawrence H., ed. *Democratick Editorials: Essays in Jacksonian Political Economy by William Leggett*. Indianapolis, Ind.: Liberty Press, 1984.

———. "William Leggett: Jacksonian Editorialist as Classical Liberal Political Economist." *History of Political Economy* 18 (1986): 307–324.

White, Shane. *Somewhat More Independent: The End of Slavery in New York City, 1770–1810*. Athens: University of Georgia Press, 1991.

Whitman, Walt. *The Gathering of the Forces*. Edited by Cleveland Rogers and John Black. New York: G. P. Putnam's Sons, 1920.

———. *Leaves of Grass*. Brooklyn: the author, 1855.

———. *Specimen Days*. Philadelphia: David McKay, 1892.

Whittier, John Greenleaf. *The Complete Poetical Works of John Greenleaf Whittier*. Boston: Houghton Mifflin, 1892.

———. *Old Portraits and Modern Sketches*. Boston: Ticknor, Reed and Fields, 1850.

———. *The Writings of John Greenleaf Whittier in Seven Volumes*. Cambridge: Riverside Press, 1888.

Widmer, Edward L. *Young America: The Flowering of Democracy in New York City*. New York: Oxford University Press, 1999.

Wiecek, William M. *The Sources of Antislavery Constitutionalism in America, 1760–1848*. Ithaca: Cornell University Press, 1977.

Wilentz, Sean. *Chants Democratic: New York City and the Rise of the American Working Class*. New York: Oxford University Press, 1984.

———. "Jacksonian Abolitionist: The Conversion of William Leggett." In *The Liberal Persuasion: Arthur Schlesinger, Jr., and the Challenge of the American Past*, edited by John Patrick Diggins, 84–106. Princeton: Princeton University Press, 1997.

———. "The Missouri Crisis Revisited: Slavery, Democracy, and the Constitution in the Early Republic." Paper delivered as the Bacon Lecture on American Constitutional History, Boston University, May 2, 2002.

———. "Slavery, Antislavery, and Jacksonian Democracy." In *The Market Revolution in America*, edited by Melvyn Stokes and Stephen Conway, 202–23. Charlottesville: University of Virginia Press, 1996.

———. "Society, Politics, and the Market Revolution, 1815–1848." In *The New American History*, edited by Eric Foner, 51–72. Philadelphia: Temple University Press, 1991.

———, ed. *Major Problems in the Early Republic, 1787–1848*. Lexington, Mass.: Heath, 1992.

Wilson, Henry. *History of the Rise and Fall of the Slave Power in America*. Boston: J. R. Osgood and Co., 1875–77.

Wilson, Major L. *The Presidency of Martin Van Buren*. Lawrence: University of Kansas Press, 1984.

———. *Space, Time, and Freedom: The Quest for Nationality and the Irrepressible Conflict, 1815–1861*. Westport, Conn.: Greenwood Press, 1974.

Wilson, William. *Great American Question: Democracy vs. Doulocracy; or, Free Soil, Free Labor, Free Men & Free Speech.* . . . Cincinnati: E. Shephard's Steam Press, 1848.

Woodford, Frank B. *Lewis Cass: The Last Jeffersonian.* New Brunswick, N.J.: Rutgers University Press, 1950.

Zahler, Helene Sara. *Eastern Workingmen and National Land Policy, 1829–1862.* New York: Columbia University Press, 1941.

Zweig, Paul. *Walt Whitman: The Making of the Poet.* New York: Basic Books, 1984.

Abolitionist petitions. *See* Antislavery petitions

Abolitionists: black, 168; criticism of, 31–32, 82–83, 115–16, 118, 136; differences from antislavery Democrats, 78, 104–5, 135, 139; immediatist, 37; in New Hampshire, 85, 96–97; in Ohio, 44–45, 148, 149, 151; in Pennsylvania, 128; questioning of political candidates, 113–14, 149; restrictions on mailings, 6, 17, 42, 43–44. *See also* Antiabolitionist violence; Gag rule; Political abolitionism

Adams, Charles Francis, 121, 161, 162

Adams, John Quincy, 40, 50, 74–75, 80, 108, 109, 126, 134, 154

Africa, colonization of American blacks in, 34, 40, 148

Albany Atlas, 69–70, 194

Albany Regency, 57, 69

Allaben, Jonathan, 169, 242 (n. 26)

Allen, Charles, 175

American Antislavery Society, 22, 42, 149, 150, 238 (n. 13)

American Colonization Society, 34

Antiabolitionist violence: Democrats supporting, 6, 18; effects on Hale's views, 84; in Massachusetts, 22, 112–13; in New York City, 21, 30, 42, 214 (n. 12); in New York state, 42; in Ohio, 42, 44, 152; in Pennsylvania, 128–29

Antimasonry, 127, 128

Anti-rent movement, 14, 59–61

Antislavery Democrats: arguments based on benefits to whites, 114, 138–39, 149, 167; banished from party, 6–7, 17–18, 25, 38, 46, 47–48; in Congress, 143, 240 (n. 53); cooperation with other parties, 79, 90–91, 93, 97–100; departures from party, 133, 194–95, 197; differences from abolitionists, 78, 104–5, 135, 139; egalitarianism, 52, 144–45; in 1830s, 18; evolution of views, 10, 18, 103, 119, 132, 134, 159, 180, 194; grassroots support for separate party, 70; influence in Republican Party, 195–97; Jacksonians, 4–5, 144–45; in New Hampshire, 79, 88–89, 94, 96–100; in Ohio, 144–45, 159–60; racial views, 14–15, 123, 131, 136, 138–39, 167; split with Polk administration, 65, 131–32, 157; Utica meeting, 73. *See also* Barnburners; Free Soil ideology; Independent Democracy; Slavery in territories

Antislavery petitions, 17, 42–43, 112. *See also* Gag rule

Appeal of the Independent Democrats, 193

Aristocracy, 49–50, 70, 71, 104, 108, 131, 133, 142

Atherton, C. G., 116, 119, 224 (n. 20)

Atkins, Q. F., 156

Bailey, Gamaliel: antislavery views, 144, 148, 149–51; background, 147–48; call for Liberty convention, 154; efforts to create antislavery party, 151, 152, 153; on election campaign of 1848, 172–73; Free Soil salon, 190–91; hard-money views, 155; and *National Era*, 158, 164, 165; national reputation, 152; and *Philanthropist*, 145, 146, 147, 149–51, 152, 153, 154–55, 159; political

Bailey, Gamaliel (*cont.*)
views, 152–53; religious beliefs,
147, 148, 152; support for cooperation with other parties, 145, 146,
151, 189; True Democracy and,
147, 152, 154–57
Bancroft, George, 3, 4, 53, 63, 66, 115,
116, 120, 166
Bankers. *See* Money Power
Bank of the United States. *See* Second
Bank of the United States
Barnburner Manifesto, 74–75
Barnburners, 62–66, 72; break with
proslavery Democrats, 65, 66, 68–
73; delegates to 1848 convention,
73, 74, 75–76; departures from
Democratic Party, 194; differences
with Hunkers, 62; election victories,
65; in Free Soil movement, 71, 77,
161; in Free Soil Party, 187–90;
Herkimer Convention, 71–72, 138–
39, 222 (n. 67); involvement in
Wilmot Proviso, 67; leaders, 62, 68,
69, 73, 138; Morton and, 121; opposition to slavery in territories, 1–
4, 67; return to Democratic Party,
190; separate ticket, 69–70, 72; in
upstate New York, 57
Beckwith, Abijah C., 11–12, 14, 16,
36–37, 70–71, 77, 188, 194, 197
Beecher, Henry Ward, 190
Benton, Thomas Hart, 68, 166, 190
Berry, Nathaniel S., 98
Biddle, Nicholas, 17
Bingham, Kingsley, 195
Birney, James G.: at Liberty Party convention, 156; as Liberty Party presi-
dential candidate, 150–51, 153–54,
155, 171, 225 (n. 31), 238 (n. 25),
239 (n. 43); and *Philanthropist*, 44,
149
Birney, William, 155
Blair, Francis, 166
Boston: antiabolitionist mobs, 112–13;
Customs House, 116; Morton as col-

lector in, 104, 120, 121, 166; power
elite, 108
Boutwell, George, 186
Bowdoin College, 79
Bradford County, Pennsylvania, 126,
128
Bradford County Antislavery Society,
128
Brinkerhoff, Jacob, 2, 175, 233 (n. 1),
240 (n. 53)
Brooklyn Eagle, 67, 69, 71, 73, 163
Brooklyn Freeman, 163–64
Brownson, Orestes, 8, 9
Bryant, William Cullen, 52, 68, 163,
188; departure from Democratic
Party, 194; Leggett and, 20, 21, 25,
26; opposition to Texas annexation,
63, 64–65; on Republican Party,
196
Buchanan, James, 3, 139, 141, 142,
177, 195
Bucktails, 56–57
Buffalo Free Soil convention, 77, 141,
160–62, 163, 168
Burke, Edmund, 80
Burned-Over District, 12, 55, 171
Butler, B. F., 121, 161
Byrdsall, Fitzwilliam, 8–9

Calhoun, John C., 116; attempts to bar
abolitionist petitions, 42, 43; bill to
restrict abolitionist mailings, 42,
43–44; break with Jackson, 110, 231
(n. 28); Hunkers' support of, 62;
Morton's friendship with, 106, 108,
109–11; presidential campaigns, 9,
109; proslavery resolutions, 45–46,
47, 68, 137; support for nullifiers,
110; support for Texas annexation,
63; support of slavery, 8, 88, 110–
11; support of states' rights, 88,
109, 110; as vice president, 6, 109;
on Wilmot Proviso, 138
Cambreleng, C. C., 25, 69
Canton Resolutions, 58

Capitalists, 8, 47, 131, 142, 153, 195.
    See also Money Power
Cass, Lewis, 142; election results, 121,
    169, 173, 233 (n. 76); opponents,
    74, 77; popular sovereignty doc-
    trine, 141; presidential campaign,
    76, 159, 160, 165; supporters, 63,
    165, 166, 184
Chaddock, Calvin, 106
Chase, Salmon P.: address to conven-
    tion, 156; antislavery views, 144; call
    for Free Soil convention, 160; calls
    for Liberty conventions, 154, 155–
    56; defense of fugitive slave, 158,
    240 (n. 57); Free Soil Party and,
    101, 161–62, 164, 167, 172, 173–
    75, 190; hard-money views, 155; on
    Herkimer Convention, 71–72; Lib-
    erty Party and, 154, 158–59, 239
    (n. 39); on Morris, 37; Ohio Free
    Territory convention, 160, 242
    (n. 19); opposition to Kansas-
    Nebraska Act, 193; as senator, 175,
    184; Sumner and, 71, 186; support
    for cooperation with other parties,
    145–46, 158, 160; support for Free
    Soil–Democratic coalition, 183–84,
    191; support for presidential nomi-
    nation of, 196; True Democracy
    and, 145–46, 147, 154–57, 162;
    Wilmot and, 141
Chemung County, N.Y., 55, 169–71
Cincinnati: antiabolitionist mobs, 42,
    44, 152; antislavery Democrats,
    144–45; Free Soil supporters, 164;
    Jackson's visit, 45; settlers, 145, 151
Cincinnati Antislavery Society, 148
Clay, Henry, 6, 29, 40, 46, 65, 81, 107,
    185
Clayton Compromise, 141
Clermont County Antislavery Society,
    44–45
Clinton, DeWitt, 56–57
Colby, Anthony, 99
Cole, Donald B., 96

Colonization movement, 34, 40, 148
Compromise of 1850, 182, 185, 187,
    189, 191
Congregational Church, 96, 105, 108,
    125
Congress: debates on slavery in territo-
    ries, 1–4, 141; land reform peti-
    tions, 168; North-South divisions, 3;
    sovereignty over territories, 141;
    Texas annexation issue, 65–66, 223
    (n. 3). *See also* Gag rule; Wilmot
    Proviso
Connecticut: coalition of Democrats
    and Free Soil, 184; western land
    claims, 124, 125
Conscience Whigs. *See* Whigs, antislav-
    ery
Constitution: absence of mention of
    slavery, 34, 215 (n. 21); arguments
    against slavery based on, 4, 6, 23–
    25, 34; Fifth Amendment, 23; fugi-
    tive slave clause, 34; Hale's view of,
    92; seen as proslavery, 32, 92; slav-
    ery seen as local institution, 149;
    strict constructionist views, 23;
    three-fifths clause, 34, 92
Conway, Moncure, 190
Coös County, N.H., 86, 87–88, 228
    (n. 80)
Corwin, Tom, 165
Craven, Avery, 123

Davis, Jefferson, 5
Delaware County, N.Y., 55, 56, 57,
    169–71, 172
Democratic Party: association with
    slaveholders, 4, 8, 15, 197; coali-
    tions with Free Soil Party, 184–87;
    divisions over slavery, 8–9, 65; in
    Midwest, 192–93; national conven-
    tion (1844), 63, 64–65; national
    convention (1848), 68, 73, 74, 75–
    77, 118; North-South alliances, 6,
    71, 142; North-South divisions, 63,
    118–19; platform planks on slavery

Democratic Party (*cont.*)
extension, 76–77; popular sov-
ereignty advocates, 9, 141, 192–94;
potential coalitions with Free Soil
Party, 182–84, 188–89, 191; south-
ern support, 15, 142; states' rights
faction, 22; Van Buren's coalition,
50. *See also* Antislavery Democrats;
Jacksonian Democrats; Northern
Democrats
Devyr, Thomas, 61
District of Columbia, slavery in, 42–43,
45, 99, 107, 159, 185
Dix, John A., 66, 68, 72, 77, 121, 169
Dodge, Augustus, 193
Dodge, Henry, 121
Doolittle, James R., 69
Douglas, Stephen A., 5, 192, 193–94
Douglass, Frederick, 168
Dunlap, Robert P., 2

Earle, Thomas, 154
Egalitarianism, 19, 52, 144–45, 153
Elections. *See* Presidential elections
Ellis, G. W., 157
Emancipation Proclamation, 15, 197
Emancipator, 112–13, 119–20
Emerson, Ralph Waldo, 111–12
Equality, racial, 14, 15, 24–25
Erie Canal, 55, 56
Erie County, N.Y., 55, 56
Eustis, William, 107
Evans, George Henry: antislavery views,
27, 30–31, 33–35, 59; correspondence with Gerrit Smith, 60, 61,
198; early life and family of, 27–28;
freedom concept, 197–98; free soil
term coined by, 13, 59; hard-money
views, 27, 30; influence of, 27, 36–
37, 58–61, 161, 162; Jackson and,
29; labor movement and, 27; land
reform program, 18, 27, 35, 59, 60,
130, 168; Liberty Party and, 158;
political views, 27, 30; as printer, 28;
reaction to Turner rebellion, 30–

31, 32–33, 34; refusal to join Free
Soil Party, 169; view of Democrats,
29
Everett, Edward, 111–12, 113, 114

Fairfield, John, 119
Federalists, 6, 49
Field, David Dudley, 52, 72, 190, 194
Fillmore, Millard, 72
Finney, Charles Grandison, 12
Fisher, Sydney George, 133
Fitzhugh, George, 36
Flagg, Azariah C., 66, 69, 70, 71, 72,
74, 77, 189, 221 (n. 57)
Floyd, John, 31
Fogg, George G., 93, 101, 177
Foner, Eric, 14, 15, 195–96, 198
Ford, Seabury, 172
Forrest, Edwin, 25, 26
Free blacks: abolitionists, 168; in New
Hampshire, 82, 224 (n. 19); news-
papers, 24; in Ohio, 40, 152; sup-
port for Free Soil Party, 168; voting
rights, 25, 37, 82
Free Democracy (Vermont), 177
Free Democratic Party, 191, 192, 196
Free labor, 14, 15, 198
Freemasonry, 127–28
Free Soil ideology: contribution of anti-
renters, 60; incorporation of slavery
expansion issue, 35–36, 71–72;
meaning of term, 13–14, 35, 59;
origins, 7–8, 10–13, 51, 54; rhetoric, 68; right to land, 59, 60. *See
also* Land reform
Free Soil movement: Barnburners in,
71, 77, 161; characteristics of supporters, 10–13, 14–15; contributions of New Hampshire
Independent Democracy, 101–2; in
early 1850s, 191; newspapers, 163–
64, 172, 177; in New York, 51–54;
in Ohio, 144; Utica meetings, 74, 77
Free Soil Party: Buffalo convention
(1848), 77, 141, 160–62, 163, 168;

call for free farms, 167–68, 169;
coalitions with Democrats, 184–87;
convention of 1852, 191; debates
on coalitions with Democrats, 182–
84, 188–89, 191; former Democrats
in, 133; former Whigs in, 101, 160,
161, 165, 175, 177; free blacks and,
168; Hale as presidential candidate
(1852), 191, 192; in Massachusetts,
121, 169, 175, 184–88, 233 (n. 76);
members of Congress, 175, 181,
190; members of state legislatures,
181; midwestern support, 177; in
New York, 51, 169–71, 187–90, 218
(n. 3); in Ohio, 172–75, 184, 187–
88, 241 (n. 5); in Pennsylvania, 177;
platform (1848), 14, 161–62, 167–
68, 169, 177, 184, 196; platform
(1852), 191, 245 (n. 27); prospects
after 1848 election, 181, 182; racism in, 14–15, 167; ratification
meetings, 164; reunion, 101; satires
of, 181–82; significance of founding, 162
Free Soil Party, presidential campaign
(1848): candidates for nomination,
161; election results, 121, 169–71,
218 (n. 3), 233 (n. 76); optimism,
164, 172, 241 (n. 3); problems in,
164–66; support in New York state,
51, 169–71, 187–89; Van Buren's
candidacy, 162, 167–69; votes from
former Democrats, 121, 171–72,
175–77, 187–88; Whig voters, 175–
77; Wilmot's role, 143
Free Soil Party of 1846, 61–62
Freewill Baptists, 83–84, 95–96, 228
(n. 77)
Frémont, John C., 172, 175, 195
French, B. V., 175
Fugitive Slave Act (1850), 182, 185,
186
Fugitive slave laws, 147, 150, 153, 159
Fugitive slaves: Chase's defense of, 158,
240 (n. 57); constitutional clause,

34; in Massachusetts, 107, 118, 120,
187; in New Hampshire, 99; in
Ohio, 158; in Pennsylvania, 128

Gag rule: Democratic opponents, 6,
18, 80, 221 (n. 43), 224 (n. 12);
Democratic supporters, 6, 82, 134,
224 (n. 20); end of, 80, 224 (n. 12);
Hale's opposition, 80, 84–85, 88;
Morris's opposition, 8; votes on, 65,
80, 224 (n. 12); Whig opponents,
80, 134
Gallup, John J., 61
Garnet, Henry Highland, 168
Garrison, William Lloyd, 15, 89, 103;
criticism of, 101, 102; followers,
149; on Freewill Baptists, 97; on
Hale, 226 (n. 53); mob violence
against, 112; reaction to Turner rebellion, 30, 32, 33; view of Constitu-
tion, 92
Gates, Seth, 80
George, Henry, 27
Gibbs, John T., 93
Giddings, Joshua: antislavery views,
134, 136; Chase and, 156, 157; in
Congress, 80, 134, 175; Free Soil
Party and, 167, 173, 183, 190, 191;
opponents, 243 (n. 40); opposition
to Free Soil–Democratic coalition,
183; opposition to gag rule, 80; op-
position to Kansas-Nebraska Act,
193; speech at Ohio Free Territory
convention, 160
Goodell, William, 158
Goodwin, Ichabod, 90, 227 (n. 67)
Greeley, Horace, 89, 173, 190
Griffith, Camillus, 107
Grover, Martin, 2
Grundy, Felix, 43

Hale, John P., 191; antislavery views,
92, 100–101, 227 (n. 62); in Congress, 78–79, 80–81, 84; congressional election and runoffs (1845),

Hale, John P. (*cont.*)
90–94, 227 (n. 67); conversion to
antislavery views, 83–85; debate with
Pierce, 93–94; family of, 79, 223
(n. 4); Free Soil Party and, 101, 161,
190; Jacksonian views, 79; leadership
of Independent Democracy, 91–94,
177; letters to wife, 80–81, 83, 86;
Letter to the Democratic Republican Electors of New Hampshire, 81, 85–86, 226
(n. 53); opposition to abolitionism,
82–83; opposition to gag rule, 80,
84, 88; opposition to Texas annexation, 78–79, 80–81, 83–84, 85–88,
93, 157, 224 (n. 13); plans to retire
from politics, 81, 86, 91; political career, 79–81, 82, 88; presidential candidacy (1848), 73, 101, 158, 164;
presidential candidacy (1852), 191,
192; religious beliefs, 83–84, 93, 97;
as senator, 99, 100–101; in state legislature, 98, 99; supporters, 86–89,
90–91, 94, 95, 97, 100, 226 (n. 57)
Hale, Lucy Lambert, 80, 83, 84
Hallett, B. F., 118
Hamer, Thomas, 40
Hamilton, Alexander, 49
Hamlin, Hannibal, 2, 184, 190, 196
Hammond, Jabez D., 63, 190
Hard-money Democrats, 7, 9; Leggett's
arguments, 19, 20–21, 23, 52; Morton among, 108; in New York state,
219–20 (n. 26); support for antirenters, 60; in upstate New York,
55–58. *See also* Evans, George
Henry; Morris, Thomas
Harrison, William Henry, 62, 126
Harvard College, 106, 186
Haverhill, Mass., 22
Hawthorne, Nathaniel, 79
Hayes, John L., 89, 92, 101
Henshaw, David, 109, 111, 116, 118,
119, 120
Herkimer Convention, 71–72, 138–
39, 222 (n. 67)

Herkimer County, N.Y.: economy, 56,
213 (n. 33); free-soil supporters, 13,
51, 55–56, 70, 169–71; radical
Democrats, 57, 58; Republican
voters, 195. *See also* Beckwith,
Abijah C.
Hill, Isaac, 79, 80, 81, 82, 224 (n. 17)
Hoffman, Michael, 58
Hofstadter, Richard, 20
Homestead Act, 15, 180, 197, 246
(n. 48). *See also* Land reform
Homesteads. *See* Free Soil ideology;
Land reform
Hone, Philip, 20
Hoyt, Joseph G., 89, 91
Hunker Democrats, 61, 62, 65, 66, 68–
69, 188, 189, 194
Huston, James L., 108

Illinois, Free Soil Party support, 177
Independent Democracy, 78, 89–95,
97–100, 101, 177
Independent Democrat, 91, 94, 177
Independent Treasury, 26, 46, 58, 80,
127

Jackson, Andrew: bank veto message,
30, 41; break with Calhoun, 110,
231 (n. 28); Evans and, 29; farewell
address, 17; Hale and, 79; on limiting abolitionist mailings, 42; Morton and, 106; New England
Democrats' views of, 109; presidential campaigns, 6, 50, 81, 109, 110,
126; support in Ohio, 40; visit to
Cincinnati, 45
Jacksonian Democrats: contribution to
political abolitionism, 4–5, 101–2;
departures from party, 194–95; divisions among, 6; equal rights doctrine, 24, 25; Jackson
administration, 6; newspapers, 40–
41; in Ohio, 144–45, 150, 159–60;
opposition to Texas annexation, 54,
63, 64–65; in Pennsylvania, 126; po-

litical success, 50; racism, 4, 180; in Republican Party, 7, 14, 15–16, 101, 171–72, 195–97; supporters of slavery, 8–9; in upstate New York, 56; view of freedom, 198; view of Money Power, 7, 17. *See also* Antislavery Democrats; Barnburners; Hard-money Democrats

Jay, William, 154

Jefferson, Thomas, 32, 49, 163–64. *See also* Northwest Ordinance

Jeffersonians, 6, 39–40, 106, 126. *See also* Morris, Thomas

Jennings, Robert, 28

The John-Donkey, 181–82

Julian, George W., 191

July Days riots, 21, 30

Kansas-Nebraska Act, 192, 193–94

Kemble, Fanny, 53

King, Leicester, 154, 159

King, Preston: address to national convention, 75–76; Canton Resolutions, 58; coalition with Hunkers, 190; in Congress, 52, 65, 181, 190; departure from Democratic Party, 194, 197; Free Soil Party and, 161, 181, 189, 192; hard-money views, 58; leadership of antislavery Democrats, 52, 69, 77, 138; opposition to Texas annexation, 65; political career, 56, 58; Wilmot Proviso and, 2, 67–68, 135

Know-Nothings, 177

Kohl, Lawrence F., 9

Labor movement, 27, 28–30, 35

Land reform: farmers' support for, 36–37, 51; Free Soil agenda, 5, 7, 13; Free Soil Party platform, 167–68, 169; inclusion of ex-slaves and Indians, 59, 60, 197–98; labor support for, 36; link to abolitionism, 36, 59, 130; link to Wilmot Proviso, 132–33; petitions supporting, 129–

30, 168, 235 (n. 35); slaveholders' opposition to, 36. *See also* Free Soil ideology; Homestead Act

Lane Theological Seminary, 148

Leavitt, Joshua, 112–13, 119–20, 162, 190

Leggett, William: antiabolitionism, 21; antislavery views, 18, 23–25, 26, 34, 144–45, 215 (n. 19); attacks on Money Power, 18, 20–21; background, 14, 19; conversion to abolitionism, 21–23; death, 26; Democratic excommunication of, 25, 26–27; editorials, 19, 20–21, 22, 23, 24, 52–53; egalitarianism, 19, 144–45; on equal rights for blacks, 24–25; hard-money views, 19, 20–21, 23, 52; influence of editorials, 8, 24–25, 26–27, 52, 55–58, 73, 127, 142; influence on Free Soil platform, 161, 162; nomination for congressional seat, 25–26; reaction to July Days riots, 21, 30; Sedgwick and, 52–53; support for Van Buren, 23, 26; worldview, 20; writings, 19–20

Lewis, Samuel, 154, 160

Liberator, 32, 97

Liberia, colonization proposals, 40

Liberty League, 158, 168, 169, 171, 240 (n. 60)

Liberty Party: Birney as presidential candidate, 150–51, 153–54, 155, 171, 225 (n. 31), 238 (n. 25), 239 (n. 43); Buffalo convention (1847), 158–59; competition with Whigs, 154–55, 156; cooperation with other parties, 79, 90–91, 93, 97–100, 145–47, 151, 157; equal rights doctrine, 153; Hale as presidential candidate, 73, 101, 158, 164; hard-money policies, 155; in Massachusetts, 115, 116, 117, 232 (n. 55); in New Hampshire, 79, 85, 90–91, 93, 97–100, 225 (n. 31); in

Liberty Party (*cont.*)
New York state, 154, 171; in Ohio, 145–47, 150–51, 152, 153–55; platforms, 24, 158–59; Southern and Western Convention, 155–57; support for free homesteads, 158; votes from former Democrats, 65, 116
Lincoln, Abraham, 8, 15–16, 47, 133, 172, 175, 196–97
Lincoln, Levi, Jr., 108
Locke, Richard Adams, 26
Locofoco Party, 8, 19, 25, 127, 218 (n. 9)
Longfellow, Henry Wadsworth, 79
Loomis, Arphaxed, 58

Madison, James, 106
Mahan, John B., 150
Maine: coalition of Democrats and Free Soil, 184; statehood, 6
Mann, Horace, 190
Marcy, William, 188, 191
Masonry, 127–28, 235 (n. 24)
Masquerier, Lewis, 61
Massachusetts: abolitionist groups, 103; antislavery views, 111; Free Soil Party, 121, 169, 175, 184–88, 233 (n. 76); fugitive slaves in, 107, 118, 120, 187; legislature, 181, 185; Liberty Party in, 115, 116, 117, 232 (n. 55); mob violence against abolitionists, 22; Morton as governor of, 104, 107–8, 113, 114–16, 118, 185; Morton's supporters, 109–10, 111, 112, 113, 122; Republican Party support, 175; Whigs, 104, 108–9, 111, 112–13, 115, 121, 175, 184, 185
Massachusetts Antislavery Society, 84, 226 (n. 53)
Massachusetts Democrats: antislavery resolutions, 185; coalition with Free Soil Party, 184–87; effects of Free Soil Party, 175; emergence of party, 109, 111; factions, 116, 120; in Free Soil Party, 121–22

Matilda (fugitive slave), 158, 240 (n. 57)
McDuffie, George, 22
McLean, John, 160
Medary, Samuel, 41, 157
Methodist Protestant Church, 147, 148, 152
Mexican War, 14, 66, 139–41. *See also* Wilmot Proviso
Meyers, Marvin, 7, 20
Michigan, Free Democrats, 195, 196
Miller, Josiah, 195
Missouri Compromise, 6, 107, 192, 193, 194
Missouri Crisis, 4, 6, 106–7
Money Power: Leggett's attacks on, 18, 20–21; radical Democrats' view of, 7, 9, 17, 108; replaced by Slave Power, 47, 132, 139
Monopolies, 19, 30, 57, 108
Morgan, Levi, 38
Morris, Thomas: antislavery views, 37–38, 43–48, 100, 144–45; call for Liberty convention, 154; early life and family of, 38–39; egalitarianism, 144–45, 153; hard-money views, 41–42, 46; influence of, 37, 38, 47–48, 152, 158, 161; Jacksonian views, 37; law practice, 39, 41; leadership of Ohio political abolitionists, 146; Liberty Party and, 154; opposition to fugitive slave law, 147; opposition to gag rule, 8; petition to abolish slavery in District of Columbia, 42–43; political career, 39–48; political excommunication, 38, 46, 47–48, 100, 146; religious beliefs, 39; "Report on Colonization," 40; as senator, 8, 41–46, 149; on Slave Power, 8, 18, 38, 43–44, 47–48, 139, 149, 153; support for Birney's presidential bid, 151; support for black suffrage, 37; support for Jackson, 40
Morrison, Michael A., 9, 192

Morton, Marcus: abolitionism charge against, 116, 117–20; antislavery views, 103–5, 106–7, 111, 113–14, 118, 230 (n. 3); on aristocracy, 104, 108; Barnburners and, 121; as collector of Boston port, 104, 116–20, 121, 166; in Congress, 106–7, 230 (n. 3); criticism of abolitionists, 115–16, 118; departure from Democratic Party, 121–22; early life and family of, 105–6; Free Soil Party and, 160–61, 165–66, 175; friendship with Calhoun, 106, 108, 109–11; as governor, 104, 107–8, 113, 114–16, 118, 185; gubernatorial candidacies, 104, 109, 113–14; hard-money views, 108; law practice, 106, 230 (n. 12); opposition to slavery in territories, 4, 6, 230 (n. 3); political career, 103–5, 106–11, 113–17; political supporters, 109–10, 111, 112, 113, 122; religious beliefs, 114; on state supreme court, 108; support for Nantucket postmaster, 117–18, 232–33 (n. 61); support of states' rights, 109, 110; support of Van Buren, 111

National Era, 158, 164, 165, 189
National Negro Convention, 168
National Reform Association (NRA), 58–61, 235 (n. 35)
New Hampshire: abolitionist groups, 85, 96–97; abolition of slavery in, 82; antislavery political groups, 177; constitution, 82; elections (1846), 98; free blacks in, 82, 224 (n. 19); Free Soil Party support, 175–77; Hale supporters, 86–89, 90–91, 94, 95, 97, 100, 226 (n. 57); legislature, 85, 97, 98, 99, 223 (n. 2); Liberty Party in, 79, 85, 90–91, 93, 97–100, 225 (n. 31); Republican Party support, 177; Texas annexation issue,

78–79, 85, 87–88, 223 (n. 2). *See also* Independent Democracy
New Hampshire Antislavery Society, 82–83
New Hampshire Democrats: antislavery group, 88–89; cooperation with Free Soil Party, 184; divisions within, 81–82; effects of Free Soil Party, 175; election victories, 82; opposition to railroads, 81–82; reprimand of Hale, 86; responses to Independent Democracy, 98, 100; split over slavery extension, 78, 79; supporters of Texas annexation, 223 (n. 2); support for slavery, 81, 82; support of Wilmot Proviso, 100
New York City: antiabolitionist mobs, 21, 30, 42, 214 (n. 12); Workingmen's Party, 27, 28, 29–30
New York Democrats: Albany Regency, 57, 69; antislavery, 11–12, 50–51; attempts by Free Soilers to reconcile with, 187–90; county clubs, 57; divisions among, 25, 189–90, 194; hard-money supporters, 57–58; Hards and Softs, 189–90; importance of slavery issue, 50–51; patronage, 57; schism, 62, 68–73, 121; support from Freewill Baptists, 96; Tammany Hall, 25, 26–27, 29, 218 (n. 9). *See also* Barnburners; Beckwith, Abijah C.; Hunker Democrats; Van Buren, Martin
New York Evening Post, 20, 25, 52, 68; Leggett's editorials, 8, 19, 20–21, 22, 23; Sedgwick's essays, 53, 54
New York state: antiabolitionist mobs, 42; anti-rent movement, 14, 59–61; Burned-Over District, 12, 55, 171; constitution, 25; elections (1847), 72; free blacks, 25; Free Soil counties, 13, 51, 55–58, 169–72, 195–96, 218 (n. 3); Free Soil Party candidates, 61, 192; Free Soil Party support, 51, 169–71, 187–89, 218

New York state (*cont.*)
(n. 3); hard-money views, 219–20
(n. 26); landowners, 59; legislature,
57–58, 60, 70–71; Liberty Party in,
154, 171; market gardens, 55–56;
Republican voters, 171–72, 195;
Stop and Tax Law, 58; tenant
farmers, 51, 58
Nichols, Eli, 153
Niles, John M., 119
Norris, Moses, Jr., 98
Northern Democrats: concern with
southern dominance of party, 7, 52;
doughfaces, 15; growing opposition
to slavery, 10, 119, 132, 134; Missouri Crisis and, 6; need for southern support in national campaigns,
142; opposition to gag rule, 65, 221
(n. 43), 224 (n. 12); opposition to
slavery in territories, 6, 7; Polk administration and, 65, 131–32, 157;
split over slavery issue, 94; support
of Polk, 63; votes on Kansas-
Nebraska Act, 194; Wilmot as archetype of, 129. *See also* Antislavery
Democrats; *and individual states*
Northwest Ordinance, 2, 40, 141, 193,
240 (n. 57)
NRA. *See* National Reform Association
Nullification crisis, 41, 110

Ohio: abolitionists in, 44–45, 148, 149,
151; antiabolitionist violence, 42,
44, 152; black laws, 149–50, 153,
184; free blacks in, 40, 152; Free
Soil Party, 172–75, 184, 187–88,
241 (n. 5); Free Territory convention, 160, 242 (n. 19); fugitive slave
law, 147, 150, 153; fugitive slaves in,
158; legislature, 39–40, 41, 150,
181, 184; Liberty Party in, 145–47,
150–51, 152, 153–55; political abolitionists, 144–47; presidential election (1848), 172–75; settlers, 145,
151–52; support of Wilmot Proviso,
159–60; Whigs in Western Reserve,
145, 150, 151, 173. *See also* Cincinnati
Ohio Antislavery Society, 149, 153
Ohio Democrats: in Cincinnati, 145;
Liberty Party cooperation with,
145–46, 157; newspapers, 40–41;
soft-money, 9; support for Wilmot
Proviso, 159–60; treatment of
Morris, 38, 45, 46, 47–48, 146
Oneida County, N.Y., 55, 56
Oregon, 66, 130, 141, 221 (n. 46),
235–36 (n. 37)
Ossippee, N.H., 88, 95, 96, 97
O'Sullivan, John L., 63
Otis, Harrison Gray, 112
Owen, Robert, 28
Owen, Robert Dale, 2, 28, 29, 30

Paine, Tom, 27, 28, 32, 38
Palfry, John G., 160, 161
Parker, Theodore, 103
Parkman, John, 84
Parsons, S. B., 86
Penn, William, 125
Pennsylvania: abolitionists in, 128; abo-
lition of slavery in, 128; antiaboli-
tionist violence, 128–29; canal
companies, 126; Free Soil Party sup-
port, 177; fugitive slaves in, 128; leg-
islature, 131; settlers in northern
tier, 124–25; tariff issue, 130–31,
134, 177, 234 (n. 17), 236 (nn. 38,
39)
Pennsylvania Democrats: opposition to
Wilmot Proviso, 139; votes for Free
Soil Party, 177; in Wilmot District,
126–27, 177, 191, 234 (n. 15)
People's Resolutions, 58
Perry, Gardiner B., 112
Phelps, Amos, 175
Philanthropist: Bailey and, 145, 146,
147, 149–51, 152, 153, 154–55,
159; James G. Birney and, 44, 149
Phillips, Wendell, 102

Pierce, Franklin: at Bowdoin, 79; Hale and, 81, 82, 86, 93–94; leadership of state party, 81, 82, 89, 90, 98; Morton and, 119; opposition to railroads, 81–82; as president, 194, 195; presidential campaign, 93, 177, 191–92; support of Kansas-Nebraska Act, 194

Plaindealer, 8, 19, 24

Political abolitionism: achievements, 102; contribution of Jacksonians, 4–5, 101–2; evolution of, 149, 150; in Massachusetts, 105; Morris's contribution, 44, 47–48; in New York state, 61; in Ohio, 144–47, 149, 151; Wilmot's role, 123, 134. *See also* Antislavery Democrats; Liberty Party

Polk, James K.: administration, 66, 131–32; appropriations bill, 1–4, 132, 135, 137; Oregon Territory and, 221 (n. 46); patronage appointments, 131–32; presidential campaign, 63, 64, 65, 126, 129, 171, 223 (n. 2); on Wilmot Proviso, 67, 134–35

Popular sovereignty, 9, 141, 192–93

Presidential elections: of 1824, 50, 126; of 1828, 6, 109, 126; of 1832, 81, 110, 126; of 1836, 17; of 1840, 62, 126, 150–51, 153–54; of 1844, 63–65, 126, 129, 154, 155, 171; of 1848, 73–76, 121, 169–71, 172–75; of 1852, 177, 191–92; of 1856, 172, 175, 195; of 1860, 172, 175, 196–97

Property rights, 23–24

Racism, 4, 14–15, 123, 131, 136, 138–39, 167, 180. *See also* White supremacy

Railroads, 81–82, 224 (n. 18)

Randall, Benjamin, 95–96, 228 (n. 77)

Randall, Henry S., 188

Rantoul, Robert, Jr., 186–87, 190

Rathbun, George, 65, 74, 132

Reeve, Tapping, 106

Republican Party: convention of 1860, 196, 245 (n. 42); election of 1856, 172, 175, 195; election of 1860, 172, 175, 196–97; focus on slavery issue, 196; former Democrats in, 7, 14, 15–16, 101, 133, 171–72, 195–97; former Whigs in, 16, 196; founding, 195; opposition to Slave Power, 8; platforms, 101, 196; voters, 10, 171–72, 175, 177, 195

Richards, Leonard L., 137

Ritchie, Thomas, 6, 50

Robinson, Frederick, 15

Root, Joseph, 175

St. Lawrence County, N.Y.: Democrats, 57–58; economy, 56; free-soil supporters, 51, 55, 70, 169–71; market gardens, 56; shift to Republican Party, 172, 195; split among Democrats, 72; votes in presidential elections, 169–72

Schlesinger, Arthur, Jr., 4–5, 9, 19

Scott, Winfield, 3

Second Bank of the United States, 9, 17, 30, 41–42, 47, 49, 50, 108, 157

Sedgwick, Catherine Maria, 53

Sedgwick, Theodore, I, 53

Sedgwick, Theodore, II, 53

Sedgwick, Theodore, III, 8, 52–54, 63, 81, 218 (n. 9)

Sewall, Samuel, 115

Seward, William H., 25, 154, 156, 173, 190, 196

Sewell, Richard, 167

Seymour, Horatio, 188, 189

Shafer, Thomas, 61

Shays's Rebellion, 57, 105

Shunk, Francis R., 129

Sims, Thomas, 187

Slade, William, 177, 190

Slaveholders: coalition with northern workers, 50; seen as aristocrats, 70, 71, 131, 133, 142

Slave Power: coining of phrase by Morris, 8, 18, 38, 43–44; Democratic views of, 9, 132; seen as allied with capitalists, 8, 47, 131, 142, 153, 195; use of term, 18

Slavery: abolition in northern states, 82, 128; Calhoun's resolutions supporting, 45–46; evolution of northern views on, 10, 18, 103, 119, 132, 134, 159, 180, 194; as issue in national politics, 4; Jacksonian supporters of, 8–9; as local issue, 88, 107, 137, 149; Nat Turner rebellion, 30–33, 34; three-fifths clause of Constitution, 34, 92. *See also* Abolitionists; Antislavery Democrats; Fugitive slaves

Slavery in territories: Barnburner opposition to, 1–4, 67; Calhoun's support for, 45, 46, 137; Clayton Compromise, 141; congressional debates on, 1–4, 141; constitutional arguments against, 4, 6; disagreements among Democrats, 69, 137; importance of issue, 69; incorporation of issue into Free Soil ideology, 35–36, 71–72, 130; issue before Mexican War, 66; Kansas-Nebraska Act, 192, 193–94; Liberty Party opposition to, 159; opposition to, 4, 6, 7, 14, 67, 132, 136; prohibition in Northwest Ordinance, 40, 193, 240 (n. 57); restriction as first step to abolition, 15, 133–34, 136–37, 138; Van Buren on restriction of, 74–75. *See also* Wilmot Proviso

Smith, Adam, 125

Smith, Gerrit, 115; abolitionism, 61; correspondence with Evans, 60, 61, 198; Free Soil Party and, 191; Liberty Party and, 158; link between abolitionism and land reform, 36; on Ohio abolitionists, 153; opposition to Kansas-Nebraska Act, 193; presidential candidacy, 168, 169, 171

Smith, John, 38–39, 217 (n. 76)

South Carolina nullifiers, 41, 110

Stanton, Henry B., 100, 189

States' rights: arguments against gag rule, 80; Calhoun's support for, 88, 109, 110; Democratic supporters, 22; Liberty Party platform, 159; Morton's support of, 109, 110; nullification crisis, 41, 110; support in New Hampshire, 81, 82

Stetson, Lemuel, 64, 65

Stevens, Thaddeus, 128, 190

Stewart, Alvan, 24, 149

Storrs, George, 82–83

Sumner, Charles, 53, 71, 121–22, 185, 186, 190, 193

Susquehanna County, Pa., 125, 126

Tammany Hall, 25, 26–27, 29, 218 (n. 9)

Tappan, Benjamin, 46, 119

Tariffs, 130–31, 134, 155, 177, 186, 236 (nn. 38, 39)

Taylor, Zachary, 159, 165, 169, 172, 183, 233 (n. 76)

Territories: congressional sovereignty, 141; migration to, 68. *See also* Northwest Ordinance; Oregon; Slavery in territories

Texas annexation: boundaries, 185; congressional approval, 66, 223 (n. 3); constitution, 85; debate in Congress, 65–66; opposition to, 54, 63, 64–65, 78–79, 80–81, 83–84, 85–88, 93; supporters, 63, 85, 223 (n. 2); Tyler's signature, 227 (n. 60)

Third party politics, 182. *See also* Free Soil Party; Liberty Party

Thompson, James, 2

Tilden, Samuel J., 52, 74, 75, 77

Tocqueville, Alexis de, 24, 53

Towanda, Pa., 126, 127, 132

True Democracy, 147, 152, 154–57, 162

Tuck, Amos, 86–87, 89, 90, 91, 92, 100, 101–2, 160–61, 184

Turner, Nat, rebellion of, 30–33, 34, 42

Tyler, John, 116, 186, 227 (n. 60)

Underground Railroad, 128
Utica, N.Y., 42, 55
Utica Convention, 74, 77

Van Buren, John, 69, 74, 75, 138, 167–68, 188–89, 190

Van Buren, Martin: address on slavery restriction, 74–75; Albany Regency, 57, 69; attempts to ally with southerners in 1820s, 6, 71; in Free Soil Party, 188; Independent Treasury doctrine, 26, 127; leadership of Barnburners, 62, 73; leadership of Bucktails, 56; Leggett and, 23, 26; on Mexican War, 66; Missouri Compromise and, 6; Morton's support of, 111; opposition to monopolies, 57; opposition to Texas annexation, 63; position on Wilmot Proviso, 71, 74–75; presidential campaign (1836), 17, 23; presidential campaign (1840), 62, 126; presidential campaign (1844), 63–65, 118; presidential campaign (1848), 73–76, 77; as senator, 6, 57; southern opponents, 22; support for Pierce in 1852, 192; support for slavery restriction in territories, 74–75; on threat of aristocracy, 49–50; as vice president, 53, 127; view of free-soil supporters, 71. *See also* Free Soil Party, presidential campaign (1848)

Vance, Joseph, 150

Vermont: Free Democracy, 177; Free Soil Party support, 169, 177

Wadsworth, James, 63, 189
Walker, Amasa, 120, 121, 175, 184–85
Walker, David, 103
Walker, Enoch, 125
Walker, Robert, 62

Walker Tariff, 131, 177, 186, 236 (n. 39)

Wayne County, N.Y., 169–71

Webb, James Watson, 31, 33–34

Webster, Daniel, 185

Weld, Theodore, 97, 148

Weller, J. B., 172, 243 (n. 40)

Welles, Gideon, 66, 73–74

Wentworth, John, 132, 165, 177

Wetmore, Robert C., 91

Whig Party: cooperation with other parties, 79, 90–91, 93, 97–100; in Massachusetts, 104, 108–9, 111, 112–13, 115, 121, 175, 184, 185; in New Hampshire, 79, 90–91, 93, 94, 96, 97–100, 161, 175–77; in New York state, 61, 72, 189; in Ohio, 145, 150, 165, 172–73; in Pennsylvania, 128, 177; in the South, 15; Taylor as presidential candidate, 159, 165, 183

Whigs, antislavery: competition with Liberty Party, 154–55, 156; in Congress, 134; in Free Soil Party, 101, 160, 161, 165, 175–77; in New Hampshire, 93, 177; in New York state, 171; in Ohio, 151, 153, 154–55, 160; in Republican Party, 16, 196; in Vermont, 177

Whitefield, George, 95

White supremacy, 5, 24–25, 82, 123, 124, 136, 138–39. *See also* Racism

Whitman, Walt, 7; antislavery views, 163; *Brooklyn Freeman*, 163–64; editorials in *Brooklyn Eagle*, 67, 69, 71, 73, 163; at Free Soil convention, 163; opposition to slavery in territories, 67; relationship with Lincoln, 196–97; support for Free Soil, 52, 77

Whitmarsh, Seth, 121

Whittier, John Greenleaf, 100, 186, 190, 226 (n. 53); on Leggett, 22, 26, 27; Morton and, 113, 115; poems on New Hampshire politics, 89–90, 98–99

Wilmot, David: antislavery views, 14–15, 123, 124, 131, 133–34, 135–36, 232 (n. 45); as archetype of northern Democrat, 129; arguments for slavery restriction, 124, 133–34, 135–36, 141–43; Barnburners and, 138; in Congress, 129–32, 134–36, 139–43, 235 (n. 32); criticism of abolitionists, 128–29; departure from Democratic Party, 194; early life and family of, 124, 125; Free Soil Party and, 143, 160–61, 167, 190; hard-money views, 127; at Herkimer Convention, 72, 138–39; historians' views of, 123; importance in political abolitionism, 123; introduction of proviso, 2–4; in journalism, 127; land reform issue, 129–30, 132–33; law practice, 126; motives for proviso, 132–34; political career, 138; political views, 5, 127, 129; racism of, 14–15, 123, 131, 136, 138–39; religious and social affiliations, 127–28; in Republican Party, 196; retirement, 191; satires of, 181–82; speeches supporting proviso, 135–36, 138–39; support of gag rule, 134; tariff issue and, 130–31, 134; Van Buren and, 71
"Wilmot, the Wizard," 181–82
Wilmot District, 126–27, 177, 191, 234 (n. 15)
Wilmot Proviso: authorship of, 123, 233 (n. 1); as first step to abolition, 133–34, 136–37, 138; introduction in 1846, 2–4, 66–67, 132, 158; link to land reform, 132–33; motives of originators, 132–34; opposition to, 74–75; originators of, 2, 67, 132, 236 (n. 48); passage in House, 3; political impact, 133–34, 138; reactions to, 134, 138; reintroduction by King, 67–68, 135; significance, 14; supporters, 69, 70, 138, 159–60, 164, 165, 181–82, 189; Van Buren's position on, 71, 74–75; votes on, 137
Wilmot Proviso Leagues, 138
Wilson, Henry, 160, 175, 185, 190, 191
Wilson, Major L., 9
Wisconsin: Democratic Party, 184; Free Soil Party, 184; Free Soil Party support, 177; Republican Party, 195
Wood, Bradford, 132
Woodbury, John, 88, 90, 94, 98, 227 (n. 67)
Woodbury, Levi, 81, 224 (n. 17)
Woodward, George W., 125
Woodworth, William, 137
Working Man's Advocate, 27, 28–29, 32–35, 130
Workingmen's Party, 27, 28, 29–30
Wright, Elizur, 115
Wright, Frances, 28
Wright, Silas, 56, 57–58, 63, 65, 68, 72, 73

Yost, Jacob S., 2